MACMILLAN / McGRAW-HILL

LANGUAGE ARTS TODAY

Great literature is an inspiration. Katherine Paterson's *The Great Gilly Hopkins* inspired artist Don Daily to create the illustration on the cover of your book. The story begins on page 192. We hope that you enjoy the story and the illustration!

SENIOR AUTHORS

ANN McCALLUM WILLIAM STRONG TINA THOBURN PEGGY WILLIAMS

Literature Consultant **Joan Glazer**

Macmillan / McGraw-Hill School Publishing Company

New York Chicago Columbus

ACKNOWLEDGMENTS

The publisher gratefully acknowledges permission to reprint the following copyrighted material:

"The Enormous Egg" is excerpted from *The Enormous Egg* by Oliver Butterworth. Copyright © 1956 by Oliver Butterworth; Copyright © renewed 1984 by Oliver Butterworth. By permission of Little, Brown and Company and Sidgwick & Jackson Ltd., London.

"The Great Gilly Hopkins" from *The Great Gilly Hopkins* by Katherine Paterson. (Thomas Y. Crowell). Copyright © 1978 by Katherine Paterson. Reprinted by permission of Harper & Row, Publishers, Inc.

"Japanese Houses" excerpted from *Shelters: From Tepee to Igloo* by Harvey Weiss (Thomas Y. Crowell). Copyright © 1988 by Harvey Weiss. Reprinted by permission of Harper & Row, Publishers, Inc.

"Lucy Looks Into a Wardrobe" from *The Lion, the Witch and the Wardrobe* by C. S. Lewis. Copyright © C. S. Lewis Pte Ltd. 1950. Published by William Collins Sons & Co Ltd. and used with their permission.

"Maggie Marmelstein for President" from *Maggie Marmelstein for President* by Marjorie Weinman Sharmat. Copyright © 1975 by Marjorie Weinman Sharmat. Reprinted and recorded by permission of Harper & Row, Publishers, Inc.

"Project Turtle" from *Turtle Watch* by George Ancona. Copyright ©1987 by George Ancona. Used by permission of the author.

"Zeely" is excerpted from *Zeely* by Virginia Hamilton. Copyright © 1967 by Virginia Hamilton. Reprinted with the permission of Macmillan Publishing Company. Reprinted also and recorded by permission of McIntosh and Otis, Inc.

Poems, Brief Quotations, and Excerpts
"They're Tearing Down a Town" by Jed Strunk from *The Saturday Evening Post*, 1974. © 1974 The Curtis Publishing Co. Reprinted by permission.

Excerpt from "Surprises" by Jean Conder Soule is used by permission of the author.

Haiku by Gaki and by Kyorai from *Birds, Frogs, and Moonlight* translated by Sylvia Cassedy and Kunihiro Suetake. Reprinted by permission of Sylvia Cassedy.

"Hog-Calling Competition" by Morris Bishop from *Spilt Milk* (G. P. Putnam's Sons). Copyright © 1936, 1964 Alison Kingsbury Bishop. Originally in *The New Yorker*. Used by permission.

Excerpt from "National Book Award Acceptance Speech" by Katherine Paterson. Copyright © 1979 by Katherine Paterson. Reprinted by permission of the author.

Excerpt from "The Door" from *Selected Poems* by Miroslav Holub, translated by Ian Milner and George Theiner (Penguin Modern European Poets, 1967). Copyright © Miroslav Holub, 1967, translation copyright © Penguin Books, 1967. Reprinted by permission of the publisher.

"Sea Shell" from *The Complete Poetical Works of Amy Lowell*. Copyright © 1955 by Houghton Mifflin Company. Copyright © 1983 renewed by Houghton Mifflin Company, Brinton P. Roberts, Esquire, and G. D'Andelot Belin, Esquire. Reprinted by permission of Houghton Mifflin Company.

"Seal" from *Laughing Time, Nonsense Poems* by William Jay Smith. Published by Delacorte Press, 1980. Copyright © 1955, 1980 by William Jay Smith. Reprinted by permission of William Jay Smith.

Excerpt from "The Elephant" in *Laughing Time: Nonsense Poems* by William Jay Smith, published by Delacorte Press, 1980. Copyright © 1955, 1957, 1980 by William Jay Smith. Reprinted by permission of William Jay Smith.

Brief quotation from Oliver Butterworth from *Fourth Book of Junior Authors & Illustrators*, edited by Doris de Montreville and Elizabeth D. Crawford. (Bronx, NY: HW Wilson, 1978) All rights reserved. Reprinted by permission of the publisher.

Haiku by Sho-u from *Cricket Songs*, Japanese haiku translated by Harry Behn. Copyright © 1964 by Harry Behn. All rights reserved. Reprinted by permission of Marian Reiner.

(Acknowledgments continued on page 553.)

Cover Design: Barnett-Brandt Design
Cover Illustration: Don Daily

Copyright © 1993 Macmillan / McGraw-Hill School Publishing Company

Macmillan/McGraw-Hill School Division
10 Union Square East
New York, New York 10003

Printed in the United States of America

ISBN: 0-02-244115-8

9 8 7 6 5 4 3 2 1

MACMILLAN / McGRAW-HILL

LANGUAGE ARTS TODAY

CONTENTS

THEME: *SURPRISES*

Language Study

Unit 1: SENTENCES xx

Writing

Unit 2: WRITING PERSONAL NARRATIVES 40

AWARD WINNING SELECTION

THEME: *PATTERNS*

Unit 3: NOUNS 74

Language Study

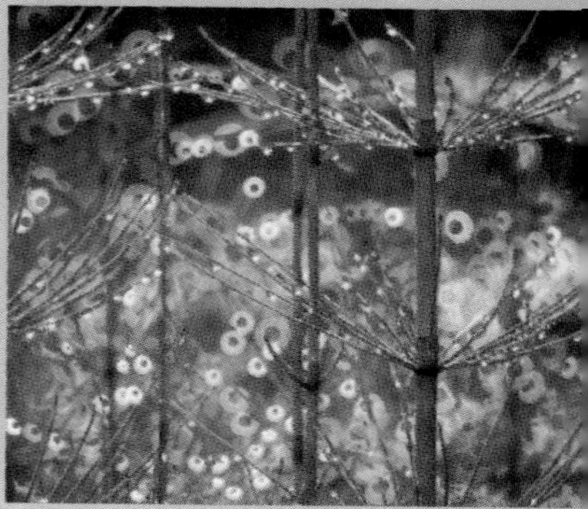

Unit 4: WRITING INSTRUCTIONS 112

Writing

THEME: *PRIZES*

Language Study

Unit 5: VERBS

Writing

Unit 6: WRITING LETTERS

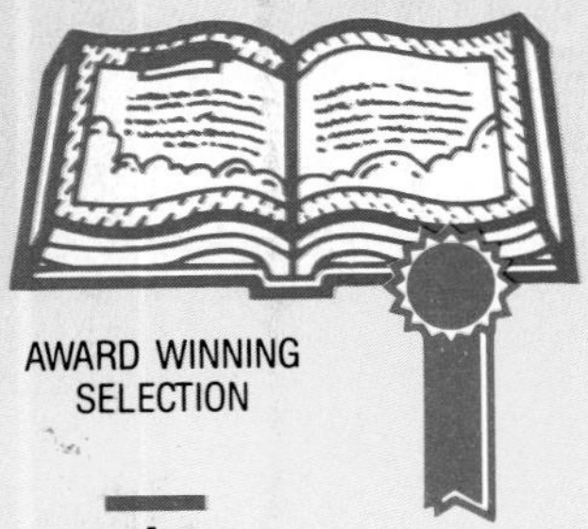

AWARD WINNING SELECTION

THEME: *IMAGES*

Unit 7: ADJECTIVES 224

Language Study

Unit 8: WRITING DESCRIPTIONS 258

Writing

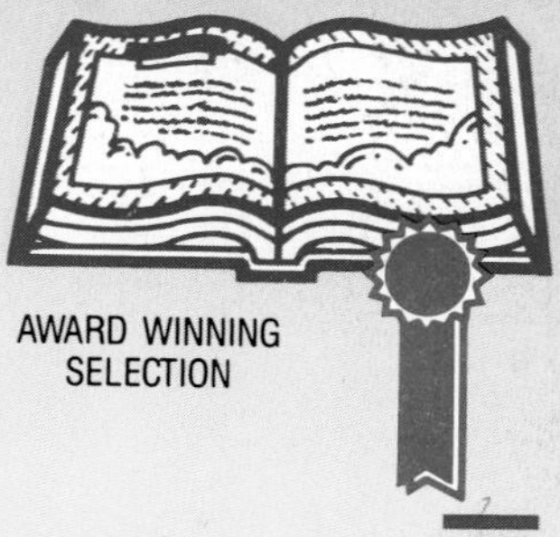

AWARD WINNING SELECTION

THEME: *VIEWS*

Language Study

Unit 9: PRONOUNS 290

Writing

Unit 10: WRITING PERSUASIVE PARAGRAPHS 330

THEME: *ADVENTURES*

Unit 11: ADVERBS

Language Study

Unit 12: WRITING STORIES

Writing

AWARD WINNING SELECTION

THEME: *INVESTIGATIONS*

Language Study

Writing

AWARD WINNING SELECTION

WRITER'S REFERENCE

WRITER TO WRITER

I'm here to answer some questions about writing, writer to writer, you might say. Ready? Let's begin!

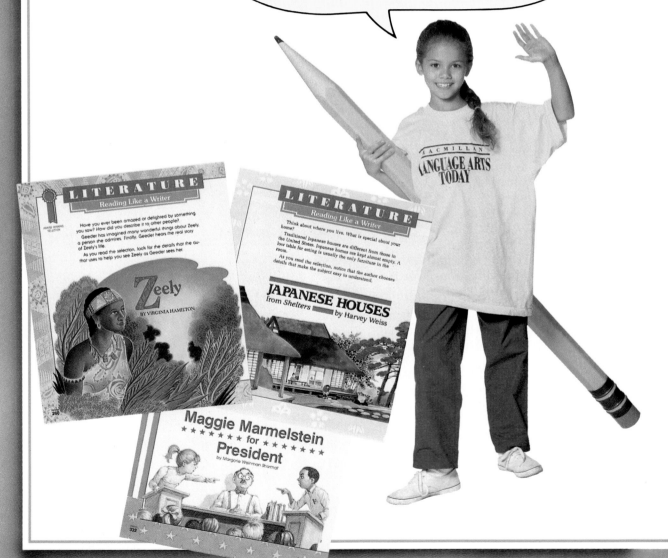

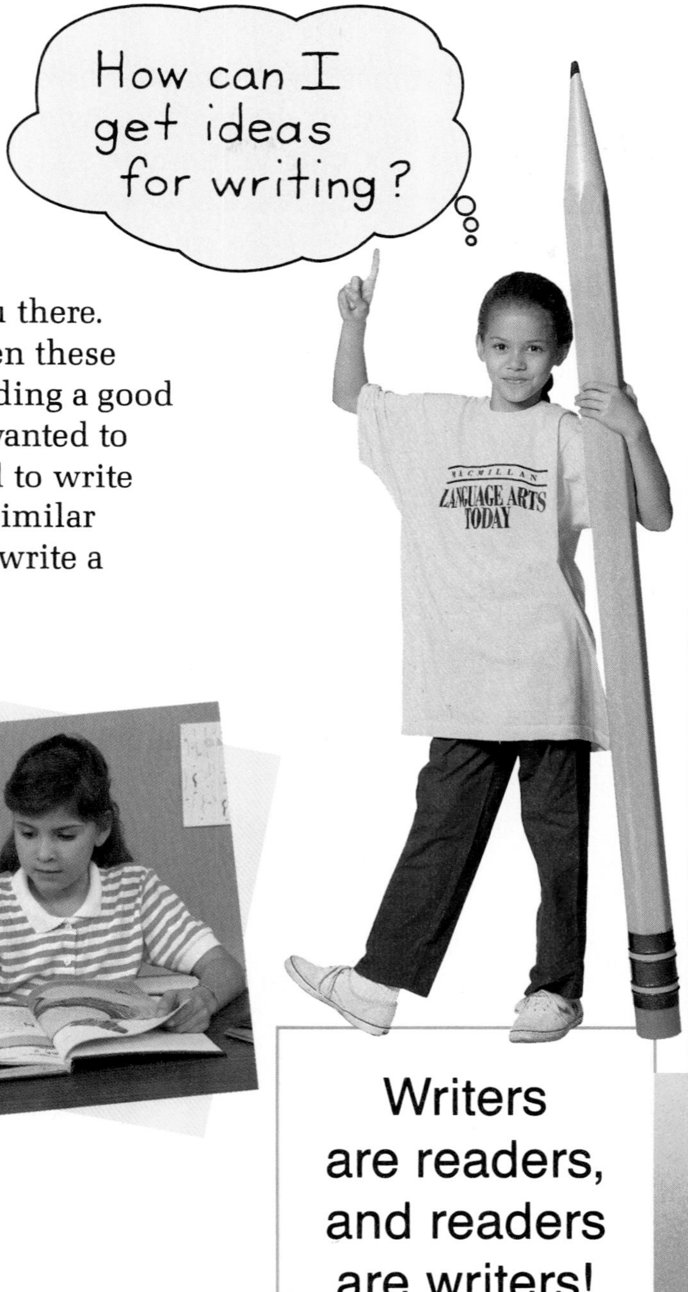
How can I get ideas for writing?
LANGUAGE ARTS TODAY

This book can really help you there. There's great literature between these covers. I noticed that after reading a good story, biography, or poem, I wanted to respond. Sometimes I wanted to write about the same topic or in a similar style. Sometimes I wanted to write a journal entry.

Writers are readers, and readers are writers!

I know that sometimes, no matter how hard I try, the ideas won't come. Reading a story doesn't work. Talking with my friends doesn't help. Then, I take a look at the **PICTURES** *SEEING LIKE A WRITER* section in this book, and presto! Ideas start to flow. The pictures turn up the volume on my imagination.

IMAGINE

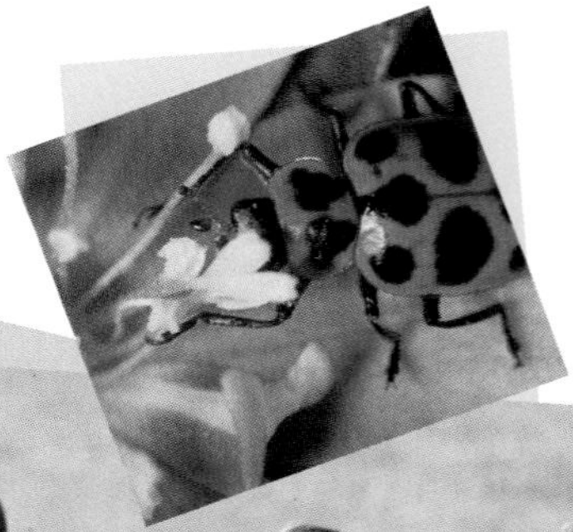

What will I write about today?

Writers observe, and observers can find lots of ideas for writing.

JOURNAL

Personally, I don't know how I'd keep all my ideas straight without my journal. I write in it every day—facts, thoughts, feelings. I draw pictures, too. A journal is a great place to keep track of what you've learned.

A journal is a writer's best friend.

How does working with a group help?

Writing doesn't have to be something that you do alone. I get lots of ideas when I work with my classmates. During group writing, we write and conference together. When it's time to write on my own, I'm all warmed up and ready to go.

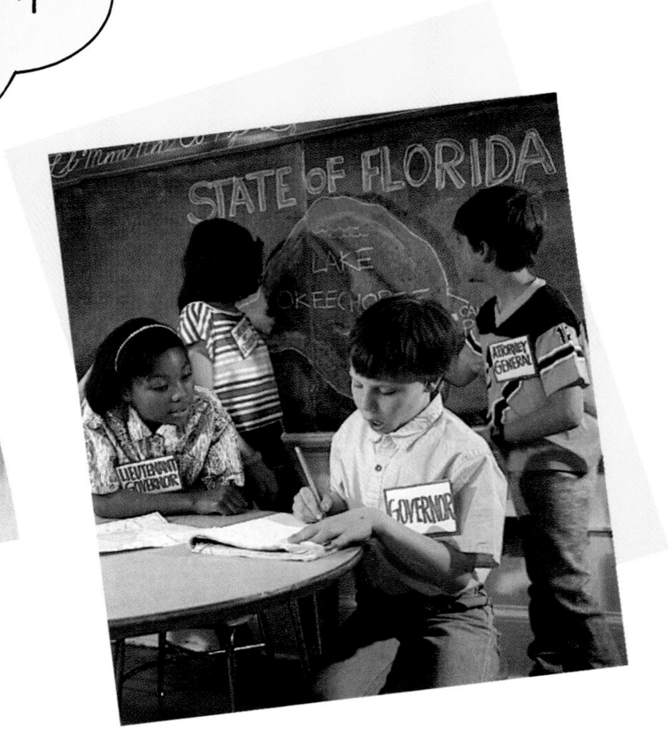

Writing together builds confidence; conferences get the ideas flowing.

How do thinking and writing go together?

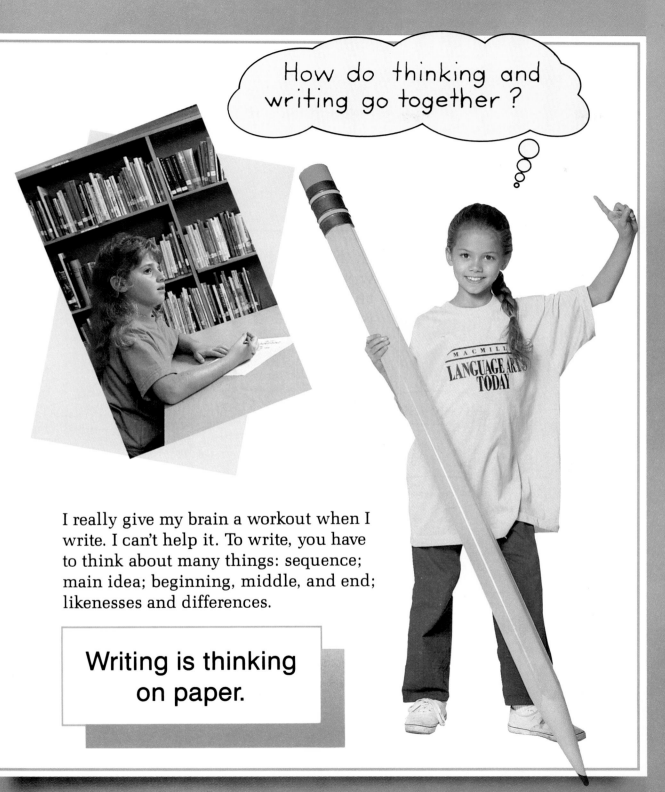

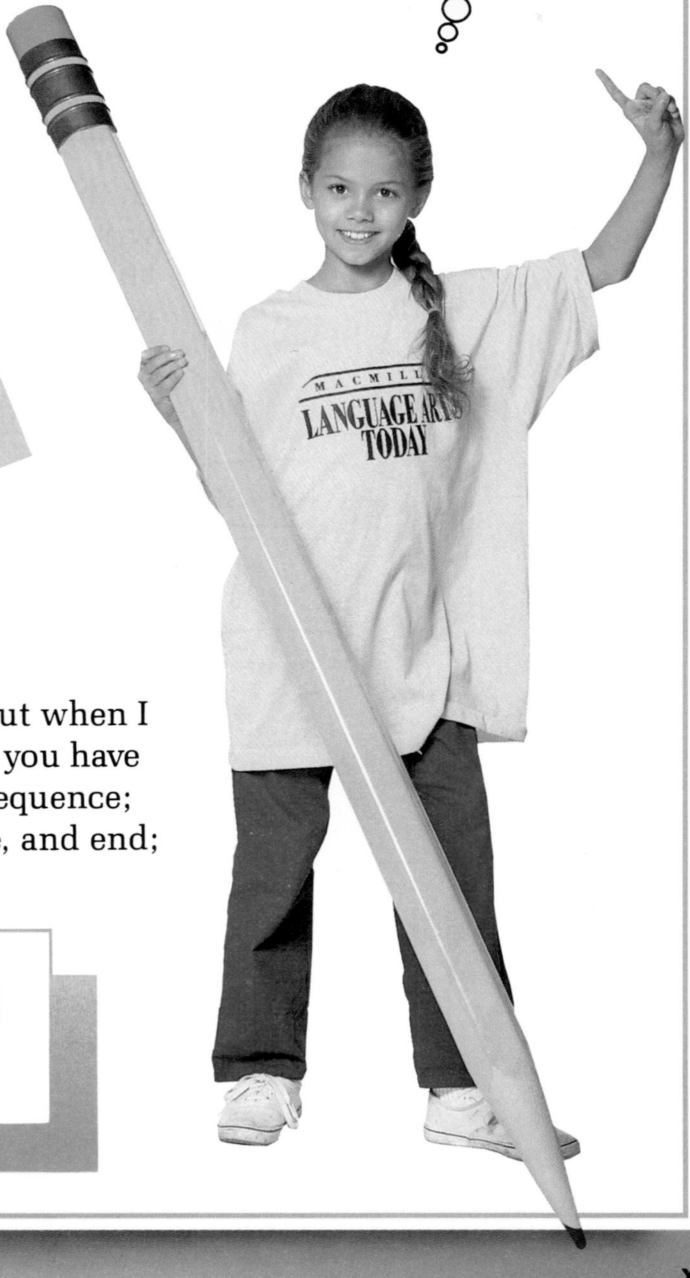

I really give my brain a workout when I write. I can't help it. To write, you have to think about many things: sequence; main idea; beginning, middle, and end; likenesses and differences.

Writing is thinking on paper.

What is the writing process, and how will it help me?

Writing isn't something that just happens 1-2-3. It takes time to write. The writing process allows me the time I need.

Prewrite

At this stage I can get ideas and plan my writing. I need to think about my purpose and audience. Graphic organizers can really help here.

Write a First Draft

This is the stage when I overcome the "blank paper blues." I don't let small mistakes hold me up. I like this stage because I finally get to *see* what I think. I guess that's what it means to be a writer.

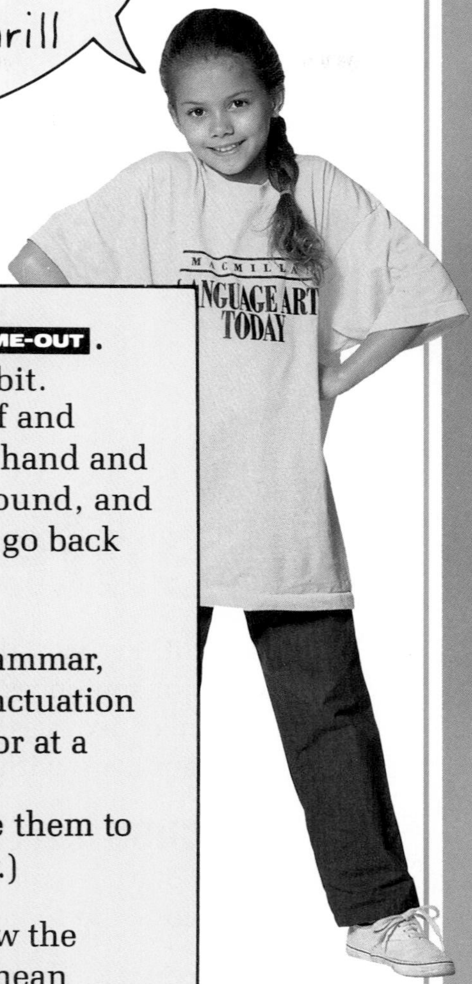

Don't tell anyone, but I feel most like a writer when I revise. It's such a thrill to be in control!
TODAY

Revise

Before I revise, I take some TIME-OUT. I need to let my writing settle a bit. Then I read my writing to myself and to a friend. I then take pencil in hand and go to it. I add, take out, move around, and combine some sentences. I even go back to prewriting for more ideas.

Proofread

During this stage, I fix all my grammar, spelling, capitalization, and punctuation mistakes. I proofread for one error at a time. (Take my advice. Learn the proofreading marks. You can use them to make changes simply and easily.)

Publish

I knew I was an author when I saw the word "publish." Publishing can mean reading your writing out loud or taking it home to show your family—anything that involves sharing your writing with your audience.

GRAMMAR

UNIT 1

Sentences

In Unit 1 you will learn about sentences. There are many kinds of sentences. Some sentences ask questions, and some sentences express strong feeling. All sentences help you to communicate with others.

Discuss Read the poem on the opposite page. The poet uses poetry to communicate with others. What does the poem communicate to you?

JOURNAL

Creative Expression The theme of this unit is *Surprises*. What surprises have you received lately? Write a few sentences to tell about a surprise. You may want to illustrate your sentences. Write your sentences in your journal.

THEME: *SURPRISES*

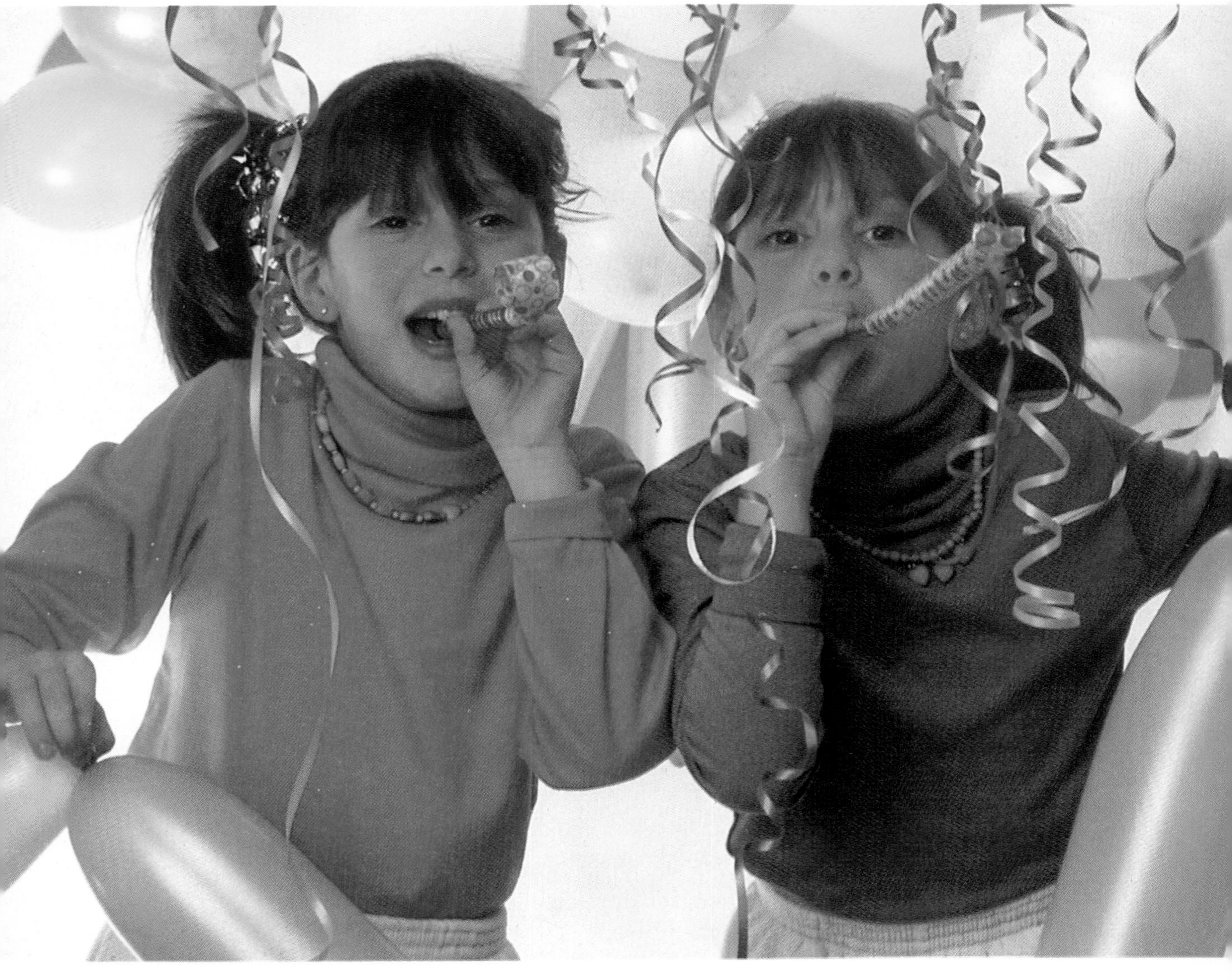

Surprises are round
Or long and tallish.
Surprises are square
Or flat and smallish.

Surprises are wrapped
With paper and bow,
And hidden in closets
Where secrets won't show.

—Jean Conder Soule, from "Surprises"

1 WHAT IS A SENTENCE?

A sentence is a group of words that expresses a complete thought.

A sentence states an idea. A sentence is complete if it can stand alone and make sense. Every sentence begins with a capital letter and ends with a punctuation mark.

Sentences	Not Sentences
We planned Diane's birthday party. Sabrina and Peter made the decorations.	Served fruit and snacks. Sabrina and others.

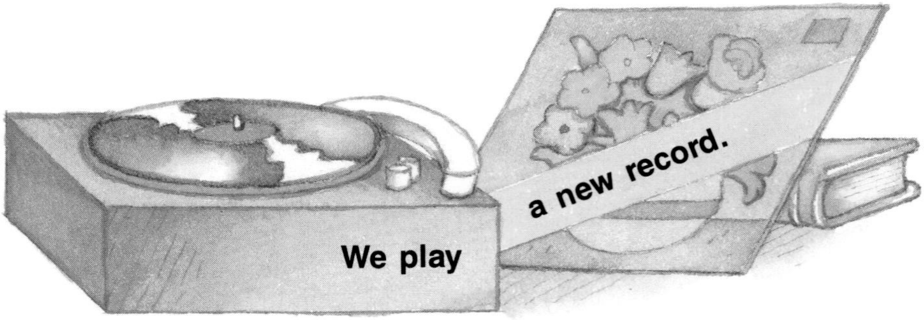

Guided Practice

Tell which groups of words are sentences and which are not sentences.

Example: A lovely dress. *not a sentence*

1. Made streamers for the party.
2. Barbara brought flowers.
3. Kept a secret.
4. Miguel found an interesting gift.
5. The records on the record player.

?! **THINK**

■ How can I decide if a group of words is a sentence?

REMEMBER

- A **sentence** is a group of words that expresses a complete thought.
- A sentence begins with a capital letter and ends with a punctuation mark.

More Practice

A. Write each group of words. Next to each group write **sentence** or **not a sentence.**

Example: a lonely morning. *not a sentence*

6. Diane was sad.
7. No one wished her a happy birthday.
8. She did not know about the party.
9. The surprise party was a secret.
10. Started at seven o'clock.
11. Carlos, Roberta, Michele, and Diane's father.
12. Looked for the perfect gift.
13. Gave money for the gift.
14. Alan took the money to the pet store.
15. He bought a wonderful gift for Diane.

B. Add words to each fragment to make it complete.

Example: An interesting pet.
I have an interesting pet.

16. Never saw one with white fur.
17. Would not hold it in his hand.
18. Always loved animals.
19. Punched holes in a box for the pet.
20. The most wonderful birthday.

Extra Practice, page 28

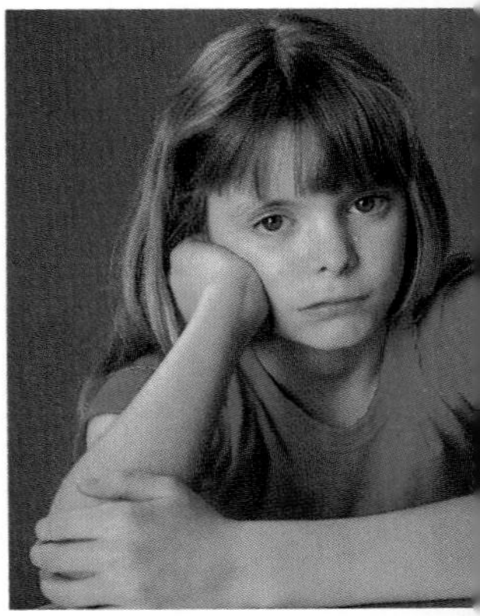

WRITING APPLICATION A Description

Write a paragraph that describes the best party you ever went to or imagined. What did you eat? What music was played? Who was there? Have a partner underline any group of words that does not express a complete thought.

2 FOUR KINDS OF SENTENCES

There are four kinds of sentences: **declarative, interrogative, imperative,** and **exclamatory.** The chart below lists each type and gives an example.

Begin every sentence with a capital letter. Notice the punctuation mark that ends each kind of sentence. Study the chart below.

Declarative Sentence

Purpose: makes a statement
Example: I am tired of winter.
End Punctuation: period (.)

Imperative Sentence

Purpose: tells or asks someone to do something
Examples: Wear your scarf. Please stay home.
End Punctuation: period (.)

Interrogative Sentence

Purpose: asks a question
Example: Is it snowing?
End Punctuation: question mark (?)

Exclamatory Sentence

Purpose: expresses strong feeling
Example: That poor cat looks frozen!
End Punctuation: exclamation mark (!)

Guided Practice

Identify each sentence as **declarative**, **interrogative**, **imperative**, or **exclamatory**.

Example: Are you cold? *interrogative*

1. How deep the snow is!
2. Where are my warm gloves?
3. Please wear your snowshoes.
4. We did not expect snow in May.
5. Are the telephones working?

?! THINK

- How can I decide if a sentence is declarative, interrogative, imperative, or exclamatory?

REMEMBER

- The four types of sentences are **declarative, interrogative, imperative,** and **exclamatory.**
- Sentences end with a **period,** a **question mark,** or an **exclamation mark.**

More Practice

A. Write each sentence. Then write whether each sentence is **declarative, interrogative, imperative,** or **exclamatory.**

Example: Do snowstorms scare you?
interrogative

6. Turn on the radio.
7. Is there news about the hurricane?
8. The weather reporter made a big mistake!
9. She predicted sunshine for today.
10. Are schools closed because of the storm?
11. How heavy the rainfall is!
12. Make sure the windows are closed.

B. Write each sentence. Add the correct end punctuation.

Example: The floor is soaked *The floor is soaked!*

13. Have you seen a tornado before
14. How dark the sky looks
15. Is the basement the safest place in the house
16. Yes, we will wait downstairs in the playroom
17. The weather reporter says the tornado is near
18. Where do animals hide during a tornado
19. Pets stay indoors
20. Birds and squirrels hide in the trees

Extra Practice, page 29

WRITING APPLICATION A Comic Strip

COOPERATIVE LEARNING

Draw a comic strip that shows how people prepare for a big storm. Under each picture in your comic strip, write a sentence that describes what you have drawn. Have a partner identify each type of sentence in your comic strip.

3 COMPLETE SUBJECTS AND COMPLETE PREDICATES

Every sentence has two main parts, the subject and the predicate. Both the subject and the predicate can be one word or more than one word.

The **complete subject** of a sentence includes all the words that tell whom or what the sentence is about. The **complete predicate** of a sentence includes all the words that tell what the subject does or is.

The children hear strange noises.
The boys and girls are curious.

The noises
came
from
upstairs.

Guided Practice

Tell the complete subject and the complete predicate in each sentence.

Example: The quiet house became filled with noises.
The quiet house complete subject
became filled with noises. complete predicate

1. Louie heard the noises first.
2. Harry and Brenda heard them, too.
3. The sounds came from upstairs.
4. The children called Uncle Sydney.
5. Uncle Sydney brought a flashlight.

?! **THINK**

- How can I find the complete subject and the complete predicate in a sentence?

REMEMBER

- The **complete subject** of a sentence includes all the words that tell whom or what the sentence is about.
- The **complete predicate** of a sentence includes all the words that tell what the subject does or is.

More Practice

A. Write each sentence. Draw one line under the complete subject. Draw two lines under the complete predicate.

Example: Mysterious noises disturb the family.

6. Celia and Rosa went up to the attic.
7. Strange noises came from that room.
8. The attic was dusty.
9. The light was dim.
10. Uncle Sydney seemed puzzled.
11. The night sounds remained a mystery.
12. Uncle Sydney and the children went downstairs.
13. The scratching noises started again during dinner.

B. Add a complete subject or a complete predicate to each group of words. Write the new sentence.

Example: joined the search
The children joined the search.

14. left their meal on the table
15. Uncle Sydney and the children
16. looked carefully around the attic
17. heard a tiny, scratching sound in the corner
18. looked beneath a pile of old magazines
19. saw a furry tail
20. a mother squirrel and two babies

Extra Practice, page 30

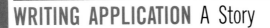

WRITING APPLICATION A Story

COOPERATIVE LEARNING

Write a story about mysterious sounds or shadows. Have a partner draw one line under each complete subject and two lines under each complete predicate.

4 SIMPLE SUBJECTS

The complete subject of a sentence includes all the words that tell whom or what the sentence is about. Within the complete subject you can find the simple subject. The **simple subject** is the main word or words in the complete subject.

A mysterious **envelope** lay on the table.
Mary Ann was surprised.

Sometimes, the simple subject is the same as the complete subject.

Mary Ann thought about the problem.

Guided Practice

Tell which word or words make up the simple subject.

Example: The surprise confused Mary Ann.
surprise

1. Mary Ann showed her mother the envelope.
2. Her mother noticed the address.
3. The envelope had only Mary Ann's name on it.
4. Who sent Mary Ann five dollars?
5. The girl was puzzled by the mysterious gift.

?! THINK

- How can I decide which word or words make up the simple subject?

REMEMBER

- The **simple subject** is the main word or words in the complete subject.
- The **simple subject** can be the same as the complete subject.

More Practice

A. The complete subject is underlined in each sentence. Write the simple subject.

Example: The letter raises questions. *letter*

6. Mary Ann's birthday was months away.
7. The letter came from her town.
8. Her mother thought about the mystery.
9. The envelope gave no clue about the sender.
10. Mary Ann put it into her drawer.
11. She asked her friends many questions.
12. Nobody had the right answer.
13. Mary Ann thought about the envelope all day.

B. Write each sentence. Add a simple subject to each group of words.

Example: had a plan *Mother had a plan.*

14. ______ finally asked her neighbors.
15. ______ had an idea.
16. "______ shoveled snow for Mrs. Jefferson, Mary Ann."
17. "Maybe ______ sent the money."
18. ______ asked Mrs. Jefferson about the envelope.
19. ______ smiled kindly at Mary Ann.
20. ______ had a secret.

Extra Practice, page 31

WRITING APPLICATION A Map

Make a map that shows the way to a hidden treasure chest. Write a paragraph about how your friend will use the map to find the treasure. Ask a partner to draw one line under the simple subject in each of your sentences.

GRAMMAR

5 SIMPLE PREDICATES

The complete predicate of a sentence includes all the words that tell what the subject does or is. The **simple predicate** is the main word or words in the complete predicate. The simple predicate is also called the **verb**. Read the sentences below. Notice the words in dark type.

Jeanne **looked** through the window.
A boy **was** at the front door.
He **wore** a red jacket.
Jeanne **thought** for a moment.

Guided Practice

The complete predicate is underlined in each sentence. Tell which word or words make up the simple predicate.

Example: Jeanne wondered about him. *wondered*

1. Jeanne walked to the door.
2. The little boy ran to the corner.
3. He waited by the tree.
4. Jeanne remembered his face.
5. The boy stood silently by the tree.

?! **THINK**

■ How can I find the simple predicate in a sentence?

REMEMBER

- The **simple predicate** is the main word or words in the complete predicate.
- The simple predicate is also called the verb.

More Practice

A. The complete predicate in each sentence is underlined. Write the simple predicate.

Example: Jeanne felt curious. *felt*

6. Jeanne and the boy went to the same school.
7. The boy spoke only with pencil and paper.
8. Jeanne brought a pencil and notebook from the house.
9. The boy wrote a message on the paper.
10. The message was the boy's name and phone number.
11. Jeanne understood the boy's problem.
12. She took Paul into her house.
13. She called the boy's mother.

B. Write each sentence. Add a simple predicate to complete each sentence.

Example: Jean and Paul _____ a snack. *ate*

14. Paul _____ a deck of cards from his pocket.
15. He _____ Jeanne a magic trick with the cards.
16. Jeanne _____ magic tricks.
17. Jeanne _____ her paint set from a drawer.
18. Paul _____ a picture.
19. He _____ something on a piece of paper.
20. The message _____ Jeanne for the visit.

Extra Practice, page 32

WRITING APPLICATION A Paragraph

Think about a time you met a new friend. Write a paragraph telling about the meeting. Include any details that will help the reader to understand what made the event fun or unusual. Exchange paragraphs with a classmate. Underline the simple predicates.

6 COMPOUND SUBJECTS AND COMPOUND PREDICATES

Your sentences can be about more than one person, thing, or action. A sentence with a **compound subject** has two or more simple subjects with the same predicate. The simple subjects are joined by *and* or *or*.

A sentence with a **compound predicate** has two or more simple predicates with the same subject. The predicates can also be joined by *and* or *or*. Some sentences have both a compound subject and a compound predicate.

JoJo and **Merry** are birds. They **chirp** and **sing**.
Selina and **Tomas watched** and **laughed**.

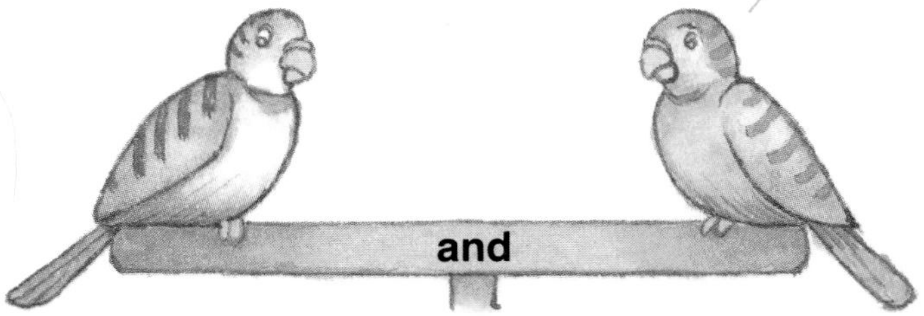

Guided Practice

Tell whether each sentence has a compound subject, a compound predicate, or both.

Example: Selina and Thomas look for the birds.
compound subject

1. The blue parakeet hops or flies around the cage.
2. The green parakeet eats and sleeps on the perch.
3. The children stand and watch the birds.
4. Selina and Tomas bought and named the birds.
5. Jojo and Merry chirped all afternoon.

?! **THINK**

- How can I tell if a sentence has a compound subject, a compound predicate, or both?

REMEMBER

- A **compound subject** has two or more simple subjects with the same predicate.
- A **compound predicate** is two or more simple predicates with the same subject.

More Practice

A. Write each sentence. Draw a line under the word that connects the simple subjects or the simple predicates.

Example: Mom and Dad wait with the children.

6. Tomas stops and notices something in the cage.
7. Tomas or Selina checks the box each day.
8. JoJo watches and guards an egg.
9. The children and Mom go to the pet store.
10. The clerk welcomes and shows them some supplies.
11. The children look and choose a special box for the egg.
12. JoJo and Merry like the nesting box.
13. Mom and Dad buy a book about parakeets.

B. Write each sentence. Draw one line under the compound subject. Draw two lines under the compound predicate.

Example: Boys and girls ask about the birds.
Selina sketches and photographs the birds.

14. JoJo or Merry sits on the eggs.
15. Mom chooses and buys food for the parakeets.
16. Selina and Tomas tell their classmates about the eggs.
17. Friends visit and see the birds.
18. The children watch and protect the birds.
19. Parakeets develop and hatch in three weeks.
20. Sheryl and Greg each want a baby parakeet.

Extra Practice, page 33

WRITING APPLICATION A Caption

Draw or find a picture that shows a group of baby animals. Write a caption describing the animals. Label each compound subject and compound predicate.

7 COMPOUND SENTENCES

Sentences can also be compound. A **compound sentence** contains two sentences joined by a comma and the words *and*, *or*, or *but*. You can form compound sentences by joining two or more sentences that contain similar ideas. Each sentence that makes up the compound sentence has a subject and a predicate of its own.

My friends enjoy the movies, **and** I like movies, too.
I like all movies, **but** James prefers Westerns.
June reads reviews, **or** she asks other people for their opinions.

Guided Practice

Tell which sentences are compound sentences.

Example: My friends chose a movie, and I met them at one o'clock. *compound sentence*

1. Everybody met at the school, and we were ready for the movie.
2. *Master of the World* sounded like an adventure movie.
3. I bought tickets, and June bought snacks.
4. James sat in the front, but we sat farther back.
5. We can sit near the aisle, or we can sit in the middle of the row.

?! **THINK**

■ How can I recognize a compound sentence?

REMEMBER

■ A **compound sentence** contains two sentences joined by a comma and *and*, *or,* or *but*.

More Practice

Write each compound sentence. Add the correct punctuation. Label correct sentences *correct*.

Example: I like old movies, and Carol likes them, too.

6. The lights dimmed and the audience became quiet.
7. The beginning was too boring and the music was too loud.
8. Maurice and Carol were bored by the movie.
9. Maurice was disappointed and Carol was restless.
10. Ten minutes passed and I liked the story less and less.
11. We did not expect this kind of movie.
12. The movie title had sounded exciting but this was not an adventure story.
13. The movie was about a scientist.
14. We could wait outside in the cold or we could stay inside and watch the movie.
15. The movie started slowly but it became more exciting.
16. Carol watched the movie eagerly, now.
17. The scientist began a dangerous experiment and the movie took a surprising turn.
18. The audience was completely silent.
19. The movie seemed short but it was more than two hours long.
20. It was a thrilling movie and I hope for a sequel.

Extra Practice, page 34

WRITING APPLICATION A Movie Review

Write a review, or summary, of a movie you have seen recently. In your review, explain what happens in the movie. Exchange papers with a classmate. Underline the compound sentences in each other's reviews.

8 CORRECTING SENTENCE FRAGMENTS

A sentence has a subject and a predicate, and it expresses a complete thought. Sometimes a group of words may look like a sentence but is actually a sentence fragment. A **sentence fragment** is a group of words that does not express a complete thought. You must add words or phrases to sentence fragments to form complete sentences.

Sentences

Jennifer and I planned a surprise.
We thought about the surprise all week.

Sentence Fragments

As a present for our mother.
Made a shopping list.

Guided Practice

Tell which groups of words are sentences and which are sentence fragments.

Example: Looked through a cookbook. *sentence fragment*
I found a simple recipe. *sentence*

1. Sat at the kitchen table.
2. Jennifer watched me gather the ingredients.
3. I put the utensils on the counter.
4. Studied the recipe.
5. To the store for ingredients.

?! THINK

■ How can I decide if a group of words is a sentence fragment?

REMEMBER

- A **sentence fragment** is a group of words that does not express a complete thought.
- You must add words or phrases to sentence fragments to form complete sentences.

GRAMMAR

More Practice

Decide which group of words in each pair is a sentence fragment. Add words to make the fragment a complete sentence. Write the new sentence. Label each complete sentence *sentence*.

Example: Took the list. *Jennifer took the list.*

6. Gone for a long time.
7. Jennifer often takes a long time at the store.
8. Reads the labels carefully.
9. I cleaned up the house.
10. Made the beds and washed the dishes.
11. Still had time for more work.
12. The floor needed.
13. I used the buffing machine.
14. Came into the kitchen.
15. She had bought the wrong kind of flour.
16. No time for another shopping trip.
17. I was not angry at her.
18. We can surprise our mother another time.
19. Mother came home.
20. Really pleased and happy.

Extra Practice, page 35

WRITING APPLICATION A Recipe

Write a recipe or set of instructions for preparing a dish. In your recipe, include the ingredients needed to make this dish. Then tell your reader what to do with each ingredient. Exchange recipes with a classmate. Underline any sentence fragments in each other's recipes.

GRAMMAR

9 MECHANICS: Capitalizing and Punctuating Sentences

Sometimes writers combine sentences to form run-on sentences instead of compound sentences. A **run-on sentence** joins together two or more sentences that should be written separately. You can correct a run-on sentence by dividing it into separate sentences. You can also fix a run-on sentence by making it into a compound sentence.

North America was unexplored in the early 1800s, no one had traveled from coast to coast.

North America was unexplored in the early 1800s. No one had traveled from coast to coast.

North America was unexplored in the early 1800s, and no one had traveled from coast to coast.

Which of the sentences above is a run-on? Which is a compound sentence? Which sentences have been correctly punctuated and capitalized?

Guided Practice

Tell which sentences are run-on sentences.

Example: Most people lived in the eastern part of the country it was safe territory. *run-on*

1. People were curious about the wild country, and they dreamed of adventure.
2. The Rocky Mountains were dangerous people needed a clear path to the West.
3. In 1803, America bought the Louisiana Purchase the new territory was huge.
4. The addition of this new land doubled the size of the United States.
5. There were no roads in the new land, and the country was mostly forest.

?! THINK

■ How can I recognize and correct run-on sentences?

REMEMBER

- You can rewrite a **run-on sentence** as separate sentences or as a compound sentence.

GRAMMAR

More Practice

Correct the run-on sentences by separating them into two sentences or by forming a compound sentence. Write each new sentence. Label each correct sentence *correct.*

Example: The explorers drew maps they made careful studies. *The explorers drew maps, and they made careful studies.*

6. Meriwether Lewis led an expedition through the new territory.
7. Lewis needed a partner, and he hired William Clark.
8. They looked for a path to the West they searched for a waterway to the Pacific Ocean.
9. They started their expedition in 1804, and they traveled for three years.
10. They had a Native American guide her name was Sacajawea.
11. Everyone waited for news the expedition took three years.
12. Sacajawea led them through the Rockies she was a knowledgeable guide.
13. On the return trip, Lewis and Clark separated they traveled two different rivers.
14. The expedition showed the size of the country, everyone was surprised.
15. It was a country of many natural resources it was bountiful.

Extra Practice, Practice Plus, pages 36–38

WRITING APPLICATION An Explanation

Imagine that you are about to set out on an expedition or a trip to a strange land. Write a paragraph explaining how you will prepare for your expedition. Have a partner check for any run-on sentences.

10 VOCABULARY BUILDING: Using Context Clues

The words that you already know can help you to figure out the meaning of new words. The familiar words in a sentence are the **context**, or setting, for a word that you do not recognize. Which words in the sentence below give clues about the meaning of the word *wilted*?

It did not rain, so the flowers *wilted* and became limp.

The word *limp* describes what happened to the flowers when *it did not rain*. These words are **context clues** that help you guess the meaning of *wilted*.

Guided Practice

Use the context clues in each sentence to tell the meaning of the underlined words.

Example: Our country cousins live on a farm and love rural life. *Clues: country, farm*

1. Since we grew up in the city, we only knew urban life.
2. Most campers did not say anything, but Mary was quite vocal.
3. She dug with her trowel because a shovel was too big.
4. She watched the farmer shear wool from the sheep and pile the soft fleeces on the ground.
5. Tod was cautious in the woods because he knew hikers must be careful.

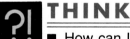

?! THINK

- How can I use context clues to figure out the meaning of unfamiliar words?

REMEMBER

- **Context clues** are familiar words that help you understand the meaning of unknown words in a sentence.

More Practice

Write each sentence. Draw a line under each familiar word that helps you to define the underlined word in each sentence.

Example: The thick foliage of the woods gave us shade.
woods, shade

6. The trail was concealed by the leaves and branches that covered it.
7. We found only a narrow path instead of the wide trail marked on the map.
8. We heard a loud crash, and the tent swayed and shook.
9. A huge limb from the tree fell between the other branches.
10. We saw two deer, a fawn and its mother.
11. Sharp rocks and poison ivy are two hazards of hiking in the woods.
12. Although his voice was gruff, the ranger was a kind person.
13. Nora was usually happy, but she felt forlorn when we left her alone.
14. Our team finally defeated the other team after losing to them all season.
15. I can smell the soup because its aroma is reaching us from the forest.

Extra Practice, page 39

WRITING APPLICATION A Letter

Write a letter to a friend describing an event that you enjoyed. Use a dictionary to find some unfamiliar words to use in your letter. Give context clues in your sentences so that others can understand any difficult words. Exchange letters with a classmate. Use context clues to guess the meaning of any unfamiliar words in each other's letters.

GRAMMAR AND WRITING CONNECTION

Combining Sentences

In your writing, you can show that the ideas in two separate sentences are related. You can show the relationship between the sentences by using a comma and the word *and* to join or connect the sentences.

The circus is in town. We will see it.
The circus is in town, **and** we will see it.

You can also use *but* or *or* to show a relationship between the sentences.

Dad usually works on the weekends, **but** he has the day off today.
Are we going by bus, **or** will Mom drive the car?

Working Together

COOPERATIVE LEARNING

With your classmates, discuss how to join sentences with *and*, *but*, or *or*. Look at each pair of sentences. Then tell how you would join them to make a single sentence.

Example Dad wore a new tie.
He looked handsome.
Dad wore a new tie, and he looked handsome.

1. Sally put on her new dress.
   I shined my shoes.
2. We were ready five minutes later.
   It took Mom an hour to get a baby-sitter.
3. Can we leave now?
   Should we wait?

Revising Sentences

Tommy wrote the following sentences in his journal about his family's trip to the circus. Help Tommy revise his notes by joining each pair of sentences. Use a comma and *and*, *but*, or *or* to show the connection between the ideas.

4. It was a beautiful day.
   The sky was clear.
5. Are we going into the big tent?
   Will we go to the sideshow first?
6. There was a huge crowd today.
   The tent had enough room for everyone.
7. At first Sally was startled by the clowns.
   She was soon laughing with everyone else.
8. The acrobats were graceful.
   Their act was thrilling.
9. The elephants were the biggest animals in the circus.
   The lions were scarier.
10. The circus was exciting.
    The trip brought the family closer together.

WRITER AT WORK

Think about some of the other surprises you read about in this unit. Brainstorm to choose a surprise you would like to write about. Write a story. Be sure to include a description of the setting and the characters. When you revise, look for any pairs of sentences that you can combine.

UNIT CHECKUP

LESSON 1

What Is a Sentence? (page 2) Write each group of words. Next to each group write **sentence** or **not a sentence**.

1. Stood in line for the bus.
2. Steve, Sam, and Mary.
3. They waited for an hour.
4. I was impatient.
5. Realized it was Saturday!

LESSON 2

Four Kinds of Sentences (page 4) Write each sentence. Add the correct end punctuation.

6. Who is at the door
7. Open the door
8. I am so surprised
9. My oldest friend has arrived
10. Did you receive my letter

LESSONS 3-5

Subjects and Predicates (pages 6–11) Write each sentence. Draw a line between the complete subject and the complete predicate. Then, draw one line under the simple subject and two lines under the simple predicate.

11. Our school expected another defeat.
12. The team lost every game last year.
13. This year was a good year.
14. We had a secret weapon.
15. Our star player saved the day.

LESSON 6

Compound Subjects and Compound Predicates (page 12) Write each sentence. Draw one line under the compound subject. Draw two lines under the compound predicate.

16. Yolanda and Wally made a collage.
17. They painted and added photos.
18. We begged and pleaded for a peek.
19. Howard and I have made collages.
20. The collage shows and tells a story.

LESSON 7

Compound Sentences (page 14) Write each sentence. Write **simple** or **compound** next to each.

21. The light will not work, and the room is dark.
22. I called the repair crew, but they were gone.
23. The bulb is new and is not broken.
24. We are impatient, or we would have looked more carefully.
25. The plug is out and lying on the floor!

LESSON 8

Correcting Sentence Fragments (page 16) Write each group of words. Write **sentence** or **fragment** next to each group.

26. My friend Sara.
27. I have a big umbrella.
28. With this umbrella.
29. Sara was surprised.
30. Even though it rained.
31. Sara likes the rain.

LESSON 9

Mechanics: Capitalizing and Punctuating Sentences (page 18) Correct and rewrite the run-on sentences.

32. The king was proud he never smiled.
33. No one smiled at him they were scared of his anger.
34. Fran wanted to tell a joke she was afraid of the king.
35. We saw the king sit down on his throne it broke into pieces.
36. We were silent soon the king actually laughed.

LESSON 10

Vocabulary Building: Using Context Clues (page 20) Write the correct definition of each underlined word.

37. I used binoculars to see things that were far away.
a. special lenses for seeing long distances
b. walking shoes c. large umbrella

38. Janice spotted a heron with its wings folded.
a. type of snake b. small water plant c. bird

39. I saw some toxic plants and stayed far away from them.
a. leafy b. poisonous c. beautiful

40.–45.

Writing Application: Complete Sentences (pages 2–19) The following paragraph contains 6 errors. Rewrite the paragraph correctly.

My visit to Aunt Jane's house. It was more fun this year than last my little cousin was finally old enough for games. Like softball and volleyball. Summer is pretty in Massachusetts the trees are shady. Cool weather, too. Lovely time.

ENRICHMENT

WORD VOLLEYS

Think of an interesting or funny subject for a sentence. Have a partner complete the sentence with a predicate. Then, let your partner begin a sentence with the same subject, while you supply the predicate. Form a compound sentence.

Pantomime Play this game in a small group. Take turns performing a simple action. For example, one person could pretend to make a campfire. The others should each write a complete sentence that describes what the person is doing. One person might write, "You are having trouble making a fire." Another might write, "You are building a fire with sticks and branches."

SENTENCE SALAD

Try this game with a group of classmates. Each student will write a sentence on a large sheet of paper.

Then, cut the paper so that one half contains the subject and one half contains the predicate.

Put all the pieces of paper in a pile. Take turns choosing slips from the pile until everyone has a whole sentence that makes sense.

WORD DETECTIVES

Play this game with a small group. Find three unfamiliar words in your dictionary. Write each word on a separate slip of paper. Next to the word, draw a picture showing something that would help a person to guess the meaning of the word. Exchange slips with the other players. The first player to guess the meaning of all the words wins.

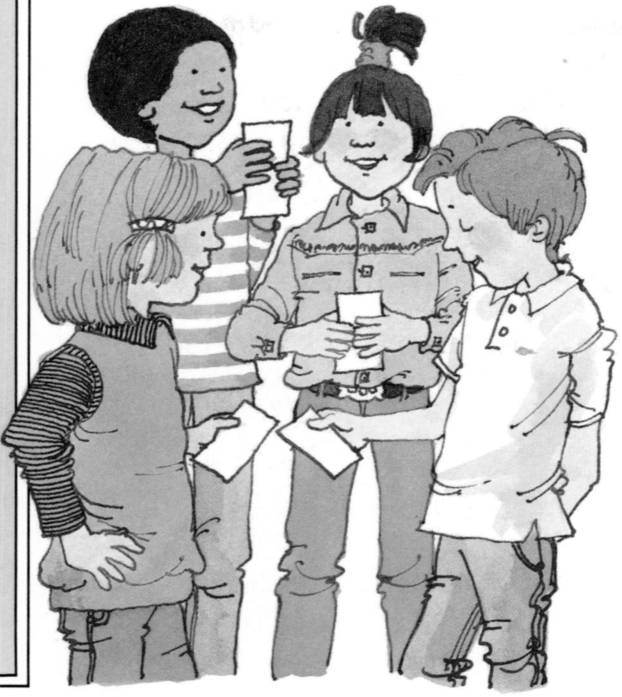

★ ★ ★ MEET THE PRESS ★ ★ ★

Did you ever watch a journalist interview someone? Try this activity with a partner. Write three questions that you could ask your partner. Write his or her answers in your

notebook. Then, add the correct punctuation and capitalization to your recorded interview. When you have finished, let your partner interview you.

EXTRA PRACTICE

Three levels of practice

What Is a Sentence? (page 2)

LEVEL **A.** Write each group of words. Next to each group write **sentence** or **not a sentence**.

1. We spent the gloomy morning alone.
2. The rain fell heavily.
3. Jim, Peter, and David.
4. A loud knock at the door.
5. Uncle Harry stood in the doorway.
6. Had not warned us of his visit.
7. Felt so happy!
8. Uncle Harry had a mysterious box.
9. Had holes in the top.

LEVEL **B.** Write each group of words. Then, add words to each group to make a complete thought. Write the new sentence.

10. Opened the box.
11. Inside the box.
12. Gave a kitten to each of us.
13. My favorite one.
14. Played with us.
15. Forgot about the rainy day.
16. None of us.
17. Always makes us happy.

LEVEL **C.** For each pair, write the group of words that is a sentence. Then, add words to the other group to make a complete thought.

18. Then, Uncle Harry went outside. To his car.
19. He came back to the house. Carried a big green sack.
20. We screamed and jumped with surprise. Excited by the surprise.
21. Made us sit down. Jim put his hand over his mouth.
22. A moment later. The bag moved!
23. We were amazed at first. All four of us.
24. Opened the bag. There was a puppy inside.
25. Mother came home later. Decided we could keep the pets.

EXTRA PRACTICE

Three levels of practice

Four Kinds of Sentences (page 4)

LEVEL **A.** Write each sentence. Next to each, write **declarative, interrogative, imperative,** or **exclamatory**.

1. Mr. and Mrs. Sanchez woke up suddenly.
2. What is that sound?
3. Go downstairs and look.
4. The basement is flooded!
5. Please do not shout.
6. Where did the water come from?
7. There is a leak somewhere.
8. Call the plumber.
9. Here is his telephone number.

LEVEL **B.** Write each sentence. Add the correct end punctuation.

10. When will the plumber come
11. He will be here soon
12. It is so cold down here
13. Turn off the faucet in the sink
14. Is that where the flood started
15. Help me move these boxes out of the water
16. What a terrible surprise this is
17. Do you hear the doorbell

LEVEL **C.** Change each declarative sentence into an imperative sentence. Change each exclamatory sentence into an interrogative sentence. Write the new sentences and add the correct end punctuation.

18. You can turn off the faucet.
19. You can see where all the water ran out!
20. The basement is completely ruined!
21. The plumber is here!
22. Let us go down to the basement.
23. You could ask him if he needs a flashlight.
24. This is a terrible mess!
25. We will need more than a mop!

EXTRA PRACTICE

Three levels of practice

Complete Subjects and Complete Predicates (page 6)

LEVEL A. Write each sentence. Draw one line under the complete subject. Draw two lines under the complete predicate.

1. Mona and I saw a funny play.
2. The play is about a detective.
3. He owns a very smart dog.
4. His dog helps him solve mysteries.
5. The man and his dog make a good team.
6. The front doorbell rang three times.
7. A woman rushed into the room.
8. Someone had stolen her necklace!
9. The detective had a new job.

LEVEL B. Add a complete subject or a complete predicate to each group of words. Write the new sentence.

10. Played the detective.
11. Broke into sobs.
12. About her necklace.
13. Was an interesting stage set.
14. Her cats Daisy, Tab, and Louie.
15. Acted guilty.
16. The whole third act.
17. Gathered all the clues.

LEVEL C. Match each subject with a predicate. Write a complete sentence.

	Subjects	Predicates
18.	My friends and I	were covered with red velvet.
19.	The main actors	was surprising.
20.	The play	guessed the ending.
21.	The theater seats	were very professional.
22.	The ending of the play	discussed the play.
23.	Nobody	was the detective's helper.
24.	The best actor	concerned a strange crime.
25.	The young assistant	solved the crime by himself.

EXTRA PRACTICE

Three levels of practice
Simple Subjects (page 8)

LEVEL **A.** The complete subject is underlined. Write the simple subject.

1. The children looked in the attic.
2. The windows were broken.
3. The wooden floor was full of splinters.
4. The whole attic smelled dusty.
5. The two youngsters had a plan.
6. Their father kept an old trunk there.
7. The wooden trunk was covered with cobwebs.
8. Curious Jules wondered about the trunk.
9. Annie thought of pirates and lost treasure.

LEVEL **B.** Write each sentence. Draw a line under the simple subject.

10. The dark room was dangerous.
11. Annie found a flashlight.
12. Her brother discovered a key.
13. The children both looked at the trunk.
14. Jules handed the key to Annie.
15. His sister held the key for a moment.
16. The old trunk probably contained treasure.
17. The attic was dark and mysterious.

LEVEL **C.** Add a simple subject to each group of words. Write the new sentence.

18. The _____ seemed more exciting than ever.
19. _____ walked toward it.
20. The _____ opened the trunk together.
21. The brass _____ fit the lock.
22. The heavy _____ swung open suddenly.
23. Many old _____ were inside the trunk!
24. _____ laughed and laughed.
25. _____ told their father about their discovery.

EXTRA PRACTICE

Three levels of practice

Simple Predicates (page 10)

LEVEL **A.** The complete predicate is underlined. Write the simple predicate.

1. The boys planned an interesting trip.
2. Stanley and Burt visited a museum.
3. The two friends looked at a map of the city.
4. They chose a museum in their neighborhood.
5. The museum had many fascinating exhibits.
6. Burt requested a map of the exhibits.
7. Stanley bought a book about dinosaurs.
8. Each room held exhibits of plants, rocks, or animals.
9. The museum was very famous.

LEVEL **B.** Write the simple predicate in each sentence.

10. The boys found the dinosaur exhibit.
11. Stanley heard a noise.
12. The noise came from a skeleton of a dinosaur.
13. The dinosaur made strange sounds.
14. Burt looked closely at the dinosaur.
15. He laughed suddenly.
16. The sounds were the clicks of someone's camera.
17. A man photographed the huge skeletons.

LEVEL **C.** Add a simple predicate to each group of words. Write the new sentence.

18. The boys ______ an interesting room.
19. It ______ many rows of old rocks.
20. A card near the rocks ______ "Fossils."
21. Fossils ______ animal traces left in rock.
22. Stanley ______ at the fossils again and again.
23. The boys ______ that exhibit.
24. The museum ______ at five o'clock.
25. Stanley and Burt ______ until closing time.

EXTRA PRACTICE

Three levels of practice

Compound Subjects and Compound Predicates (page 12)

LEVEL **A.** Write each underlined group of words. Then write **compound subject** or **compound predicate** after each group of words.

1. Saturday and Sunday were boring days.
2. Susan and I miss our old friend Bonnie.
3. Her family packed and moved away.
4. Tuesday and Wednesday passed.
5. My sister and brother asked about Bonnie.
6. The house and yard were empty.
7. I wait and hope for a letter soon.
8. Aunt Paula and Uncle Edward must know Bonnie's address.
9. I call and ask them for any news.

LEVEL **B.** Write each sentence. Draw one line under each compound subject. Draw two lines under each compound predicate.

10. Susan and I received a letter from Bonnie.
11. Friends and neighbors heard about Bonnie's new home.
12. We dressed and ran to school.
13. Richard and Jenny showed each other post cards from Bonnie.
14. Her phone number and address were both on the cards.
15. My classmates talked and laughed during recess.
16. The teacher and students were all excited.
17. Everyone knew and liked Bonnie.

LEVEL **C.** Write the compound subject or the compound predicate in each sentence. Then write the joining word in each sentence.

18. The teacher smiled and welcomed the whole class.
19. She and a student had a secret.
20. Susan giggled and whispered to me.
21. The boys and girls got a surprise.
22. Bonnie and her friends were together again.
23. Bonnie grinned and waved at her classmates.
24. The teacher and the class voted for a celebration.
25. A party or picnic was an excellent idea.

EXTRA PRACTICE

Three levels of practice

Compound Sentences (page 14)

LEVEL **A.** Write each sentence. Then write whether the sentence is a **simple sentence** or a **compound sentence**.

1. I read a good book this week.
2. The librarian recommended it, and I took it home.
3. Annie liked the book, too, and she told Joe about it.
4. The story was funny and full of surprises.
5. I waited until the weekend and read all morning.
6. On Saturdays I often read, or I visit my friends.
7. I read until Saturday night, and I could not stop!
8. The hero was a cat named Max, but he was just like a person.
9. He lived in the country, and he had many friends.

LEVEL **B.** Draw a line under the word that joins the two separate sentences in each compound sentence. Add the correct punctuation.

10. The book was funny and it was exciting.
11. The cat needed excitement or he became bored.
12. He was brave and he was also intelligent.
13. Max had adventures but he always escaped.
14. One day Max found a path and he faced a decision.
15. The cat could go to the right or he could go to the left.
16. He chose the left path and he admired the scenery.
17. Everything seemed safe but danger was ahead.

LEVEL **C.** Add a sentence to each one below to make a compound sentence. Write the new compound sentence.

18. A strange animal appeared.
19. He had a huge, square head.
20. Max could run.
21. Max approached the enemy.
22. He looked closely at the animal.
23. The animal had a problem.
24. A bag was stuck on his head.
25. Max almost laughed out loud.

EXTRA PRACTICE

Three levels of practice

Correcting Sentence Fragments (page 16)

LEVEL **A.** Write each group of words. Write **sentence** or **sentence fragment** next to each.

1. One sunny morning.
2. Dreams of treasure.
3. Lenore walked through the park.
4. On the ground near the swings.
5. She saw a golden object.
6. It was shiny.
7. Wondered what it was.
8. Could it be gold?
9. An exciting idea.

LEVEL **B.** Join each group of words to make a complete sentence. Write the new sentence.

10. Without stopping, the girl. Ran all the way home.
11. Maybe it was worth. A hundred dollars.
12. As she ran. She thought about her new wealth.
13. Perhaps she could. Spend it on a new bike.
14. A hundred dollars. Was a wonderful discovery.
15. Now she had money. For presents.
16. A number of ideas. Popped into Lenore's mind.
17. In her pocket. Was the golden treasure.

LEVEL **C.** Add words to these fragments to make them complete sentences. Write the new sentences.

18. Reached the front door.
19. Her brother and sister.
20. As she explained her discovery.
21. Held her breath.
22. Showed them her treasure.
23. Laughed and laughed at her.
24. When she showed them the chocolate wrapped in gold paper.
25. Laughed with the others.

EXTRA PRACTICE

Three levels of practice

Mechanics: Capitalizing and Punctuating Sentences (page 18)

LEVEL **A.** Write **correct** or **run-on** after each word group.

1. Dr. Porter lived in his laboratory.
2. He had a special project it took all his time.
3. The scientist worked every day he worked hard and long.
4. He was uncertain about his new project.
5. The chemicals he mixed were new they were not tested yet.
6. What could happen?
7. The experiment might succeed it could fail.
8. Dr. Porter dreamed of success he longed for fame.
9. He continued with his experiment.

LEVEL **B.** Correct the punctuation and capitalization in each sentence. Write the new sentence.

10. dr. Porter sat and worried about his work.
11. he mixed two red chemicals.
12. the mixture was red but he wanted something purple.
13. it was not the correct result and he threw out the chemicals and started over.
14. he mixed two blue chemicals and made a dark powder.
15. the scientist became angry.
16. he was frustrated by his mistakes.
17. his experiment was important to him.

LEVEL **C.** Correct the run-on sentences. Write the new sentence.

18. The scientist yelled he was very upset.
19. He made one last attempt he began again.
20. Purple stuff suddenly filled the tube it smelled sweet.
21. It was a fabulous new invention it was a success.
22. Maybe it was a new food maybe it was a type of fuel.
23. He smelled the mixture it was grape jelly.
24. Dr. Porter made a sandwich he ate every bit of it.
25. He is famous now and his invention is delicious.

PRACTICE + PLUS

Three levels of additional practice for a difficult skill

Mechanics: Capitalizing and Punctuating Sentences (page 18)

LEVEL **A.** Read each sentence. Write **correct** or **run-on** for each.

1. Bill plays the guitar he also plays the drums.
2. His best friend plays the piano.
3. They know twenty songs they write songs, too.
4. Bill and Robin play rock music and jazz.
5. Audiences love them they are wonderful.
6. Their band played ten times last week.
7. We listened to the band they played for hours.
8. They played fast songs I danced all evening.
9. I like funny songs and serious ones, too.
10. Horace can sing and dance well he is talented.
11. Debby is also a good dancer she is graceful.
12. We can watch the show or dance again.
13. The orchestra plays tonight the ballet performs tomorrow I like them both.
14. Darnell plays the violin and the cello.
15. I like classical music it is beautiful and it is restful.
16. We rehearse every afternoon the music is difficult we also rehearse on weekends.
17. The orchestra still needs an oboe player we could also use another flute player.
18. The conductor is here and ready for the rehearsal.

LEVEL **B.** Rewrite each run-on sentence as two correct sentences or one compound sentence.

19. The morning was cool the sun shone brightly.
20. Patricia had no plans she felt restless.
21. Her mother suggested some ideas Patricia did not like any of them.
22. She called a friend the friend was not at home.
23. Patricia sat on the steps the cement was too hot.
24. The neighborhood was deserted the girl saw no one.
25. Patricia walked to the end of the block she noticed a sign.

PRACTICE + PLUS

26. The sign was on a tree it said, "Help Wanted."
27. Patricia read the words they gave her a new idea.
28. A neighbor had a dog the dog needed a bath.
29. Patricia ran home she found a pencil and notepad.
30. She ran to the corner again the sign was still there.
31. She copied down the phone number she also wrote the address.
32. Patricia's mother met her on the steps Patricia told her about the job.
33. Her mother liked the idea Patricia could wash the dog.
34. They went inside together her mother dialed the number.

LEVEL **C.** Rewrite each run-on sentence correctly.

35. Mrs. Blake was happy her spaniel needed a bath now someone was available for the job.
36. Patricia and her mother met Mrs. Blake the woman had a broken arm she needed help with her dog.
37. The spaniel's name was Jinx Jinx was a funny dog.
38. Patricia patted the dog Jinx licked Patricia's hand.
39. Mrs. Blake got a bucket she also brought some soap.
40. Patricia and Jinx went to the garden Patricia put Jinx into a special tub.
41. She used the garden hose water filled the tub Jinx barked happily.
42. Patricia soaped the dog's fur the shampoo made thick suds.
43. She used warm water the dog enjoyed it.
44. Patricia rinsed the soap away Mrs. Blake and Patricia's mother watched the whole bath.
45. Jinx jumped from the tub he shook the water from his ears.
46. Patricia brushed his wet fur the dog stood calmly the sun quickly dried his fur.
47. Mrs. Blake brought a tray of sandwiches to the patio everyone ate a sandwich Jinx had one also.
48. Mrs. Blake paid the girl five dollars she thanked Patricia and offered her another job.
49. Jinx needed a dog walker Patricia was delighted she liked Jinx.
50. Everyone was happy Mrs. Blake had a helper Patricia and her mother had a new friend.

EXTRA PRACTICE

Three levels of practice

Vocabulary Building: Using Context Clues (page 20)

LEVEL **A.** Write a definition for each underlined word. Draw a line under the familiar words that you used as context clues.

1. The composer startled the listeners with surprising music.
2. At first the tune was soothing, soft, and gentle.
3. He deceived us by tricking us with this quiet beginning.
4. The instruments blared loud notes at the end.
5. Anyone who dozed was awakened suddenly.

LEVEL **B.** Write each sentence. Use context clues to select the correct definition of the underlined word. Write the correct definition.

6. The band played popular pieces, so we heard our favorite songs.
   a. unpleasant   b. well-liked   c. lively
7. The crowd was enthusiastic and loved every song the band played.
   a. angry   b. strongly responsive   c. loud
8. Last time, the music was awful, but this time, it was superb.
   a. terrible   b. musical   c. excellent
9. I appreciated the concert, but Bill hated it.
   a. disliked   b. enjoyed   c. learned
10. The concert included Jan's favorite song, one that he adored.
    a. hated   b. wrote   c. loved

LEVEL **C.** Write each sentence. Use context clues to help you guess the meaning of the underlined words. Write a definition for the word.

11. If I could select tonight's concert, I would opt for a rock band.
12. At the last classical concert I was bored, and I do not think this one will delight me.
13. I expected something dull, so I was astonished by the exciting music.
14. The conductor beamed, and the audience smiled back at him.
15. Before, I thought that nothing could alter my opinion of classical music, but this concert has given me different ideas.

WRITING

UNIT 2

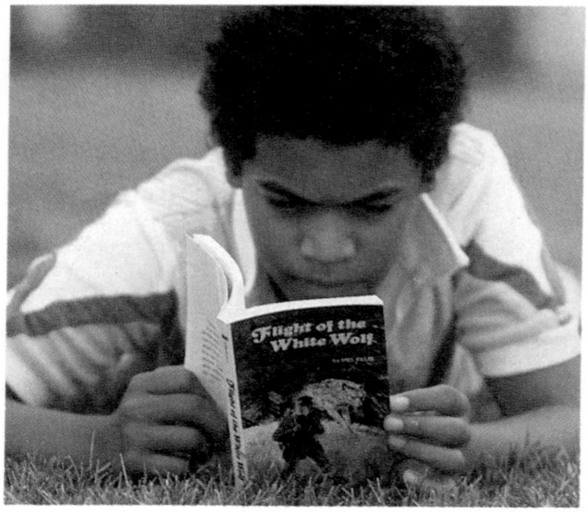

Writing Personal Narratives

Read the quotation and look at the picture on the opposite page. Oliver Butterworth wrote the story that you will read in this unit. How does Oliver Butterworth feel about writing?

When you write a personal narrative, you will want your audience to understand the way you felt about an event that was important to you.

Focus A personal narrative tells about something that happened in your life.

What event would you like to write about? On the following pages you will find a story that tells of a momentous event in one person's life. You will see some photographs, too. You can use both the story and the photographs to find ideas for writing.

THEME: *SURPRISES*

Sometimes I think I might pinch myself and wake up and find that I just dreamed about writing books. It seems too good to be true.

—Oliver Butterworth

LITERATURE

Reading Like a Writer

AWARD WINNING SELECTION

Did you ever have a surprise that was too exciting to enjoy alone? How did you share the experience with other people?

In this story, a boy named Nate and his family discover that their ordinary hen has hatched the surprise of the century.

As you read the selection, look for the specific details that the author uses to describe the amazing event.

from THE ENORMOUS EGG

by Oliver Butterworth

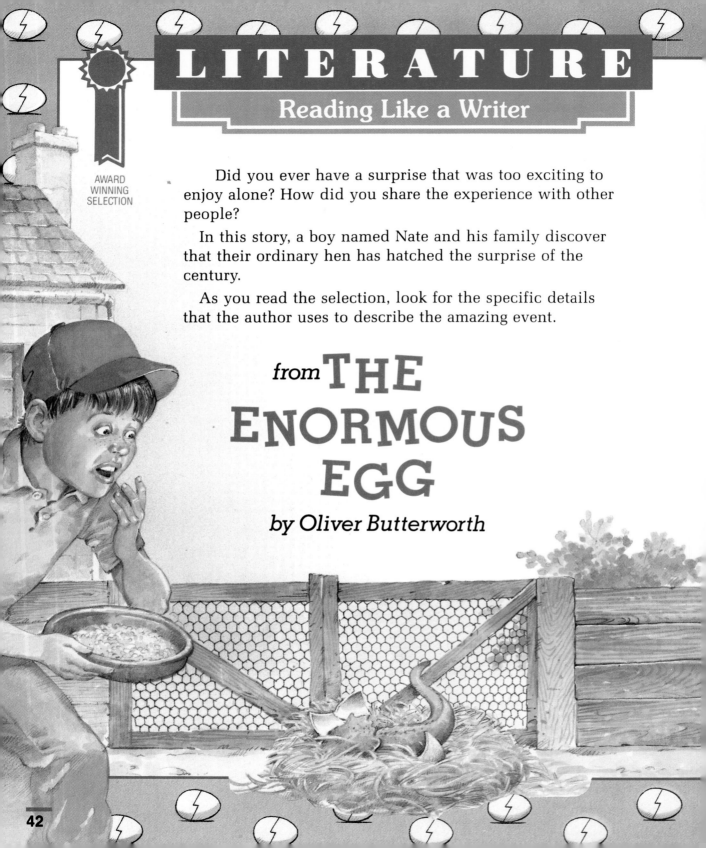

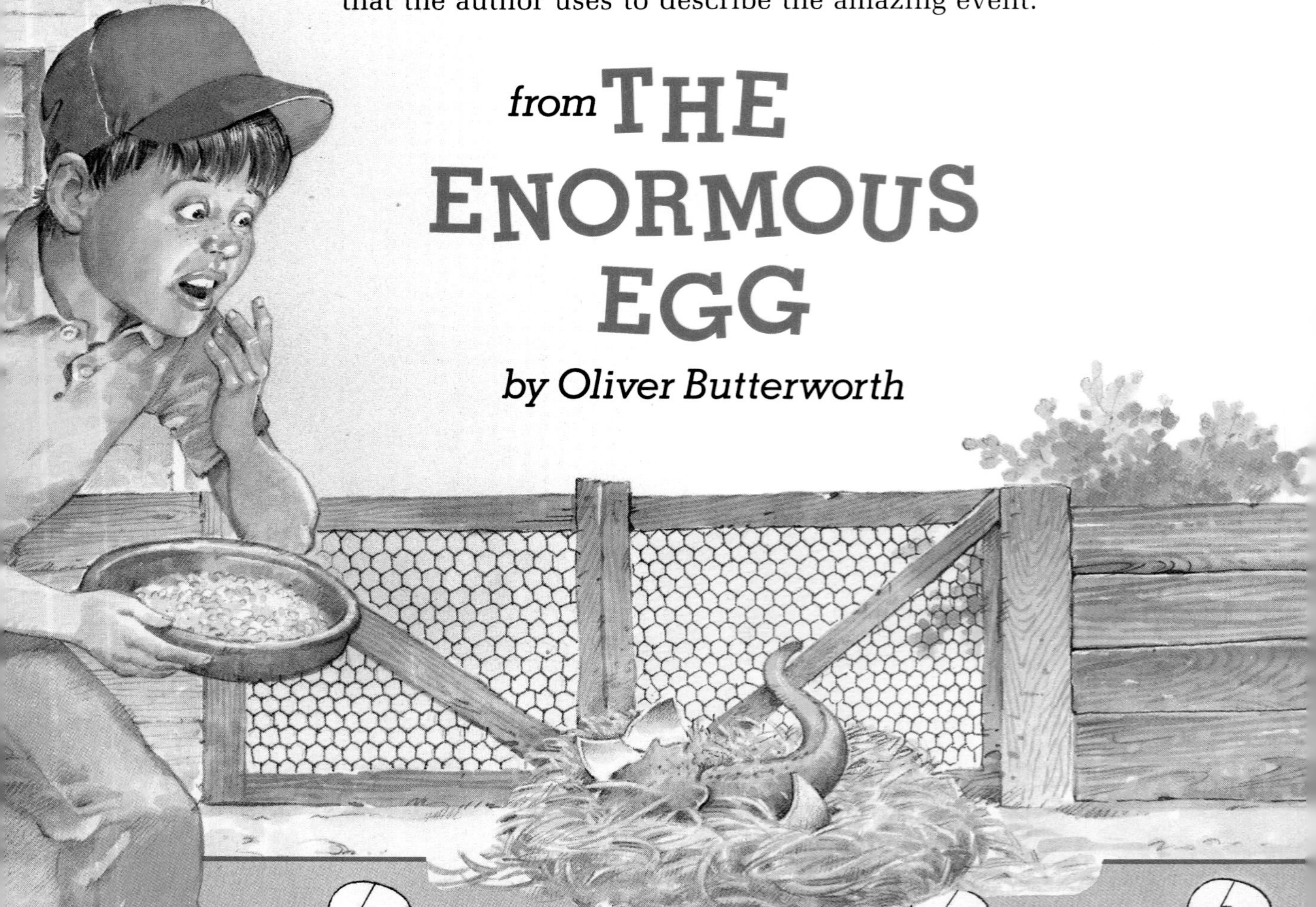

I just went over to the nest and put a little grain down for that poor old hen, and started to turn away, when I realized all at once that something had changed. The hen wasn't sitting on the nest any more. She was walking back and forth with a kind of wild look in her eye, and every time she came near the nest she gave a little hop and fluttered away again. I bent down to look in the nest, and—wow! There was something in there, and it was alive! It was moving around.

The first paragraph introduces the main idea of the selection and prepares you for the details in the narrative.

I thought at first that it was a rat or something that had busted the egg and eaten it. But after I got a good look I could see that it wasn't any rat. It was about the size of a squirrel, but it didn't have any hair, and its head—well, I couldn't believe my eyes when I saw it. It didn't look like anything I'd ever seen before. It had three little knobs sticking out of its head and a sort of collar up over its neck. It was a lizardy-looking critter, and it kept moving its thick tail slowly back and forth in the nest. The poor hen was looking pretty upset. I guess she hadn't expected anything like this, and neither had I.

Notice the author's use of details to help you "see" the strange animal in the hen's nest.

I just stood there for a minute, I was so surprised all I could do was look. Then I started yelling, and lit out across the yard as fast as I could go. When I busted into

the kitchen Mom was so startled that she dropped a saucepan in the sink. Pop came running down the stairs with lather over one side of his face and a razor in his hand, and Cynthia was right behind.

"For goodness' sakes!" Mom said. "What's the matter with you?"

"It's alive!" I shouted. "It's alive! And it moves around, and it wiggles its tail and has horns and it looks like a lizard, and it doesn't have any fur, and the hen's running round and round and doesn't know what to do about it, and—"

"Hold on there, Nate," Pop said. "You look as if you'd seen a ghost. What's all the excitement about?"

I was so out of breath that I couldn't talk for a while. "It's the egg," I said. "It's hatched!"

"What!" Pop shouted. "It did? Why didn't you say so?" And he ran out the door and down the steps, still holding on to his razor. I grabbed Mom's hand and pulled her along, and Cynthia was just ahead of us. She'd forgotten to put on her shoes, and Mom was saying, "All this excitement over an egg. My goodness!"

When we all got out to the nest, Pop was leaning over, looking hard at it. Mom was still saying, "Why we should all come running out here only half dressed, just to see an egg that hatched out—I can't see anything in there, it's too dark. Walt, why don't you bring it out here so we can look at it, whatever it is?"

Pop was still leaning over staring at the thing in the nest. All he said was, "By jing!" under his breath, sort of. By that time Cynthia had squeezed in beside Pop. She took one good look and then let out a screech that you could have heard way down to the post office. That started the hen off, and she began squawking and flapping around in circles, and Ezekiel started crowing, and the goat started bleating. There was an awful lot of commotion, and everybody was talking at the same time and nobody could hear anything.

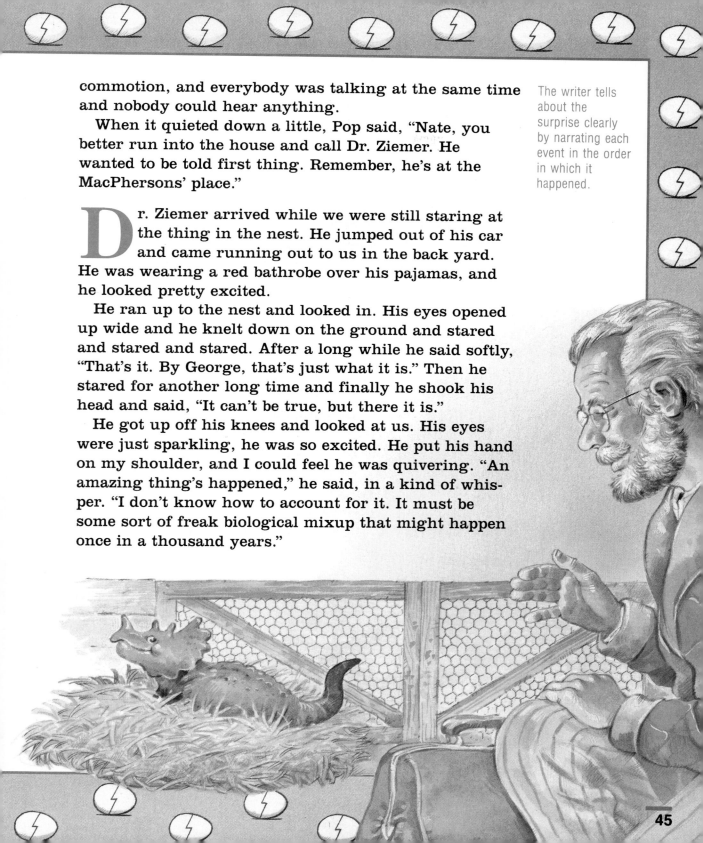

When it quieted down a little, Pop said, "Nate, you better run into the house and call Dr. Ziemer. He wanted to be told first thing. Remember, he's at the MacPhersons' place."

The writer tells about the surprise clearly by narrating each event in the order in which it happened.

Dr. Ziemer arrived while we were still staring at the thing in the nest. He jumped out of his car and came running out to us in the back yard. He was wearing a red bathrobe over his pajamas, and he looked pretty excited.

He ran up to the nest and looked in. His eyes opened up wide and he knelt down on the ground and stared and stared and stared. After a long while he said softly, "That's it. By George, that's just what it is." Then he stared for another long time and finally he shook his head and said, "It can't be true, but there it is."

He got up off his knees and looked at us. His eyes were just sparkling, he was so excited. He put his hand on my shoulder, and I could feel he was quivering. "An amazing thing's happened," he said, in a kind of whisper. "I don't know how to account for it. It must be some sort of freak biological mixup that might happen once in a thousand years."

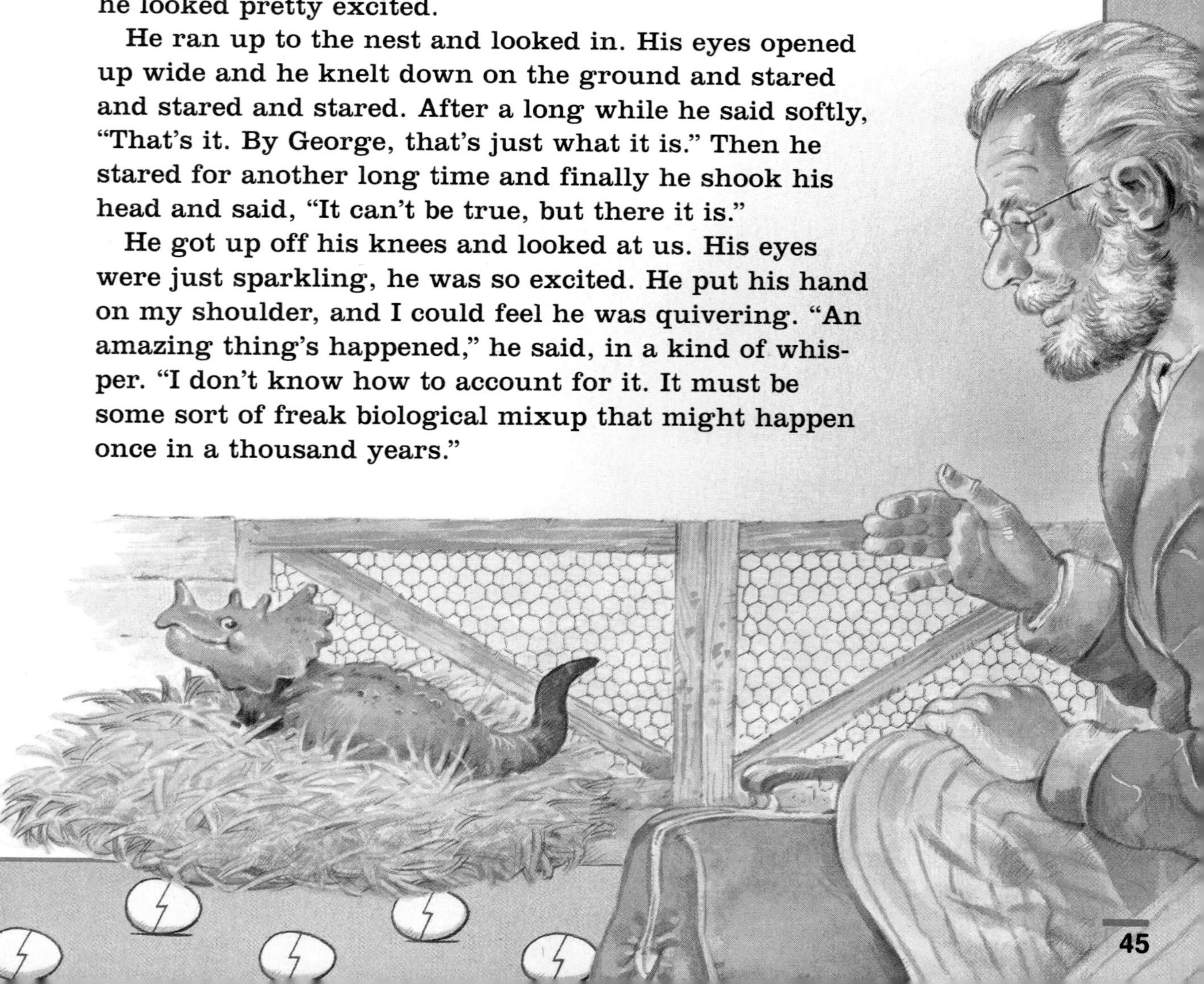

"But what is it?" I asked.

Dr. Ziemer turned and pointed a trembling finger at the nest. "Believe it or not, you people have hatched out a dinosaur."

We just looked at him.

"Sounds incredible, I know," he said, "and I can't explain it, but there it is. I've seen too many Triceratops skulls to be mistaken about this one."

"But—but how could it be a dinosaur?" Pop asked.

"Goodness gracious!" Mom spluttered. "And right here in our back yard. It doesn't seem hardly right. And on a Sunday, too."

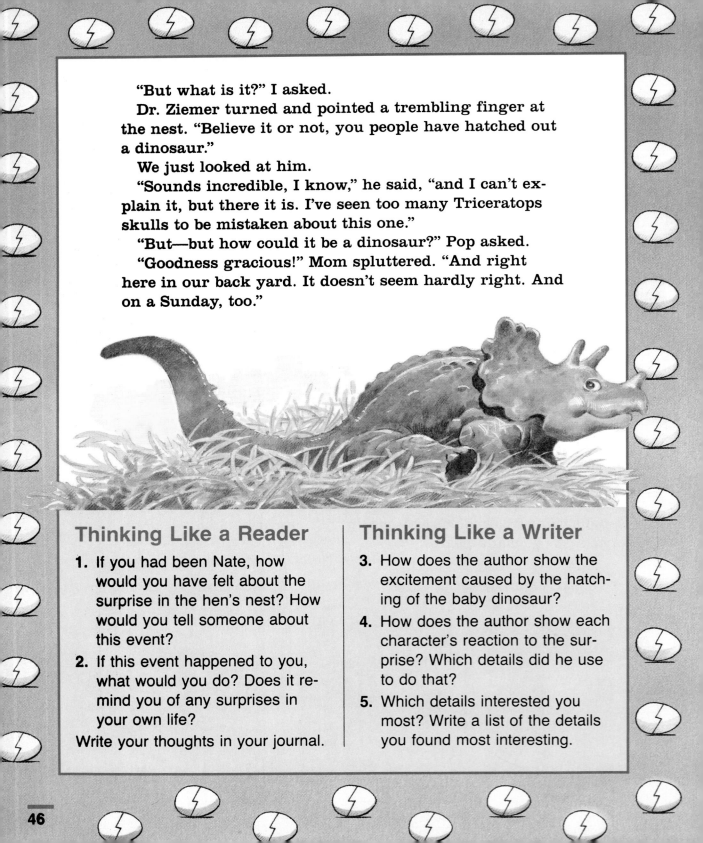

Thinking Like a Reader

1. If you had been Nate, how would you have felt about the surprise in the hen's nest? How would you tell someone about this event?

2. If this event happened to you, what would you do? Does it remind you of any surprises in your own life?

Write your thoughts in your journal.

Thinking Like a Writer

3. How does the author show the excitement caused by the hatching of the baby dinosaur?

4. How does the author show each character's reaction to the surprise? Which details did he use to do that?

5. Which details interested you most? Write a list of the details you found most interesting.

Responding to

LITERATURE

Brainstorm

Vocabulary

In "The Enormous Egg," Nate uses words like "screech," "commotion," and "excitement" to show how the characters respond to the arrival of the dinosaur. Think of an exciting event that has happened to you. What words might describe the surprise? In your journal write any words or phrases that come to mind. Begin to create a personal vocabulary list.

Talk It Over

Talk About a Surprise

Nate is amazed to find a dinosaur in the hen's nest where he expected to find an unhatched egg or a baby chick. Imagine that you have just experienced a surprise. Talk about the surprise with a partner. Tell him or her what happened, using as many clear details as possible. Ask your partner if your description needs more details in order to be precise. Then, let your partner tell you about a surprise while you listen carefully.

Quick Write *Write a Letter*

You have been thinking about surprises and how people respond to them. Think about a surprise that you have experienced. Write a brief letter to a friend that describes the surprise. For example, you might write to a friend to share your surprise at a sudden bad storm.

Keep your letter in your folder.

> Dear Karla,
> I know it's the middle of May, but we just had the biggest snowstorm of the year. Mother was getting ready to plant tomatoes when she heard about the storm on the radio. The

Idea Corner

Things That Surprised Me

You have already thought about some surprises that you might want to share. Take time to record some of them in your journal. You may write down words or phrases, topics for writing, or even drawings that illustrate events that have happened to you.

PICTURES SEEING LIKE A WRITER

Finding Ideas for Writing

Look at the pictures. Think about what you see.
What ideas for narrative writing do the pictures give you?
Write your ideas in your journal.

WRITING

TOGETHER

1 GROUP WRITING: A Personal Narrative

COOPERATIVE LEARNING

In a personal narrative, your purpose is to share an event with your readers. How can you help your audience to experience the event?

- Main-Idea Sentence
- Supporting Details
- Time Order

As you write, think about your **purpose** or reason for writing a personal narrative. You may be writing to entertain your reader or to communicate a particular idea. Your readers, or **audience**, may be other students, friends, a teacher, or someone whom you have never met.

Main-Idea Sentence

Read the paragraph below. Notice how the first sentence prepares you for what follows.

> Before our camping trip, we prepared for every possibility except one. On Monday, Mary packed the maps and compass. Then she reminded Rufus to bring the first-aid kit. On Thursday, Sue bought extra water containers, and we packed enough food for a whole army. The only thing for which we were not prepared was rain.

The first sentence in the paragraph is the **main-idea sentence.** It states the main, or overall, idea of the paragraph and catches the reader's attention.

Guided Practice: Main-Idea Sentence

Imagine that you and your friends have made plans to take a trip together. Work with your class to write a main-idea sentence for a narrative about the unexpected events that happened during your trip.

Supporting Details

Details support the main idea in a personal narrative. They give more information about the event or situation. Each detail sentence further develops the main idea and helps the reader to understand the narrative.

Time Order

In a personal narrative, the sentences that support the main idea often appear in **time order**, the order or sequence in which events occur.

Look at the paragraph about the camping trip. Notice the sentences that support the main idea.

- Which words in these sentences show time order?
- What other words could you use to show the order of events?

Read the paragraph again, replacing each of the time-order words or phrases with a time-order word from the following list.

after, always, before, finally, first, last, later, meanwhile, now, soon, then

Do the time-order words you have chosen make the sequence of events clear?

Guided Practice: Charting Supporting Details

Your class has written a main-idea sentence for a personal narrative. With your class, make a chart like the one that follows. Fill in the chart with details that tell about the experience.

Example: My camping trip was filled with unexpected events.

saw a bear
fell into a creek
lost my knapsack
decided to give up camping

Putting a Personal Narrative Together

With your class, you have written a main-idea sentence for a narrative. You have charted supporting details and used time-order words.

Think about your main-idea sentence. Then, look at your chart of supporting details. You will need to decide which details best support the main idea of your narrative. Which supporting details will you include? What details might you add to your narrative?

Here is one student's personal narrative. The student used the main-idea sentence and some of the details you have already seen to write her own paragraph. She ordered her sentences carefully to make her narrative clear. As you read the paragraph, look for the time-order words that show the sequence of events.

> My camping trip was filled with unexpected events. First, the weather turned overcast and rainy. Then, there were unexpected animals. Raccoons and bears ate our food. They knocked over the garbage pails, too. Finally, Joey had an accident. He fell into the little creek on the campgrounds and got completely soaked. In the future, we have to prepare more carefully.

Guided Practice: Writing a Personal Narrative

Use the main-idea sentence you wrote with your class to write a personal narrative. Write three or four detail sentences that support the main idea. Include some supporting details from your chart. Use time-order words to arrange the sentences in a logical order.

Exchange paragraphs with a classmate. Underline the detail sentences in each other's narratives. Ask your partner which detail sentences helped him or her to understand your narrative. Then, ask your partner if more details are needed to make your meaning clear.

Checklist: Narrative Writing

When you write a personal narrative, you will want to keep some points in mind. You can use the checklist below to remind you to include these points.

Make a copy of the completed checklist. You can add other points to it to help you write. Keep a copy of it in your writing folder. You can use it when you write your personal narrative.

CHECKLIST

✔ Purpose and audience
- ■ ______________________
- ■ ______________________

✔ Main idea ____________
- ■ ______________________
- ■ ______________________

✔ Supporting details
- ■ ______________________
- ■ ______________________

✔ Time-order words ______
- ■ ______________________
- ■ ______________________

WRITING TOGETHER

WRITING TOGETHER

2 THINKING AND WRITING: Main Idea and Details

You have learned that writing a personal narrative is one way to share an experience with a reader. In a narrative you tell your reader about an event or events. You help the reader to understand what happened by selecting and ordering details carefully.

Every narrative begins with a main, or an overall, idea. The detail sentences in the narrative support the main idea by giving more information about the event. Look at this page from a writer's journal. This writer is preparing to write a personal narrative about a short trip on a ferryboat. On the page, details are listed.

My first trip on the ferryboat was the most exciting part of summer vacation.

Mother's dog, Willie, got lost in the engine room.

The trip took three hours.

My little sister Carmen wandered away.

Carmen's birthday is tomorrow.

Thinking Like a Writer

■ Which details support this writer's main idea?

Not all of the details in the writer's journal add to the main idea of the narrative. For instance, the sentence about Carmen's birthday does not give more information about the ferryboat trip.

THINKING APPLICATION Choosing Supporting Details

COOPERATIVE LEARNING

Each of the writers below is planning to write a personal narrative. Help each one to decide which detail sentences support his or her main idea. Write the details to include on a separate piece of paper. You may work with a group of students to discuss your ideas. Share the reasons for your choices with your classmates.

1. Lisa's personal narrative will tell about the exciting day on which she first saw her newborn twin sisters. Which details should she include? What might she add?

My favorite baby-sitter read to me.
Mom came home with twins!
I like to read aloud.
Dad brought Mom and the babies home.

2. Brian's personal narrative will tell about his first night at camp. Which details should he include? What might he add?

The bunkhouse was warm and stuffy.
Strange noises kept me awake.
I grew up in the city.
Dad promised us a puppy in the fall.

3. Gabriella's personal narrative will tell about the day she learned to play baseball. Which details should she include? What might she add?

I watched other players hit the ball.
I felt eager to try, too.
I already knew how to play tennis.
I hit a home run that day.

4. Mel's personal narrative will tell about his visit to a bakery. Which details should he include? What might he add?

The air smelled delicious.
The bakers rolled out trays of dough.
I tasted a piece of fresh bread.
Bread at the supermarket is already sliced.

3 INDEPENDENT WRITING: A Personal Narrative

Prewrite: Step 1

You have learned some important ideas about narration. Now you are ready to choose your own topic for writing. Louis, a student in the fifth grade, decided his **audience** would be other students. He chose a topic in this way.

Choosing a Topic

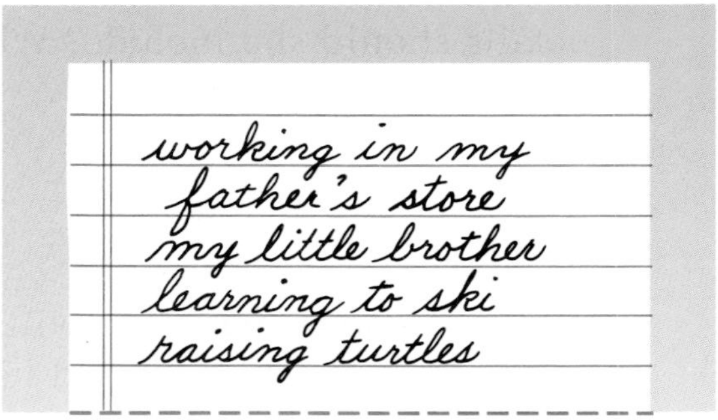

1. First, Louis wrote a list of events that might interest other students.
2. Next, he thought about narrating each event.
3. Last, he selected the event he thought would make the most interesting narrative.

Louis decided to write about learning to ski. He narrowed his topic to the first time he skied. His **purpose** was to show what his first day on the ski slopes was like.

Louis made a **cluster** that helped him to explore ideas for writing. Louis's cluster looked like this.

Exploring Ideas: Clustering Strategy

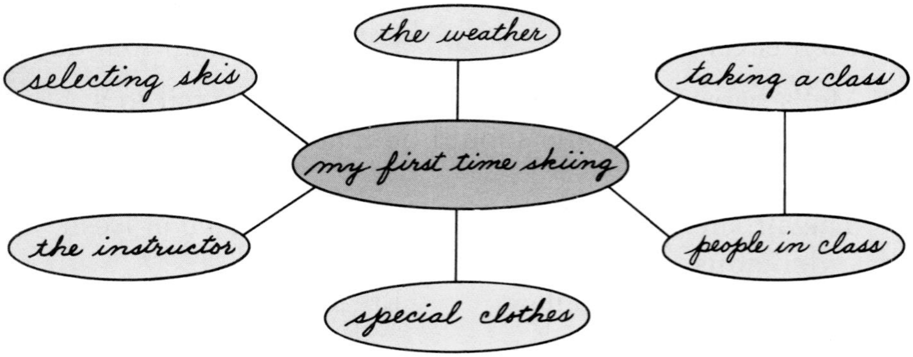

Before beginning to write, Louis tried to remember as many details as he could about that day. He wanted to give a clear account of the event. Louis also added some more details to his cluster.

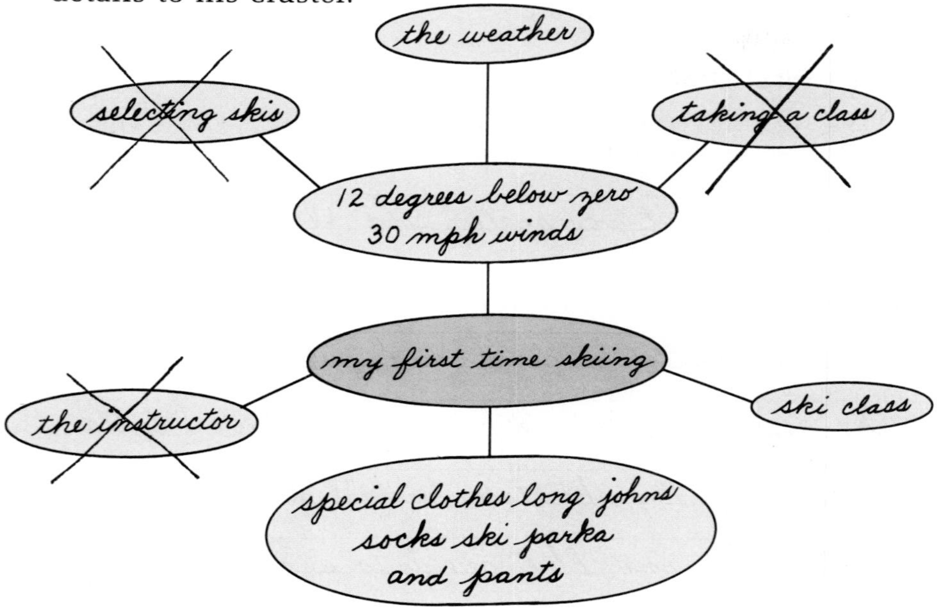

Thinking Like a Writer

- What did Louis add?
- What did he cross out?
- Why do you think he decided to leave out certain details?

YOUR TURN

JOURNAL

Think of an experience that you would like to share. Use **Pictures** or your journal for ideas. Follow these steps.

- Make a list of events or experiences.
- Choose one that you would like to share.
- Narrow the topic if it is too broad.
- Decide on the main idea of your personal narrative.
- Think about your purpose and audience.

Make a cluster. Remember, you can add to or take away from the cluster at any time.

WRITING PROCESS

Write a First Draft: Step 2

Louis has decided which details to include in his personal narrative. He used a planning checklist. Louis is ready to write his first draft.

Louis's First Draft

First because it was really cold. I put on two pairs of long johns and socks. The wind howled and it blue really hard. Then I put on my ski parka and ski pants. When I went outside I could hardly walk. My ski class hadn't prepared me for this. The wind blue me into a snowdrift. Later I heard the temperature was 12 degrees below zero with 30 mile-an-hour winds.

While Louis was writing his first draft, he did not worry about errors. He wanted to put all of his ideas down on paper.

YOUR TURN

Write your first draft. As you prepare to write, ask yourself these questions.

- What is my main idea? How can I best explain it?
- Which details would my audience want to know?

TIME-OUT You might want to take some time out before you revise. That way you will be able to revise your writing with a fresh eye.

Planning Checklist

- Remember purpose and audience.
- State a main idea.
- Use supporting details.
- Use time-order words.

Revise: Step 3

After Louis finished his first draft, he read it over to himself. He decided to share his narrative with his classmate Fernando. Fernando had some suggestions for improving the narrative.

Louis reviewed his planning checklist. He saw that he had forgotten an important point. He checked it off so that he would remember it when he revised. Louis now has a checklist to use as he revises.

Louis made some changes to his personal narrative. Notice that he did not correct small errors. He knew he could correct them later.

The revisions Louis made changed his paragraph. Turn the page. Read Louis's revised paragraph.

Revising Checklist

- ■ Remember purpose and audience.
- ✓ ■ State a main idea.
- ■ Use supporting details.
- ■ Use time-order words.

WRITING PROCESS

Louis's Revised Draft

My first day skiing, I thought I was prepared for everything. First because it was really cold. I put on two pairs of long johns and socks. The wind howled and it blue really hard. Then I put on my ski parka and ski pants. When I went outside I could hardly walk. My ski class hadn't prepared me for this. The wind blue me into a snowdrift. Later I heard the temperature was 12 degrees below zero with 30 mile-an-hour winds.

Thinking Like a Writer

WISE WORD CHOICE

- Which sentence did Louis add? How does adding the sentence improve the paragraph?
- Which sentences did Louis put in a different order? Do you think the changes improve the paragraph?

YOUR TURN

Read your first draft. Make a checklist. Ask yourself these questions.

- Is my main idea clear?
- Do my supporting details develop the main idea?
- Have I used time-order words correctly?

If you wish, ask a friend to read your narrative and make suggestions. Then revise your paragraph.

Proofread: Step 4

Louis knew that his work was not complete until he proofread his paragraph. He used a proofreading checklist while he proofread.

Louis's Proofread Draft

My first day skiing, I thought I was prepared for everything.
First, because it was really cold, I put on two pairs of long johns and socks. The wind howled and it blew (blue) really hard. Then I put on my ski parka and ski pants. When I went outside I could hardly walk. My ski class hadn't prepared me for this. The wind blew (blue) me into a snowdrift. Later I heard the temperature was 12 degrees

YOUR TURN

Proofreading Practice

Use the paragraph below to practice your proofreading skills. Find the errors. Write the paragraph correctly on a separate piece of paper.

I thought I new everything about Ronnie. He was my age and he had two sisters. Because he was knew at skool. He didn't have a lot of friends. He was smart. He liked to study. The girls liked him because he was really nice to them. When I finally met his parents, they were French. Ronnie talked to them in perfect French, and translated for me!

Proofreading Checklist

- Did I indent my paragraph?
- Did I spell all words correctly?
- What punctuation errors do I need to correct?
- What capitalization errors do I need to correct?

Applying Your Proofreading Skills

Use your checklist to proofread your personal narrative. Review **The Grammar Connection** and **The Mechanics Connection**, too. Use the proofreading marks to mark changes.

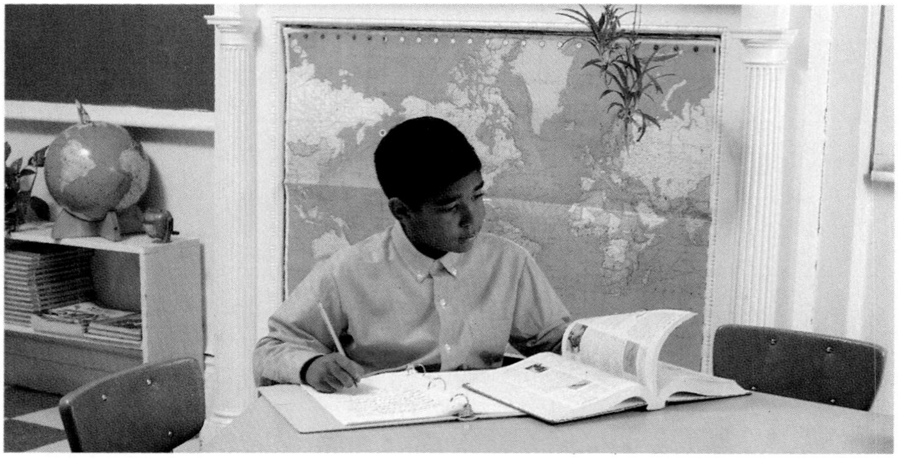

THE GRAMMAR CONNECTION

Remember these rules about sentences.

- A sentence expresses a complete thought.
- A sentence contains both a subject and a predicate.

  Must guard against frostbite. *not a sentence*
  Skiers must guard against frostbite. *sentence*

Check your narrative. Have you used complete sentences?

THE MECHANICS CONNECTION

Remember these rules about punctuating sentences.

- A sentence begins with a capital letter and ends with a period, an exclamation mark, or a question mark.
- To join two or more sentences, use a comma and a joining word.

  Tomorrow we will ski**, and** we will ride the chair lift.

Check your narrative paragraph. Have you used the correct punctuation to combine your sentences?

Proofreading Marks

¶ Indent
∧ Add
Take out
≡ Make a capital letter
/ Make a small letter

Publish: Step 5

Louis shared his personal narrative by having it published in the school newspaper. He copied his work neatly and sent it to the editor. The editor printed Louis's paragraph in the sports section. Several students wanted to know if Louis actually managed to ski during that freezing day.

YOUR TURN

Make a final copy of your narrative paragraph. Think of a way to share your work. Some ideas are listed in the **Sharing Suggestions** box below.

SHARING SUGGESTIONS

Create a notebook of personal narratives. Ask others for their work.

Read your work aloud to the class. Invite questions from your listeners.

Mail your work to a friend in another city. Ask him or her to respond to your narrative.

4 SPEAKING AND LISTENING: Having a Class Discussion

You have just written a narrative about an event that happened to you. You told your ideas and experiences to readers. In a good conversation, you speak *and* listen to others. You can learn a great deal by listening to someone's ideas, and you can also share some of your own knowledge.

In a class discussion, students take turns offering ideas and responding to them. Every class discussion has a specific purpose. Often, the purpose of a discussion is to share information about a topic.

Suppose your class has been given a social studies project. The assignment is to prepare for a group discussion about what makes your school's neighborhood special. Each student thinks about or researches one interesting or unusual thing about the neighborhood. Each student records some main points and details on a note card to prepare for the class discussion. Look at this note card.

Notes on What the Neighborhood Looks Like

1. has a beautiful park planned 100 years ago
2. has many wide streets shaded by tall trees
3. is located in a part of the city in which there are many old houses
4. school stands on a hill and has a nice view of the river

Notice that this student's main idea appears in the title at the top of the note card. How do the details add to the main idea that she will bring up in the class discussion?

When you prepare for a class discussion, it will help you to keep your **purpose** and **audience** in mind. These speaking guidelines will help you to focus your talk.

SPEAKING GUIDELINES: A Class Discussion

1. Remember your **purpose** and **audience**.
2. Make a note card. Practice speaking in class, using the note card as a memory aid.
3. Tell the main idea. Add supporting details. Use time-order words.
4. Look at your classmates as you speak.
5. Speak clearly when it is your turn.

- How do I prepare to join in a class discussion about a specific topic?
- How can I use details to support the main idea I wish to contribute to a class discussion?

SPEAKING APPLICATION A Class Discussion

Work with your class to decide on an interesting topic for a class discussion. Think about the main idea you would like to contribute to the discussion. List some points that support and develop this main idea. Prepare a note card with the specific information that you will use in the discussion. Use the speaking guidelines to help you prepare. Your classmates will be using the following guidelines as they listen to your ideas.

LISTENING GUIDELINES: A Class Discussion

1. Listen for each speaker's main idea.
2. Listen for the supporting details.
3. Listen for the logical order of details.

WRITING

EXTENSION

5 WRITER'S RESOURCES: Finding Words in a Dictionary

You have learned that choosing precise words helps you to share your experiences. When you wrote a personal narrative, you were careful to select just the exact details you needed. Using a dictionary correctly allows you to find and spell many additional words you can use in your writing.

You use a dictionary to look up the correct spelling and meaning of a word. Words appear in a dictionary in **alphabetical order**. The first letter of a word determines whether it can be found in the **front**, **middle**, or **back** of the dictionary. Each word in dark type is an **entry word**. The entry word is the basic form of the word, without endings such as *ed*, *ing*, *s*, *er*, and *est*.

On the top of each page of the dictionary, there are two **guide words**. The guide word on the left is the first word on the page. The guide word on the right is the last word on the page. The entry words on each page fall alphabetically between the two guide words. Look at the dictionary entry below. What are the guide words that appear above the first entry word?

mesquite/metaphor

mes·quite (mes kēt′) *n.* a small thorny tree or shrub that grows in desert regions from the southwestern United States to Chile, bearing small flowers and slender seed pods containing beans used as feed for livestock.

mess (mes) *n., pl.* **mess·es. 1.** an untidy, disorderly, or dirty state or condition: *The closet is a mess.* **2.** a person or thing that is in such a state or condition: *The room was a mess after the party.* **3.** an unpleasant, difficult, or confusing situation: *to make a mess of one's life.* **4.** an untidy or confused mass or collection; jumble: *a mess of newspapers on the floor.* **5.** an indefinite amount: *to catch a mess of fish.* **6.a.** a group of people who take meals together regularly, especially in the army or navy. **b.** the meal eaten by such a group. **c.** the place where such a meal is eaten; mess hall. —*v.i.* **1.** to interfere or tamper: *Don't mess with my typewriter.* **2.** to take one's meals in a mess hall.

mes·sage (mes′ij) *n.* **1.** a communication sent from one person or group to another. **2.** a formal or official communication: *the president's message to Congress.* **3.** the point of view or idea meant to be communicated: *The movie's message was that crime doesn't pay.*

Practice

A. Look at these guide words. Which of the words listed below appear on the page of the dictionary that has these guide words at the top? Write the words on a separate piece of paper.

1. fiesta/ figure

a. fire	d. fig
b. fifth	e. fib
c. figure	f. film

2. hibachi/high frequency

a. hibernate	d. height
b. highchair	e. hide
c. hiccup	f. highlight

B. Read each definition for the word *buckle*. On a separate piece of paper, write three different sentences in which you use *buckle* correctly.

> **buck·le** (buk′əl) *n.* **1.** a clasp used to fasten together two loose ends, such as the ends of a belt or strap. **2.** something that resembles this, such as an ornament on a shoe. **3.** a bend or sag in a surface: *a buckle in the counter top.* —*v.,* **buck·led, buck·ling.** —*v.t.* **1.** to fasten with a buckle. **2.** to cause (something) to sag or bend, especially from strain or heat. —*v.i.* **1.** to be fastened or joined by a buckle. **2.** to sag or bend: *A beam supporting the roof buckled.*

WRITING APPLICATION A Narrative

Choose two words from the list below. Look up the meaning of each word. Write the definitions on a separate piece of paper. Then write a narrative paragraph in which you use both words correctly. Exchange paragraphs with a group of classmates. Read each other's paragraphs and check for the correct use of each word.

horizon	gauge	taut
standard	permit	zone
mode	legend	fund

6 WRITER'S RESOURCES: Using a Dictionary

When you see an unfamiliar word, use a dictionary to learn its meaning. Often, there is more than one definition of a word in the dictionary. You use the **context**, or setting, of the word to select the correct dictionary definition.

Here is a dictionary entry for the word *transfer*.

> **trans·fer** (*v.*, trans fûr′, trans′fər; *n.*, trans′fər) *v.*, **trans·ferred, trans·fer·ring.** —*v.t.* **1.** to move or remove from one person, place, or the like, to another: *to transfer money from one pocket to another.* **2.** to give or sell the title or possession of to another: *to transfer property from parents to children.* **3.** to convey (a drawing, design, pattern, or the like) from one surface to another. —*v.i.* **1.** to transfer oneself: *to transfer to a new school.* **2.** to be transferred: *The office will transfer to new quarters.* **3.** to switch from one bus, train, airplane, or the like, to another, usually with little or no extra charge: *to transfer at Chicago.* —*n.* **1.** the act of transferring or the state of being transferred: *the transfer of property by a will.* **2.** something that is transferred, especially a drawing, design, pattern, or the like, moved from one surface to another. **3.** a ticket allowing a passenger to continue a journey on another vehicle, usually with little or no extra charge. **4.** the place or means of transferring. —**trans·fer′ a·ble,** *adj.*

Many words can be used as more than one part of speech. If you look closely at the dictionary entry for the word *transfer*, you will notice a small letter *v*. or *n*. before some of the definitions. This letter tells you whether the word is defined as a verb or as a noun in the definition and example sentences. The word *transfer* can be used as either a verb or a noun. Notice that the pronunciation of *transfer* depends upon whether it is used as a noun or as a verb.

After each entry word, you will find a phonetic respelling of the word, which also shows how many syllables the word contains. The pronunciation key at the bottom of the dictionary page tells you how to pronounce the word.

> **a**t; **ā**pe; f**ä**r; c**â**re; **e**nd; m**ē**; **i**t; **ī**ce; p**î**erce; h**o**t; **ō**ld; s**ô**ng, f**ô**rk; **oi**l; **ou**t; **u**p; **ū**se; r**ü**le; p**u̇**ll, t**û**rn, **ch**in; si**ng**; **sh**op; **th**in; th̲is; **hw** in **wh**ite; **zh** in treasure. The symbol **ə** stands for the unstressed vowel sound heard in **a**bout, tak**e**n, penc**i**l, lem**o**n, and circ**u**s.

Practice

A. Choose one word from the following list. Look up the word in your dictionary. Copy the first and second definitions of the word. Write one sentence for each definition. Be sure that you have used the word in its correct context, or setting.

parade rugged hurdle common

B. Look back at the definitions for the entry word *transfer* on page 68. Figure out the meaning of the word in each of the sentences below. Write the number of the correct definition and whether it is a noun or a verb. Write the two phonetic respellings of the last syllable. Then, write three sentences in which you use the word *transfer*.

a. Please transfer your bicycle to the bicycle rack outside.
b. Do we transfer to a different bus at Elm Street?
c. I will transfer to a jazz dance class next term.
d. Did the bus driver give you a transfer?
e. The artist made a transfer of his drawing.

WRITING APPLICATION A Paragraph

Look up the word *history* in your dictionary. Write a paragraph in which you use *history* in two separate sentences. See if you can use the word differently in each sentence. Exchange paragraphs with a classmate. Ask your partner to tell you what the word means in the two different sentences. If you wish, you can illustrate each of your sentences with a sketch or painting.

Writing About Social Studies

When you think of social studies, you may think of history. What we call history is often a record of facts and dates. Sometimes history is recorded as personal narratives like those you wrote with your class and on your own.

The building of a road through your town is a historical fact. The fact might be recorded in the town hall. You could write a letter describing the road and how it changed the way you live. Your letter would become a part of history, too.

ACTIVITIES

Imagine a Highway Imagine that a highway was built right through the middle of your town or city. Your home has been separated from your school and the stores in the neighborhood. Write a paragraph describing how you would go to school and the stores to shop.

Write a Family History What types of experiences has your family had? Where were your parents and your grandparents born and raised? Write a narrative that includes information about your family's life over the years. You may need to interview some of your relatives to find out some facts.

Look at the Scene Look at the picture on the opposite page. Think about how you would feel if you were in this picture. Write a narrative based on what you think the picture tells you about life in that place at that particular moment. What would you see and hear? Would you be frightened? Use your imagination to add exciting details to your narrative.

Respond to Literature The following personal narrative is taken from the book *My Prairie Year, Based on the Diary of Elenore Plaisted*. Elenore's experiences on the prairie in 1889 were different from her life in Maine. Read the following narrative in which the author and her family protect themselves from a tornado. Then, write a narrative about an incident you found exciting, such as a storm, a sudden change in the weather, or another incident. You might also choose to write a summary of the narrative below. If so, you can mention specific details that helped you to picture the tornado.

Tornado!

At sunset, after one of these scorching days, great clouds began to gather, all reddish brown and orange and flame-colored. They came so close you felt you could touch them, and they were rolling and boiling, but we felt no wind. Suddenly there was a draft of cold air and off in the distance, a snakey black cloud was rushing toward us. The men came running in from the fields shouting, "Tornado!" The oxen were turned loose, and we all crowded into the cellar. As we crouched in that dark, quiet place, the sky seemed to tear loose, as if a freight train were passing right over us. When we came out everything was silent and dripping wet, and the house still stood.

UNIT CHECKUP

LESSON 1

Group Writing: A Personal Narrative (page 50) Read the following paragraph. On a separate sheet of paper, write a sentence that tells the main idea of the paragraph.

First, Leon started yelling. Then, Marcy froze in her tracks. Finally, Dad picked up the little garter snake with a stick and put it in the bushes.

LESSON 2

Thinking: Main Idea and Details (page 54) Imagine that you are going to write a narrative about why you decided to learn photography. Which of the following details would you include?

1. want to have pictures of family and friends
2. start a scrapbook
3. started a stamp collection last year
4. an expensive hobby

LESSON 3

Writing a Personal Narrative (page 56) Imagine that you have traveled through time and landed in another century. Write a personal narrative in which you describe what life is like in this other time. Tell your reader how life in the past or future is different from life in the twentieth century.

LESSON 4

Speaking and Listening: A Class Discussion (page 64) Imagine that your class will discuss adopting a classroom pet. Prepare a note card with some ideas for the discussion.

LESSONS 5-6

Writer's Resources: The Dictionary (pages 66-68) Look at the guide words. Which of the entry words listed below will you find on this page of the dictionary?

mantle/march

1. map
2. marigold
3. maple
4. miller
5. nine
6. marble

THEME PROJECT ART EXHIBIT

You have been reading and writing about surprises, the unusual or unexpected events that make life exciting. In your personal narrative, you shared your experience and feelings with readers. You have created a personal narrative that may have surprised your audience, too!

Writing a personal narrative is one way to share a surprise. You can also share a surprise by creating a picture and letting your audience study it.

Think of an object that might surprise or seem mysterious to your classmates.

- Draw or paint a picture of this special object.
- Hang your drawing or painting where your classmates can see it clearly. Have the other students make guesses about the mystery item in the picture.
- Make a museum show by hanging these pictures around the classroom.
- With your class write a brochure, or booklet, that describes each artwork in the museum show.

UNIT 3

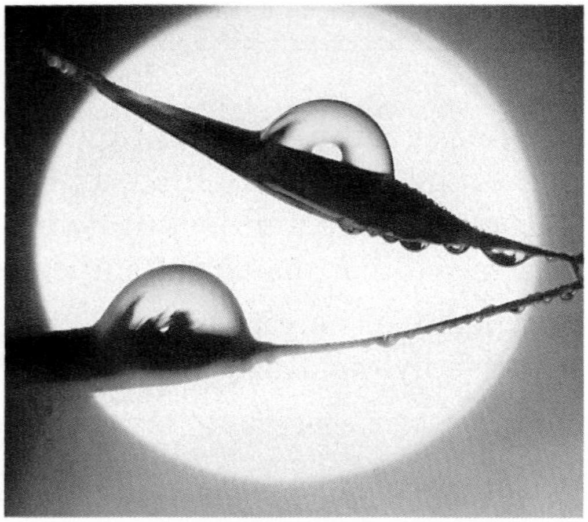

Nouns

In this unit you will learn about nouns. Nouns name people, places, things, and ideas. Think of how many times you use nouns in your writing.

Discuss Read the poem on the opposite page. What different things are mentioned in the poem?

Creative Expression The theme of this unit is *Patterns*. Look at the poem again. What kinds of patterns might the rain make on the grass? What other kinds of patterns do you know? Draw a picture that shows a pattern. You might want to draw a quilt pattern or the pattern the clouds make in the sky. Write your ideas in your journal.

THEME: *PATTERNS*

Rain went sweeping on
in the twilight, spilling moons
on every grass blade.

—Sho-u

1 WHAT IS A NOUN?

A noun is a word that names a person, place, thing, or idea.

Nouns are the words that you use to tell others about the persons, places, things, or ideas that are important to you. A noun can be a single word or two or more words used together.

	Nouns	
Persons	lawyer woman student	Michael Jackson singer plumber
Places	state island country	Texas valley park
Things	bicycle book tree	quilt sewing machine table
Ideas	happiness goodness sadness	courage liberty truth

Guided Practice

Tell which words are nouns.

Example: A quilt is a special kind of blanket. *quilt blanket*

1. Quilts are difficult to make.
2. Sometimes people work together.
3. Choose pretty fabric for the quilt.
4. Many patterns can be made.
5. Look for diagrams in a book.

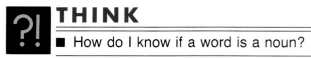

?! THINK

- How do I know if a word is a noun?

REMEMBER

- A **noun** is a word that names a person, place, thing, or idea.
- A **noun** can be more than one word.

More Practice

A. Write each sentence. Draw a line under each noun.

Example: The quilt in my room is very old.

6. People can sew a quilt by hand.
7. Now sewing machines can be used, too.
8. Quilts are made in this way.
9. Stitch two pieces of fabric together.
10. Place stuffing between the layers of fabric.
11. Use soft materials.
12. Feathers are a good choice.
13. Goose down is also an excellent material.

B. Write each sentence. Draw a line under each noun. Then write whether the noun names a **person, place, thing,** or **idea.**

Example: Read these instructions carefully. *thing*

14. Next, sew the layers together.
15. A person needs patience for this craft.
16. Some quilts are made from scraps.
17. Patchwork quilts are popular with many people.
18. The scraps are sewn together in a pattern.
19. Squares and circles are common designs.
20. A sewing room is a busy place.

Extra Practice, page 100

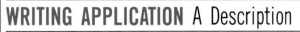

WRITING APPLICATION A Description

COOPERATIVE LEARNING

Write a description of an object in your home or classroom that is interesting. Describe what the object looks like and why it is interesting. If you like, illustrate your description with a drawing of the object. Exchange descriptions with a group of classmates. Look for nouns in each other's writing.

GRAMMAR

2 SINGULAR NOUNS AND PLURAL NOUNS

A **singular noun** names one person, place, thing, or idea. A **plural noun** names more than one person, place, thing, or idea.

Many plural nouns are formed by adding *s* to the singular form of the noun. The spelling of some nouns changes when they become plural.

SINGULAR: The *town* looks sleepy, but the *city* looks lively.

PLURAL: The *towns* look sleepy, but the *cities* look lively.

How to Form Plural Nouns

Singular	Plural	Examples
most nouns	Add *s*	student—students
nouns that end in *s, x, ch, zz* or *sh*	Add *es*	guess—guesses box—boxes branch—branches bush—bushes buzz—buzzes
nouns that end with a vowel and *y*	Add *s*	toy—toys day—days
nouns that end with a consonant and *y*	Change *y* to *i* and add *es*	country—countries body—bodies

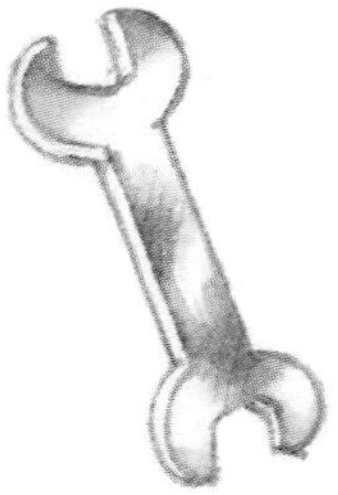

one wrench—$5

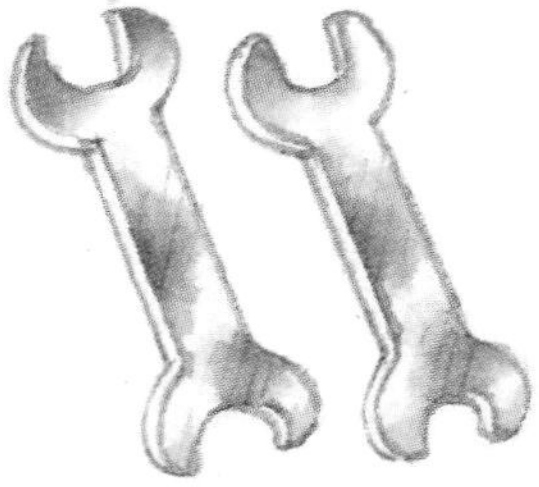

two wrenches—$9

Guided Practice

Tell the plural form of each noun.

Example: story *stories*

1. girl

2. wrench

3. ray

4. puppy

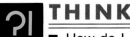

?! **THINK**

■ How do I decide whether a noun is singular or plural?

REMEMBER

- A **singular noun** names one person, place, thing, or idea.
- A **plural noun** names more than person, place, thing, or idea.

More Practice

A. Write each noun. Then, write its plural form.

Example: peach *peaches*

5. band
6. dish
7. berry
8. chorus
9. box
10. singer
11. choir
12. chimney
13. lunch
14. bus

B. Write the plural form of each underlined noun.

Example: The singer sang beautifully. *singers*

15. The song had the best verse.
16. The composer repeated the line several times.
17. My friend sang in the concert.
18. The ditty told of life on the ranch.
19. The cowboy had lost the fastest horse.
20. He follows the animal through the scratchy bush.
21. The stallion roamed the county in Montana.
22. The searcher traveled the range.
23. The cloud in the sky wept for him.
24. The rain made the grass muddy.
25. The cowboy sang about the missing pony.

Extra Practice, page 101

WRITING APPLICATION A Caption

Draw a picture that shows what your favorite song is about. Write a summary of the song as a caption for your drawing. Exchange work with a classmate. Look for singular and plural nouns in each other's captions.

GRAMMAR

3 MORE PLURAL NOUNS

You can form the plural of many nouns by adding *s* or *es*. There are special rules for forming the plural of some nouns.

Special Endings for Plural Nouns		
Noun	**Noun**	**Examples**
Nouns that end in *f* or *fe*	Change the *f* to v and add *es* to some nouns. Add *s* to other nouns.	wife—wives calf—calves bluff—bluffs
Nouns that end with a vowel *and o*	Add *s.*	stereo—stereos video—videos
Nouns that end with a consonant and *o*	Add *s* or *es.*	silo—silos hero—heroes
Nouns that have special plural forms		tooth—teeth foot—feet man—men woman—women
Nouns that have the same forms in singular and plural		deer—deer sheep—sheep

Guided Practice

Tell the plural form of each noun.

Example: calf *calves*

1. potato
2. rodeo
3. half
4. wolf
5. knife

?! **THINK**

■ How can I remember to form the plural of special nouns correctly?

REMEMBER

- The plural forms of certain nouns are made by following special rules.

More Practice

A. Write each noun. Then write its plural form. You can use a dictionary to check your spelling.

Example: batch *batches*

6. trout
7. alto
8. reef
9. deer
10. tooth
11. man
12. radio
13. bluff
14. pinto
15. studio

B. Write each sentence. Complete the sentences with the correct plural form of each noun in parentheses.

Example: People sit on _______ of grass. (patch) *patches*

16. _____ and adults enjoy games. (Child)
17. Three _____ and three boys form a team. (man)
18. Two _____ play water polo. (woman)
19. A family brought their _____ so they can play musical chairs. (radio)
20. These soccer players can run as fast as _____. (deer)
21. The players' voices created _____. (echo)
22. Boys and girls fish for _____ in a pool. (trout)
23. _____ cover the water. (Leaf)
24. A baseball flew over the _____. (roof)
25. Some girls imitate cowgirls in the _____. (rodeo)

Extra Practice, page 102

WRITING APPLICATION A Set of Rules

Write a set of rules for playing your favorite game. Tell how the game is played and how the score is kept. Exchange rules with a classmate. Find the singular and plural nouns in each other's set of rules.

GRAMMAR

4 COMMON NOUNS AND PROPER NOUNS

You know that a noun is a naming word. A **common noun** names any person, place, thing, or idea. A **proper noun** names a particular person, place, thing, or idea. Proper nouns begin with a capital letter.

Common Nouns	Proper Nouns	Common Nouns	Proper Nouns
building	Sears Tower	river	Mississippi River
holiday	Veterans Day	day	Friday
month	October	lake	Lake Charles
state	Nebraska	city	Chicago
bridge	Oakland Bay Bridge	mountain	Mt. Mansfield
author	Mark Twain	continent	Africa

Guided Practice

Tell which nouns are **common nouns** and which are **proper nouns.**

Example: The water in Lake Superior is bright blue in this photograph.
water common Lake Superior proper
photograph common

1. Students can make a design with photographs.
2. Magazines such as *Life* or *Newsweek* have many illustrations.
3. Cut the pictures out with scissors.
4. Look for photographs of Paris, London, or Rome.
5. Chris found a painting of the Eiffel Tower in one issue.

?! THINK

- How can I decide if a word is a common noun or proper noun?

REMEMBER

- A **common noun** is a noun that names any person, place, thing, or idea.
- A **proper noun** is a noun that names a particular person, place or thing.

More Practice

A. Write the nouns below. Capitalize the proper nouns.

Example: country—spain—capital *Spain*

6. author—toni morrison—edgar allan poe
7. the persian gulf—caribbean sea—lake
8. texas—state—county
9. the lincoln tunnel—the golden gate bridge—road
10. the declaration of independence—paper—document
11. stonington—bakersfield—town
12. africa—australia—continent

B. Write each sentence. Draw one line under each common noun. Draw two lines under each proper noun.

Example: The teacher assigns a project on Tuesday.

13. Materials for artwork are everywhere.
14. Some artists use macaroni, string, photographs, and paint.
15. Objects for a design can come from a particular place.
16. Jaime made a picture of things from the Mojave Desert.
17. The picture showed cactus, pebbles, dried flowers, and insects.
18. Frances made a poster about big cities in the United States.
19. The poster showed photos of Seattle, Chicago, and Dallas.
20. José made a poster about lakes and rivers in America.

Extra Practice, page 103

WRITING APPLICATION A Set of Directions

Write a set of directions for creating an artwork from things found outdoors. Exchange your set of directions with a classmate. Identify the common and proper nouns in each other's work.

GRAMMAR

5 SINGULAR POSSESSIVE NOUNS

One of the ways you can use nouns in your sentences is to show ownership. A noun that shows ownership is called a **possessive noun.**

Singular Possessive Nouns
The **cat's** whiskers are long.
The **girl's** paintbrush is dry.
The **dog's** paws are wet.

Form the possessive of a singular noun by adding an apostrophe (') and *s* ('s) to the noun.

the home of Mr. Stein	**Mr. Stein's** home
the land of the farmer	**the farmer's** land
the hobbies of the student	**the student's** hobbies

Guided Practice

Tell the possessive form of each singular noun.

Example: farm *farm's*

1. Nell
2. painter
3. child
4. clerk
5. horse

?! THINK

■ How do I decide if a word is a singular possessive noun?

REMEMBER

- A **singular possessive noun** shows that one person, place, or thing owns something.
- Form the possessive of a singular noun by adding an apostrophe (') and *s*.

More Practice

A. Write the singular possessive form of each noun.

Example: eagle *eagle's*

6. president
7. artist
8. driver
9. baker
10. man
11. sculptor
12. gardener
13. lion

B. Write each sentence. Change the words in parentheses to include the singular possessive form of the underlined noun.

Example: (The studio of the artist) is cheerful.
The artist's studio is cheerful.

14. (The sculptures of Jenny Grove) are wonderful.
15. (The lions of Jenny) are majestic.
16. (The birds of the sculptor) are graceful.
17. (The work of the artist) delights people.
18. There is always a visitor in (the studio of Jenny).
19. (The friend of my father) bought a seal and a dove.
20. (The wings of the dove) are opened wide.

Extra Practice, page 104

WRITING APPLICATION An Explanation

Design a sculpture that you might make out of wood, clay, or metal. Then write a paragraph that explains your sculpture. You could include details about how it will be made, how big it will be, and the materials from which it will be made. Exchange your work with a classmate. Look for possessive nouns in each other's writing.

6 PLURAL POSSESSIVE NOUNS

A plural noun that shows ownership is called a **plural possessive noun.** When a plural noun ends in *s*, the possessive is formed by adding *only* an apostrophe (') after the *s*.

The dresses of the girls hang on the rack.
The **girls'** dresses hang on the rack.

The tools of the gardeners are new.
The **gardeners'** tools are new.

When a plural noun *does not* end in *s*, the possessive is formed by adding an apostrophe (') and *s*.

The clothes of the children are colorful.
The **children's** clothes are colorful.

Guided Practice

Tell the plural possessive form of each noun.

Example: sheep *sheep's*

1. men
2. workers
3. adults
4. women
5. boys

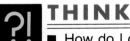

?! THINK

■ How do I decide if a word is a plural possessive noun?

REMEMBER

- Form the possessive of a plural noun that ends in *s* by adding an apostrophe (') after the *s*.
- Form the possessive of a plural noun that does not end in *s* by adding an apostrophe (') and *s*.

More Practice

A. Write the plural form of each noun. Then write the plural possessive form of the noun.

Example: goose *geese geese's*

6. child
7. doctor
8. lawyer
9. farmer
10. engineer
11. kitten
12. horse
13. mother

B. Write each sentence. Change the words in parentheses to the plural possessive form.

Example: (The return of the birds) signals the new season.
The birds' return signals the new season.

14. (The gardens belonging to the neighbors) are beautiful.
15. (The children of the gardeners) help with the work.
16. Every spring (the work of the gardeners) begins.
17. (The goal of the people) is the improvement of the area.
18. (The job of the young children) is done after school.
19. Vegetable seeds are planted in (the gardens of the neighbors).
20. (The labor of the workers) will be rewarded.

Extra Practice, page 105

WRITING APPLICATION A Description

Imagine that you and your friends have entered a garden contest. You each enter a special flower, vegetable, or fruit. Write a paragraph in which you use possessive nouns to describe what each person's flower, vegetable, or fruit looks like. Show your description to a classmate. Circle the possessive nouns in each other's descriptions.

7 USING POSSESSIVE NOUNS

You often use nouns to show ownership. If you are not sure how to form the possessive of a particular noun, review these rules. You may need to use your dictionary to check the spelling of certain plural nouns.

Study the chart below.

The gloves of the **men** protect their hands.
The **men's** gloves protect their hands.

The gymnasium of the **children** gets a new floor.
The **children's** gymnasium gets a new floor.

Singular Possessive Nouns
Add an apostrophe (') and an *s* to a singular noun to form the possessive. *Mom'***s** *pies* *Charles'***s** *comb*

Plural Possessive Nouns Ending with *s*
Add an apostrophe (') to a plural noun ending with *s* to form the possessive. *boys' gymnasium* *teachers' meeting*

Plural Possessive Nouns Not Ending with *s*
Add an apostrophe (') and an *s* to a plural noun not ending with *s*. *children'***s** *desks* *women'***s** *rights*

Guided Practice

Tell the possessive noun in each sentence.

Example: The principal's project teaches the students good safety rules. *principal's*

1. The children listen to Mrs. Denkar's speech.
2. The woman's words are important.
3. She has the students' attention.
4. The children's safety is important.
5. The speaker is the principal's guest.
6. Mr. Isaac's ideas about safety are good.

?! THINK

- How do I form a possessive noun?

REMEMBER

- Form the possessive of singular nouns and plural nouns that do not end in *s* by adding an apostrophe (') and an *s*.
- Form the possessive of plural nouns that end with *s* by adding an apostrophe (').

GRAMMAR

More Practice

A. Write each sentence. Underline the possessive noun.

Example: The teachers' words were heard.

7. He told students about the fire warden's drills.
8. Mr. Issac praised the fifth graders' safety habits.
9. Mrs. Denkar sees Cindy's raised hand.
10. Cindy is this year's crossing guard.
11. She needs people's cooperation.
12. Parents' help is very important.
13. Children's safety involves everyone.

B. Write each sentence. Change each underlined phrase to include a possessive noun.

Example: The remarks of the chief are intelligent.
The chief's remarks are intelligent.

14. The safety habits of the students should be perfect.
15. The students listen to the opinions of adults.
16. The comments of the visitors are helpful.
17. The hands of many pupils are raised now.
18. The work of the hall monitors improves safety in our school.
19. The principal reminds students to use the office of the nurse.
20. The goals of the assembly have been met.

Extra Practice, Practice Plus, pages 106–107

WRITING APPLICATION A Poster

Make a poster that shows good safety habits. Write clear captions that explain your drawings. Have a classmate check your poster for possessive nouns.

8 MECHANICS: Abbreviations

An **abbreviation** is the shortened form of a word. Most abbreviations begin with a capital letter and end with a period. Abbreviations are often used in addresses, lists, and titles.

Initials are also a kind of abbreviation. Initials can be used instead of a whole name. Initials are capitalized and are followed by a period.

Some Common Abbreviations and Initials

Addresses	Avenue–Ave.	Drive–Dr.	Street–St.
Titles	Doctor–Dr.	Senior–Sr.	Junior–Jr.
States	Ohio–OH	New Mexico–NM	Rhode Island–RI
Time and Initials	before noon–A.M.	after noon–P.M.	Joseph Peter Gordon–J.P. Gordon
Businesses	Company–Co.	Corporation–Corp.	Incorporated–Inc.
Days	Monday–Mon.	Thursday–Thurs.	Sunday–Sun.
Months	November–Nov.	April–Apr.	August–Aug.

Guided Practice

Tell the abbreviation or initial for each underlined word.

Example: Davis and Davis, <u>Incorporated</u> *Inc.*

1. Lakeville, <u>Ohio</u>
2. Four o'clock in the <u>afternoon</u>
3. Seven o'clock in the <u>morning</u>
4. 421 Bryant <u>Avenue</u>
5. <u>Doris Jane</u> Bailey

?! **THINK**

■ How do I decide when to use an abbreviation?

REMEMBER

- An **abbreviation** is a shortened form of a word. Most abbreviations are capitalized and end with a period.
- An **initial** is the first letter of a name. Initials are capitalized and are followed by a period.

More Practice

A. Write the correct abbreviation for the following words. Be sure to use correct punctuation.

Example: Sunday *Sun.*

6. Doctor
7. Company
8. Drive
9. New Mexico
10. before noon
11. Street
12. Avenue
13. April

B. Write each group of words. Abbreviate the underlined word or words in each group.

Example: Sam Dugan, Junior *Jr.*

14. Paul James Tyler
15. 129 Ocean Road
16. Doctor Benson
17. November 1, 1951
18. Monday, April 15
19. Jamestown Railway Company
20. Dogwalkers, Incorporated

Extra Practice, page 108

WRITING APPLICATION A Telegraph Message

Write a telegraph message to a friend about the opening of an art show. In your message, be sure to include the date, time, place, and the name of the artist. Abbreviate words to save space in your message. When you have finished, exchange messages with two classmates. Check to see that all abbreviations are spelled and punctuated correctly in each other's work.

COOPERATIVE LEARNING

G R A M M A R

9 VOCABULARY BUILDING: Compound Words

A **compound word** is a word made from two or more words joined together. You can often tell the meaning of a compound word from the two separate words in the compound. You can also use your dictionary to look up the definition of a compound word.

Many compound words are written as one word.

basket + ball = basketball   news + paper = newspaper

Some compound words are written as two words.

brain wave   fairy tale   fire engine   peanut butter

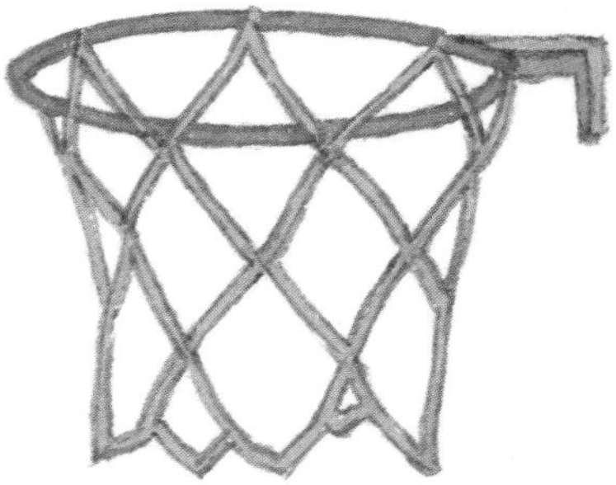

basket

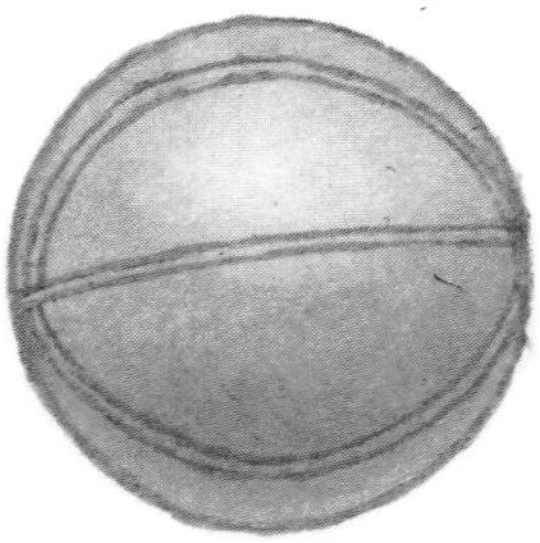

ball

Guided Practice

Tell the compound word that can be made from each pair. Then tell the meaning of the new word.

Example: mail box   *mailbox*   *a box where mail is put*

1. door   bell
2. board   walk
3. dog   house
4. vault   pole
5. note   book

?! THINK

■ How can I decide if a word is a compound word?

REMEMBER

■ A **compound word** is made from two or more words.

More Practice

A. Write each sentence. Draw a line under the compound word in each sentence.

Example: This fish comes from a fishpond.

6. Marty has three fish in a fish tank.
7. He bought the fish at a pet shop.
8. He put them into the water with a fishnet.
9. Marty bought a model lighthouse for the tank.
10. His fish need warm saltwater.
11. The plastic top on the tank works as a safeguard.
12. It keeps Marty's house cat away from the fish.
13. The cat thinks the fish are playthings.

B. Match the words in Column A and Column B to form compound words. Look up any words that you do not know in the dictionary.

Example: fire place *fireplace*

	Column A	Column B
14.	river	hook
15.	board	car
16.	bell	bar
17.	fish	bank
18.	box	card
19.	salad	bath
20.	bird	fruit

Extra Practice, page 109

WRITING APPLICATION A Description

Imagine a new type of animal. Write a description of the imaginary animal. Exchange papers with a classmate. Circle any compound words in each other's writing.

GRAMMAR AND WRITING CONNECTION

Combining Sentences

When you revise your writing, you may want to combine two sentences that contain related information. When words in two sentences are repeated, the sentences may often be combined into one by using *and* or *or*.

Separate: Will our team be *victorious*?
Will our team be *defeated*?

Combined: Will our team be *victorious or defeated*?

Look at the example sentences above. Notice that the two separate sentences share the subject *team*. When the sentences are combined, none of the meaning is lost.

Working Together

COOPERATIVE LEARNING

Discuss each pair of sentences with your classmates. Then tell how you would combine them to make a single sentence.

Example: **In tennis,** players earn points.
In racquetball, players earn points.
In tennis and racquetball, players earn points.

1. In football, players score goals.
In hockey, players score goals.
2. Our uniforms are colorful.
Our uniforms are attractive.
3. Will East be the winner?
Will West be the winner?

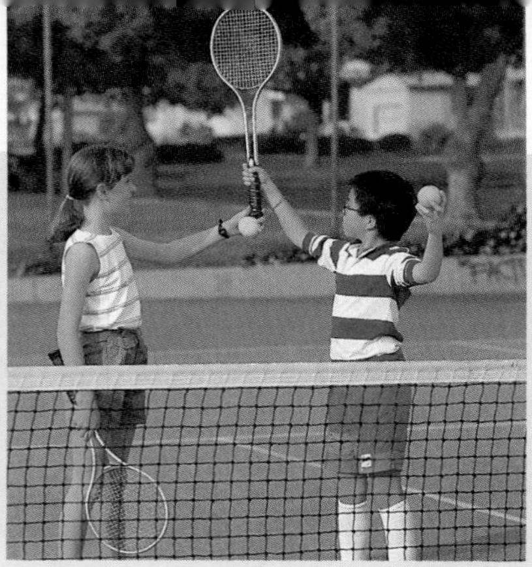

Revising Sentences

Andrew wrote these sentences as captions for a comic strip about his favorite sport. Help Andrew to improve the sentences in his caption. Rewrite these pairs of sentences by combining them.

4. Referees enforce the rules in sports.
Umpires enforce the rules in sports.

5. The quarterback is strong.
The quarterback is fast.

6. Will Sal be on our team?
Will Vic be on our team?

7. The coach can choose Marty.
The coach can choose Ben.

8. Is Saturday's game out of town?
Is Saturday's game at home?

9. Did number forty catch the pass?
Did number forty fumble the pass?

10. I enjoyed last year's games.
I enjoyed this year's games even more.

11. Did you try out for the team?
Did you change your mind?

12. The fans cheered for hours.
The fans waved bright pennants.

WRITER AT WORK

Below is the beginning of Dale's letter describing a game of hide-and-seek at a picnic. Help Dale to improve her letter by combining sentences where possible. Add sentences of your own to complete the letter.

Dear Cathy,

I wish you had been at our picnic. José wishes you had been there, too. The boys in our class played hide-and-seek. The girls in our class played hide-and-seek. The woods were dark. The woods were scary. I enjoyed the suspense. The other students enjoyed the suspense.

UNIT CHECKUP

LESSON 1

What Is a Noun? (pages 76–77) Write each sentence. Draw a line under each noun.

1. Two groups can sing a song.
2. Singers start at different places in the song.
3. This song is called a round.
4. The parts make a beautiful sound.
5. The end comes when the last group finishes.

LESSONS 2-3

Singular Nouns and Plural Nouns (pages 78–81) Write each noun. Then write its plural form.

6. mouse
7. fox
8. survey
9. bunch
10. video

LESSON 4

Common and Proper Nouns (pages 82–83) Write each noun. Next to each noun write **common** or **proper**.

11. Susan takes the bus to school.
12. Her route follows the river.
13. The driver turns left on Elm Street.
14. The bus stops at Pine Road and Oak Street.
15. Martin walks to school from his house on Ohio Road.

LESSONS 5-6

Singular and Plural Possessive Nouns(pages 84–87) Write each sentence. Change the underlined group of words to include a possessive noun.

16. Marjorie brought <u>a picture of the cats</u> to school.
17. <u>The ears of one cat</u> are white.
18. <u>The family of Marjorie</u> found a cat in an alley.
19. <u>The cat belonging to Marjorie</u> will soon have kittens.
20. <u>The wish of the children</u> is to have one of the kittens.

LESSON 7

Using Possessive Nouns (pages 88–89) Write each sentence. Change the underlined group of words to include a possessive noun.

21. The book that belongs to Wayne has many pictures.
22. They show the work of a scientist.
23. The experiments of Dr. Wong are important.
24. I like the explanations of the doctors.
25. The research of the scientists is fascinating.

LESSON 8

Mechanics: Abbreviations (pages 90–91) Write the abbreviation or initials for each underlined group of words.

26. September 8, 1978
27. Doctor Gray
28. Perry James, Senior
29. 57 Kiley Drive
30. Gretchen Lewis Brown

LESSON 9

Vocabulary Building: Compound Words (pages 92–93) Match the words (Columns A and B; C and D) to form compound words. Look up any words that you do not know in the dictionary.

Column A	Column B	Column C	Column D
31. cracker	walk	**36.** rain	boat
32. ice	nut	**37.** tree	air
33. bag	skate	**38.** life	door
34. side	hand	**39.** plane	bow
35. ground	play	**40.** mat	house

Writing Application: Noun Usage (pages 76–88) The following paragraph contains 10 errors with nouns. Rewrite the paragraph correctly.

41.-50.

I really like interesting autoes. i want a Car of my own. My sister brenda drives me place sometimes. Brendas car is nice. It is a blue convertibles. Her friends car is not as comfortable. She bought it Sep. 20 of last year. She keeps it parked on oak Road.

ENRICHMENT

WORD SAFARI

Play this game in a small group. One person chooses a noun from the list below. Then, he or she will begin a story with a sentence using that noun. The next player will continue the story with a sentence that uses one of the other nouns. Take turns until all the nouns have been used.

elephant jungle trail
gasoline water food truck
game warden hunter

WORD BLENDS

You have learned that compound words are made by joining two or more words. Another type of word is made by blending parts of two words together.

breakfast + lunch = brunch
smoke + fog = smog
motor + hotel = motel

Make up some new words of your own. Pick two words and use parts of each to make the new word. Have a classmate guess the meaning of your words.

WORD-WICH

Any number of people can play this game. The first player says a word. The second player turns the word into a compound word. The next player takes the second part of the compound and makes it the first part of a new compound. Keep going until you run out of words.

CREATIVE EXPRESSION

Concrete Poems

Seal

See how he dives
From the rocks with a zoom!
See how he darts
Through his watery room
Past crabs and eels
And green seaweed,
Past fluffs of sandy
Minnow feed!
See how he swims
With a swerve and a twist,
A flip of the flipper,
A flick of the wrist!
Quicksilver-quick,
Softer than spray,
Down he plunges
And sweeps away;
Before you can think,
Before you can utter
Words like "Dill pickle"
Or "Apple butter,"
Back up he swims
Past Sting Ray and Shark,
Out with a zoom,
A whoop, a bark;
Before you can say
Whatever you wish,
He plops at your side
With a mouthful of fish!

—William Jay Smith

TRY IT OUT!

The poem "Seal" is a concrete poem. It suggests the shape of a swimming seal. Think of something that you would like to describe. Write a concrete poem about this subject.

EXTRA PRACTICE

Three levels of practice

What Is a Noun? (page 76)

LEVEL **A.** Write each sentence. Write **person, place, thing,** or **idea** above each underlined noun.

1. Summer is a wonderful season.
2. My sister goes to the country for vacation.
3. Sylvia throws a rock into the still lake.
4. A small wave races across the surface.
5. The stone makes ripples.
6. Sunlight makes the water sparkle.
7. Many people enjoy the scenery.
8. I prefer the beach to the mountains.
9. My holiday begins next month.

LEVEL **B.** Write each sentence. Draw a line under each noun.

10. Wind blows across the hot sand.
11. The sands of the desert are in constant motion.
12. A small tornado hovers in the distance.
13. A man rides a mule over a dune.
14. In a day the dune will be much smaller.
15. More sandy mounds will form.
16. The land looks different each morning.
17. Only cactuses grow on this dry earth.

LEVEL **C.** Complete each sentence with a noun from the list below. After the noun write **person, place, thing,** or **idea.**

shore excitement wave seal people sound sun boat

18. At the beach huge waves crash onto the ______.
19. Children express their ______ with shouts.
20. The waves break with a thunderous ______.
21. A ______ swims in the surf.
22. Each ______ breaks and then falls.
23. ______ watch the changing patterns of the ocean.
24. The ______ makes everyone squint.
25. I can barely see the ______ in the distance.

EXTRA PRACTICE

GRAMMAR

Three levels of practice

Singular Nouns and Plural Nouns (page 78)

LEVEL **A.** Write each sentence. Draw a line under the plural nouns.

1. Many animals have special markings.
2. Certain creatures are almost invisible.
3. Some bears are white and blend in with the snow.
4. Many jungle animals are green.
5. They can hide easily in leafy trees.
6. The deserts of the world contain many brown rodents.
7. Garter snakes look like sticks.
8. People sometimes wear special outfits that blend into the background.
9. Safari clothes are usually in shades of green and brown.

LEVEL **B.** Write each noun. Then write its plural form.

10. plain
11. brush
12. ax
13. bay
14. watch
15. dress
16. bounty
17. buzz
18. country

LEVEL **C.** Write the plural form of each underlined noun.

19. The <u>lobster</u> looks just like the <u>rock</u> behind it.
20. A brown <u>bird</u> is invisible in a winter <u>bush</u>.
21. A <u>leopard</u> blends easily into its <u>setting</u>.
22. The <u>lizard</u> is famous for its <u>change</u> of color.
23. The <u>seahorse</u> also changes <u>color</u> and hides from its <u>enemy</u>.
24. A <u>butterfly</u> can look like a <u>flower</u>.
25. The <u>insect</u> looks just like a <u>twig</u>.

EXTRA PRACTICE

Three levels of practice

More Plural Nouns (page 80)

LEVEL **A.** Draw a line under the plural noun in each sentence.

1. Interesting sounds fill the hall.
2. Three radios play the same music.
3. Four videos show different movies.
4. Two sopranos sing a song.
5. Twenty feet dance across the floor.
6. Fifty echoes are heard.
7. The movie studios are hard at work.
8. The director suggests changes in the music.
9. The composer writes more songs for the movie.

LEVEL **B.** Write each noun. Then write its plural form.

10. piano
11. fish
12. moose
13. solo
14. man
15. hero
16. horse
17. branch

LEVEL **C.** Write each sentence. Complete each sentence with the correct plural form of the noun in parentheses.

18. Three _____ were born in the barn this year. (calf)
19. _____ build their nests in the hayloft. (Mouse)
20. Two _____ hold grain. (silo)
21. _____ graze in the pasture. (Sheep)
22. Ten _____ float on the pond. (goose)
23. _____ are kept in the cellar. (Potato)
24. _____ roam the woods. (Deer)
25. Owls perch on the _____ of the house and barn. (roof)

EXTRA PRACTICE

Three levels of practice

Common Nouns and Proper Nouns (page 82)

LEVEL **A.** Write the nouns below. Capitalize the proper nouns.

1. marie curie — scientist — person
2. river — hudson river — stream
3. atlantic ocean — water — sea
4. oakdale — town — place
5. thanksgiving — holiday — feast
6. city — rome — capital
7. volcano — mount saint helens — mountain
8. mark twain — man — author
9. statue — statue of liberty — tower

LEVEL **B.** Write each sentence. Draw one line under each common noun and two lines under each proper noun.

10. Washington, D.C. is the capital of the United States.
11. There are many monuments in this city.
12. People visit the Lincoln Memorial every year.
13. Tourists always enjoy the Washington Monument.
14. Perhaps the most beautiful monument is the Jefferson Memorial.
15. The Smithsonian is a wonderful museum.
16. Many people admire the White House.
17. Students visit the Library of Congress.

LEVEL **C.** Write the nouns in each sentence. Next to each noun write **common** or **proper**. Capitalize the proper nouns.

18. All countries have famous monuments and buildings.
19. In paris, france, there are the eiffel tower and the louvre museum.
20. The sphinx and the tomb of king tut are in egypt.
21. The taj mahal is a famous memorial in india.
22. The ruins of the city of troy lie in turkey.
23. Ancient buildings such as the colosseum are in rome, italy.
24. The parthenon is in greece.
25. The kremlin is a famous building in moscow, russia.

EXTRA PRACTICE

Three levels of practice

Singular Possessive Nouns (page 84)

LEVEL **A.** Each sentence contains an underlined singular possessive noun. Write each sentence. Draw two lines under the word that names what is owned.

1. The doctor's office is crowded.
2. The designer's pattern is simple.
3. The architect's blueprints are complex.
4. The builder's plans are on the table.
5. The musician's cello is in a black case.
6. The girl's report is excellent.
7. The man's ideas are interesting.
8. The student's questions are intelligent.
9. The teacher's lecture is fascinating.

LEVEL **B.** Write each noun. Then write its singular possessive form.

10. lawyer
11. nurse
12. author
13. plumber
14. sailor
15. pilot
16. painter
17. dancer

LEVEL **C.** Write each sentence. Change the words in parentheses to include a singular possessive noun.

18. (The mitt of the catcher) is made of leather.
19. (The ship of the captain) is off course.
20. (The script of the actor) is long.
21. (The tools of the electrician) are handy.
22. (The briefcase of the judge) is full.
23. (The truck of the farmer) is loaded with potatoes.
24. (The mane of the horse) is braided with ribbons.
25. (The slippers of the dancer) are pink.

EXTRA PRACTICE

Three levels of practice

Plural Possessive Nouns (page 86)

LEVEL **A.** Write the possessive form of each plural noun.

1. gardeners
2. mice
3. leaves
4. neighbors
5. geese
6. heroes
7. bushes
8. dogs
9. trout

LEVEL **B.** Write the plural form of each noun. Then write its plural possessive form.

10. soldier
11. inventor
12. wife
13. officer
14. sculptor
15. child
16. grandfather
17. actor

LEVEL **C.** Rewrite each phrase to include a plural possessive noun.

18. the paints of artists
19. the bicycles of the boys
20. the tools of the workers
21. the dresses of women
22. the letters from the children
23. the smiles of the aunts
24. the speed of the runners
25. the applause of the people

GRAMMAR

EXTRA PRACTICE

Three levels of practice

Using Possessive Nouns (page 88)

LEVEL **A.** Write each sentence. Underline the possessive noun.

1. Tom's new telescope is fun.
2. We study stars in Mrs. Williams's class.
3. The children's books explain constellations.
4. The ancient Greeks' legends about stars are fascinating.
5. The three stars show Orion's belt.
6. Tomorrow we will stargaze from our neighbor's roof.
7. Mr. Anderson's building is many stories high.
8. I borrowed my cousin's telescope.
9. Our friend's telescope is too weak.

LEVEL **B.** Write each sentence. Change each underlined phrase to include the possessive noun.

10. <u>The picture of the boy</u> was unusual.
11. <u>The life of the artist</u> is hard.
12. <u>The work of the weavers</u> was beautiful.
13. They used <u>the picture by the painter</u> as a pattern.
14. Jim explained <u>the job of the dyer</u>.
15. <u>The colors of the dyers</u> must match the original art.
16. <u>The knowledge of the historians</u> is helpful.
17. <u>The delight of the viewers</u> makes the work worthwhile.

LEVEL **C.** Write and complete each sentence with a possessive noun.

18. The _____ visit to the park was fun.
19. The _____ favorite part was the playground.
20. _____ dog ran through the grassy field.
21. Molly held the _____ leash.
22. The _____ friend brought his dog, too.
23. A sudden shower soaked the _____ clothes.
24. The _____ paws were muddy and wet.
25. The rain did not spoil the _____ pleasure.

PRACTICE + PLUS

Three levels of additional practice for a difficult skill

Using Possessive Nouns (page 88)

LEVEL **A.** Write each sentence. Change the underlined group of words to include a possessive noun.

1. The farm of my aunt is in Nebraska.
2. The school of my cousins is in a nearby town.
3. The truck of my uncle takes them to school.
4. The sister of my mother plants corn and wheat.
5. The husband of my aunt is a farmer, too.
6. The produce of my relatives is sold throughout the country.
7. The work of Aunt Maggie is very hard.
8. The hours of a farmer are long.
9. The day of the farmer begins at dawn.

LEVEL **B.** Rewrite each sentence using a possessive noun.

10. The apartment of Uncle Brad is in the city.
11. The day of my uncle is spent at an office.
12. The wife of Uncle Brad works in the city, too.
13. The brother of my father is a lawyer.
14. The daughter of Uncle Brad goes to my school.
15. The name of my cousin is Celia.
16. The favorite subject of Celia is history.
17. Many of the books belonging to Celia are about history.

LEVEL **C.** Write a sentence for each of the possessive nouns below.

18. brother's
19. friend's
20. parent's
21. cat's
22. speaker's
23. visitor's
24. doctor's
25. artist's

GRAMMAR

EXTRA PRACTICE

Three levels of practice

Mechanics: Abbreviations (page 90)

LEVEL A. Write the word for which each abbreviation stands.

1. Mon.
2. Dr.
3. Blvd.
4. Corp.
5. Co.
6. Ave.
7. NM
8. Sr.
9. St.

LEVEL B. Write the correct abbreviation for each of the following words.

10. Junior
11. afternoon
12. Friday
13. November
14. New Jersey
15. before noon
16. Road
17. New York City

LEVEL C. Write each group of words. Complete each group with the correct abbreviation or initials for the word or words in parentheses.

18. _____ 9, 1972 (September)
19. Mayfair, _____ (Incorporated)
20. _____, July twenty-third (Tuesday)
21. _____ Griggs (John Paul)
22. _____ Box 2221 (Post Office)
23. Jennings and _____ (Company)
24. San Diego, _____ (California)
25. _____ 52 B (Apartment)

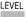

EXTRA PRACTICE

G R A M M A R

Three levels of practice

Vocabulary Building: Compound Words (page 92)

LEVEL **A.** Write each sentence. Draw a line under the compound word in each sentence.

1. Only an expert tracker can follow a trail in grassland.
2. Footprints are very light.
3. Even a horseshoe may not leave much of a mark.
4. After a rainstorm, tracking is easier.
5. A muddy riverbank shows the tracks of an animal.
6. The dry streambed shows no marks at all.
7. At night, trackers can use a flashlight.
8. Torchlight can also reveal tracks.
9. Sunlight is the best light of all.

LEVEL **B.** Make compound words by matching the nouns in the two columns.

10.	way	boat
11.	tug	path
12.	teller	knob
13.	suit	barrow
14.	house	story
15.	flower	case
16.	wheel	dog
17.	door	sun

LEVEL **C.** Make compound words by matching the nouns in the two columns. Then, write the definition of each word.

18.	place	fish
19.	gold	market
20.	dog	shift
21.	holder	paint
22.	book	sheep
23.	gear	window
24.	pane	pot
25.	brush	picture

MAINTENANCE

UNIT 1: Sentences

Complete Subjects and Complete Predicates (p. 6) Write each sentence. Draw one line under the complete subject. Draw two lines under the complete predicate.

1. The ducks swim on the pond.
2. A heron flies overhead.
3. The sun sparkles through the trees.
4. Many people enjoy the day.

Simple Subjects and Simple Predicates (p. 8, 10) Write each sentence. Draw one line under the simple subject and two lines under the simple predicate.

5. The food is gone!
6. Perhaps the dog ate it.
7. I doubt that.
8. Roger saw a raccoon out here.

Compound Subjects and Compound Predicates (p. 12) Write each sentence. Draw one line under each compound subject. Draw two lines under each compound predicate.

9. Pat and Jo went to the fair.
10. They rode and enjoyed the rides.
11. Jo won and kept a prize.

Compound Sentences (p. 14) Write each sentence. Write **simple sentence** or **compound sentence** next to each.

12. The music is beautiful.
13. The band plays more, and the audience is pleased.
14. The concert ends, and it is time to go home.

Correcting Sentence Fragments (p. 16) Rewrite each group of words to make a complete sentence.

15. Valerie plays the flute. But does not like the piano.
16. Some people can whistle and dance. At the same time.
17. The first time Henry painted. He liked it.

Vocabulary Building (p. 20) Write the meaning of the underlined word in each sentence. Then, write the word or words you used as context clues.

18. The robber's accomplice aided him.
19. John felt blissful about the beautiful weather.

UNIT 3: Nouns

What Is a Noun? (p. 76) Write each sentence. Draw a line under each noun.

20. Many flowers grow in the garden.
21. Alexandra is growing corn and peas.
22. Frank shovels the soil.
23. Birds fly around and land in trees.

Singular Nouns and Plural Nouns (p. 78, 80) Write each noun. Then write its plural form.

24. deer
25. moose
26. dairy
27. wish
28. potato
29. box
30. boy
31. wife

Common Nouns and Proper Nouns
(p. 82) Write each sentence. Draw one line under each common noun. Draw two lines under each proper noun.

32. The pyramids are in Egypt.
33. The capital of Egypt is Cairo.
34. Tourists from every continent visit this country.
35. The pyramids were built long before Europeans came to North America.

Singular and Plural Possessive Nouns (p. 84, 86) Write each noun. Then write its singular and plural possessive forms.

36. lady
37. fox
38. prince
39. hound

Using Possessive Nouns
(p. 88) Write each sentence. Replace the words in parentheses with a phrase that includes a possessive noun.

40. (The bicycle belonging to Juan) is new.
41. (The father of Miriam) works at home.
42. (The names of the patients) are written in red on the list.

Mechanics: Abbreviations
(p. 90) Write the abbreviations or initials for each word.

43. Doctor
44. Road
45. Sunday
46. Paul Jerry Smyth

Vocabulary Building: Compound Words (p. 92)
Match words in the columns to make compound words.

47. horse	light
48. drop	care
49. sun	shoe
50. free	dew

UNIT 4

Writing Instructions

Read the quotation and look at the picture on the opposite page. Ezra Jack Keats is a famous writer. You may have read some of his books. What creative activity is Ezra Jack Keats explaining? What sort of pattern did he see in his work?

Instructions are most helpful to people when they are clear and in step-by-step order. When you write instructions, you will want to be sure that your audience clearly understands them.

Focus Instructions present information about how to do something in a clear and orderly way.

What do you know how to do or create? What would you like to explain? In this unit you will find an article and some interesting photographs. You can use the article and the photographs to find ideas for writing.

THEME: *PATTERNS*

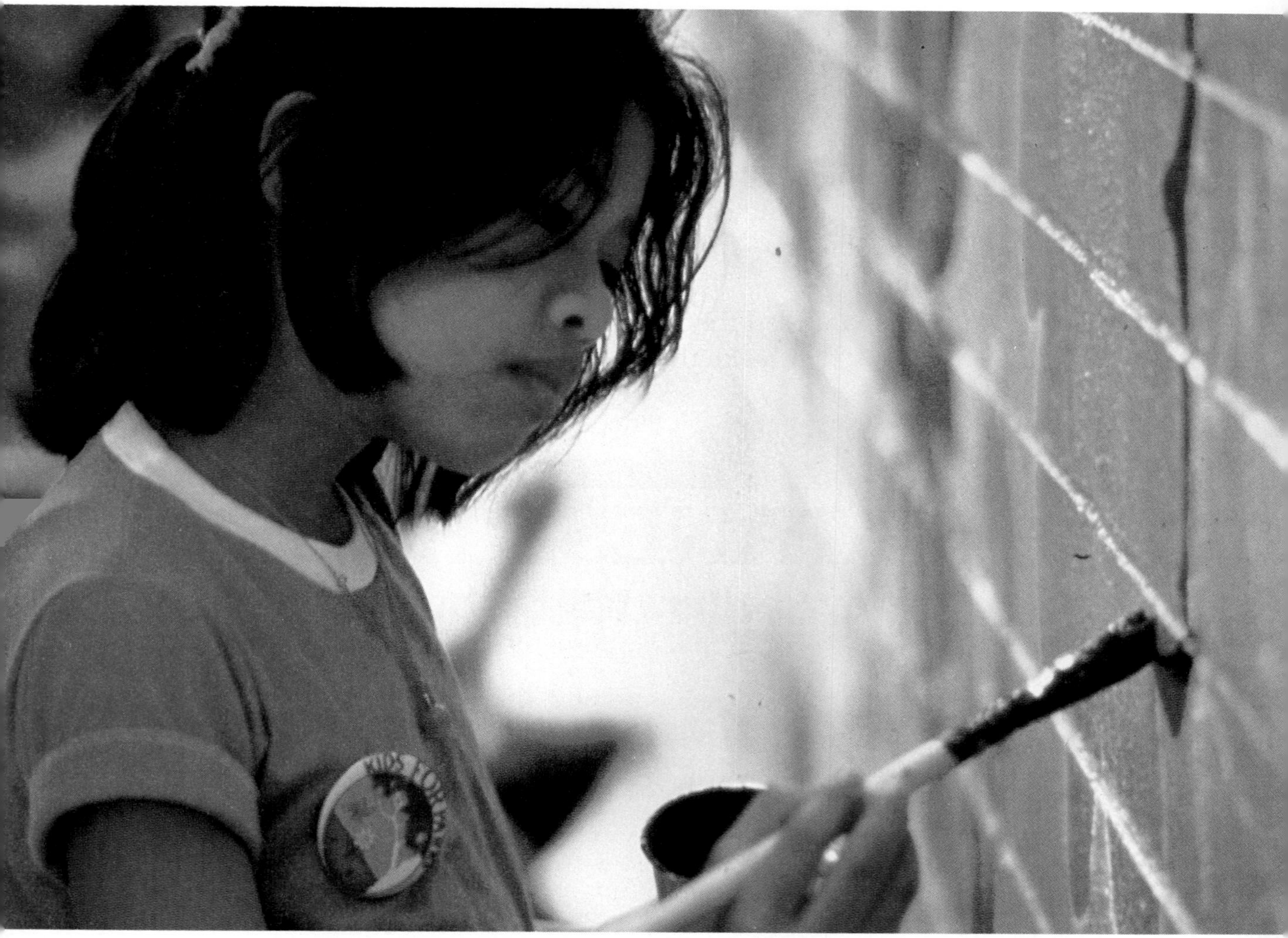

I taught myself to paint, using any kind of material I could find. Once, I covered a board with blue paint, then dipped my brush into the white and dabbed it onto the board, shook the brush a little and let it trail off. I stepped back and got the greatest thrill I can remember. I saw a little cloud floating across a blue sky.

—Ezra Jack Keats

LITERATURE

Reading Like a Writer

Think about where you live. What is special about your home?

Traditional Japanese houses are different from those in the United States. Japanese homes are kept almost empty. A low table for eating is usually the only furniture in the room.

As you read the selection, notice that the author chooses details that make the subject easy to understand.

JAPANESE HOUSES

from *Shelters* by Harvey Weiss

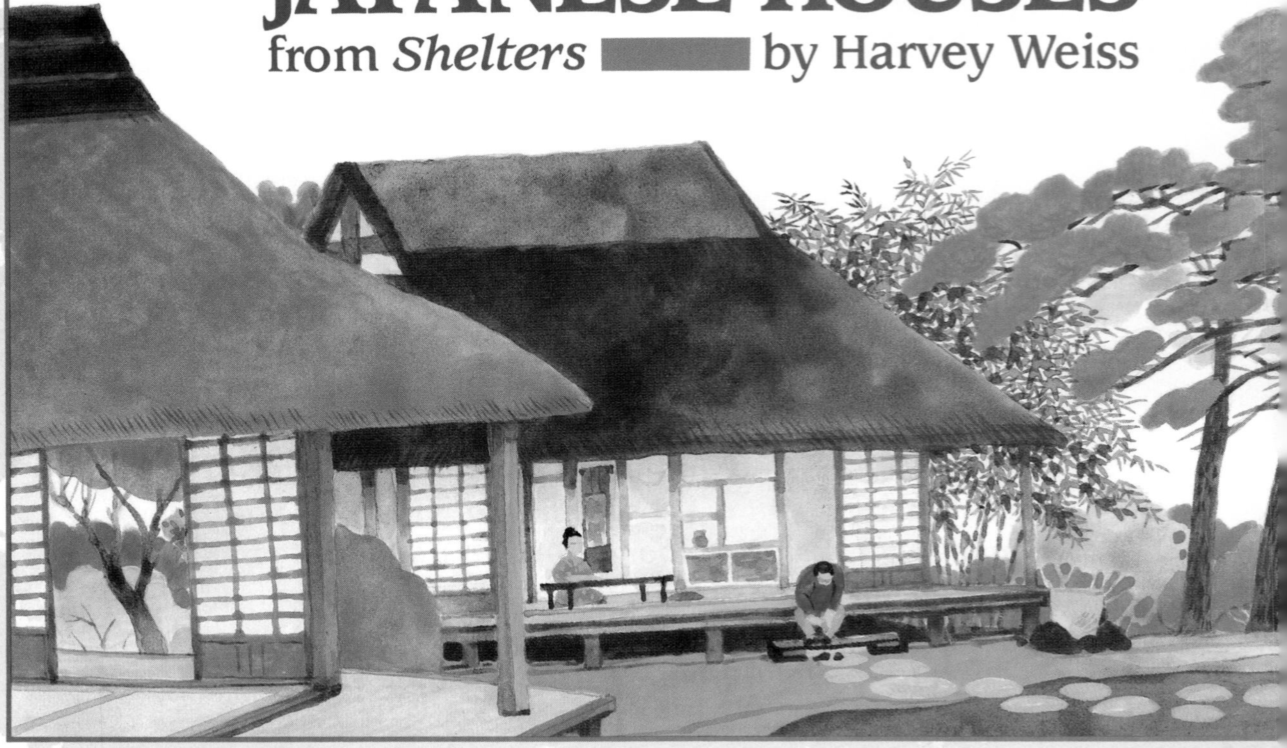

Japan is one of the world's most modern countries. It has large industrial centers and cities such as Tokyo, Osaka, and Yokohama, teeming with people, cars, and trucks. Japanese cities have all the advantages and problems found in large urban areas anywhere. There are steel and concrete skyscrapers, business buildings and apartment complexes jammed close together, and houses of all sorts.

But one kind of dwelling is typical of the warmer parts of Japan, although it is not as common as it once was. That is a small, light, airy family house built with simple, traditional materials. It is put together with enormous skill, delicacy, and attention to detail.

Notice that the author introduces the topic sentence as the second sentence in paragraph 2. The topic sentence prepares you for the details that follow.

Many of these houses are built with movable walls. You won't find walls made of massive logs or the weighty solidity of an African adobe dwelling. The walls are lightweight wood frames covered with paper or a light wood lattice. These screen-like walls slide back and forth to open up a space or close it off. In winter the thin walls are sometimes replaced by heavier ones, or panels to protect against the cold, dry winds that blow in over the Sea of Japan from Siberia.

This kind of lightweight Japanese house is practical and works well in the particular climate where it is found. But there is another reason it is built this way. The Japanese are very aware of their history and cultural heritage. Where

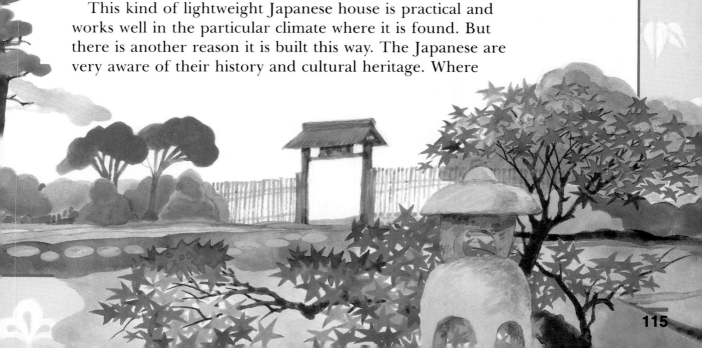

The body of the selection contains many clear details that help you to picture the rooms in a Japanese house.

possible, they like to continue this heritage by building in the traditional manner.

The traditional Japanese house has very little furniture. In fact it looks quite bare to the foreign visitor. The reason is that its inhabitants sit on cushions on the floor. There are no chairs, benches, end tables, or sofas. Usually, the only furniture is a low table around which the family gathers to eat.

There are no beds. A mat or quilt on the floor is used for sleeping and put away during the day. Clothing, blankets, and other household materials are folded up and placed in storage areas set into the walls.

The floors are covered with grass mats. These are fairly fragile, and to protect them and keep them clean, visitors and family remove their shoes before entering the house.

To the Japanese, a house is more than a place to keep out of the weather or a place to store one's possessions. The house is considered a part of the natural world, like a field, or a mountain, or a forest. It is regarded with appreciation, care, and sensitivity. The house is an important part of the world, and something to be made as beautiful as possible. It is a work of art.

Thinking Like a Reader

1. Do you think you would enjoy living in a Japanese house? Why or why not? Record your ideas in your journal.
2. What are houses in your neighborhood like? How do they compare with Japanese houses?

Write your responses in your journal.

Thinking Like a Writer

3. What does the author explain about Japanese houses?
4. Which details does he use to explain his topic?
5. Which details do you find most interesting? Make a list of these details.

Write your responses in your journal.

Responding to

LITERATURE

BRAINSTORM *Vocabulary*

The author of "Japanese Houses" uses some nouns that may be new to you. Read the selection again and look for words that describe Japanese houses. In your journal write any nouns that come to mind. Begin to create a personal vocabulary list. You can use these words when you write an explanation.

Talk It Over

Explain Your Work

In the selection you read, the author explains how traditional Japanese houses are built. Think of something you have made. Explain to a partner how you did it. Tell what steps the task included. Then, listen as your partner tells you about something she or he made.

Example: "I made a diorama. I used a shoebox, thin cardboard, paint, and string. I cut figures of people and buildings out of the cardboard. Then, I painted each piece. Next, I glued the string to the back of each piece. I punched holes through one side of the shoebox and threaded the string through the holes so that the pieces hung down. I knotted each string. When I was finished, I had a scene of a city street with people."

Quick Write *Write a Label*

When you buy a product, it often comes with a set of directions that tells you how to use it. Write a set of directions that includes clear instructions for making something. Here is an example:

Brownie Mix

1. Preheat oven to 350 degrees.
2. Place brownie mix in a large bowl.
3. Add half a cup of water.
4. Add one egg, then stir mixture.
5. Pour mixture into baking pan.
6. Bake for thirty minutes.

Keep your set of directions in your folder.

Idea Corner

Giving Explanations

You have already started to think about problems or tasks you could explain. How could you help your reader to understand and solve a problem? In your journal make some notes about the steps involved in solving a problem. Use these notes when you write an explanation.

PICTURES SEEING LIKE A WRITER

Finding Ideas for Writing

Look at the photographs. What ideas for writing instructions do the photographs give you? Write your ideas in your journal.

WRITING TOGETHER

COOPERATIVE LEARNING

1 GROUP WRITING: Instructions

The **purpose** of a written explanation is to provide clear, useful instructions about how to do something. An explanation states a problem (what is to be done) and then goes on to solve it (steps to follow). What makes an explanation easy for an audience to follow?

- Topic Sentence
- Transition Words
- Clear Details

Topic Sentence

Read the following set of instructions. Notice the underlined sentence.

How to Find a Book in the Library

Finding a book in the library is not difficult if you follow three main steps. First, recall the title of the book you want to find. Second, look for the title in the card catalog. The cards are in alphabetical order. Then, find the number on the card. The number tells you on which shelf the book can be found. After you know the number, find the correct shelf.

The underlined sentence is called the **topic sentence**. A topic sentence states the main idea of a paragraph. In an explanation, the topic sentence introduces what will be explained or what problem will be solved.

Guided Practice: Writing a Topic Sentence

With your class, choose a topic on which you all agree. Brainstorm ideas with your classmates. Then write a topic sentence that states the problem to be solved.

Example: Making wind chimes takes only a few simple materials.

Transition Words

Look back at the paragraph on page 120. Notice that the writer takes you from one step to the next by using words such as *first* and *second*. These words are called **transition words**. They show the *order* of steps to be followed.

The paragraph clearly shows how to find a book in the library. The instructions are simple and clear. Reread the paragraph.

- What other transition words does the writer use?
- How do these words make the instructions clear?

Guided Practice: Using Transition Words

Remember the problem you have chosen to solve in your explanation. Your instructions will tell your audience how to make something. With your classmates, discuss the steps needed to make this object. As a class, make a list of transition words like the one below.

first, second, third
now, next, then
later, last, finally

Clear Details

Each detail in a set of instructions must be clear. The reader has to be able to follow the writer's explanation. In the directions for finding a book in the library, the details tell the reader just what to do. Look back at the paragraph.

- Which details are given?
- Are the steps easy to understand?

Guided Practice: Listing Clear Details

Look at the list of transition words you made with your class. Which words would help you to order your details? Is there enough information in your explanation?

Make a list of details to include in your explanation. Work with your classmates to fill in any missing steps in your instructions.

Putting a Set of Instructions Together

With your classmates you have written a topic sentence for a paragraph that explains how to make something. You have listed some details and some transition words, too.

Think about your topic sentence. Then look at your list of details. Which details would your reader need to understand your instructions? Be sure to include those details. Cross out any details that do not help to make your explanation clear.

A student listed some steps that show how to make wind chimes. These are the steps he chose to include. Look at the details below.

could use glass, metal, or wood	need 6–8 pieces
need larger piece of material	use medium-weight string

This student listed details that tell more about what materials are needed for a wind chime than about how to put the pieces together.

Guided Practice: Writing Instructions

Use your topic sentence and detail sentences to write a set of instructions. Include transition words to order the steps correctly. Choose words that tell the reader exactly what to do in each step of the instructions.

Share your instructions with a classmate. Ask your partner if he or she could make the object by following your instructions.

Checklist: Instructions

When you write a set of instructions, you will want to keep some points in mind. A checklist will remind you of the things you will want to include in your instructions.

Look at this checklist. Some points need to be added. Make a copy of the checklist and complete it. Keep a copy of it in your writing folder. You can use it when you write your instructions.

CHECKLIST

- ✓ Purpose and audience
- ✓ Topic sentence
- ✓ Transition words
- ✓ Clear details ______________________

____

____

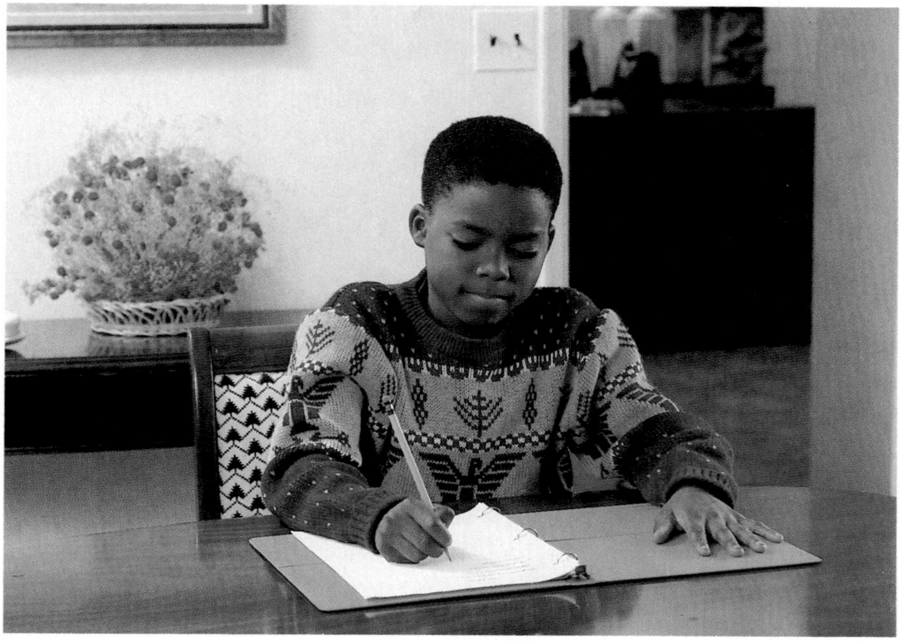

2 THINKING AND WRITING: Solving Problems

You know that when you write a set of instructions, you state a problem and then go on to solve it. The steps of your instructions must be clear.

Writers think carefully about the **purpose** of their explanations and state the problem in a topic sentence. Writers decide which details are important for the **audience** to know and arrange them in logical step-by-step order.

Look at this page from a student writer's journal.

Making Your Own Photo Album
heavy cardboard for covers
thick paper or thin cardboard
string or yarn and paste

Thinking Like a Writer

- Is there enough information here to show a reader how to make an album for photographs?

In your set of instructions, you will have to explain the problem to be solved and how to solve it.

Making your own photograph album is easy and requires only a few simple steps. You need two pieces of heavy cardboard, some sheets of light cardboard or heavy paper for the inside leaves, string or yarn, and paste. First, punch three holes on the left-hand side of each piece of cardboard or paper. Put as many sheets inside the covers as you want. Thread the string through the holes and tie it so that your album stays together. Apply paste to the backs of the photographs, and arrange them as you like.

THINKING APPLICATION Making Details Clear

COOPERATIVE LEARNING

WRITING TOGETHER

Each of the writers named below is planning to write a set of instructions. The instructions should be as precise as possible. Help each student to decide which details are clear. Write the details on a separate piece of paper. Do you think you could make the object by following the steps in each set of instructions? You may wish to discuss your thinking with other students. In your discussion, explain your choices to each other.

1. Linda's instructions will tell readers how to make a terrarium. Which details are clear? What details could be added?

   get glass or plastic tank
   put in plants
   fill with grass or pebbles
   small animals can live in terrarium.

2. Daryl's instructions will tell readers how to make a layer cake. Which details are clear? What details could be added?

   buy round or square cake pans
   make batter and pour into pans
   bake layers for 30 minutes
   let cool before icing

3. Terry's instructions will tell readers how to make a skateboard. Which details are clear? What details could be added?

   get a 12″ by 6″ piece of wood
   fasten wheels with screwdriver
   could use wheels from roller skates
   make sure board is balanced

4. Jill's instructions will tell readers how to make a window box for flowers. Which details are clear? Which details are unclear?

   wood or aluminum box
   small plants or flowers
   pack with soil
   place on window

3 INDEPENDENT WRITING: Instructions

Prewrite: Step 1

You have seen how writers put together instructions. Now you can write instructions of your own. Lily, a student your age, wanted to write instructions for the members of her cooking club. She chose a topic in this way.

Choosing a Topic

1. First, Lily thought of foods she liked.
2. Next, she started a list of foods she knew how to cook.
3. Last, she chose the recipe she thought she could explain the most clearly.

making a stew
making a tuna casserole
making chili
making corn bread

Lily decided to explain how to prepare chili. Once she had narrowed her topic, she was ready to explore her idea.

Exploring Ideas: Using a Flow Chart

Lily used a flow chart to organize the steps of her instructions. Notice her topic sentence.

This is how to make the world's best chili.

Chop onion, garlic
↓
Add ground beef
↓
Add beans and other ingredients
↓
Brown onions and ground beef

Lily knew that the **purpose** of her writing was to explain how to make chili. She thought about the steps she would need to explain.

Before she actually wrote her instructions, Lily decided it was important to review each step carefully. She made some changes to her flow chart.

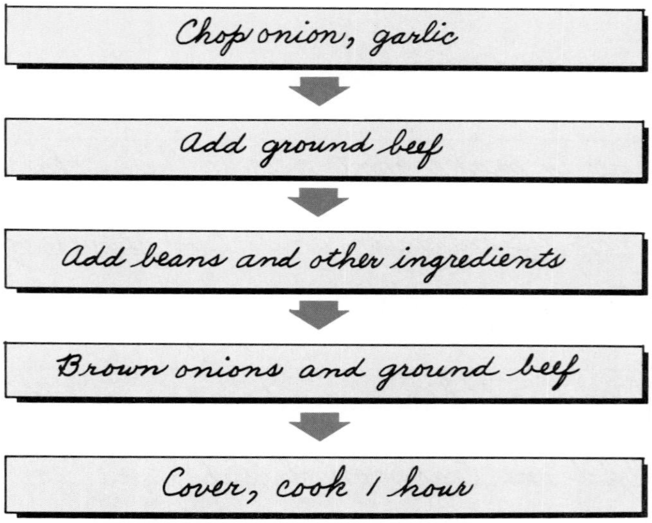
Chop onion, garlic
Add ground beef
Add beans and other ingredients
Brown onions and ground beef
Cover, cook 1 hour

Thinking Like a Writer

- What changes did Lily make to her flow chart?
- Do her changes make sense?

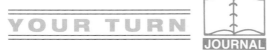

YOUR TURN

JOURNAL

Think of something you have made that you would enjoy explaining. Use **Pictures** or your journal for ideas. Follow these steps.

- Write a list of things you know how to make.
- Choose one that you can easily explain.
- Narrow the topic if it is too broad.
- Think about your purpose and audience.

Make a flow chart. Remember, you can change the order of steps on the flow chart later.

Write a First Draft: Step 2

Lily knows what to include in her set of instructions. She has made a planning checklist. Lily is now ready to write her first draft.

Lily's First Draft

aunt bess's Chili

This is how to make aunt bess's chili, the World's best chili. Chop up one onion and two cloves of garlic. Add one to two pounds of ground beef. Add five cups of canned beans and two cups of canned tomatos. Add one teaspoon of salt and four tablespoons of chili powder. Stir and cook for about one hour until chili is brown.

As Lily wrote, she did not worry about errors. She wanted to put her ideas down on paper.

Planning Checklist
- Remember purpose and audience.
- Include a topic sentence.
- Use transition words.
- Choose clear details.

YOUR TURN

Write your first draft. As you prepare to write, ask yourself these questions.

- What will my audience need to know?
- How can I best explain my ideas?

TIME-OUT You might want to take some time out before you revise. That way you will be able to revise your writing with a fresh eye.

Revise: Step 3

After she finished her first draft, Lily read it over to herself. Then she shared her writing with her friend, David. She asked David to suggest ways she could improve her work.

The chili sounds good, but I'm not sure I completely understand the steps in the recipe.
OK. I'll make the order of steps clearer.

Lily then looked at her planning checklist. She realized that she had forgotten one point. She checked it off so that she would remember it when she revised. Lily now has a checklist to use as she revises her instructions.

Lily made changes to her work. She did not correct small errors. She knew she could fix them later.

The revisions Lily made changed her set of instructions. Turn the page. Look at Lily's revised draft.

Revising Checklist

- Remember purpose and audience.
- Include a topic sentence.
- ✓ Use transition words.
- Choose clear details.

WRITING PROCESS

Lily's Revised Draft

aunt bess's Chili

This is how to make aunt bess's chili, the World's best chili. First, melt two tablespoons of butter in a pan. Then, Chop up one onion and two cloves of garlic. Next, Add one to two pounds of ground beef. After that, Add five cups of canned beans and two cups of canned tomatos, Add one teaspoon of salt and four tablespoons of chili powder. Finally, Stir all the ingredients and cook for about one hour until chili is brown. Aunt bess's chili serves six.

Thinking Like a Writer

WISE WORD CHOICE

- Which words did Lily add? How did this make her instructions clearer?
- Which sentences did she combine? How does this improve her writing?
- Which sentences are new or changed? How does this revision help make the instructions clear?

YOUR TURN

Read your first draft. Ask yourself these questions.

- What is my topic sentence?
- What transition words have I included to show the order of the steps in my instructions?
- How can I make my details clearer?

If you wish, ask a friend to read your instructions and make suggestions. Then revise your set of instructions.

Proofreading: Step 4

Lily knew that her work was not complete until she proofread her instructions. She used a proofreading checklist while she proofread.

Part of Lily's Proofread Draft

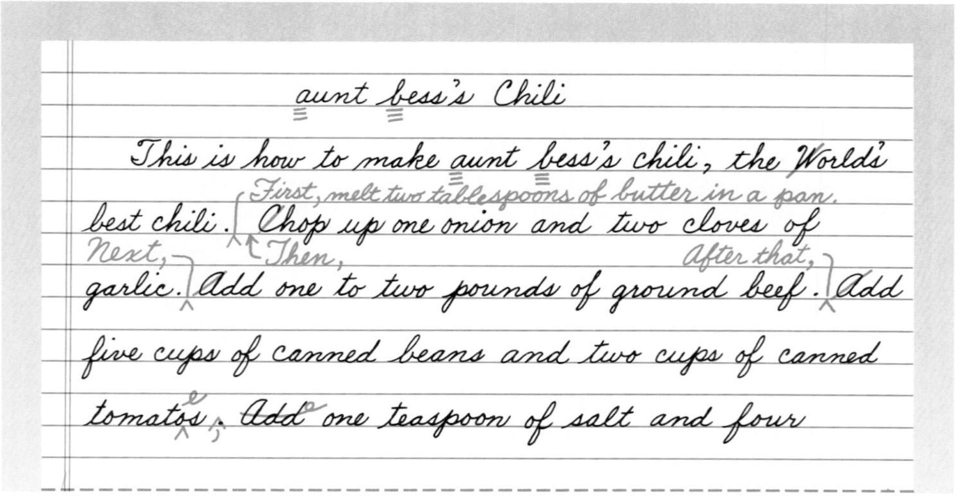
aunt bess's Chili

This is how to make aunt bess's chili, the Worlds'
First, melt two tablespoons of butter in a pan.
best chili. Chop up one onion and two cloves of
Next, Then, After that,
garlic. Add one to two pounds of ground beef. Add
five cups of canned beans and two cups of canned
e
tomatos. Add one teaspoon of salt and four

YOUR TURN

Proofreading Practice

Below is a paragraph that you can use to practice your proofreading skills. Find the errors. Write the paragraph correctly on a separate sheet of paper.

> First remove all the furniture and rugs. Then spread a drop cloth over the floor Be sure it covers up to the walls. Wear a mask to protect you from the paint fume. Open the paint and stir it well. Next paint around the edges of the ceiling with a brush Then roll paint on the ceiling with a roller. After that, paint the four corners with a brush. Then roll paint on the wall finally, clean up and put back the furniture when the paint is dry.

Proofreading Checklist

- Did I indent at the beginning of each paragraph?
- Did I spell all words correctly?
- What punctuation errors do I need to correct?
- What capitalization errors do I need to correct?

WRITING PROCESS

WRITING PROCESS

Applying Your Proofreading Skills

Now proofread your set of instructions. Read your checklist again. Review **The Grammar Connection** and **The Mechanics Connection**, too. Use the proofreading marks to mark changes.

THE GRAMMAR CONNECTION

Remember these rules about nouns.

- Most nouns form the plural by adding *s*.
- Nouns ending in *s*, *x*, *ch*, or *sh* form the plural by adding *es*.
- Nouns ending with a vowel and *y* form the plural by adding *s*.
- Nouns ending with a consonant and *y* form the plural by changing the *y* to *i* and adding *es*.

  The gift**s** were under the tree.
  The tree branch**es** were decorated with tinsel.
  The boy**s** thought of their cousin**s** in other cit**ies**.

Check your work. Have you formed plural nouns correctly?

Proofreading Marks
¶ Indent
∧ Add
ℓ Take out
≡ Make a capital letter
/ Make a small letter

THE MECHANICS CONNECTION

Proper nouns are those that name a particular person, place, or thing. All proper nouns must be capitalized.

river	→	Nile River	country	→	Egypt
mountain	→	Mt. Rainier	state	→	California

Publish: Step 5

Lily shared her instructions with her cooking club. She copied the instructions in her best handwriting and gave them to the members of the club. Several members of her cooking club made Aunt Bess's chili. They said it was easy to make and tasted delicious.

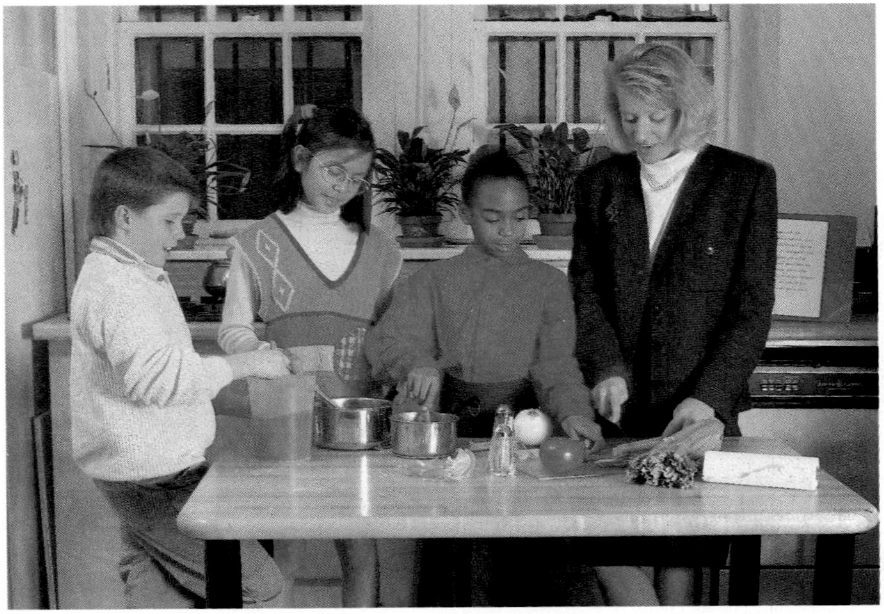

YOUR TURN

Make a final copy of your instructions. Write as neatly as you can. Think of a way to share your work. You might find some ideas in the **Sharing Suggestions** box below.

SHARING SUGGESTIONS

Create a how-to book that includes instructions for making various things.	Exchange instructions with a classmate. Try to make the thing described.	Read your instructions aloud to your class. Ask other students to tell you if the instructions are clear.

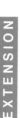

WRITING

EXTENSION

4 SPEAKING AND LISTENING: Giving Instructions

You have just written a set of instructions. Your instructions have shown readers how to make something. You included transition words and clear details in a logical order. Now you can use what you know about writing instructions to give a talk in which you explain to an audience how to make something.

First, you will want to make a flow chart for your explanation. The flow chart should include your topic and some details. Each detail in the flow chart should appear in the order in which you plan to discuss it.

Look at the flow chart below.

Making a Papier-Mâché Sculpture

sculpt an object from torn paper

↓

tear strips of newspaper

↓

find object to mold paper around

↓

make a flour paste

↓

layer paper and paste on form

↓

let sculpture dry, then paint

Notice that the title at the top of the flow chart gives the topic or main idea of the student's explanation. How does the order of steps help you to understand the instructions?

Keep in mind that as the student explains each step to his classmates, he will use appropriate transition words. These words will help his classmates to understand the order of steps in the process.

When you give a talk, it will help you to keep your **purpose** and **audience** in mind. These speaking guidelines will help you to focus your explanation.

SPEAKING GUIDELINES: Giving Instructions

1. Remember your **purpose** and **audience**.
2. Make a flow chart. Practice using the flow chart.
3. Begin with a topic sentence.
4. Use transition words to show the order of details.
5. Look at your listeners and speak in a strong, clear voice.

- What is the purpose of my explanation?
- Do the instructions serve this purpose?

SPEAKING APPLICATION A Set Of Instructions

Think of something you know how to make. Prepare a flow chart to use as you organize the details of your explanation. Use the speaking guidelines to help you prepare. Your classmates will be using the following guidelines as they listen to your instructions.

LISTENING GUIDELINES: Instructions

1. Listen for the purpose of the explanation.
2. Listen for the logical order of the steps in the instructions.
3. Listen for clear details.

5 WRITER'S RESOURCES: The Thesaurus

In this unit you have prepared instructions explaining how to make several things. You have learned that it is important to find the precise words to explain your meaning in each step of your instructions.

A useful resource for the writer is a **thesaurus**. This is a book that contains lists of **synonyms**, words that mean almost the same thing as the word you have looked up. The thesaurus helps you to find words that say exactly what you mean.

Sample Entry
laugh, chuckle, giggle, guffaw, snicker
antonyms: *See* **cry**.

A list of **entry words** can be found in the thesaurus. Entry words are written in **dark type** and are listed in alphabetical order. The words listed after each entry word are synonyms. At the end of some entries is a list of **antonyms**, words that mean the opposite of the **entry word**. The number next to the entry word in the **index** of a thesaurus tells you where the word is listed in the book. Some thesauruses give the definition of the entry word and an example sentence.

Practice

A. Use the Thesaurus on page 507 to find synonyms for the following entry words. Make a list of these synonyms on a separate sheet of paper.

1. big
2. look
3. smile
4. nice
5. run
6. interesting
7. good
8. like
9. plain
10. neat
11. sad
12. strong
13. think
14. surprised
15. little
16. ready
17. shy
18. see
19. hard
20. many

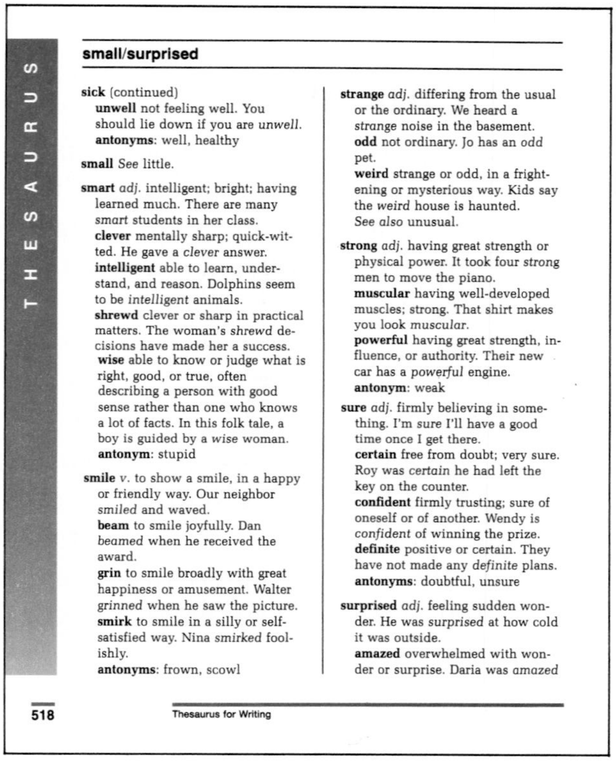

THESAURUS

small/surprised

sick (continued)
unwell not feeling well. You should lie down if you are *unwell.*
antonyms: well, healthy

small See little.

smart *adj.* intelligent; bright; having learned much. There are many *smart* students in her class.
clever mentally sharp; quick-witted. He gave a *clever* answer.
intelligent able to learn, understand, and reason. Dolphins seem to be *intelligent* animals.
shrewd clever or sharp in practical matters. The woman's *shrewd* decisions have made her a success.
wise able to know or judge what is right, good, or true, often describing a person with good sense rather than one who knows a lot of facts. In this folk tale, a boy is guided by a *wise* woman.
antonym: stupid

smile *v.* to show a smile, in a happy or friendly way. Our neighbor *smiled* and waved.
beam to smile joyfully. Dan *beamed* when he received the award.
grin to smile broadly with great happiness or amusement. Walter *grinned* when he saw the picture.
smirk to smile in a silly or self-satisfied way. Nina *smirked* foolishly.
antonyms: frown, scowl

strange *adj.* differing from the usual or the ordinary. We heard a *strange* noise in the basement.
odd not ordinary. Jo has an *odd* pet.
weird strange or odd, in a frightening or mysterious way. Kids say the *weird* house is haunted.
See also unusual.

strong *adj.* having great strength or physical power. It took four *strong* men to move the piano.
muscular having well-developed muscles; strong. That shirt makes you look *muscular.*
powerful having great strength, influence, or authority. Their new car has a *powerful* engine.
antonym: weak

sure *adj.* firmly believing in something. I'm *sure* I'll have a good time once I get there.
certain free from doubt; very sure. Roy was *certain* he had left the key on the counter.
confident firmly trusting; sure of oneself or of another. Wendy is *confident* of winning the prize.
definite positive or certain. They have not made any *definite* plans.
antonyms: doubtful, unsure

surprised *adj.* feeling sudden wonder. He was *surprised* at how cold it was outside.
amazed overwhelmed with wonder or surprise. Daria was *amazed*

518 Thesaurus for Writing

B. Choose two of the entry words from Practice A. Write a sentence for each word. Then, replace each entry word with a **synonym** from your list.

WRITING APPLICATION Sentences

Choose three words that you used in your set of instructions. Write these words on a separate sheet of paper. Look up each word in your Thesaurus. Then, write two synonyms for each word. Finally, use each synonym in a sentence. Keep your list of words in your writing folder. You can use it in **The Curriculum Connection** on page 138.

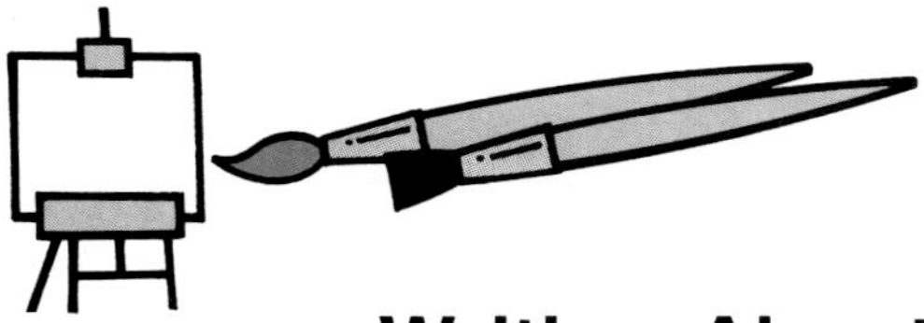

Writing About Art

You can read about art in books, magazines, and newspaper reviews. There are many ways to write about art. A writer may describe a particular work of art or explain how it was created. An artist may tell something about his or her life and work.

ACTIVITIES

Describe a Painting Look at the illustration on the opposite page. Write an explanation of what you see happening in the picture. Which details in the picture make you think your explanation is a good one? Include these details in your writing so that your reader can "see" the picture.

Explain How to Make a Work of Art What kinds of things have you made in art class or outside of school? Think of the steps needed to make a painting, a photograph, a drawing, or other artwork. Recall the order of the steps. Then write an explanation of how to make the artwork. Be sure to order your steps clearly.

Respond to Literature The following explanation is taken from a book about drawing living things. The author believes it is important to understand how an animal or a plant moves. He says that an artist must watch animals in action before trying to capture them on paper.

After reading the explanation, try drawing a living animal or plant. After you finish your drawing, write a description of what you did in order to understand how to draw the animal or plant.

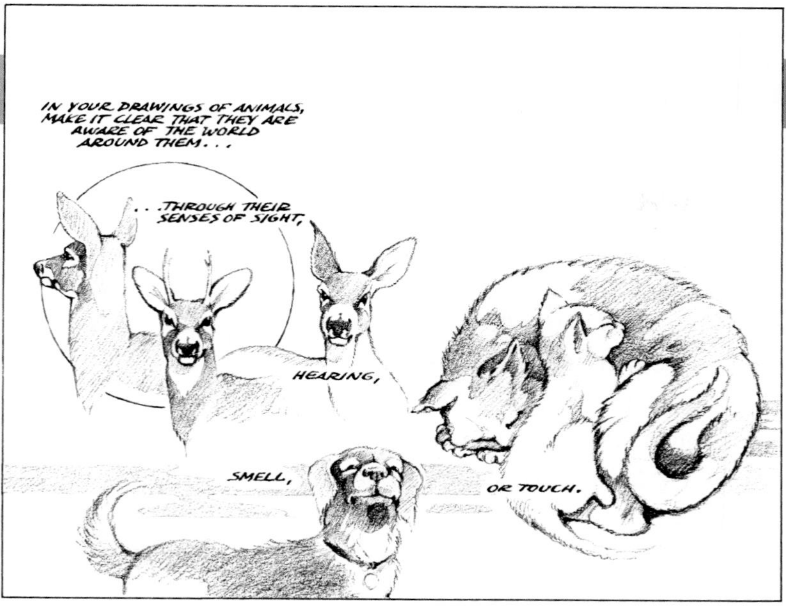

IN YOUR DRAWINGS OF ANIMALS, MAKE IT CLEAR THAT THEY ARE AWARE OF THE WORLD AROUND THEM . . .
. . .THROUGH THEIR SENSES OF SIGHT,
HEARING,
SMELL,
OR TOUCH.

From Drawing Life in Motion

Animals move freely. Many are conscious of where and why they move. Life is moving around them. They can sense it. Life is pulsing within them. They can hardly contain it. Even when standing still, animals move with breaths or blinks, always ready for action.

You can breathe life into your drawings of still animals by giving them a look of awareness or by poising some part of their bodies on the verge of, or at the end of, a move.

Animals can move from place to place by pushing or pulling on other things. An inchworm crawls by pushing against the ground with its hind end and then pulling on the ground with its front end.

A toad's muscular hind legs push against the ground with every hop. A lizard climbing up a boulder pulls on the rock with each clawed step.

The most effective way I know to draw animals in motion is to show them in the midst of pushing or pulling themselves along.

UNIT CHECKUP

LESSON 1 **Group Writing: Instructions** (page 120) On a separate sheet of paper, arrange the following details in an order that makes sense. Begin each sentence with a transition word that shows the order of steps.

How to Make a Collage

—Arrange materials on paper or cardboard.
—Paste down paper and other loose objects.
—Collect materials like paper, string, paint, and paste.
—Paint or draw on paper before pasting any objects.

LESSON 2 **Thinking: Solving Problems** (page 124) Help your reader solve the following problem. Next to each detail, write a complete sentence that explains a step in the instructions. Then write your sentences in a clear, orderly paragraph.

Making a Set of Flashcards

—index cards without lines
—words you want to remember
—magic marker
—purpose of set of flashcards

LESSON 3 **Writing Instructions** (page 126) Imagine that a classmate will visit you. Write a set of instructions that explains how to get to your home from the school. Put each step of your directions in a logical order.

LESSON 4 **Speaking and Listening: Giving Directions** (page 134) Imagine that you will give an oral report in which you tell your classmates how to do or make something. Make a flow chart that includes each step in the proper order.

LESSON 5 **Writer's Resources: The Thesaurus** (page 136) Choose four words. Look them up in your thesaurus. Then choose a synonym for each word. On a separate sheet of paper, write a sentence for each synonym.

THEME PROJECT — QUILT DESIGN

You have been reading about patterns of many kinds. Patterns exist everywhere. In art, music, science, cooking, gardening—anywhere you look, you can find a pattern.

Think of some of the patterns you have seen. They may be small or large. Sometimes, a pattern is hard to see. Once you see it, though, it seems quite clear.

Collection of the Museum of American Folk Art; Gift of David Pottinger. 1980.37.27

Quilt; Sunshine and Shadow, Amish, Susan Beechy, Topeka, Indiana. Cotton. 1935-40 83″ × 70″

The quilt in this photograph has patterns or designs that you can see easily. Talk with your classmates about the patterns you find in the quilt. Think of the kinds of patterns you like.

- Draw a design for a quilt that you would like to make or own.
- Begin by brainstorming some ideas.
- After you have drawn or painted the design for your quilt, write an explanation of its pattern. What does it look like? Why did you choose this particular pattern?
- Share your quilt design and written explanation with your classmates. Look for the patterns in each other's quilt designs.

UNIT 5

Verbs

In this unit you will learn about verbs. Some verbs express action, and others do not. Which verbs can you think of that do not express action?

Discuss Read the poem on the opposite page. What are the people doing? Which verb can you find that does not express action?

JOURNAL

Creative Expression The theme of this unit is *Prizes*. What kinds of prizes do you know about? Draw a medal or a ribbon that might be given as a prize. Write a few words on your drawing to explain the prize. You may wish to put your drawing in your journal.

THEME: *PRIZES*

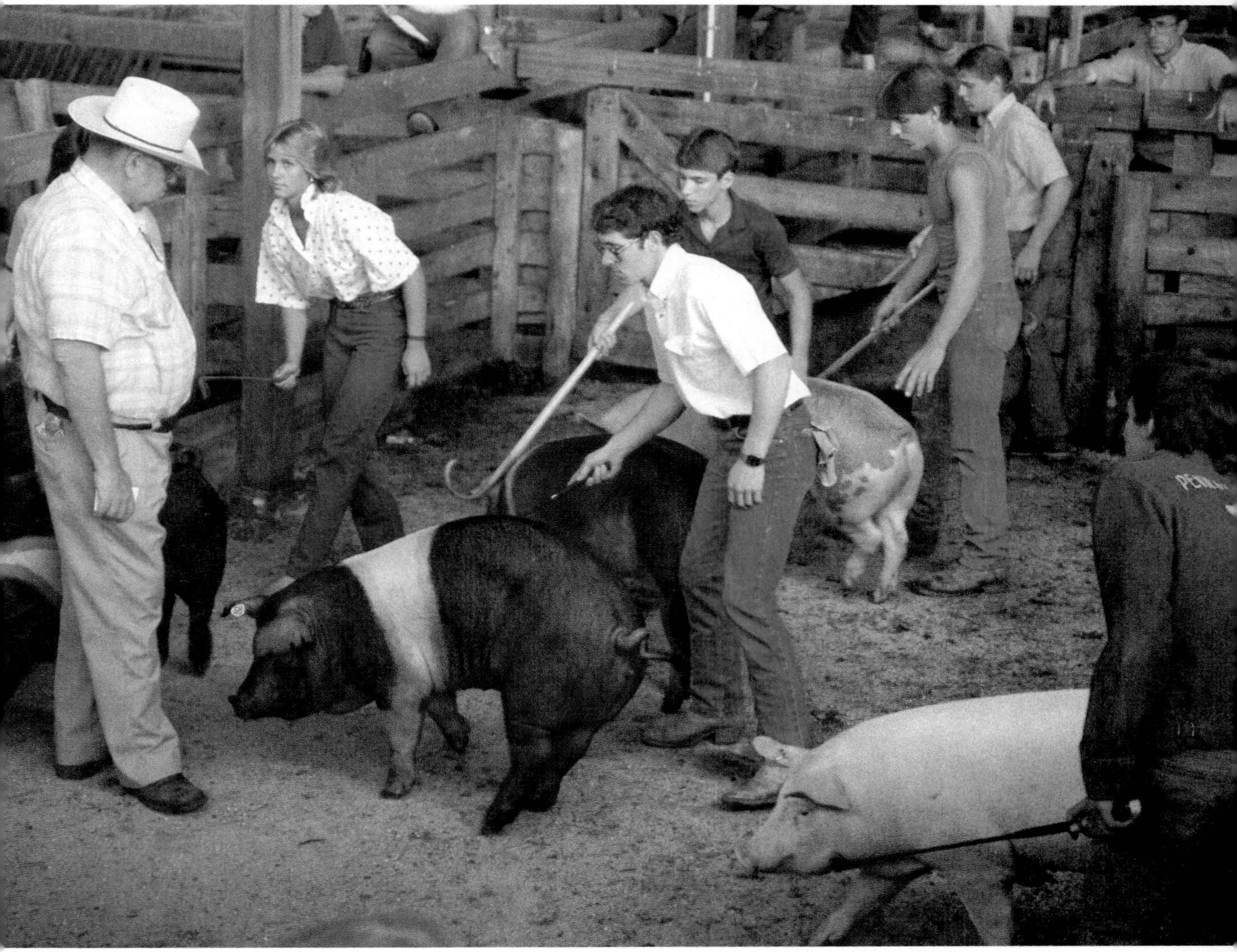

Hog-Calling Competition

A bull-voiced young fellow of Pawling
Competes in the meets for hog-calling;
The people applaud,
And the judges are awed,
But the hogs find it simply appalling.

—Morris Bishop

1 WHAT IS AN ACTION VERB?

An action verb is a word that expresses action.

Every sentence you write has two parts, a subject and a predicate. The main word in the predicate is often an **action verb.** The action verb tells what the subject of the sentence does or did. What kinds of actions are expressed in the sentences below?

Sylvia **entered** the short story contest.
Now many people **read** her story.
We **enjoy** her tale about a leprechaun.

Verbs can also express action you cannot see.

I **wonder** about the contest.
Robin **hoped** for a prize.

Sylvia typed her story.

Guided Practice

Tell which word is the action verb in each sentence.

Example: The teacher discusses our stories. *discusses*

1. We read the contest rules.
2. The judges outlined the rules.
3. Only fifth graders enter the contest.
4. We work on our stories all week.
5. Sylvia planned her story carefully.

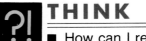

?! **THINK**

■ How can I recognize an action verb?

REMEMBER

- An **action verb** expresses action.
- An action verb tells what the subject of the sentence does or did.

More Practice

A. Write each sentence. Draw a line under the action verb in each sentence.

Example: The contest begins today. *The contest begins today.*

6. Sylvia writes in a diary.
7. Her story comes from her diary.
8. Details interest Sylvia.
9. Past prize winners visited the state capital.
10. Sylvia hopes for a good prize.
11. Robin enters the contest, too.
12. He works slowly but carefully.

B. Write the sentences. Complete each sentence with an action verb.

Example: I _____ my story first. *I finish my story first.*

13. Everyone _____ about his story.
14. No one _____ it except Robin.
15. Sylvia _____ about the contest.
16. Robin _____ eagerly.
17. We _____ for the judge's decision.
18. They _____ the winner on Friday.
19. The announcement _____ everybody.
20. Robin and Sylvia both _____ prizes.

Extra Practice, page 176

WRITING APPLICATION A List

COOPERATIVE LEARNING

Imagine that you must judge a short story contest. Write a list of the contest rules. Include your ideas about what makes a short story good. Read your work to a group of your classmates. Ask them to find the action verbs.

GRAMMAR

2 VERBS WITH DIRECT OBJECTS

Often, a subject and a verb express a complete thought.

Subject	**Verb**
The dog	barked.
The sound	echoed.

Sometimes an action verb is followed by a direct object. A **direct object** is a noun or pronoun in the predicate that receives the action of the verb. A direct object answers the question *what?* or *whom?* after action verbs.

Elaine judges **dogs.**
She gives **prizes** to the winners.
Dogs love **her.**

The spaniel wants the prize.

Guided Practice

Tell the action verb and the direct object in each sentence.

Example: The pet owners follow the rules.
follow *action verb* rules *direct object*

1. We plan a dog show.
2. Each owner enters a dog.
3. Elaine judges our show.
4. George owns a spaniel.
5. The spaniel carries a bone.

?! THINK

■ How can I recognize the direct object in a sentence?

REMEMBER

- A **direct object** receives the action of the verb.
- A direct object answers the question *what?* or *whom?* after action verbs.

More Practice

A. Write each sentence. Draw one line under the action verb and two lines under the direct object.

Example: The dogs wear tags. *The dogs wear tags.*

6. A beagle shows her hunting skills.
7. Each owner wants the best prize.
8. Elaine brings dog biscuits.
9. The pets love the treats.
10. They all wag their tails.
11. The dogs obey the handlers.
12. They treat the dogs well.

B. Write each sentence. Complete each sentence with a direct object.

Example: The judges choose the _____. *The judges choose the winners.*

13. We enter the _____.
14. Elaine pats a frightened _____.
15. Susan brushes a _____.
16. A collie chases a _____.
17. The judge announces the _____.
18. Ricky holds a _____.
19. A sheepdog wins the _____.
20. The audience applauds the _____.

Extra Practice, page 177

WRITING APPLICATION An Announcement

Write an announcement for a dog show. Include important information about the event. Have a classmate find the action verbs and direct objects in your work.

GRAMMAR

3 MAIN VERBS AND HELPING VERBS

You know that a simple predicate can be more than one word. Some sentences have a main verb and a helping verb. The **main verb** shows what the subject does or is. The **helping verb** helps the main verb to show an action in the sentence. By itself, a helping verb cannot show action.

The main verbs in the sentences below are in red. The helping verbs are in blue.

Stan and Jan **are entering** the talent contest.
I **can help** them rehearse.
They **have created** a dance routine.
They **will dance** together.

Study the chart below.

Common Helping Verbs					
am	are	were	shall	has	can
is	was	will	have	had	could

Guided Practice

Tell the main verb in each sentence. Then, tell the helping verb in each sentence.

Example: The dancers will perform soon.
perform *main verb* *will* *helping verb*

1. Gerald is practicing for the contest.
2. He has danced in many talent shows.
3. He will perform some difficult dance steps.
4. We have started our rehearsals.
5. We can meet every afternoon.
6. Judson and I could use more practice.

?! **THINK**

- How can I recognize the main verb and the helping verb in a sentence?

REMEMBER

- The **main verb** shows what the subject does or is.
- The **helping verb** helps the main verb to show an action.

More Practice

A. Write each sentence. Draw one line under the helping verb. Draw two lines under the main verb.

Example: We are participating in the event. *We are participating in the event.*

7. We have met every day after school.
8. Other students are planning their acts.
9. Everybody is making fancy costumes.
10. Sandy has made a decision.
11. She shall enter the contest without a partner.
12. She is performing a solo act.

B. Write the sentences. Complete each sentence with a helping verb.

Example: My brother _____ coaching me. *My brother is coaching me.*

13. We _____ practice very hard.
14. I _____ attend all the rehearsals.
15. Lucy _____ singing in her act.
16. My friends _____ come to the show.
17. The judges _____ make fair decisions.
18. We _____ planning a party after the contest.
19. We _____ invited many guests to the party.
20. We _____ waiting eagerly for that day.

Extra Practice, page 178

WRITING APPLICATION An Article

Imagine that you are writing for your school paper. Write a brief news article about a special event at the school. Have your classmates find the main verbs and the helping verbs in your article.

4 WHAT IS A LINKING VERB?

Some verbs do not show action. Verbs that do not show action are called linking verbs. A **linking verb** is a verb that links the subject of a sentence to a noun or an adjective in the predicate. The word that follows the linking verb names or describes the subject of the sentence. Many linking verbs are forms of the verb *to be*.

The state fair **is** a treat.

Some verbs can be either linking verbs or action verbs.

The fairgrounds **look** pretty. (linking verb)
You can **look** at the Ferris wheel. (action verb)

Common Linking Verbs

am	was	seem	taste
is	were	appear	smell
are	will be	look	feel

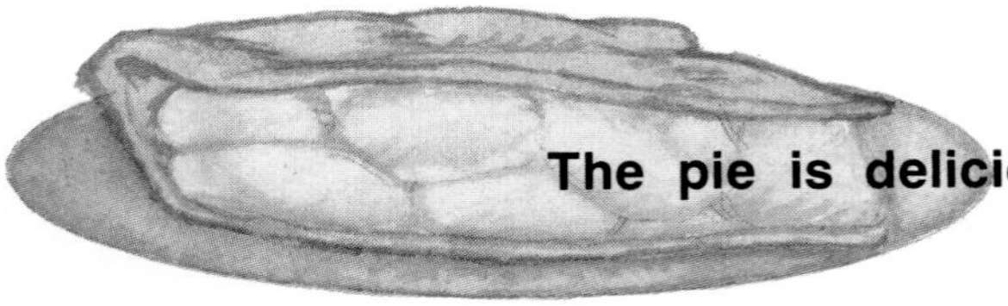

The pie is delicious.

Guided Practice

Tell the linking verb in each sentence.

Example: The muffins smell good.
smell linking verb

1. Mrs. Lowe's pies taste wonderful.
2. She is an excellent baker.
3. The cakes look beautiful.
4. They smell delicious.
5. The prizes are red and blue ribbons.

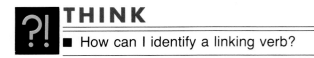

?! THINK

■ How can I identify a linking verb?

REMEMBER

- A **linking verb** links the subject of a sentence to a noun or an adjective in the predicate.
- The word that follows the linking verb names or describes the subject of the sentence.

More Practice

A. Write each sentence. Draw a line under the linking verb.

Example: The fairgrounds are crowded. *The fairgrounds are crowded.*

6. The animal shows are my favorite exhibits.
7. The farmers seem friendly.
8. The animals look healthy.
9. The judges are experts.
10. People are excited by the contests.
11. One judge is a farmer.
12. He appears knowledgeable about the animals.

B. Write each sentence. Draw one line under the linking verb. Draw two lines under the word that describes or names the subject.

Example: Hank is confident. *Hank is confident.*

13. Sheila seems quite skilled.
14. Her sewing appears perfect.
15. The dress is a blue ribbon winner.
16. Hans and Jody are relaxed, too.
17. They were contestants in last year's show.
18. That flower show looks interesting.
19. I am fond of flowers.
20. I will be a gardener one day.

Extra Practice, page 179

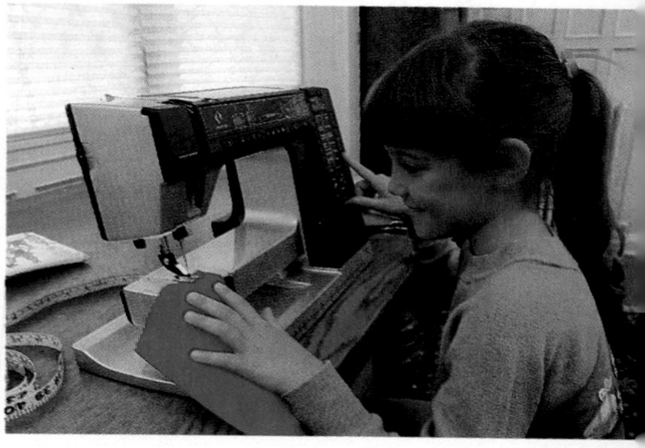

WRITING APPLICATION A Story

Imagine that you have just won first prize in a contest. Write a story about the events that took place during the contest. Have a classmate circle the linking verbs.

5 VERB CONTRACTIONS

When you speak, you sometimes use contractions. A contraction is a word made from two words. Contractions are often used in informal writing and conversation. They should not be used in formal reports or business letters. Sometimes you can combine a verb with the word *not* to form a **verb contraction.**

Use an apostrophe (') in place of the letter or letters that have been left out. Remember, *not* is a negative word and is not part of the verb phrase.

Contractions with Verbs Plus the Word *not*

should not	shouldn't	would not	wouldn't
is not	isn't	cannot	can't
will not	won't	has not	hasn't
must not	mustn't	were not	weren't
was not	wasn't	are not	aren't
could not	couldn't	had not	hadn't
do not	don't	have not	haven't
does not	doesn't	has not	hasn't

Guided Practice

Tell the contraction of the underlined words.

Example: I could not decide upon a project. *couldn't*

1. Sylvia will not display her painting yet.
2. She does not feel ready.
3. I have not seen it.
4. She should not worry about her work.
5. We are not finished, either.

?! THINK

- How can I decide where to use an apostrophe in a contraction?

REMEMBER

- Contractions are formed from some verbs and the word *not*.
- Use an apostrophe (') to show the letter or letters that have been left out of the contraction.

More Practice

A. Write the word or words from which the contraction has been made.

Example: wouldn't *would not*

6. mustn't
7. doesn't
8. aren't
9. haven't
10. don't
11. can't
12. isn't
13. won't
14. didn't
15. hadn't

B. Write each sentence, using a contraction of the underlined words.

Example: The students <u>are not</u> ready. *The students aren't ready.*

16. The art show <u>was not</u> planned until last week.
17. There <u>is not</u> much time left!
18. Joe <u>will not</u> talk about his sculpture.
19. He <u>would not</u> explain his silence.
20. Mindy <u>cannot</u> stand secrets.
21. She <u>has not</u> hidden her pottery from viewers.
22. Many students <u>could not</u> stop for conversation all week.
23. Now we <u>are not</u> worried any longer.
24. The judges <u>were not</u> wrong about the artwork.
25. We <u>should not</u> forget to congratulate the winners.

Extra Practice, page 180

WRITING APPLICATION An Advertisement

Write an advertisement for a contest. Your language can be informal, so feel free to use contractions. Have a partner look for the contractions in your work.

6 VERB TENSES

The verb you use in a sentence helps you to tell when something happens. The time expressed by a verb is called its **tense**. Verbs show time by changes in tense. The three main tenses are the **present, past,** and **future** tenses.

Present-tense verbs show something that is happening now.

Johanna always **wants** something different.

➡ Add *s* or *es* to a present-tense verb when a singular noun is its subject.

Past-tense verbs show action that has already happened.

Yesterday she **wanted** an Olympic medal.

➡ Add *ed* to the present tense of the verb to form the past tense of most verbs.

Future-tense verbs show something that has not yet happened.

Tomorrow Johanna **will want** something else.

➡ Add *shall* or *will* before the present tense of the verb to form the future tense.

Guided Practice

Tell whether the underlined verb is in the present, past, or future tense.

Example: I ski each winter. *present tense*

1. The team skied downhill. past
2. Each team member practices daily. pres.
3. We will watch them ski. fut.
4. The best athletes will receive the prize. fut.
5. Our team earned the bronze medal. past

?! THINK

■ How can I identify the **present, past,** and **future** tenses?

REMEMBER

- The three main tenses are the **present, past,** and **future** tenses.

More Practice

A. Write **present, past,** or **future** after each underlined verb.

Example: We watched the whole show. *past*

6. I like the figure skating.
7. Winners will receive medals.
8. Machines scraped the ice this morning.
9. A skater twirled on the ice.
10. The best athletes will practice for hours.
11. My favorite skater races today.
12. I cheered for Stacy yesterday.

B. Write each sentence. Complete each sentence with the correct tense of each verb in parentheses.

Example: The ball game _____ at four o'clock. (start) *The ball game starts at four o'clock.*

13. I _____ a baseball to school tomorrow. (carry)
14. Gretchen _____ me at the games last year. (watch)
15. Now, she _____ a chance, too. (want)
16. Last spring, I _____ softball. (play)
17. Later this year, I _____ for the team. (pitch)
18. This morning, the coach _____ a victory today. (promise)
19. Last time, the team _____ heavily. (score)
20. We _____ the other teams next fall. (defeat)

Extra Practice, page 181

WRITING APPLICATION A News Story

Imagine that you are a television reporter at an important event such as a track meet or game. Write a news story about the event and what makes it exciting. Exchange stories with a partner. Identify the verb tenses in each other's writing.

7 USING THE PRESENT AND PAST TENSES

A verb changes its form to agree, or work, with the subject to show its tense.

Rules for Forming the Present Tense				
1. Most verbs: Add *s*.			stop	stop**s**
			climb	climb**s**
2. Verbs ending in *s*, *ch*, *sh*, *x*, and *z*: Add *es*.	guess	guess**es**	fix	fix**es**
	catch	catch**es**	buzz	buzz**es**
	rush	rush**es**		
3. Verbs ending with a consonant and *y*: Change the *y* to *i* and add *es*.			fry	fri**es**
			hurry	hurri**es**
Rules for Forming the Past Tense				
1. Most verbs: Add *ed*.			mend	mend**ed**
Verbs ending with *e*: Add *d*.			free	free**d**
2. Verbs ending with a consonant and *y*: Change the *y* to *i* and add *ed*.			carry	carri**ed**
			bury	buri**ed**
3. Verbs ending with a single vowel and a consonant: Double the final consonant and add *ed*.			slip	slip**ped**
			fan	fan**ned**

fanned

Guided Practice

Tell the past tense of the underlined verb in each sentence.

Example: We study the campaign issues. *studied*

1. We vote for a class president.
2. Students elect the person of their choice.
3. I pick the winner every time.
4. Sandra and I support Chris.
5. Chris believes in student government.

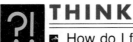

THINK

▪ How do I form the present and past tenses of most verbs?

REMEMBER

- Add *s* or *es* to form the present tense of singular verbs.
- Add *ed*, *d*, or *ied* to form the past tense of verbs.

More Practice

A. Write each sentence, using the past tense of the underlined verb.

Example: The teacher explains the rules. *The teacher explained the rules.*

6. The class votes on Tuesday.
7. The students listen to the speeches.
8. The candidates rush around the halls.
9. They worry about their chances.
10. I plan a different speech for Chris.
11. My classmates discuss the issues.
12. Many problems need our attention.

B. Write each sentence. Use the correct form of the verb in parentheses.

Example: I _____ shorthand all week. (practice) *I practiced shorthand all week.*

13. I _____ to school last Tuesday. (hurry)
14. The class _____ me as the spokesperson. (name)
15. I always _____ a pencil and notepad. (carry)
16. That way I _____ my ideas. (remember)
17. My speech _____ the candidates. (praise)
18. I _____ both the winner and the loser. (thank)
19. Everyone _____ when the election was over. (cheer)
20. The teacher _____ beverages and toasted the class. (pour)

Extra Practice, page 182

WRITING APPLICATION A Speech

Imagine that you have just finished your term as class president. Write a speech explaining what you have done to make school a better place. Check verb tenses.

GRAMMAR

8 SUBJECT-VERB AGREEMENT

A verb agrees with its subject in **number**. If the subject is singular, the verb must be singular. If the subject is plural, the verb must be plural.

Add *s* or *es* to the present-tense verb when the subject is a singular noun or *he*, *she*, or *it*.

The winner **rushes** by us. He **appears** happy.

Do not add *s* or *es* to the present-tense verb when the subject is a plural noun or *I*, *you*, *we*, or *they*.

Morris and Cora **seem** excited.
They **rush** into the room.

Notice that in the compound subject *Morris and Cora* the verb agrees with a plural subject.

Guided Practice

Tell which of the verbs in parentheses completes each sentence correctly.

Example: We (join, joins) the audience in the room. *join*

1. Bill (enter, enters) the spelling bee.
2. We (wish, wishes) him well.
3. He (tell, tells) us his plan.
4. He (study, studies) the dictionary every night.
5. Janet and I (spell, spells) well, too.

?! **THINK**

- How do I make the subject and the verb agree?

REMEMBER

- In the present tense, the subject and verb must agree in number.

More Practice

A. Write each sentence, using the correct form of the verb in parentheses.

Example: We (prepare, prepares) for the spelling bee. *We prepare for the spelling bee.*

6. The spelling bee (begin, begins) today.
7. The teachers (choose, chooses) the words.
8. Winners (receive, receives) a dictionary.
9. The words (seem, seems) difficult.
10. We all (learn, learns) quickly.
11. The contest (start, starts) in a minute.
12. I (read, reads) the rules first.

B. Write each sentence. Complete each sentence with the correct present-tense form of the verb in parentheses.

Example: Jo _____ the score. (check) *Jo checks the score.*

13. My friends _____ the spelling bee. (watch)
14. Bonnie _____ the first word. (spell)
15. She _____ the next word. (miss)
16. We _____ the next hour in that room. (pass)
17. The judge _____ all the mistakes. (catch)
18. Many students _____ from the stage. (walk)
19. Bill _____ the spelling bee successfully. (finish)
20. The judge _____ the prize to him. (award)

Extra Practice, Practice Plus, pages 183–184

WRITING APPLICATION A Poster

COOPERATIVE LEARNING

Make a poster that gives information about a contest or another event that will take place at your school. Have a group of your classmates check for subject-verb agreement in your poster.

9 USING *BE* AND *HAVE* CORRECTLY

Some verbs follow special rules to agree with their subjects. *Be* and *have* are two verbs that must change their form according to special rules in order to agree with their subjects.

Study the chart below to memorize the present and past tense forms of *be* and *have*.

Subject	Present	Past
I	am	was
you	are	were
he, she, it	is	was
we	are	were
they	are	were
Subject	**Present**	**Past**
I	have	had
you	have	had
he, she, it	has	had
we	have	had
they	have	had

are watered

is watered

Guided Practice

Tell which verb in parentheses agrees with the subject in each sentence.

Example: The garden club contest (is, are) fun. *is*

1. First prize (is, are) a watering can.
2. I (is, am) a member of the club.
3. Jean (is, am) a member, too.
4. The club (has, have) regular meetings.
5. We (has, have) good prizes for the winners.

?! **THINK**

- How do I decide which form of *be* and *have* to use in a sentence?

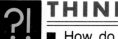

REMEMBER

- A verb and its subject must agree in number.
- The verbs *be* and *have* change in order to agree with their subjects.

More Practice

Complete each sentence, using the correct verb from the pair in parentheses.

Example: The contestants (is, are) excited. *The contestants are excited.*

6. Paul's tulips ____ the prettiest in the neighborhood. (is, are)
7. Last year, he ____ a garden full of roses. (have, had)
8. Now, he ____ a new type of flower for the garden show. (have, has)
9. The tiger lilies ____ orange and black. (is, are)
10. Dana ____ a new member of the garden club. (is, are)
11. I ____ a friend of hers. (is, am)
12. We ____ all contestants in this year's show. (is, are)
13. Flowers and plants ____ the main entries in the contest. (is, are)
14. You ____ wonderful dahlias. (has, have)
15. My sister and I ____ begonias and violets. (has, have)
16. Jim ____ a great idea. (have, has)
17. He ____ a judge in the contest. (is, are)
18. The prizes ____ all perfect for gardeners. (is, are)
19. I ____ in charge of the prizes. (is, am)
20. Jim and I ____ many good prizes in mind. (has, have)

Extra Practice, page 185

WRITING APPLICATION A Description

Imagine that you are in charge of the prizes to be awarded to the winners of a contest. Decide what the contest and prizes should be. Write a description of the prizes. Ask a classmate to read your description. Have him or her check for subject-verb agreement.

GRAMMAR

10 USING IRREGULAR VERBS I

You form the past tense of **regular** verbs by adding *ed* to the verb. **Irregular** verbs are spelled differently in the past tense.

Irregular Verbs

Present	Past	Past with helping verbs
see	saw	has, have, had seen
run	ran	has, have, had run
come	came	has, have, had come
go	went	has, have, had gone
give	gave	has, have, had given
eat	ate	has, have, had eaten
write	wrote	has, have, had written
drive	drove	has, have, had driven
ride	rode	has, have, had ridden
take	took	has, have, had taken
speak	spoke	has, have, had spoken
choose	chose	has, have, had chosen
fly	flew	has, have, had flown
draw	drew	has, have, had drawn

Guided Practice

Tell the past-tense form of the verb in parentheses.

Example: Aesop's animals (speak) like humans. *spoke*

1. Aesop (write) about clever and foolish animals.
2. He (give) them names and ideas of their own.
3. Becky (choose) a book of funny animal fables.

?! **THINK**

- How do I form the past tense of an irregular verb?

G R A M M A R

REMEMBER

- Irregular verbs do not form the past tense by adding *ed*.
- The helping verbs *has*, *have*, and *had* are used with irregular verbs.

More Practice

A. Write each sentence. Write the past-tense form of the verb in parentheses.

Example: Last week, I (find) the book. *found*

4. The last story has (give) me an amusing idea.
5. I have (write) a humorous fable, too.
6. John and I (speak) about the fables.
7. John (choose) his favorite fable.
8. The animals (run) in a race.
9. A bear (see) the entire race.
10. Birds (fly) in the race.
11. The race (take) almost an hour.
12. Many animals (come) to the event.

B. Write each sentence. Write the correct past-tense form of the verb in parentheses.

Example: The race had (begin) already. *begun*

13. A bird has (fly) to the finish line.
14. A flea had (ride) on his back.
15. John and I have (speak) of this funny fable.
16. We have (see) how the race ends.
17. John has (draw) a picture of the lazy hare.
18. The rabbit had (go) to sleep!
19. The tortoise had (ran) the best race.
20. Aesop had (choose) him as the winner.

Extra Practice, page 186

WRITING APPLICATION A Comic Strip

Draw a comic strip that shows a race between two animals. Write captions for your comic strip that explain your drawing.

GRAMMAR

11 USING IRREGULAR VERBS II

You know that irregular verbs do not form the past tense with *ed*. Remember these verb forms.

More Irregular Verbs

Present	Past	Past with helping verbs
sing	sang	has, have, had sung
swim	swam	has, have, had swum
drink	drank	has, have, had drunk
do	did	has, have, had done
grow	grew	has, have, had grown
throw	threw	has, have, had thrown
know	knew	has, have, had known
wear	wore	has, have, had worn
bring	brought	has, have, had brought
teach	taught	has, have, had taught
say	said	has, have, had said
make	made	has, have, had made
sit	sat	has, have, had sat

Guided Practice

Tell the correct past-tense form of the verb in parentheses.

Example: Who (make) the award-winning movie? *made*

1. The audience (sit) down in the theater.
2. Some of the stars (do), too.
3. An actor had (sing) the theme song already.
4. An excited director has (make) a speech.

?! **THINK**

■ How can I decide which form of an irregular verb to use in a sentence?

REMEMBER

- The helping verbs *has*, *have*, and *had* may be used with some past forms of irregular verbs.

More Practice

A. Write each sentence. Use the correct past-tense form of the verb in parentheses.

Example: We (grow) impatient. *We grew impatient.*

5. He had (know) many famous actors for years.
6. A pop star (sing) another song.
7. The judges (sit) at a table.
8. A famous actor (make) the movie on the screen now.
9. Two sharks (swim) toward the beach.
10. The sunbathers (drink) refreshments.
11. The shark (swim) toward them.
12. We (grow) terribly frightened at this point.

B. Write each sentence. Use the correct past-tense form of the verb in parentheses.

Example: The actors have (wear) fancy clothes tonight. *The actors have worn fancy clothes tonight.*

13. One star has (say) something nice.
14. She has (do) her best for her family.
15. She had (know) many talented actors.
16. All the winners have (make) long speeches.
17. They have (do) this every year.
18. Lorraine had (know) all the movies on the show.
19. She has (bring) a list of movie titles.
20. The show has (teach) us about movies and stars.

Extra Practice, page 187

WRITING APPLICATION A Review

Write a review of a movie, book, or television program that you think deserves to win an award. Explain your reasons for recommending this book or entertainment. Circle past-tense forms of verbs in your work.

GRAMMAR

12 MECHANICS: Using the Comma

You have seen how commas are used to separate the sentences that form a compound sentence. Commas are also used to separate words in a series or list.

We brought poles, hooks, and hip boots.
Peter will bring sandwiches, juice, or milk.

These sentences contain words in a series. A series is a list of three or more items.

➡ Use a comma to separate each item in a list.

➡ Use the conjunction *and* or *or* before the last item in the list. The sentence below has only two items. This is not a series and does not need commas.

We brought poles and hooks.

Guided Practice

Tell where commas are needed in the following sentences.

Example: Sam Lily and Bob enter the fishing contest.
Sam, Lily, and Bob enter the fishing contest.

1. The fish are judged by size weight and beauty.
2. We can sign up on Monday Tuesday or Wednesday.
3. The fish are red blue green and silver.
4. Linda caught a bass and a trout.
5. We can fish from the boat the shore or the dock.

?! **THINK**

■ How do I use commas to separate items in a series?

REMEMBER

■ Use commas to separate three or more items in a series.

More Practice

A. Write and correctly punctuate each sentence that contains a series. Underline the word that joins the items in each series.

Example: We wear hats gloves and sneakers. *We wear hats, gloves, and sneakers.*

6. We fish with hooks lines and sinkers.
7. I brought a fishing rod a bait box and extra hooks.
8. There are contests for adults and children.
9. Russell and Holly relax on the dock.
10. They eat sandwiches talk or read.
11. I caught three trout two sunfish and a crab.
12. Is that a starfish a sea urchin or a sea horse?

B. Write and punctuate each sentence correctly.

Example: Mom Dad and Sue stay on shore. *Mom, Dad, and Sue stay on shore.*

13. For bait we use worms bread or plastic flies.
14. Bob caught a fish threw it back and caught a bigger one.
15. We count our fish weigh them and bring them to the judges.
16. A red a blue and a gold ribbon are the prizes.
17. Bob Lily and Sam all won ribbons.
18. I reel in my line clean the rod and pack my gear.
19. We are hungry from the long day the fresh air and the excitement.
20. At home we scale clean and broil the fish.

Extra Practice, page 188

WRITING APPLICATION A Letter

Imagine that you have won a fishing contest. Write a letter to a friend describing the experience. With your partner, look at your writing to see if you have used commas correctly.

13 VOCABULARY BUILDING: Homophones and Homographs

Homophones are words that sound alike but have different spellings and meanings.

> There were already **two** taco stands at the fair.
> Barney wanted **to** open a taco stand, **too.**

In these sentences *two*, *too*, and *to* are homophones. You must look at the **context** or overall meaning to tell which spelling is correct.

Homographs are words that are spelled the same but have different meanings and sometimes have different pronunciations.

> We hoped the **wĭnd** would not blow our stand down.
> Maurice wanted to **wīnd** up our awning.

In the first sentence, *wind* (wĭnd) names the movement of air. In the second sentence, *wind* (wīnd) is a verb that means "to roll up." You can tell the correct meaning of a homograph from its context.

Guided Practice

Use the context clues to select the correct homophone. Tell which word from the pair in parentheses completes each sentence correctly.

Example: (Our, Hour) taco recipe will win an award. *Our*

1. Jeremy was (scene, seen) at the taco stand.
2. Our tacos are (maid, made) with secret ingredients.
3. Mouth (pain, pane) is caused by too much hot sauce.
4. The cook (ate, eight) another taco.
5. His special recipe was (great, grate).

?! **THINK**

- How can I recognize homophones and homographs?

GRAMMAR

REMEMBER

- **Homophones** are words that sound alike but have different spellings and meanings.
- **Homographs** are words that are spelled alike but have different meanings and sometimes different pronunciations.

More Practice

A. Write each sentence, using the correct homophone.

Example: Mary (peaks, peeks) into the saucepan.

6. George (red, read) a secret recipe.
7. George did not (right, write) the recipe for us.
8. He had to (by, buy) special peppers.
9. He (blew, blue) on the cooking fire.
10. He had entered the contest, (to, two, too).
11. His sauce simmered all (night, knight).
12. We could (hear, here) him at work.
13. We (sent, cent) Mary to George's stand.
14. George put (flower, flour) in his sauce.
15. Now we (no, know) the secret ingredient!

B. Write each sentence. Use your dictionary to write the correct definition of the underlined homograph.

Example: We dove into the crowd. *plunged*

16. We saw the ingredients that went into the sauce.
17. His recipe was ours at last.
18. Jeremy and George clearly lead all competitors in the taco competition.
19. Jeremy will record the victory in his diary.
20. The judges called it a very close contest.

Extra Practice, page 189

WRITING APPLICATION A Billboard

COOPERATIVE LEARNING

Imagine that you are going to open a booth at a fair. With a group of classmates, make a billboard or sign advertising the items for sale. Use some homophones and homographs in your writing.

GRAMMAR AND WRITING CONNECTION

Keeping Verb Tenses Consistent

You know that verb tenses express time, or tell when something takes place. When you write, think about your choice of verb tenses. Does the action you are writing about take place in the present, the past, or the future? Once you can answer this question, you have decided on the right verb tense for your writing.

> We watched as our dog walked around the rink. Simba raised his head properly and waited quietly when the judge touched him. He stopped when the trainer gave him the command.

All of the verbs in the paragraph above show action that has already happened. The writer has used the past tense.

COOPERATIVE LEARNING

Working Together

With your classmates, discuss ways to keep verb tenses consistent. Look at the tense of each verb in the sentences below. Tell whether the verbs in each sentence are in the same tense or different tenses.

Example: Our dog was a winner, and he will know it. *different*

1. Simba circles the rink again and stood.
2. He is a champion, and we love him.
3. The judge recognizes and called each dog by name.

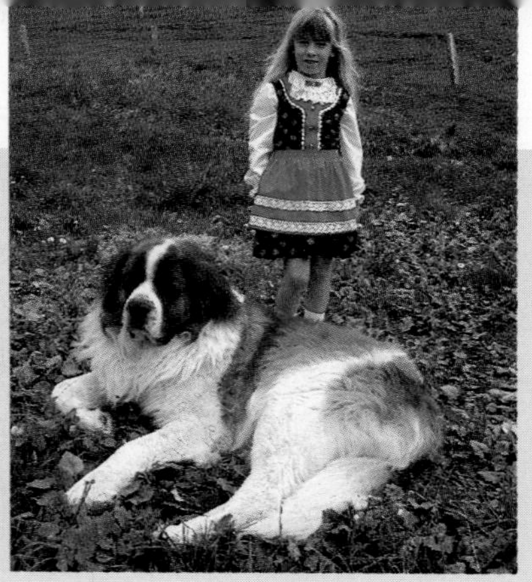

Revising Sentences

Marianna wrote these sentences about her summer vacation. Help her revise her work by changing the tense of the verb in the second sentence in each pair of sentences so that the verbs in the sentences are in the same tense. Write the new sentences on a separate piece of paper.

4. I have made my plans already.
   I arranged a visit to Europe.
5. I am excited about the trip.
   My parents were happy for me.
6. I will go to Switzerland soon.
   My plane left on June 30.
7. I will visit the Swiss Alps.
   I stay in a hotel on Lake Garda.
8. My aunt will meet me at the airport.
   She and my uncle also stay at the hotel.
9. I love my aunt's dog, Berry.
   He was a beautiful Saint Bernard.
10. Berry will compete in a dog show.
    He had won a prize for beauty and good behavior.

WRITER AT WORK

Where would you like to go on your summer vacation? Think of a place you would enjoy visiting. Write an itinerary or travel plan for your vacation.

Work with a classmate to revise your work. Ask him or her to help you check to see that you have used verb tenses properly. Change the tense of any verb that seems out of place in your itinerary.

UNIT CHECKUP

LESSONS 1-2 **Action Verbs and Direct Objects** (pages 144–147) Write each sentence. Draw one line under the action verb in each sentence. Draw two lines under the direct object.

1. Joe's jump earns points.
2. The judge measures the distance.
3. Joe wins the event, to everyone's surprise.
4. He carries his trophy home proudly.

LESSON 3 **Main Verbs and Helping Verbs** (page 148) Write each sentence. Complete each sentence with a helping verb.

5. We _____ enjoyed our holiday.
6. We _____ raced to the pool.
7. The sun _____ shone all day.
8. Bob _____ played water tag with Cindy.

LESSON 4 **What Is a Linking Verb?** (page 150) Write each sentence. Draw one line under the linking verb. Draw two lines under the word that describes or names the subject.

9. I am ready for the test.
10. The test seems important to the class.
11. We all feel prepared for the questions.
12. The teacher looks happy.

LESSON 5 **Verb Contractions** (page 152) Write each sentence, using a contraction of the underlined words.

13. Hilary does not feel shy.
14. She will not forget her lines.
15. Acting is not hard for her.
16. She cannot wait for the first performance.

LESSONS 6-7 **Using Verb Tenses** (pages 154–157) Write the correct tense of each verb below.

17. plan (future)
18. wrap (past)
19. placed (present)
20. dance (future)

LESSONS 8-9

Subject-Verb Agreement (pages 158–161) Write each sentence, using the correct present-tense form of the verb.

21. Jean _____ the bus would come. (wish)
22. She _____ at the bus stop on time this morning. (arrive)
23. An art show _____ at school today. (open)
24. The students _____ each other's best critics. (be)

LESSONS 10-11

Using Irregular Verbs (pages 162–165) Write each sentence. Complete each sentence with the correct tense of the verb.

25. The students (be) at a talent show at the moment.
26. We (see) the entire assembly now.
27. The last contestant (have) great talent.
28. The school has (grow) excited about the show.

LESSON 12

Mechanics: Using the Comma (page 166) Write each sentence, using correct punctuation.

29. We worked planned and practiced.
30. Performances took place on Friday Saturday and Sunday.
31. I invited my friends family and neighbors.
32. The audience applauded the actors the director and the writer.

LESSON 13

Vocabulary Building: Homophones (page 168) Write each sentence, using the correct homophone.

33. We (by, buy) a ticket for the raffle.
34. The tickets are (blew, blue) and red.
35. We (right, write) our addresses on the tickets.
36. We wait to see who (one, won).

37.–40.

Writing Application: Subject-Verb Agreement with Irregular Verbs (page 160) The following paragraph contains 4 errors with subject-verb agreement. Rewrite the paragraph correctly.

There is several main types of transportation. Cars moves slowly enough for a good view of the scenery. Trains rides along smoothly and comfortably. Airplane travel take passengers rapidly across long distances.

ENRICHMENT

ACTION TALES

Play this story game with a small group of classmates. Together, make twenty small slips of paper. On each slip, write an action verb. Put the slips in a bag. The first player selects a verb and begins a story using the verb. The next player selects another verb and continues the story using the new verb. Keep playing until all of the verbs have been used.

Word Chameleons

Try this activity with a partner. The following words are used as both nouns and verbs. Select a word from the list and use it in a sentence as a noun. Your partner should then use the word in a sentence as a verb. You can use a dictionary to check the meaning of any word you do not know how to use.

frame	core	form
copy	beat	drive
exit	drink	fire
flip	howl	lace

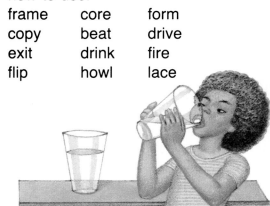

ACTORS' WORKSHOP

Play this game with a small group. Have one member of the group act out an action verb. The other members of the group should try to guess the verb. The person who identifies the verb correctly takes the next turn.

TRICKY BUSINESS

You remember homophones, those tricky words that sound the same but have different spellings and meanings. Enter this contest with a partner. Time yourselves for five minutes. Within that time, see how many words that are homophones you can write down. Whoever has written the greatest number of correct homophones wins the contest.

CHAIN LINKS

Play this game with a partner. Start a sentence that begins with a subject and a linking verb, like "I feel . . ." Your partner completes the sentence with a word that makes sense. Then, your partner starts a sentence with another subject and linking verb, and you complete the sentence. Keep going until you can't think of any more linking verbs.

EXTRA PRACTICE

GRAMMAR

Three levels of practice

What Is an Action Verb? (page 144)

LEVEL **A.** Write each sentence. Draw a line under the action verb in each sentence.

1. Three green frogs jump in this contest.
2. The first frog lands ten feet away.
3. The next frog passes him.
4. The longest jump earns the prize.
5. One frog wanders off the track.
6. Another frog sleeps in the sun.
7. Sleeping frogs never hop far.
8. The frogs learn their lesson.
9. The owners laugh at their pets.

LEVEL **B.** Write each sentence. Complete the sentence with an action verb.

10. I _____ my frog Jumper.
11. I _____ Jumper in a contest.
12. He _____ three feet down the track.
13. The judge _____ a prize.
14. Jumper _____ proudly at me.
15. Jumper _____ another leap.
16. He always _____ for me.
17. We all _____ him.

LEVEL **C.** Complete each sentence with an action verb.

18. I _____ a frog in a lake.
19. I _____ a nice home for my frog.
20. I _____ his home a terrarium.
21. I _____ plants, water, and sand in a glass box.
22. I _____ the top loosely.
23. My frog _____ his comfortable home.
24. I _____ some moss in the terrarium today.
25. He _____ around the terrarium all day.

EXTRA PRACTICE

Three levels of practice

Verbs with Direct Objects (page 146)

LEVEL **A.** Write each sentence. Draw a line under the action verb.

1. We planned a talent show.
2. Jan read poetry.
3. Andy played the flute beautifully.
4. Jeremy performed magic tricks for the crowd.
5. I memorized a song.
6. The audience judged our acts.
7. Our parents applauded our efforts.
8. Everyone really liked the show.
9. The acts certainly deserved attention.

LEVEL **B.** Write each sentence. Draw a line under the direct object of the action verb in each sentence.

10. Every student enjoyed the show.
11. Stanley's poem earned applause.
12. He crossed the stage slowly.
13. A judge displayed the trophy.
14. Stanley heard a cheer from his friends.
15. He received the award!
16. His sister threw roses at the stage.
17. Stanley hugged the trophy tightly.

LEVEL **C.** Write each sentence. Complete the sentence with an action verb that makes sense.

18. He ______ a smile to the crowd.
19. The audience ______ their hands loudly.
20. Stanley ______ a thank you speech.
21. He ______ the audience for their attention.
22. He ______ another poem about a football hero.
23. He ______ the stage happily.
24. I ______ a picture of Stanley.
25. He ______ the trophy above his head.

EXTRA PRACTICE

Three levels of practice

Main Verbs and Helping Verbs (page 148)

LEVEL **A.** Write each sentence. Draw one line under each helping verb and two lines under each main verb.

1. My family has entered a contest.
2. We have completed the forms.
3. My sister is waiting for an answer.
4. She is counting the days.
5. I have marked the calendar.
6. The date is circled in red ink.
7. We have planned the trip already.
8. My sister has picked the hotel.
9. We have selected our vacation wardrobe.

LEVEL **B.** Write each sentence. Complete each sentence with a helping verb.

10. We ______ waited long enough.
11. A letter ______ delivered to us.
12. The letter ______ promised us a trip.
13. We ______ traveling to Hawaii.
14. I ______ hoping for good weather.
15. My sister ______ purchased a bathing suit.
16. I ______ packed my camera.
17. We ______ traveling by airplane.

LEVEL **C.** Write each sentence. Complete each sentence with a main verb from the chart on this page. Use each verb only once.

18. We have ______ by plane before.
19. Now, we are ______ a tour.
20. I am ______ about my good luck.
21. We are ______ wonderful.
22. My sister has ______ her next trip already.
23. She has ______ of a trip to France.
24. We have ______ another contest.
25. My mother is ______ entry forms, too.

enjoying
planned
dreamed
thinking
entered
completing
feeling
journeyed

EXTRA PRACTICE

GRAMMAR

Three levels of practice

What Is a Linking Verb? (page 150)

LEVEL **A.** Write each sentence. Draw a line under the linking verb.

1. I am a runner.
2. I became an athlete last year.
3. My best friend is a runner, too.
4. The team seems ready at last.
5. We all feel excellent today.
6. You look prepared.
7. The track appears dry.
8. The sawdust smells sweet.
9. The race is difficult.

LEVEL **B.** Write each sentence. Complete the sentence with a linking verb from the list below.

are became look was is feel appears seemed

10. The racetrack ______ endless to the runners.
11. You ______ very tired after the third lap.
12. The race ______ close to the viewers.
13. The team ______ confident.
14. We all ______ happy about the race.
15. The relay race ______ the most fun.
16. You ______ a wonderful teammate.

LEVEL **C.** Write each sentence. Complete the sentence with a linking verb.

17. The long jump ______ a challenge.
18. We ______ the best jumpers.
19. I ______ ready for the event.
20. George's jump ______ the longest.
21. He ______ the best athlete today.
22. Nelson ______ eager and fit.
23. His jump ______ spectacular.
24. I ______ a winner today, too.
25. We ______ proud of our team.

EXTRA PRACTICE

Three levels of practice
Verb Contractions (page 152)

LEVEL **A.** Write each sentence, using the correct contraction of the underlined words.

1. We <u>have not</u> seen the reptiles yet.
2. Peter <u>has not</u> seen any snakes before.
3. He <u>does not</u> fear most animals.
4. Snakes <u>are not</u> unfriendly.
5. Most snakes <u>cannot</u> hurt you.
6. They <u>will not</u> bite.
7. You <u>do not</u> know how pretty snakes are.
8. Peter <u>did not</u> hold the snake today.
9. There <u>are not</u> many snakes like this one.

LEVEL **B.** Write each sentence. Complete the sentence with a contraction.

10. Jean _____ seen a blue snake before.
11. I _____ tell you which snake won a prize.
12. It _____ the biggest one.
13. Anna _____ fear the reptiles.
14. She _____ wait for the turtle exhibit.
15. We _____ be late for this display.
16. The judges of the contest _____ wait.

LEVEL **C.** Change each sentence to include a contraction with the word *not*.

17. I can remember the path to the aquarium.
18. We should miss the turtles.
19. I would skip that part of the aquarium.
20. They are small reptiles.
21. The judges could pick just one winner.
22. One judge has made up his mind.
23. He should choose hastily.
24. The sea turtle has received a prize.
25. I can wait until the next contest.

EXTRA PRACTICE

GRAMMAR

Three levels of practice

Verb Tenses (page 154)

LEVEL **A.** Write the tense of each underlined verb.

1. I liked the zoo better than the circus.
2. My friends love animals, too.
3. Boys and girls will enjoy the exhibits.
4. I visit the giraffes and the tigers.
5. Sue admired the elephants and the monkeys.
6. Cory takes some photographs of the animals.
7. The trained seal will earn our applause.
8. The zookeeper tells us about the tigers.
9. I toss bread to the ducks for awhile.

LEVEL **B.** Write each sentence. Complete each sentence with the correct tense of each verb in parentheses.

10. The birds (gobble) the crumbs now.
11. The peacocks (parade) on the grass yesterday.
12. We (watch) the lions later.
13. First, we (want) our lunch.
14. Earlier, I (search) for a snack bar.
15. We (purchase) a sandwich already.
16. Soon, we (visit) the monkeys.

LEVEL **C.** Change the underlined verb in each sentence to another verb in the same tense. Write the new sentence.

17. The monkeys swing on ropes.
18. These monkeys show talent.
19. Their tails look amazing.
20. We will award the monkeys prizes.
21. One monkey performed a double flip on the ropes.
22. The smallest monkey climbed a tree.
23. He will learn more monkey tricks.
24. I liked the monkey show the best.
25. You applaud the furry contestants with me.

EXTRA PRACTICE

Three levels of practice

Using the Present and Past Tenses (page 156)

LEVEL **A.** Write the present-tense verb in each sentence.

1. Our class plans an event.
2. The students arrange an art show for today.
3. I carry my painting to school.
4. Mary Louise brings her collage.
5. We choose our best work for the occasion.
6. Our artwork shows our talent.
7. We invite the other students.
8. We admire each other's exhibits.
9. Christina praises my winter landscape.

LEVEL **B.** Change each underlined verb to the past tense. Write the new sentence.

10. Mary Louise <u>applies</u> paper and paint to her collage.
11. I <u>use</u> watercolors in my painting.
12. Deirdre <u>works</u> with clay.
13. She <u>molds</u> beautiful sculptures of dancers.
14. Peter <u>sketches</u> with charcoal and chalk.
15. The judges <u>recognize</u> the talent of the students.
16. They <u>admire</u> all of the artwork.

LEVEL **C.** Change each underlined verb to the present tense. Write the new sentence.

17. Daniel's tapestry <u>glowed</u> with bright colors.
18. Gloria's portraits <u>proved</u> her talent.
19. Barbara's quilt <u>looked</u> wonderful.
20. The quilt <u>displayed</u> a circle pattern.
21. Bill's pottery <u>deserved</u> a blue ribbon.
22. The judges <u>whispered</u> to one another.
23. They <u>discussed</u> the artwork carefully.
24. They <u>handed</u> everyone an award.
25. Our exhibit <u>pleased</u> them.

EXTRA PRACTICE

GRAMMAR

Three levels of practice

Subject-Verb Agreement (page 158)

LEVEL **A.** Write each sentence, using the correct form of the verb.

1. My class (plan, plans) an election.
2. We (need, needs) a class president.
3. Harold (run, runs) for the position.
4. He (tell, tells) us his ideas.
5. We (likes, like) his speech.
6. Harold (talk, talks) to the class for an hour.
7. We (vote, votes) on Tuesday of this week.
8. Harold (leave, leaves) the room during the election.
9. The teacher (show, shows) us the blank ballots.

LEVEL **B.** Write each sentence. Complete each sentence with the correct present-tense form of the verb in parentheses.

10. We ______ slips of paper as ballots. (use)
11. The other candidate ______ votes. (lose)
12. Harold ______ my vote with his honesty. (earn)
13. He ______ my respect. (command)
14. I ______ in this election. (believe)
15. Jake ______ the ballots from the class. (collect)
16. The students ______ for the tally. (wait)

LEVEL **C.** Change each singular subject to a plural subject and each plural subject to a singular subject. Make sure the verb agrees with the new subject. Write the new sentences.

17. The teacher runs the election.
18. The candidates remain in the hall.
19. Our classmates guess the outcome.
20. The voters determine the result.
21. The teacher counts the ballots.
22. The elections are very exciting.
23. The shout breaks the silence.
24. The best candidates have succeeded!
25. The student congratulates the winner.

PRACTICE + PLUS

Three levels of additional practice for a difficult skill
Subject-Verb Agreement (page 158)

LEVEL **A.** Write each sentence, using the correct form of the verb.

1. Our class (plan, plans) a trip.
2. We (talk, talks) about our plan.
3. The teacher (help, helps) us with maps and information.
4. We (discuss, discusses) a field trip.
5. Julie (suggest, suggests) a visit to a lake.
6. She (remember, remembers) the perfect place.
7. We (agree, agrees) to the plan.
8. Our teacher (unfold, unfolds) a map of the countryside.
9. We (select, selects) a lake nearby.

LEVEL **B.** Change each singular subject to a plural subject and each plural subject to a singular subject. Make sure the verb agrees with the new subject. Write the new sentences.

10. The teachers ride in front.
11. The bus reaches the lakeshore.
12. The lake looks cold and clear.
13. The duck paddles on the lake.
14. The children play on the grass.
15. The cloud forms in the sky.
16. The sky becomes dark for a few minutes.
17. The cloud disappears by noon.

LEVEL **C.** Write each sentence. Complete the sentence with an action verb in the present tense. Be sure to use the correct form of the verb.

18. We all ______ to the dock.
19. Some men ______ from the end of the pier.
20. The fish ______ out of the water.
21. They ______ in the sunlight.
22. One man ______ a huge fish.
23. We ______ him for a while.
24. The teacher ______ us for lunch.
25. Everyone ______ the picnic.

EXTRA PRACTICE

Three levels of practice

Using *be* and *have* Correctly (page 160)

LEVEL **A.** Write whether the subject and verb in each sentence are singular or plural.

1. Peter is a wonderful writer.
2. He has a summer job in Alaska.
3. His sisters have a letter from him.
4. The letter was an entry in a contest.
5. The judges are three teachers from Washington, D.C.
6. They have a special prize for him.
7. The prize is a trip to Spain.
8. Peter's friends are happy for him.
9. His parents have a camera for him.

LEVEL **B.** Rewrite each incorrect sentence, using the correct form of the underlined verb. If the sentence is already correct, write **correct**.

10. Diane <u>is</u> ready for the canoe race.
11. She <u>are</u> an expert at this sport.
12. Her two pet turtles <u>is</u> with her.
13. One turtle <u>is</u> in the bottom of the canoe.
14. The other turtle <u>are</u> on the seat with her.
15. The turtles <u>has</u> a good time.
16. Both turtles <u>have</u> a love of water!

LEVEL **C.** Write each sentence. Complete each sentence with the correct form of the verb in parentheses.

17. The turtles _____ from this lake. (be)
18. The race _____ started. (have)
19. The canoes _____ swift and light. (be)
20. The racers _____ a good audience. (have)
21. Diane _____ friends with her. (have)
22. The turtles _____ her allies. (be)
23. Diane and the turtles _____ the edge! (have)
24. She _____ strength and skill. (have)
25. Diane and the turtles _____ everyone's favorite racers. (be)

EXTRA PRACTICE

Three levels of practice

Using Irregular Verbs I (page 162)

LEVEL **A.** Write each sentence. Write the past tense of the verb in parentheses.

1. The music awards (take) place tonight.
2. Jane and I (see) the awards.
3. We (make) a list of popular songs.
4. The host (introduce) the musicians.
5. Then (come) my favorite part.
6. The cameras (go) to the live acts.
7. The judges (give) an award for best album of the year.
8. The reporters (write) about the awards.
9. The big moment (come) at last.

LEVEL **B.** Write each sentence. Write the correct past-tense form of the verb in parentheses.

10. The dancers have (fly) from the stage.
11. My favorite star has (draw) an envelope.
12. I had (choose) him as the winner.
13. The voters have (spoke).
14. The journalists have (take) many photographs.
15. The winners have (ride) in a victory parade.
16. The audience has (show) enthusiasm for the spectacle.

LEVEL **C.** Change each underlined past-tense verb to its past form with a helping verb. Write the new sentence.

17. We <u>saw</u> the performance of the best song.
18. It <u>went</u> on for four minutes.
19. The song <u>won</u> an award.
20. The winners <u>showed</u> their awards to the audience.
21. The show <u>was</u> fun.
22. The winners <u>took</u> their awards home.
23. Jane and I <u>grew</u> tired at last.
24. We <u>left</u> the living room.
25. We <u>kept</u> a record of the winners in our journals.

EXTRA PRACTICE

GRAMMAR

Three levels of practice

Using Irregular Verbs II (page 164)

LEVEL **A.** Write each sentence. Write the past-tense of the verb in parentheses.

1. We (sing) at the picnic.
2. Lucy (swim) in the race.
3. She (drink) some cool lemonade.
4. We (do) many enjoyable things.
5. Kevin (draw) a picture of the scenery.
6. I (throw) a baseball to Roger.
7. You (know) some games, too.
8. We (fly) paper airplanes over the grass.
9. Jeremy (grow) tired of the sack race.

LEVEL **B.** Write each sentence. Write the correct past tense of the verb in parentheses.

10. We have (know) better games.
11. I had (wear) the sack all day.
12. Claudia has (teach) Sue the game.
13. Brett and Mike have (go) to the lake.
14. Now they have (swim) together.
15. They have (did) everything at the picnic.
16. We have (sing) songs, too.

LEVEL **C.** Change the underlined verb to the simple past-tense form of that verb. Write the new sentence.

17. We <u>have begun</u> another contest.
18. The students <u>had thought</u> of some prizes.
19. The adults <u>have brought</u> the prizes.
20. The children <u>have spoken</u> their thanks.
21. My sister <u>has made</u> a crown for the winner.
22. I <u>had thrown</u> the ball the farthest.
23. I <u>have worn</u> the crown for my sister.
24. We <u>had seen</u> the brilliant colors of the sunset.
25. We <u>have chosen</u> a wonderful spot for a picnic.

EXTRA PRACTICE

Three levels of practice

Mechanics: Using the Comma (page 166)

LEVEL **A.** Write each sentence. Add commas to separate items in a series. If the sentence does not need punctuation, write **correct** after it.

1. Jason sells seeds vegetables and fruit.
2. He works on Mondays Wednesdays Thursdays and Saturdays.
3. He can win prizes or more seeds.
4. The prizes include cameras toys and tents.
5. You can buy seeds for carrots and plums.
6. August September and October are the best months for this job.
7. People usually buy ten twenty or thirty packets of seeds.
8. Jason sold seeds for tomatoes pumpkins and squash today.
9. Jason sold seeds on wet days windy weekends and cold nights.

LEVEL **B.** Write each sentence. Add commas where they are needed. If the sentence does not need punctuation write **correct** after it.

10. He also paints furniture mows grass and baby-sits.
11. His seeds will grow into flowers fruits and vegetables.
12. His sales could be very big or very small.
13. The flower fruit and corn seeds sold fast.
14. Jason will win the camera two tents and a bike.
15. His friend won skates and a trip last year.
16. Jason waits and hopes for a prize.

LEVEL **C.** Write each sentence. Add commas where they are needed.

17. He will sell the seeds be the best salesman and win the prize.
18. Jason walks up the roads down each lane and into town.
19. Old seeds can age over time turn color in some cases and rot.
20. The rotten fruit or vegetable seeds must be thrown out.
21. He can buy more seeds sell them and apply for another prize.
22. Jason will knock on doors sell seeds and earn money.
23. His best customers are the gardener his teacher and the sheriff.
24. I admire his energy like his enthusiasm and hope he wins.
25. Next year I will work with Jason earn money and open a savings account.

EXTRA PRACTICE

Three levels of practice

Vocabulary Building: Homophones and Homographs (page 168)

LEVEL **A.** Write each sentence, using the correct homophone.

1. The teacher (red, read) us a fairy tale.
2. It was (by, buy) a Spanish writer.
3. A strange wind (blew, blue) through the villages.
4. Something was not (right, write) in the kingdom.
5. A noble (night, knight) came to the kingdom.
6. His (to, too, two) horses seemed uneasy.
7. After a (week, weak), he noticed the problem.
8. The people could (knot, not) breathe easily.
9. A bitter (scent, cent) filled the air.

LEVEL **B.** Write each sentence. Use your dictionary to write the correct definition of the underlined homograph.

10. A wise owl saw the problem in the kingdom.
11. There was a moldy object near the cow pen.
12. A giant crow had left a piece of cheese.
13. Everyone thought it was a lump of lead.
14. The age of the cheese set a record.
15. Another animal was close to the cheese.
16. When the wind blew, you could really smell that cheese.
17. You would soon tire of the odor.

LEVEL **C.** The underlined word in each sentence is wrong. Replace it with the correct homophone. Write the new sentence.

18. The farmers were very pour.
19. The knight will perform a feet to save them.
20. He will higher someone to take the cheese.
21. They will so it into a cloth bag.
22. I do knot know where they will take it.
23. Maybe a giant bare will carry away the cheese.
24. We will express hour thanks to the hero.
25. He could become the knew mayor of the town.

WRITING

UNIT

6

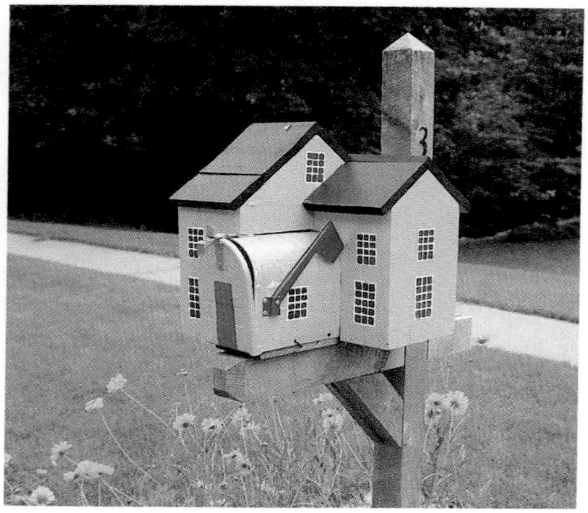

Writing Letters

Read the quotation and look at the picture on the opposite page. Why do you think it is sometimes easier to make a letter longer than shorter?

When you write a letter, your purpose and audience are very clear. You may want to write to a friend or to someone you do not know personally.

Focus A letter is a specific form of communication. There are different types of letters—friendly letters, business letters, and social notes, for example. Each type is written for a different purpose.

Is there someone to whom you would like to send a letter? What would you write? In this unit you will find the letters that one person wrote. You will find photographs, too. You can use both the letters and the photographs to find ideas for writing.

THEME: *PRIZES*

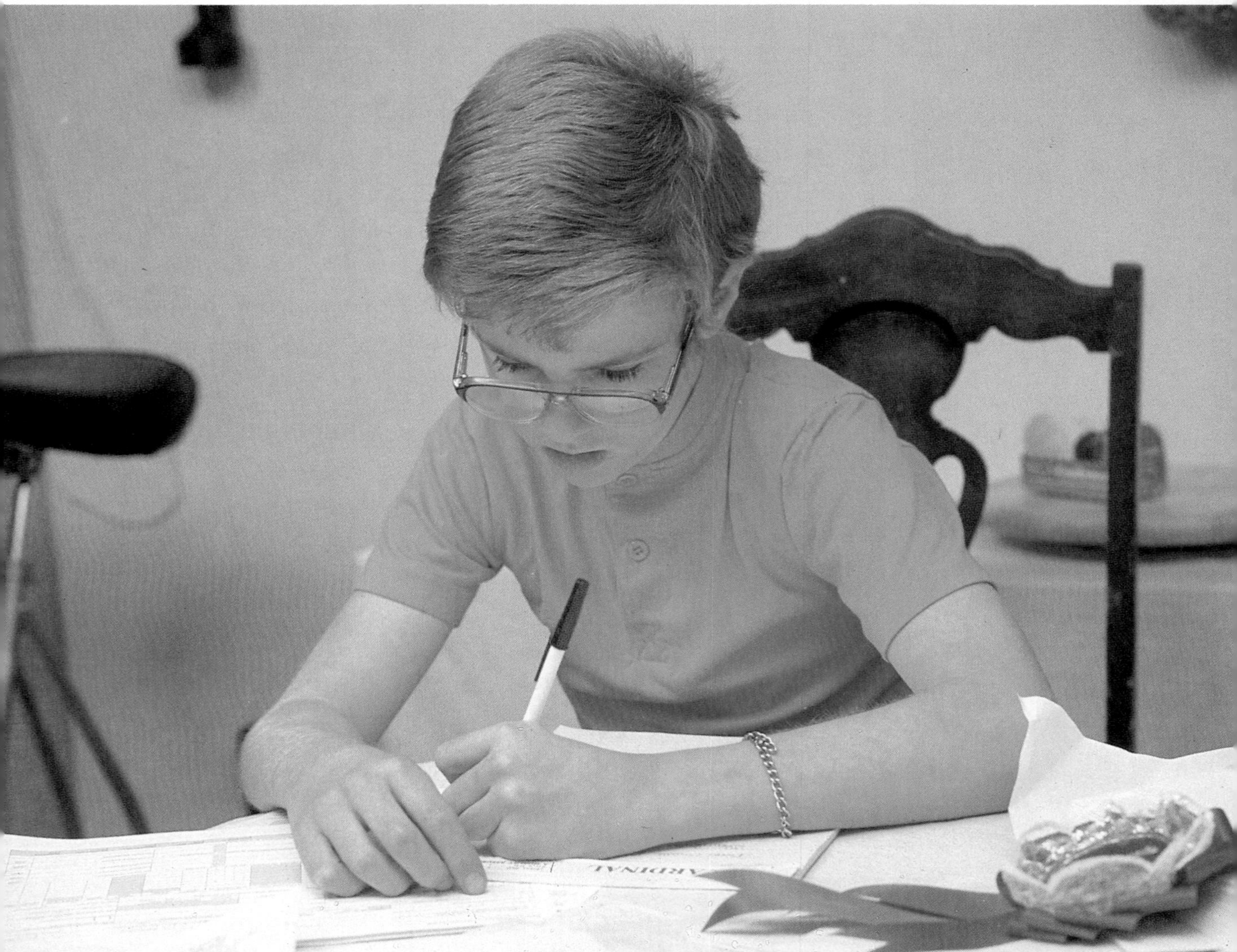

I have made this letter longer because I lack the time to make it shorter.

—Blaise Pascal

LITERATURE

Reading Like a Writer

AWARD WINNING SELECTION

Do you like to write and receive letters? To whom do you enjoy writing?

Gilly Hopkins has just moved to Virginia to live with her grandmother. In her letters, she compares her old home and school to her new ones.

As you read, notice how the author uses comparison and contrast to help you understand Gilly's feelings about her new home and friends.

P.O. Box 33
Jackson, Va.
December 5

Dear William Ernest,

Ha! I bet you thought I'd forget. But don't worry. I wouldn't forget you. I have just been so busy looking after the horses I have hardly had a minute to myself. I practically fall into bed I'm so worn out from all the work. Have you ever shoveled horse manure?

Just kidding. Actually, it is a lot of fun. We are getting six of the horses ready to race at the Charles Town track soon, so I have to help them train. I am sure one of them, named Clouds of Glory, is going to win. The prize is about a half a million dollars, so we will be even richer when he does. Not that we need the money, being millionaires and all.

How is school? I bet you zonked Miss McNair with all those new words you learned last month. You should keep in practice by reading out loud to Mr. Randolph.

Tell Trotter we have three maids and a cook, but the cook isn't half as good as she is, even though she uses lots of fancy ingredients. (Ha! Bet you knock Miss McNair over when you read her that word.)

Write soon.

Gilly

P.S. My grandmother told me to call her "Nonnie." Aren't rich people weird?

Notice that Gilly's letter starts with the appropriate heading and greeting.

In the final paragraph of her letter, Gilly contrasts something about her new life and her old one. Notice her use of words like *but* and *even though* to explain this difference.

Thompson Park Elementary School
Thompson Park, Maryland
December 7

Dear Gilly,

If anyone had told me how much I would miss having you in my class, I'd never have believed it. I hope, however, that you are enjoying your new school and that the people there are enjoying you as well. You might like to know that when I send your records to Virginia, I do not plan to include any samples of your poetry.

You will be receiving soon some paperbacks that I'd been meaning to lend you, but now that you've left us, I want you to keep them as a souvenir of our days together in Harris 6.

I certainly won't forget you even if you never write, but it would be good to hear how you're getting along.

Best wishes,
Barbara Harris

Keep in mind that the type of closing a writer uses depends upon how formal the writer wishes to be.

December 10

Dear Gilly,

How are you? I am fine. I liked your letter. I liked your horses. Write me soon.

Love,
William Ernest Teague

P.S. Did you win the race?

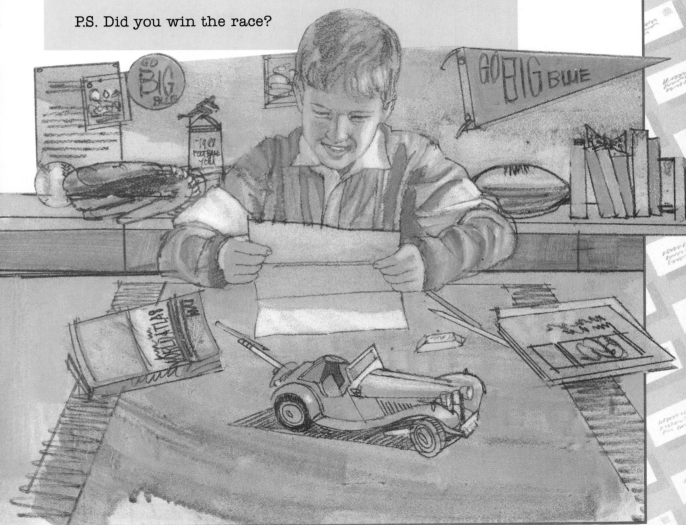

P.O. Box 33
Jackson, Virginia
December 15

Dear Miss Harris,

The books by J. R. R. Tolkien came the day after your letter. Now I know who Galadriel was.* Do you think Frodo should keep trying to take back the magic ring? I think it would be better if he kept it and took charge of things himself. Do you know what I mean? Anyhow, thank you for the books. They are really exciting.

They help a lot because school is terrible. Nobody knows anything, including the teachers. I wish I was back in Harris 6.

Your former student,
Gilly Hopkins

P.S. It's OK if you want to call me Galadriel.

* The name of a beautiful queen in J.R.R. Tolkien's book, *The Hobbit*.

Thinking Like a Reader

1. Do you think Gilly likes her new home better than her old one? How did you decide on your answer?
2. Have you ever moved, changed schools, or made new friends? What do you remember most vividly about the experience?

Write your responses in your journal.

Thinking Like a Writer

3. How does the author let you know Gilly's feelings about her new home and school?
4. How do Gilly's letters show the things that are important to her?
5. If you wanted to compare or contrast a place you know well to an unfamiliar place, what details would you include?

Write some details in your journal.

Responding to LITERATURE

BRAINSTORM *Vocabulary*

In "The Great Gilly Hopkins," Gilly wants her friends to know about her new life. In her letters, she includes words and phrases such as *hardly had a minute to myself* and *practically fall into bed*. In your journal, write words and phrases that describe your life. Begin to create your own personal vocabulary lists. You can use these words and phrases as you write a letter of your own.

TALK IT OVER
Now and Then

Gilly misses her old school and friends, but she does seem excited about some things. Think about your life this year and your life last year. Play this game with a partner. Begin by telling about something that you like this year. Then let your partner tell about something that he or she likes. Next, tell something that you dislike about this year. Give your partner a chance to do this, too. Each person should have at least three turns.

QUICK WRITE
Write a Post Card

Imagine that you have just moved to a new town or city. Write a post card to a friend. Tell your friend at least two things that are alike or different about the old home and the new.

Dear Laura,

I'm still busy unpacking, but I wanted to let you know that the move to Boston wasn't so bad, after all. My new room is much bigger than my old one, although it isn't as sunny in the morning. I have two new friends at school. They're really nice, but they aren't as funny as you and Beth!

Write back soon.

Jan

IDEA CORNER *Alike, but Different*

You have already started to think about how things can be alike, yet different. In your journal write some ideas for topics that you might use in your letter. You might write topics such as "My Two Brothers," or "Two Different Vacations." You can choose from these topics when you write your letter.

PICTURES SEEING LIKE A WRITER

Finding Ideas for Writing

Look at the photographs.
What ideas for letter writing do the photographs give you?
Write your ideas in your journal.

NISHIKI

1 GROUP WRITING: A Business Letter

COOPERATIVE LEARNING

When you write a letter, you must consider your **purpose** and **audience.** You might write a thank-you letter for a gift you received or a friendly letter to a pen pal.

If your purpose is to relate information to an audience that you do not know, you would probably write a business letter. What do you need to know about a business letter?

- Correct Letter Form
- Purpose and Audience

Correct Letter Form

As you read the business letter below, notice that the six parts of the letter are labeled.

HEADING

720 Grant Street
Baltimore, MD 20022
October 31, 1990

INSIDE ADDRESS

Halston Patima Company
405 Madison Street
Chicago, IL 60603

GREETING

Dear Sir or Madam:

BODY

I recently bought a box of your cereal. On the back of the box was an advertisement for a baseball scorecard inside the box.

The actual scorecard is disappointing. It is smaller than the advertisement, and the paper is too flimsy to last through a whole baseball game. Your advertisement is misleading, and I will not buy your cereal anymore.

CLOSING

Sincerely yours,

SIGNATURE

Allison Conner

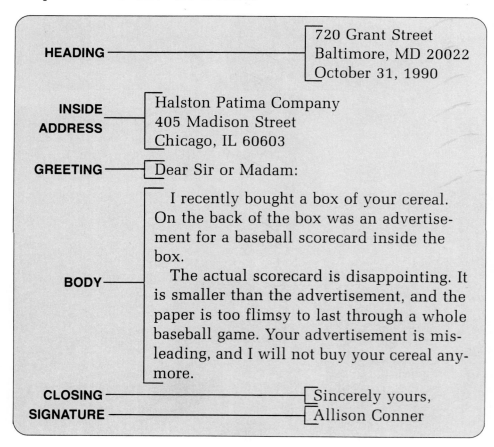

- The HEADING is the writer's address and the date. The names of the street, city, state, and month all begin with a capital letter.
- The INSIDE ADDRESS shows to whom the letter is addressed. It includes the receiver's name and the full mailing address.
- The GREETING says "hello." It begins with a capital letter and ends with a colon.
- The BODY is the main part of the letter. It contains the writer's message.
- The CLOSING says "good-by." The first word of the closing begins with a capital letter. A comma follows the last word in the closing.
- The SIGNATURE tells who wrote the letter.

Purpose and Audience

As you know, you must consider your purpose or reason for writing to a particular person or organization. Often, a business letter is the correct form for a serious letter. You would write a business letter to a business, newspaper editor, city mayor, or to any type of organization. Since in each of these cases you would have an important purpose for writing, the language of your letter should be formal, or polite. (See page 521 for other letter forms.)

Guided Practice: Selecting a Purpose and Audience

As a class, read and discuss the list below. Then, decide the purpose of a business letter written to each of these people or organizations.

the sports editor of your local newspaper
the principal of your school
The National Council on Safety and Fitness
your state senator
NASA
a department store
a famous author
your local police department

Putting a Business Letter Together

With your class, you discussed the relationship between purpose and audience in a business letter. You studied the correct form of a business letter and learned what information to include in each part.

Look again at the letter of complaint to the cereal manufacturer. The body of the letter compares and contrasts the advertisement for the scorecard and the actual card inside the box. The clear organization of the letter as a comparison and contrast makes the information easy to follow.

When you write a letter, make sure you have organized your ideas so that the letter is clear and easy to understand. Notice that a business letter's envelope contains both the sender's and the receiver's addresses.

Allison Conner
720 Grant Street
Baltimore, MD 20022

Halston Patima Company
405 Madison Street
Chicago, IL 60603

Guided Practice: Writing a Letter

Decide how you want to organize your business letter. Make sure your paragraphs are clear. Do they state the purpose of your letter?

Share your letter with a classmate. Ask your partner if the purpose of your letter is clear.

Checklist: A Business Letter

When you write a letter, you should keep some points in mind. A checklist will help you to remember important points about writing a letter. Use the checklist to make sure you have included all of the parts of a letter and organized the letter properly.

Look at this checklist. Make a copy of the checklist and keep it in your writing folder. Add any points that will help you to write a good letter. You can use the checklist when you write a letter.

CHECKLIST

- ✔ Purpose and audience
- ✔ Correct letter form
  - Heading ________
  - Inside Address ________
  - Greeting ________
  - Body ________
  - Closing ________
  - Signature ________

2 THINKING AND WRITING: Comparing and Contrasting

When you **compare** two things, you show in what ways they are alike. When you **contrast** two things, you show how they are different from one another.

A writer organizes a comparison or a contrast by first noting whether two things, or subjects, have more similarities or differences.

The writer is comparing and contrasting dogs and cats. On the page, several points of comparison and contrast are listed.

Dogs	**Cats**
need to be walked outdoors	can stay indoors
good pets for families	good pets for families
need lots of space	happy in small spaces
bark and make noise	quiet animals
need a lot of attention	can be alone much of the time
can adopt one for free	can adopt one for free

Thinking Like a Writer

- Do the notes of this writer show that cats and dogs have more similarities or more differences?

The writer will use her notes for a comparison and contrast paragraph on dogs and cats as pets. When you write to compare and contrast, remember to choose examples that clearly support your main idea.

THINKING APPLICATION Organizing Comparisons and Contrasts

COOPERATIVE LEARNING

Jeffrey has made notes about two contests. Decide which information he should use in a letter that **compares** the two contests and in a letter that **contrasts** the contests.

You may wish to discuss your thinking with other students. In your discussions, explain your choices to each other.

Baking Contest	**Spelling Contest**
costs $5.00 to enter	costs nothing to enter
for ages 10-14	for ages 10-14
$100.00 prize	$100.00 prize
takes place on Saturday	takes place on Tuesday, Wednesday
contestants bring ingredients	contestants bring no materials
sign up by November 1	sign up by November 1

Kay has made notes about two art exhibits. Decide which information she should use in a letter that **compares** the two exhibits and in a letter that **contrasts** the exhibits.

Grace Hall Exhibit	**Jennings Museum Exhibit**
paintings and sculptures	paintings and sculptures
works by nineteenth-century artists	works by twentieth-century artists
free admission for students	$6.00 admission fee
slide shows performed	slide shows performed

Make two copies of the chart below on a separate piece of paper. Then list the information in each student's notes on the chart so that the examples are organized correctly.

Points of Comparison	Points of Contrast
______________________	______________________
______________________	______________________
______________________	______________________

WRITING TOGETHER

3 INDEPENDENT WRITING: A Business Letter

Prewrite: Step 1

By this time, you know a great deal about writing letters. Now you can write a letter in which you compare and contrast. Rafael, a student in the fifth grade, wanted to write a letter to Carl Lewis, his hero.

Choosing a Topic

1. First, Rafael made a list of things to tell Lewis.
2. Next, he chose the topic that was most important to him.
3. Last, he decided upon the purpose of his letter.

Lewis compared to other runners

Lewis's 1984 and 1988 Olympic victories

Carl Lewis's success and mine

Rafael liked his last idea best. Now that he had become a runner himself, he felt he had something in common with the great Olympic athlete. He narrowed his topic to include Carl Lewis's 1984 victory in the 100-yard dash and his own victory in his school's 100-yard dash.

Exploring Ideas: Charting Strategy

Rafael used a **chart** to organize his ideas. Here is Rafael's chart.

Carl Lewis's Victory	*My Victory*
100-yard dash, Olympics	*100-yard dash, school*
represented United States	*represented my school*
set record 9.9 s	*won first place*
won gold medal	*set record 14.9 s*

Before he began his letter, Rafael recalled his own experiences and remembered details about Carl Lewis's track record. He changed the order of one of the examples on his chart.

Carl Lewis's Victory	My Victory
100-yard dash, Olympics	100-yard dash, school
represented United States	represented my school
won gold medal	won first place
set record 9.9 s	set record 14.9 s

Thinking Like a Writer

- What change did Rafael make in the order of his examples?
- How did he organize his examples?
- How do these changes improve the organization of Rafael's letter?

YOUR TURN

JOURNAL

Think of some people to whom you would like to write a letter. Be sure that each of these people is an appropriate audience for a business letter. Remember, you would write a business letter to a person that you do not know well or to an organization. Use **Pictures** or your journal for ideas. Follow these steps.

- Make a list of possible topics for your letter.
- Select a person from your list as your audience.
- Decide upon the purpose of your letter.
- Narrow the topic if it is too broad.

Make a chart like the one Rafael made. Remember, you can add to or change the order of examples at any time.

Write a First Draft: Step 2

Rafael knows the correct form for his business letter. He has made a planning checklist. Rafael is now ready to write a first draft of his letter.

Part of Rafael's First Draft

Dear Mr. Lewis:

I know how you feels after a victory. We have both won 100-yard dashes. You represented the United States at the Olympics. I represented my school at the state track meet. We both won first place. I did not win a gold medil at my race, however. I only won a blue ribbon. My times was a lot slower than yours, too. You won in 9.9 seconds, but I won in 14.9 seconds.

As Rafael wrote, he did not worry about mistakes. He tried to get his ideas down on paper.

Planning Checklist

- Remember purpose and audience.
- Use correct letter form.
heading
inside address
greeting
body
closing
signature

YOUR TURN

Write a first draft of your letter. As you get ready to write, ask yourself these questions.

- Is the purpose of my letter clear?
- Have I included the six parts of a business letter?

TIME-OUT You might want to take some time out before you revise. That way you will be able to revise your writing with a fresh eye.

Revise: Step 3

After Rafael wrote his first draft, he read it to himself. Then he gave it to his friend Rebecca to read. He asked her to suggest some improvements.

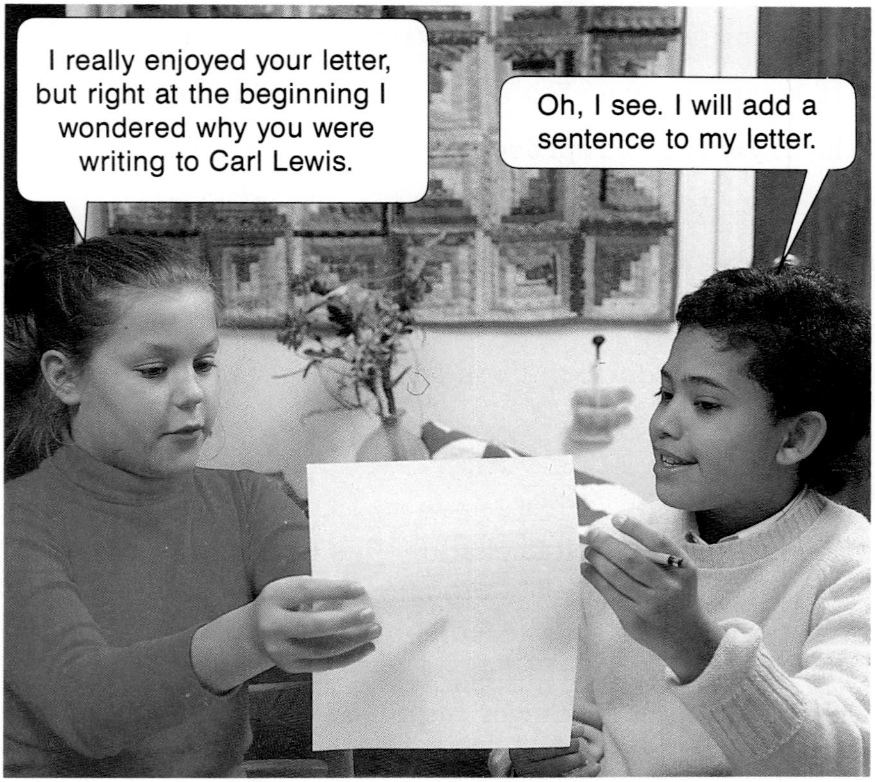

I really enjoyed your letter, but right at the beginning I wondered why you were writing to Carl Lewis.
Oh, I see. I will add a sentence to my letter.

Rafael looked at his planning checklist. He saw that he had forgotten one point. He had not explained the purpose of the letter soon enough. He checked it off so that he would remember it when he revised. Rafael now has a checklist to use as he revises his letter.

Rafael made changes to his letter. He did not correct small errors. He knew he could fix them later.

The revisions Rafael made changed his business letter. Turn the page. Look at Rafael's revised draft.

Revising Checklist

- ✓ ■ Remember purpose and audience.
- ■ Use correct letter form.
  heading
  inside address
  greeting
  body
  closing
  signature

WRITING PROCESS

Part of Rafael's Revised Draft

Dear Mr. Lewis:

I admire you more than any other Olympic athlete in the world.
^I know how you feels after a victory. We have both won 100-yard dashes. *Just as* ^You represented the United States at the Olympics, I represented my school at the state track meet. We both won first place. I did not win a gold medil at my race, however. I only won a blue ribbon. My times was a lot slower than yours, too. You won in 9.9 seconds, but I won in 14.9 seconds.

Thinking Like a Writer

WISE WORD CHOICE

- What sentence did Rafael add to his letter? How does adding this sentence make the letter clearer?
- What sentences did he combine? How does combining them improve the writing?
- How did Rafael's changes improve the organization of his letter?

YOUR TURN

Read your first draft. Make a checklist. Ask yourself these questions.

- Are my points of comparison and contrast clear?
- Is the purpose of my letter clear?
- Have I remembered to include the six parts of a business letter?

If you wish, ask a friend to read your letter and make suggestions. Then revise your letter.

Proofread: Step 4

Rafael knew that he would not send his letter before he had proofread it. He used a proofreading checklist to help him proofread and correct his letter.

Part of Rafael's Proofread Draft

won 100-yard dashes. ^Just as You represented the United States at the Olympics. I represented my school at the state track meet. We both won first place. # I did not win a gold (medil) medal at my race, however. I only won a blue ribbon. My times was a lot slower than yours, too. You won in 9.9 seconds, but I won in 14.9 seconds.

YOUR TURN

Proofreading Practice

Below is a paragraph that you can use to practice your proofreading skills. Find the errors. Write the paragraph correctly on a separate sheet of paper.

The National Baking Contest are very different from the local contest. We fly to the National contest but we take the bus to the local one. The prizes for a local victory is new baking dishes an oven and aprons but the prize for the National Contest is a new kitchen.

Proofreading Checklist

- Did I indent my paragraph?
- Did I spell all words correctly?
- What punctuation errors do I need to correct?
- What capitalization errors do I need to correct?

Applying Your Proofreading Skills

Now proofread your letter. Read your checklist one last time. Review **The Grammar Connection** and **The Mechanics Connection.** Use the proofreading marks to mark changes.

THE GRAMMAR CONNECTION

Remember these rules about subject-verb agreement.

- The verb must always agree with the subject in number.
- Singular verbs are used with singular subjects, and plural verbs are used with plural subjects.

  We **bring** a baseball bat to practice.
  Howard **brings** a catcher's mask.

Check your letter. Do the subjects and verbs agree?

Proofreading Marks

- ¶ Indent
- ∧ Add
- ℘ Take out
- ≡ Make a capital letter
- / Make a small letter

THE MECHANICS CONNECTION

Remember this rule about using commas in a series.

- Use commas to separate items in a series.

  Miranda packed a towel**,** a swimsuit**,** and goggles.

Check your letter. Have you separated items in a series with commas?

Publish: Step 5

Rafael decided to send his letter to Carl Lewis in care of the Olympic Committee in Colorado. He made a clean copy of the letter and carefully addressed the envelope. He showed the final draft to his friends before he mailed it.

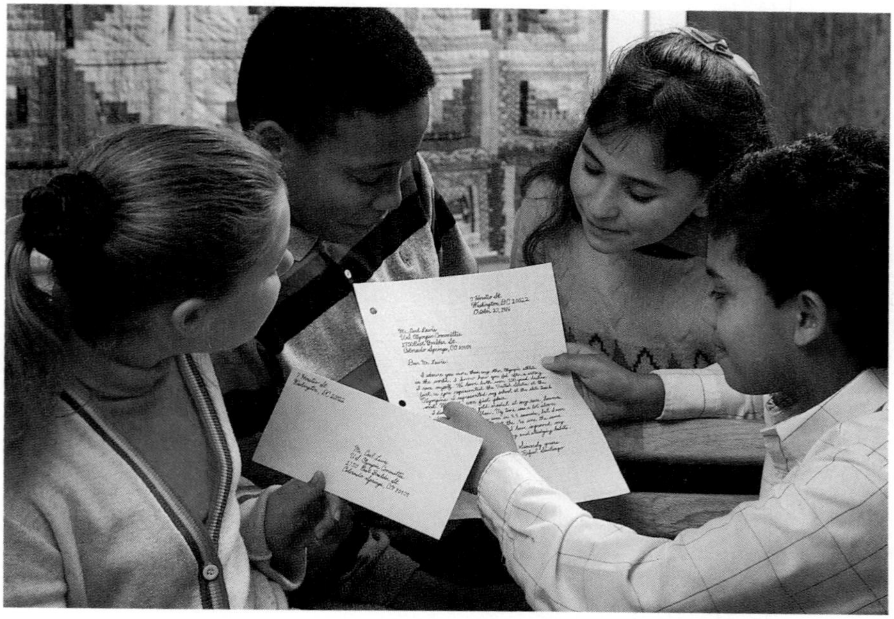

WRITING PROCESS

YOUR TURN

Make a final copy of your letter. Write as neatly as you can. Think of a way to share your work. Some ideas are given in the **Sharing Suggestions** box below.

SHARING SUGGESTIONS

Mail the letter to the person to whom it is addressed.	Read the letter in class. Ask your classmates for their comments.	Exchange letters with a friend. Answer each other's letters.

4 SPEAKING AND LISTENING: Conducting an Interview

When you write to compare or to contrast, you need to include specific information. One good way to get information is by interviewing someone who is an expert on your subject. You will want to ask questions that will help you to get the particular information you need.

First, consider the **purpose** of the interview. What do you wish to find out? Make a list of questions. Using a notebook for your questions and answers will help you to remember information.

Look at these questions from an interviewer's notebook.

Interview with Judge of a Dog Show

1. What is more important, the way the dogs look or the way they behave in the ring?

2. What types of things prove that a dog is well-trained?

3. How does a well-trained dog act during a show? How does a poorly-trained dog act?

4. How should an owner prepare a dog for a show?

Notice that these questions are specific. They allow the person being interviewed to share his knowledge and give his opinions. Remember, during an interview you might want to change some of your questions. Listening closely to the responses of the person you are interviewing will help you to avoid asking for information that you have already been given.

When you conduct an interview, keep these speaking guidelines in mind. They will help you to focus your interview.

SPEAKING GUIDELINES: An Interview

1. Remember that your **purpose** is to discover specific information about a topic from your **audience**.
2. Ask precise questions that let the other person form clear responses.
3. Use a notebook to record questions and answers. Practice asking the questions before the interview.
4. Give the person time to answer each question and to add any other information that comes to his or her mind.
5. Be polite, and thank the person you have interviewed.

■ How can I focus my questions so that they are clear and specific?

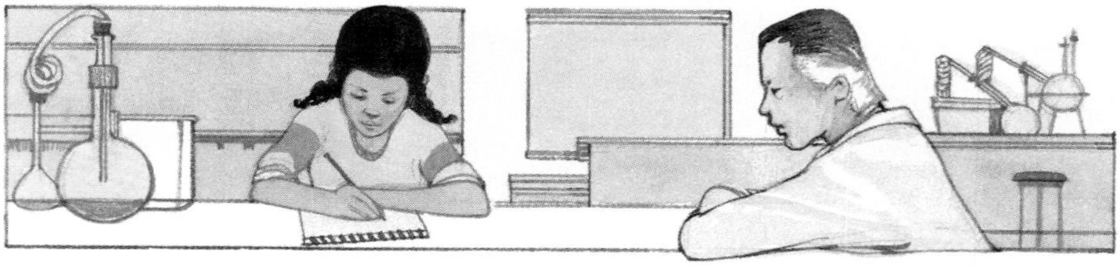

SPEAKING APPLICATION An Interview

Think of a topic that interests you. Choose a person who is an expert on this topic. Use the speaking guidelines to help you prepare. The person you interview will be using the following guidelines as he or she is interviewed.

LISTENING GUIDELINES: An Interview

1. Listen carefully to each question.
2. Listen to discover what the interviewer wants to know.

5 WRITER'S RESOURCES: Using the Library

Libraries have many different kinds of material. They have novels, collections of short stories, reference books, newspapers, and magazines. You can borrow most of these resources.

The books that you cannot remove from the library are in the **reference** section. The books in this section include dictionaries, encyclopedias, atlases, and almanacs. The other books in the library are divided into two main sections, **fiction** and **nonfiction.**

Fiction books include novels, books of short stories, poetry, and drama. In the library, all fiction books are in one section and are arranged alphabetically by the author's last name. For example, if you were looking for *Stuart Little* by E.B. White, you would go to the fiction section and look for the authors whose last names begin with *W*.

Nonfiction books contain factual information. They are arranged by subject. When you are looking for a nonfiction book on a specific subject, you will find it with books under the general category. For example, if you wanted to find a book about roses, it would be with the books about plants.

You can find magazines, journals, and newspapers in the **periodicals** section of the library.

Practice

A. Make a list of five books you would like to read. After each title, write what type of book it is, for example, a novel, book of poetry, or nonfiction book.

B. Write each item below. Then write whether you would find it in the *reference*, *fiction*, *nonfiction*, or *periodicals* section of the library.

1. *Chicago Sun Times*, September 2, 1983
2. *Charlotte's Web*
3. *The Little Engine That Could*
4. a book about sculpture
5. A Spanish-English dictionary
6. *The Columbia Encyclopedia*
7. *Newsweek*, July 5, 1988
8. an almanac
9. a book about baseball rules
10. *San Francisco Chronicle*, May 9, 1990
11. *The New York Times*, November 21, 1990
12. a book on hunting dogs
13. an article about sewing
14. a thesaurus
15. *Sports Illustrated*, October 2, 1990
16. *The Complete Poems of Emily Dickinson*
17. *The Short Stories of Mark Twain*
18. a book about the space program
19. a book on nutrition
20. an atlas

WRITING APPLICATION Questions

Write questions for an interview with a librarian. Prepare several questions the librarian can answer about where and how a student can find books about health care. Make careful notes on the information the librarian gives you. You might wish to actually conduct an interview. If you do, you could record the results in writing or use a tape recorder.

6 WRITER'S RESOURCES: Using the Card Catalog

You have learned how to find a fiction book in the library when you know both the title and the author. If you know only the title of a book, you can find it listed in the **card catalog.**

The card catalog is a file of small drawers containing cards. Each card tells about a book that is in the library. These cards are arranged in alphabetical order. The drawers are marked with letters that tell you which part of the alphabet is covered in each drawer.

Every book in the library has an **author card** and a **title card.** The nonfiction books in the library have a third card called a **subject card.**

When you know the author of a book but not its title, you can find the book by looking in the card catalog under the author's name. If you know the title, you can find the book by locating the title card. If you do not have a particular book in mind but want a book about a certain subject, you will use the subject card file. For example, if you wanted a book about fish, you would look up *fish* alphabetically in the subject cards and find listings for all of the books about fish in the library.

Here are some sample cards.

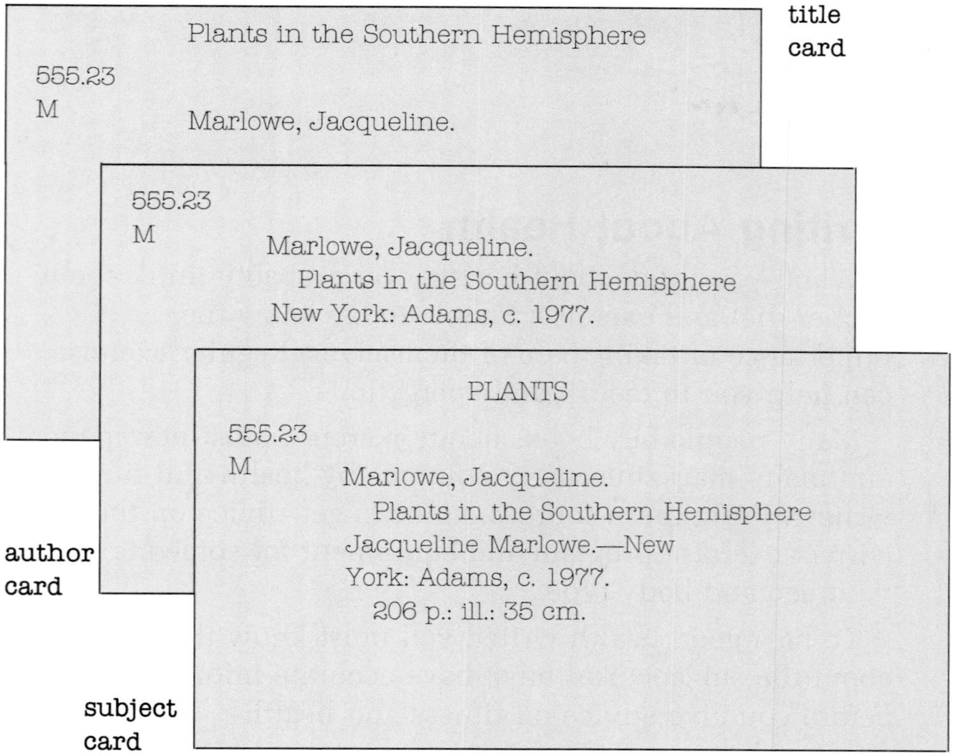

The number on each of the cards in the upper left corner is called the **call number.** You use this number to find the book in the library. You will find this book about plants among other nonfiction books numbered between 500 and 599.

Notice that each of the three cards pictured here contains the same information. Remember, the card catalog system makes it easier to find a book when you are unsure about its title, author, or both.

WRITING APPLICATION A List

Use the subject portion of the card catalog to find books about sports and fitness. Write the names of five books you find listed there. Include the author's name and the call number.

THE CURRICULUM CONNECTION

Writing About Health

When you think about health, you probably think about proper diet and exercise. People today know the importance of taking care of themselves. Regular exercise can help you to feel fit and energetic.

Many people buy books about exercise. Most newspapers and many magazines carry columns by health and fitness writers. From these sources, you can get advice on the correct exercise program and equipment for someone of your age and body type.

To be a good health writer, you must know the facts about the subject. You must have accurate information before you give advice on fitness and health.

ACTIVITIES

Keep an Exercise Log Keep a log or diary in which you record your exercise habits for an entire week. Write the date on each page and note every kind of exercise you do in one day and the amount of time you spend doing it. You might include brisk walking, biking, or sports. Write in the log each day for the whole week.

Design a Fitness Program Now that you have recorded your physical activities for a week, you can think about what a good fitness plan might include. Choose a variety of sports and exercises to fit your needs, the weather, and the amount of time you can spend on an exercise program. Make a weekly calendar that shows which sports or activities you will perform. Remember, it is necessary to exercise at least three times a week in order to keep fit.

Respond to Literature The following paragraphs are from John Gaskin's book, *The Heart*. This book explains how the heart works. The excerpt below tells how the heart works differently in the heat and in the cold. After you read these paragraphs, write a letter to a friend in which you compare and contrast the way you feel on very hot and very cold days. You might also choose to compare and contrast another health topic, such as how you feel when you do two different types of exercises. Use the friendly letter model guide on page 521.

from The Heart

Whatever the temperature is around you, your body temperature needs to stay the same. Usually it is about 98.6 ° F, although it can go up or down a little during the day.

Your blood helps to keep your temperature at the right level. On a hot day, you need to lose heat. To cool the body down, the blood vessels near the skin open wider. This means that more blood comes to the surface and can lose its heat in the air. The extra blood makes the skin look redder than usual.

When you are cold, your skin often looks paler. The blood vessels near the skin close up a little so that heat can't escape into the air. The blood stays deep inside the body to keep you warm.

UNIT CHECKUP

LESSON 1 **Group Writing: A Business Letter** (page 200) Write this information in correct letter form. 2 Adams Ave. Staten Island, NY 10306 June 6, 1990 Ms. Paula Green Woodcraft, Inc. 34 Pierce Rd. Dublin, NH 03444 Dear Ms. Green: Please send a copy of your catalog to the above address. Thank you. Sincerely, Jane Dey

LESSON 2 **Thinking: Comparing and Contrasting** (page 204) Imagine that you are going to write a paragraph that *contrasts* two prizes. Look at the list below. Copy those items that you could use in your contrast paragraph.

First Prize	Second Prize
two-week trip to Bermuda	two-week trip to Bermuda
all expenses paid	$200 for expenses
deep-sea fishing trip	bicycle trip
first-class airfare	second-class airfare

LESSON 3 **Writing a Business Letter** (pages 206–213) Imagine that you have won a trip. The actual trip was different than the trip that was described to you. Write a letter to the company that sponsored the trip in which you contrast what you were promised with what you actually received.

LESSON 4 **Speaking and Listening: An Interview** (page 214) Suppose you have been asked to interview someone in your class for the school newspaper. Pick a person whom you would enjoy interviewing about a particular topic. Prepare five questions to ask this person during the interview.

LESSONS 5-6 **Writer's Resources: The Library** (pages 216, 218) Use the subject section of the card catalog to find titles of books about one of the following topics. Write the names of three books on a separate sheet of paper.

dogs   Pulitzer Prize   Olympic Games   soccer   dance

THEME PROJECT *PLANNING AN EVENT*

People win prizes for many activities. Prizes are awarded at sporting events, dog shows, spelling bees, science fairs, county and state fairs, and even carnivals. These are only a few of the events at which prizes are given.

With your classmates, organize an event in which the whole class will take part.

- Begin by brainstorming for some ideas. You might plan a spelling or grammar bee, a poetry reading, an acting competition, or a "Beautify Our School" contest.
- Decide on the date, time, judges, and prizes for the event.

UNIT

7

Adjectives

In this unit you will learn about adjectives. Adjectives are words that describe, such as *spacious* and *amber*. Adjectives make your writing vivid and lively.

Discuss Read the words to the song on the opposite page. What images do you see?

Creative Expression The unit theme is *Images*. An image is a picture or a vision. How might you picture your area of the country? With a partner, write a description of your part of the country. You could write song lyrics or a poem. You might draw a picture, too. You might want to write your thoughts in your journal.

JOURNAL

THEME: *IMAGES*

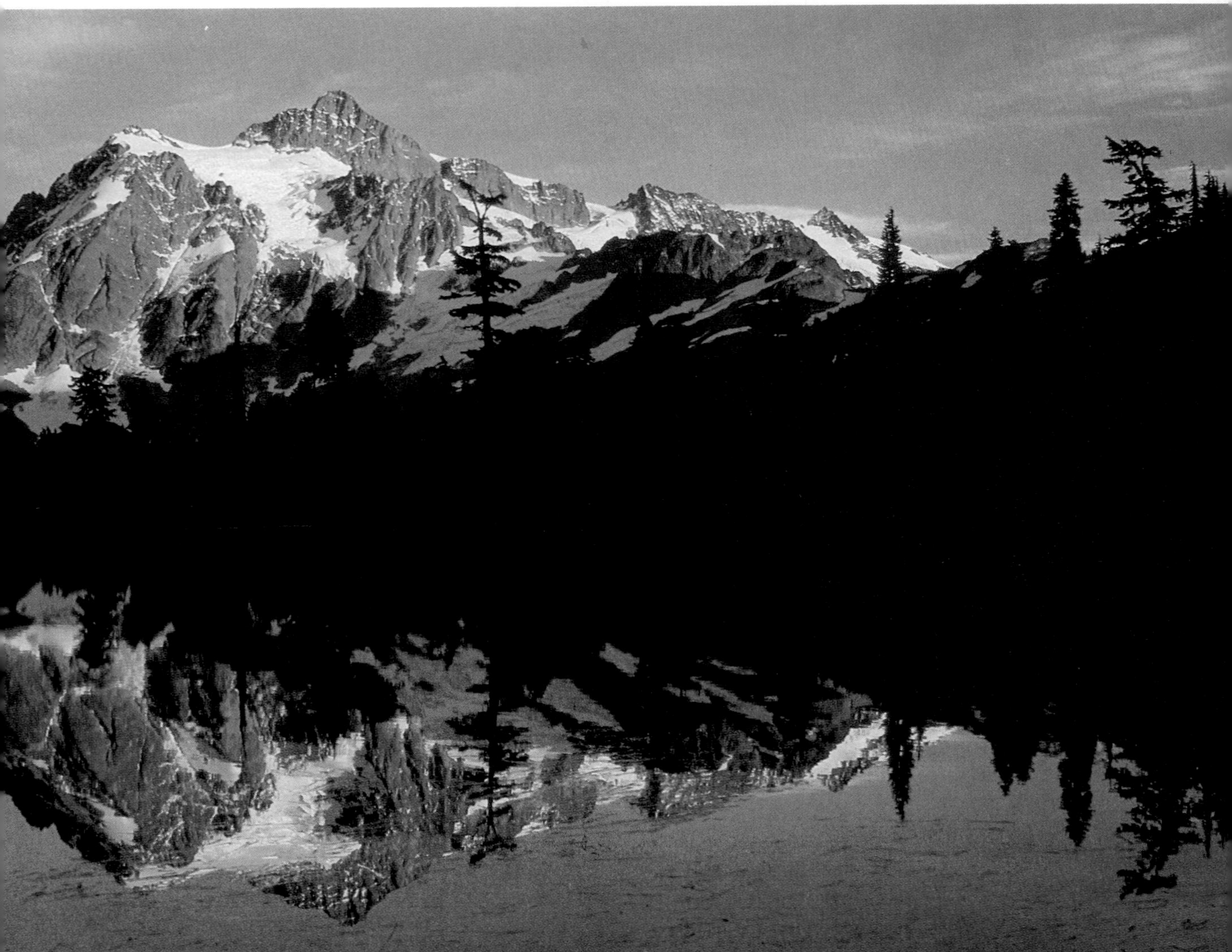

O beautiful for spacious skies,
For amber waves of grain,
For purple mountain majesties
Above the fruited plain!

—Katharine Lee Bates

GRAMMAR

1 WHAT IS AN ADJECTIVE?

An adjective is a word that describes a noun or a pronoun.

Adjectives tell *what kind* or *how many* about a noun or a pronoun. Adjectives may appear at the beginning, middle, or end of a sentence. Adjectives often come before the nouns they describe.

Vermont has **cold** winters. (what kind)

Some people enjoy winter. (how many)

Adjectives may also follow linking verbs.

The spring was **windy**.

The autumn is **beautiful.**

Two or more adjectives before a noun are usually separated by a comma.

Bright, **clear** weather arrives with spring.
Crisp, green buds unfold on trees.

A comma is not needed when one of the adjectives tells *how many*.

We had **three warm** days in March.
Several tiny birds come to our feeder.

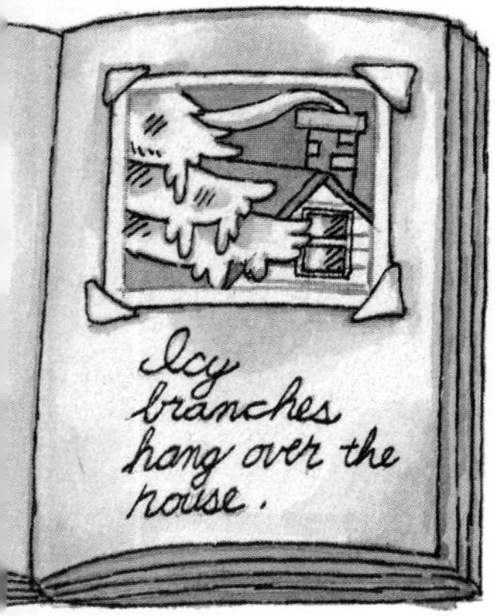
Icy branches hang over the house.

Guided Practice

Tell which word in each sentence is an adjective. Then tell which noun the adjective describes.

Example: An owl perches on the icy branch. *icy branch*

1. Snowy fields stretch to the woods.
2. The forest is still.
3. We were surprised by the sudden freeze.
4. A thin, clear frost covers the trees.
5. Two long icicles hang from a twig.

?! **THINK**

■ How can I decide if a word is an adjective?

REMEMBER

- An **adjective** describes a noun or pronoun.
- An adjective tells *what kind* or *how many* about a noun or pronoun.

GRAMMAR

More Practice

A. Write each sentence. Draw one line under each adjective that tells what kind or how many. Draw two lines under the noun that each adjective describes.

Example: We have several tall trees in our yard.

6. Summer weather is hot.
7. The cool autumn brings relief.
8. Bright, crisp leaves fall from the trees.
9. Nights become chilly.
10. Orange pumpkins grow in fields.
11. Some children wear costumes on Halloween.
12. Many animals prepare for winter.

B. Write each sentence. Complete the sentence with an adjective.

Example: The beach is a _____ place. *wonderful*

13. In July Ivan went to a _____ beach.
14. The sand was _____.
15. The _____ sun shone.
16. A _____ boat sailed on the water.
17. Ivan and his sister built a _____ sand castle.
18. They found _____ shells in the sand.
19. _____ waves rose and fell.
20. Ivan enjoyed the _____ summer.

Extra Practice, page 246

WRITING APPLICATION A Description

Write a description of your favorite season. Use words that give a clear, precise picture of the things you enjoy about the season. Circle the adjectives.

2 ADJECTIVES THAT COMPARE

Add *er* to most adjectives to compare two nouns or pronouns. Add *est* to most adjectives to compare more than two nouns or pronouns.

Spelling Adjectives That Compare

Rule	Example
Most adjectives add *er* or *est.*	short, short**er**, short**est**
Adjectives that end with *e* drop the final *e* and add *er* or *est.*	true, tru**er**, tru**est**
Adjectives that end with a consonant and *y* change the *y* to *i* and add *er* or *est.*	happy, happ**ier**, happ**iest**
Adjectives with one syllable that end with a single vowel and a consonant double the final consonant and add *er* or *est.*	wet, wet**ter**, wet**test**

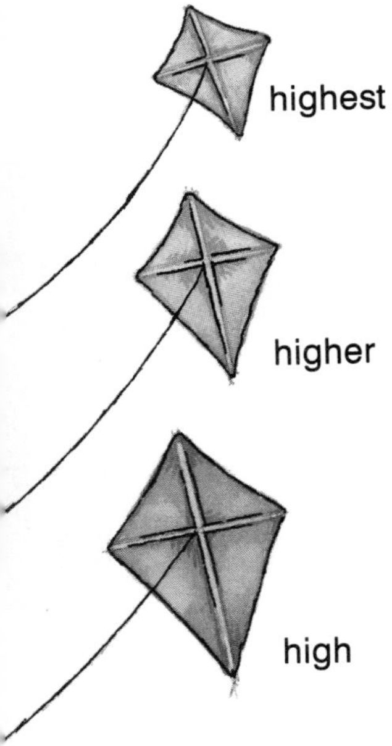

Guided Practice

Tell the correct comparing adjective.

Example: The _____ of the two boys wears a goblin mask. (taller, tallest) *taller*

1. The _____ person at the party was James. (hungrier, hungriest)
2. My costume is _____ than yours. (warmer, warmest)
3. Gabe reminds us of the _____ soldier in the world. (braver, bravest)
4. The girl in the butterfly outfit has the _____ costume of all. (prettier, prettiest)
5. The parrot costume is _____ than mine. (brighter, brightest)

?! THINK

■ How do I decide whether to add *er* or *est* to an adjective to make a comparison?

REMEMBER

- Add *er* to most adjectives to compare two nouns or pronouns.
- Add *est* to most adjectives to compare more than two nouns or pronouns.

GRAMMAR

More Practice

Write each sentence. Then complete the sentence with the correct form of the adjective in parentheses.

Example: The nights are (short) in autumn than in summer. *shorter*

6. Your costume is made of (thin) material than mine.
7. Choose a (wide) piece of cardboard than that one for a shield.
8. You can paint a (bold) design than mine on your shield.
9. The (hot) lamp of all will dry paint in ten minutes.
10. Put the pumpkin on the (high) shelf of all.
11. Tom's jack-o'-lantern has the (angry) expression of all!
12. Martha's costume is (simple) than Jean's.
13. The costume party is (scary) than last year's.
14. Myra's costume is the (strange) of all.
15. She wears the (odd) hat I have ever seen.
16. Laura's costume is (snug) than mine.
17. The (funny) outfit of all belongs to Rico.
18. He is dressed as the (huge) pumpkin in the world.
19. Our door is (narrow) than his costume.
20. Next year he will wear a (small) outfit than that one.

Extra Practice, Practice Plus, pages 247, 248

WRITING APPLICATION A Set of Instructions

Design a costume that you might wear to a Halloween party or as a character in a play. Then write instructions about how to make this costume. Be sure to include details about the kind of materials needed for the costume. Circle all the adjectives of comparison.

GRAMMAR

3 COMPARING WITH *MORE* AND *MOST*

With some adjectives of two or more syllables, you add *er* or *est*. With others you use *more* and *most* to make adjective comparisons. Never use *more* or *most* with the *er* or *est* form of an adjective.

Use *more* to compare two nouns. Use *most* to compare more than two nouns.

Incorrect: Mt. Whitney is **more bigger** than Mt. Shasta.
Correct: Mt. Whitney is **bigger** than Mt. Shasta.
Incorrect: Mt. Whitney is the **most biggest** mountain in California.
Correct: Mt. Whitney is the **biggest** mountain in California.

Guided Practice

Tell which form of each adjective you would use to compare two nouns and more than two nouns.

Example: interesting *more interesting* *most interesting*

1. serious
2. plentiful
3. enjoyable
4. wonderful
5. astonishing

?! THINK

■ How do I decide when to use *more* and *most* to make comparisons?

REMEMBER

- Use *more* to form a comparison when two nouns are compared.
- Use *most* to form a comparison when more than two nouns are compared.

GRAMMAR

More Practice

A. Write the correct form of each adjective to compare two and more than two nouns.

Example: generous *more generous* *most generous*

6. frequent
7. imaginative
8. tender
9. careful
10. courageous
11. silent
12. helpful

B. Write each sentence. Use the correct form of the adjective in parentheses.

Example: The (glorious) landscapes in this country are found in the West. *most glorious*

13. Arizona has (beautiful) scenery than my home state.
14. The Grand Canyon is the (amazing) place in the country.
15. It is one of the (spectacular) canyons in the world.
16. The Havasu Canyon is even (remote) than the Grand Canyon.
17. The Sonora Desert looks like the (rugged) land in the West.
18. The desert is (arid) than the White Mountains.
19. The (impressive) cactuses of all are the saguaros.
20. The desert has the (magnificent) air of any region.

Extra Practice, page 249

WRITING APPLICATION A Travel Guide

Write an entry for a travel guide. Describe an interesting place. Have a partner circle the adjectives that compare.

COOPERATIVE LEARNING

4 COMPARING WITH *GOOD* AND *BAD*

The adjectives *good* and *bad* have special forms for comparing two and more than two nouns.

Our science class today was **good.**
Yesterday's class was **better**.
Last week's was the **best** class of the week.
Wendy had a **bad** day.
Her headache was even **worse** than the day before.
The **worst** part of her illness was the fever.

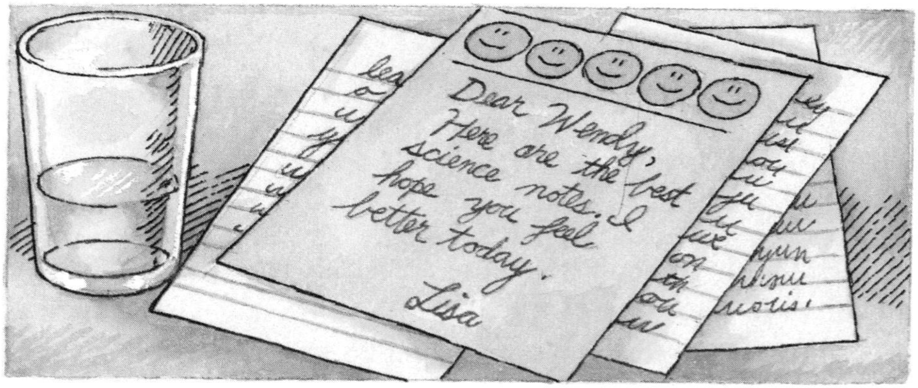

Guided Practice

Tell the correct form of *good* or *bad* in each sentence.

Example: I like science (best, better) than math. *better*

1. The teacher's lecture was (best, better) this week than last.
2. Wendy had the (worse, worst) feeling.
3. Her headache was (worse, worst) in the afternoon than in the morning.
4. I take the (better, best) notes in class.
5. I will give Wendy the (better, best) summary of the lecture.

?! **THINK**

- How can I decide which form of *good* or *bad* to use when making a comparison?

REMEMBER

- When comparing two nouns, use *better* or *worse*.
- When comparing more than two nouns, use *best* or *worst*.

More Practice

Write each sentence. Use the correct word from the pair in parentheses.

Example: Your results seem (better, best) than mine.
Your results seem better than mine.

6. Students get (better, best) results in the new laboratory than in the old one.
7. Lisa was judged to be the (best, better) scientist of all.
8. Sandra had the (worst, worse) time in the laboratory.
9. She likes lectures (best, better) than experiments.
10. Kim's experiments were (worst, worse) than Brian's.
11. Pietro got the (better, best) results in the class.
12. He thought his data was the (worse, worst) of all.
13. My projects this year are (better, best) than before.
14. Some disappointments are (worse, worst) than others.
15. Your new work is (better, best) than your old work.
16. Diane has the (worse, worst) suspicion.
17. Her results today are (worse, worst) than yesterday's.
18. Diane is a (better, best) scientist than some of us, though.
19. She may be the (better, best) researcher in the class.
20. In my (worse, worst) experiment last week, I forgot the formula.

Extra Practice, page 250

WRITING APPLICATION A Letter

Write a letter to a friend about one of your favorite subjects. In your letter, explain why this subject interests you. Try to use some forms of the adjectives *good* and *bad* in your writing. Exchange letters with a partner. Look for the words *good* and *bad* and their special forms in each other's letters.

5 USING ARTICLES AND DEMONSTRATIVE ADJECTIVES

Articles and **demonstrative adjectives** are two special kinds of adjectives that describe a noun or another adjective. *A*, *an*, and *the* are **articles.**

➡ Use *a* before a noun that begins with a consonant.
➡ Use *an* before a noun that begins with a vowel.

The refers to a specific person, place, or thing.

➡ Use *the* before a word beginning with either a vowel or a consonant.

A bird is nearby. **The** bird squawks. **An** ape roars.

This, *that*, *these*, and *those* are **demonstrative adjectives**. Demonstrative adjectives tell *which one*.

➡ Use *this* and *that* with singular nouns.
➡ Use *these* and *those* with plural nouns.

This camera needs film. **These** blankets are dirty.
That zebra runs fast. **Those** lions look majestic.

Guided Practice

Tell which word should be used in each sentence.

Example: Do you have (a, an) airplane ticket? *an*

1. (A, An) trip to Africa will be fun.
2. The scenery will make (a, an) nice photograph.
3. We are bringing (that, those) camera.

?! **THINK**

■ How do I use articles and demonstrative adjectives?

REMEMBER

- *A* and *an* refer to any singular noun, and *the* refers to a specific noun.
- *This* and *these* refer to nouns that are nearby, and *that* and *those* refer to nouns that are farther away.

G R A M M A R

More Practice

A. Write each sentence, using the correct article from the pair in parentheses.

Example: We will leave in (a, an) moment.

4. Our photographs are in (a, an) envelope.
5. We need (a, an) roll of film, too.
6. (A, An) island across the river looks inviting.
7. (A, An) camera is in the truck.
8. (A, An) lion was in our camp last night.
9. (A, An) elephant drinks from the lake.
10. (A, An) jungle is hot and damp.
11. There is (a, an) leopard on the truck.
12. There is (a, an) antelope beside the tent.

B. Write each sentence. Complete each sentence with a correct demonstrative adjective.

Example Look at _____ photograph. *this*

13. Lonny has pictures of _____ elephant.
14. Is _____ elephant dangerous?
15. _____ country is spectacular.
16. I will have _____ memories always.
17. We will never forget _____ trip.
18. We have _____ photographs.
19. We keep _____ pictures in _____ book.
20. _____ animal looks friendly in _____ picture.

Extra Practice, page 251

WRITING APPLICATION A Caption

Write a caption describing a photograph or painting. Share your caption with a partner. Circle the articles and demonstrative adjectives in each other's captions.

GRAMMAR

6 MECHANICS: Capitalizing Proper Adjectives

You know that a proper noun names a particular person, place, or thing. A **proper adjective** is an adjective formed from a proper noun. A proper adjective begins with a capital letter.

Proper Noun	Proper Adjective
Spain	Spanish
Africa	African
Greece	Greek
North America	North American

Spanish moss

Guided Practice

Identify the proper adjective in each sentence.

Example: Alaskan winters can be extremely cold. *Alaskan*

1. The Siberian climate is also harsh.
2. Canadian air will make the temperature fall.
3. The cold makes us dream of Jamaican sunshine.
4. A Mexican vacation would be nice, too.
5. A Hawaiian holiday would bring relief.

?! **THINK**

- How can I decide if a word is a proper adjective?

REMEMBER

- A **proper adjective** is formed from a proper noun.
- A proper adjective begins with a capital letter.

GRAMMAR

More Practice

A. Write each sentence. Draw a line under the proper adjective. Be sure to write each proper adjective correctly.

Example: The <u>scottish</u> moors are misty. Scottish

6. The greek islands are warm in the summer.
7. The arabian climate is very warm.
8. What have you heard about icelandic weather?
9. south american seasons are the opposite of ours.
10. I do not enjoy cold european winters.
11. It is always extremely hot in the north african deserts.
12. Wet and muggy weather comes with asian monsoons.

B. Complete each sentence with a proper adjective formed from the proper noun in parentheses. If necessary, you may use your dictionary for help.

Example: The <u>Swiss</u> winters are glorious. (Switzerland)

13. The ______ climate is often damp. (England)
14. ______ winters are severe. (Russia)
15. ______ winds bring dust storms. (India)
16. The ______ outback is hot and sunny. (Australia)
17. The ______ mountains are snowy. (Tibet)
18. The ______ deserts are famous. (Egypt)
19. How hot is a ______ summer? (Turkey)
20. Are ______ seasons similar to ours? (Japan)

Extra Practice, page 252

WRITING APPLICATION A Comparison

COOPERATIVE LEARNING

Choose three different locations in the world. Using an almanac, compare the weather in each place in the same season. When you are finished, exchange papers with a group of classmates. Underline the proper adjectives in each other's work.

7 VOCABULARY BUILDING: Synonyms and Antonyms

You can introduce variety into your sentences by using synonyms and antonyms. A **synonym** is a word that has the same or almost the same meaning as another word.

The animals of the jungle are **strong**.

The animals of the jungle are **tough**.

The words *strong* and *tough* are synonyms.

A word may have more than one synonym. Notice these synonyms for the word **quiet: calm, peaceful, silent, still.**

Antonyms are words with opposite meanings.

The blades on my skates are **sharp**.
The blades on my skates are **dull**.

A word may also have more than one antonym. Quiet has the antonyms **loud** and **noisy.**

Some antonyms are made by adding the prefix *un* or *dis* to a word. *Un* and *dis* mean "no" or "not."

untrue = not true
unlikely = not likely

Guided Practice

Tell which pairs of words are synonyms and which are antonyms.

Example: gloomy–merry *antonyms*

1. shiny–bright
2. clear–cloudy
3. unhappy–sad
4. strong–weak
5. careful–cautious

?! THINK

■ How do I decide whether words are synonyms or antonyms?

REMEMBER

- A **synonym** is a word that has the same or almost the same meaning as another word.
- **Antonyms** are words with opposite meanings.

More Practice

A. Write each sentence. Replace each underlined word with a synonym.

Example: I feel cold. *I feel chilled.*

6. A freezing winter can make people unhappy.
7. Roads glistening with ice are dangerous.
8. Many people find winter weather dreary.
9. Other people enjoy the chilly air.
10. Distant mountains look beautiful in the snow.
11. Beautiful trees sparkle under the frost.
12. Lively children sled down hills.

B. Write each sentence. Replace each underlined word with an antonym.

Example: The park bores me. *The park fascinates me.*

13. Rain forests are dry places.
14. Olympic National Park has a small rain forest.
15. The vegetation is very sparse there.
16. The woods are empty of animals.
17. Tiny ferns grow under the trees.
18. The area gets low levels of rainfall.
19. The shallow Pacific Ocean lies beyond the forest.
20. Short mountain peaks rise on the other side.

Extra Practice, page 253

WRITING APPLICATION A Weather Report

Write a weather report that describes the week's weather. Keep a record of any changes in the weather that occur from one day to another. Circle all of the adjectives in your work. Use the Thesaurus on page 507 to help you find synonyms or antonyms for these words.

GRAMMAR AND WRITING CONNECTION

Expanding Sentences

You know that adjectives can make your writing more colorful and precise. Compare these sentences.

Joanne wrote a poem about a forest.
Joanne wrote a poem about a **dark, dense** forest.

Notice that the adjectives *dark* and *dense* give the reader a clearer picture of the forest. Use adjectives in sentences to help your reader to see what you see. Read this sentence.

The cabin is near the lake.

Think of some adjectives that could describe the lake. Notice how this sentence can be expanded.

The **old** cabin is near the **blue** lake.
The **pleasant, old** cabin is near the **blue** lake.

Working Together

COOPERATIVE LEARNING

With your classmates, discuss ways to make sentences more interesting and colorful by adding adjectives. Then, identify the adjectives used in the sentences below.

Example: A playful otter catches a silver fish.
playful, silver

1. Warm, bright sunlight sparkles through the trees.
2. Soft, cool breezes ruffle the leaves.
3. The gentle motion of the clear water is peaceful.
4. I watch the playful animals during the quiet, summer day.

Revising Sentences

Peggy has written these sentences about a peaceful scene in the countryside. Help her to expand her sentences by adding adjectives to each blank.

5. The _____ eagle soars over the trees.
6. Its _____ nest is on a _____ cliff.
7. A _____ fish dangles in the bird's _____ claws.
8. The _____ eaglets have a _____ appetite.
9. A _____ bear eats _____ berries.
10. Its _____ fur shines in the _____ sun.
11. _____ squirrels scurry in the grass.
12. Their _____ tails look like _____ brushes.
13. My _____ sister photographs the _____ scene.
14. We spread a _____ blanket on the ground.
15. The _____ food satisfies us.
16. _____ animals approach our blanket.
17. A _____ raccoon appears suddenly.
18. We feed the _____ creatures _____ scraps.
19. Later, we clean up the _____ area.
20. The _____ landscape grows dark at dusk.

WRITER AT WORK

Choose a place that you have been to, or imagine a place where you would like to be. Write a paragraph that describes the place. Use as many descriptive words as you can. Check to see that you have chosen precise adjectives.

UNIT CHECKUP

LESSON 1

What Is an Adjective? (page 226) Write each sentence. Draw one line under each adjective. Draw two lines under the noun that the adjective describes.

1. Our class gave a wonderful party yesterday.
2. We played festive music.
3. We decorated the room with bright balloons.
4. The food was delicious.
5. Some students performed a traditional dance.

LESSON 2

Adjectives That Compare (page 228) Complete each sentence with the correct form of the adjective in parentheses.

6. Your pack is (heavy) than mine.
7. The (safe) place for money is your pocket.
8. That tree is (large) than the oak tree.
9. Choose the (thick) branches for the fire.
10. The ground is (wet) today than it was yesterday.

LESSON 3

Comparing with *more* and *most* (page 230) Write each sentence. Use the correct form of the adjective in parentheses.

11. It was the (beautiful) place Gerry had ever seen.
12. The building was the (elegant) in town.
13. In the museum were the (incredible) paintings.
14. The (impressive) artwork was in the main gallery.
15. Gerry was (excited) than surprised.

LESSON 4

Comparing with *good* and *bad* (page 232) Write each sentence. Use the correct form of the adjective in parentheses.

16. The jazz concert was (good) than the pop concert.
17. The saxophone player was the (good) of all.
18. The (bad) part was the long intermission.
19. Our seats were (bad) than last time.
20. Bob's view was (good) than mine.

LESSON 5

Using Articles and Demonstrative Adjectives (page 234) Write each sentence using the correct article or demonstrative adjective.

21. (An, A) play ended with a single actor on stage.
22. The actor held (a, an) orange in his hand.
23. (That, These) orange was important to the story.
24. I saw another play in (this, these) theater.
25. (These, This) actors were in the play.

LESSON 6

Mechanics: Capitalizing Proper Adjectives (page 236) Write each sentence. Capitalize each proper adjective.

26. Many mexican buildings have red tile roofs.
27. Some spanish architecture uses brown adobe.
28. Many swiss houses have steep roofs.
29. Many english buildings are made of stone.
30. Modern african buildings are made of steel.

LESSON 7

Vocabulary Building: Synonyms and Antonyms (page 238) Write each pair of words. Then write whether the words are synonyms or antonyms.

31. open–closed
32. huge–large
33. brilliant–bright
34. cool–scalding
35. loud–noisy
36. exciting–dull
37. special–ordinary
38. worse–better
39. peaceful–quiet
40. odd–weird

Writing Application: Adjective Usage (pages 226–236) The following paragraph contains 10 errors with adjectives. Rewrite the paragraph correctly.

41.-50.

We study spanish in school. Our teacher says I am the better student in the whole class. I study more harder than anyone. I have an good textbook with pictures. These one particular photograph is my favorite. It shows a old building with a garden. A smallest cat sits outside in the sunlight. Those cat looks like my cat at home. An woman in the photograph wears the big shawl I have ever seen.

ENRICHMENT

SYNONYM/ANTONYM HOTLINE

You can play this game with a small or large group. Form a circle. Say a word. The next person must say a word that is its synonym or antonym. Continue around the circle. You are out when you cannot think of a word. You can use a dictionary to settle any disagreements.

LANGUAGE STEW

Some English words come from other languages. *Kindergarten* (German) and *café* (French) are examples. Look at the definitions below. Think of the word that the definition describes. Then, add an adjective that tells more about the word.

—thin noodles with sauce
—a very popular string instrument
—a building for sports events

Write down noun and adjective pairs, such as *hungry bear*, on separate sheets of paper. Mix up the papers and pass them out. Then, silently act out the words on your paper. The other players must guess the words written on the piece of paper. The first player to guess the words takes the next turn.

CREATIVE EXPRESSION

Images

Galloping pony—
alone, against the moonlight,
on a whitened beach.

—Kyorai

Little frog among
rain-shaken leaves, are you, too,
splashed with fresh, green paint?

—Gaki

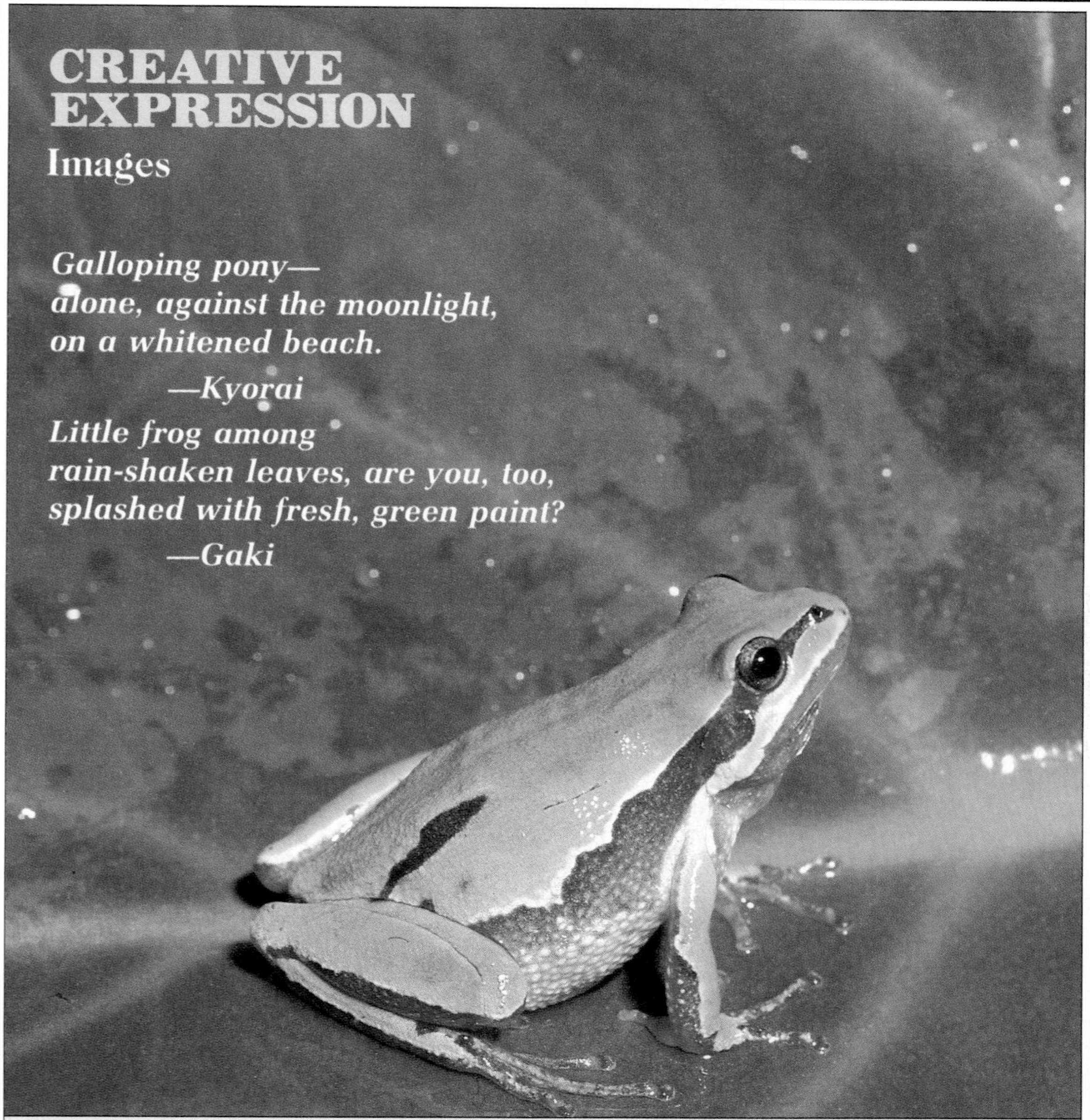

TRY IT OUT!

A haiku has three lines and seventeen syllables. The first line has five syllables, the second line has seven syllables, and the third line has five syllables. Write a haiku. Choose vivid images.

EXTRA PRACTICE

Three levels of practice

What Is an Adjective? (page 226)

LEVEL **A.** Write each sentence. Draw two lines under the adjective that describes each underlined noun.

1. Most cities contain tall <u>buildings</u>.
2. New York City has many <u>people</u>.
3. The busy <u>streets</u> attract visitors during daytime.
4. There are interesting <u>museums</u> in the city.
5. Speedy <u>subways</u> travel underground.
6. Yellow <u>taxicabs</u> take passengers around the city.
7. Blue <u>buses</u> provide comfortable <u>transportation</u>.
8. Athletic <u>tourists</u> can walk through the parks.
9. Curious <u>visitors</u> can take boat tours around Manhattan.

LEVEL **B.** Write each sentence. Draw a line under each adjective. Write **what kind** or **how many** after each underlined adjective.

10. The old building has a wide courtyard.
11. A large family owns the beautiful house.
12. Three people stand in the doorway.
13. A young child runs into the courtyard.
14. He is stopped by two geese.
15. The noisy birds have scared him.
16. The hot sun beats down on the buildings.
17. A few people sit in the shade.

LEVEL **C.** Write each sentence. Complete each sentence with an adjective.

18. Egypt has _____ pyramids.
19. They are _____ triangular buildings.
20. _____ pyramids are also found in Mexico.
21. The _____ jungle surrounds the pyramids.
22. It is a _____ climb to the top.
23. The view is _____.
24. A _____ king ordered the construction of the pyramids.
25. The workers struggled with the _____ task.

EXTRA PRACTICE

GRAMMAR

Three levels of practice

Adjectives That Compare (page 228)

LEVEL **A.** Write each sentence. Draw a line under the adjective that compares in each sentence.

1. Ocean liners are speedier than sailing ships.
2. Tugboats are smaller than freighters.
3. Tugboats are the strongest boats for their size.
4. Super tankers are the biggest ships of all.
5. There are fewer passenger ships today than there were in the past.
6. Airplanes are faster than ships.
7. Our new car is quieter than our old one.
8. The ride was bumpier in the truck than in the automobile.
9. Transportation is better now than it was in the last century.

LEVEL **B.** Write each adjective. Complete each sentence with the correct adjective from the pair in parentheses.

10. I am (busier, busiest) this year than I was last year.
11. I am a (faster, fastest) reader now than I was before.
12. I choose the (quieter, quietest) room in the house for my work.
13. The (sunnier, sunniest) spot in the room is perfect for my desk.
14. This chair is (softer, softest) than the other one.
15. I write my homework on the (cleaner, cleanest) paper of all.
16. My notes are (clearer, clearest) this week than they were last week.
17. I got the (higher, highest) grade of all on my last composition.

LEVEL **C.** Write each sentence, using the correct form of the adjective.

18. This year's class picnic was (long) than last year's.
19. It took place on the (huge) field in the town.
20. Marty and Sonya chose the (shady) spot of all.
21. The food seemed (tasty) than our usual lunch.
22. My class is (friendly) than last year's class.
23. On the way home, Franny was the (sleepy) of all.
24. That day was the (happy) of the school year.
25. The picnic was the (good) event of all.

GRAMMAR

PRACTICE + PLUS

Three levels of additional practice for a difficult skill

Adjectives That Compare (page 228)

LEVEL **A.** Write each sentence. Draw a line under the adjective that compares in each sentence.

1. Our dogs are swifter than greyhounds.
2. Tiger is bigger than Patches.
3. Patches is the fiercest dog in the neighborhood.
4. Tiger is the smarter of the two dogs.
5. My pets are cuter than the animals on television.
6. The spaniel is a better swimmer than the terrier.
7. My friend's retriever is bigger than our spaniel.
8. Our terrier has the loudest bark of all the dogs on the block.
9. The spaniel is the sweetest dog in the world.

LEVEL **B.** Write each sentence. Complete each sentence with the correct adjective from the pair in parentheses.

10. That is the (funnier, funniest) movie of the year.
11. The hero is helped by the (small, smallest) mouse in the world.
12. The mouse is (nicer, nicest) than the hero's other friends.
13. The (harder, hardest) challenge for the hero comes at the end.
14. Our hero needs the (swifter, swiftest) messenger in the world.
15. The mouse delivers the message, and their friendship becomes even (stronger, strongest).
16. The mouse becomes the (speedier, speediest) messenger in town.
17. Next time, the two friends will be (wiser, wisest) than ever.

LEVEL **C.** Write each sentence. Use the correct form of the adjective.

18. The meal was (heavy) than usual.
19. That was the (long) strand of spaghetti in the world.
20. My toast was (brown) than I like it.
21. The soup was (hot) than fire!
22. It was the (brief) meal imaginable.
23. I was (sorry) than ever about my appetite.
24. I ate (fast) than my friends.
25. I had the (bad) stomachache of all!

EXTRA PRACTICE

GRAMMAR

Three levels of practice

Comparing with *more* and *most* (page 230)

LEVEL **A.** Write each sentence. Draw a line under the adjective that compares in each sentence.

1. Mt. Everest is one of the most difficult mountains for explorers.
2. It has more severe weather than many other mountains.
3. The most strenuous part of the climb is near the top.
4. The lack of oxygen is even more dangerous than the slippery ice.
5. Explorers must use the most modern equipment of all.
6. Sherpa guides can carry the most remarkable loads.
7. One explorer was more eager than the others.
8. He became the most famous climber of all.
9. His journals are more exciting than many books.

LEVEL **B.** Write each sentence. Complete the sentence with the correct adjective from the pair in parentheses.

10. In this story, nature is _____ powerful than people. (more, most)
11. The _____ frightening event of all is a terrible storm. (more, most)
12. A girl struggles against the _____ alarming flood in history. (more, most)
13. She feels _____ tired by evening than she felt at dawn. (more, most)
14. The darkness is even _____ alarming than the flood. (more, most)
15. The story has the _____ unusual ending. (more, most)
16. The hero makes the _____ daring journey of her life. (more, most)
17. She respects nature's power _____ than she did before. (more, most)

LEVEL **C.** Write each sentence. Use the correct form of the adjective.

18. The Mona Lisa is one of the (beautiful) paintings in the world.
19. Van Gogh's paintings are even (colorful) than Picasso's.
20. Van Gogh's pictures are (striking) than many modern paintings.
21. To some people abstract art is the (exciting).
22. I like the (unusual) paintings best of all.
23. Other students prefer (realistic) art to abstract art.
24. My sister likes (startling) images than I do.
25. The (brilliant) painting in the museum is her favorite.

EXTRA PRACTICE

Three levels of practice

Comparing with *good* and *bad* (page 232)

LEVEL **A.** Write each sentence. Use the correct form of *good* or *bad*.

1. Our city has become one of the (better, best) in the country.
2. Most of the (worse, worst) problems have been solved.
3. Traffic is (better, best) than it was in past years.
4. The (worse, worst) pollution occurred ten years ago.
5. Unfortunately, the noise today is (worse, worst) than ever.
6. The planners will make the city even (better, best).
7. The (better, best) buildings in the city have received awards.
8. The (worse, worst) hazards of all have been corrected.
9. The city's (worse, worst) problem now is too many visitors!

LEVEL **B.** Write each sentence. Complete the sentence correctly.

10. The _____ movie of the year received many awards. (good)
11. The new movies are _____ than the old ones. (bad)
12. To others, movies have gotten _____ each year. (good)
13. Color movies may be _____ than black and white movies. (bad)
14. Both kinds of movies could be _____ than they are. (good)
15. The _____ movies of all often lose money for the producers. (bad)
16. My father is the _____ reviewer in the family. (good)
17. He avoids the _____ movies of all. (bad)

LEVEL **C.** Write each sentence. Choose the correct word in parentheses.

18. The weather today is _____ than it was yesterday. (worse, worst)
19. We were _____ prepared for the tornado than for the hurricane. (better, best)
20. We had the _____ storms of the year in March. (worse, worst)
21. The damage today is _____ than it was before. (worse, worst)
22. Our repair crews are _____ than most crews. (better, best)
23. The corn suffered the _____ damage of all. (worse, worst)
24. Our state has a _____ erosion problem than it had before. (worse, worst)
25. The _____ result of the storms is greater cooperation among the people in the state. (better, best)

EXTRA PRACTICE

GRAMMAR

Three levels of practice

Using Articles and Demonstrative Adjectives (page 234)

LEVEL A.

Write each sentence, using the correct word in parentheses.

1. (A, An) apple tree stands on the hill.
2. (A, An) ripe apple hangs just out of reach.
3. A hungry boy wants (that, these) apple.
4. (A, The) branches of the tree tempt him.
5. The climb is (an, the) effort for the boy.
6. (Those, This) branches are rough and uncomfortable.
7. (This, These) time he succeeds in his attempt.
8. (The, This) apples are within his grasp.
9. Should he pick (this, those) one or that one?

LEVEL B.

Write each sentence. Complete the sentence with the correct article or demonstrative adjective from the pair in parentheses.

10. _____ photograph is beautiful. (This, These)
11. Pat showed us _____ pictures yesterday. (that, those)
12. I want _____ one in my hand for myself. (this, that)
13. Choose _____ nice photograph from this pile. (a, an)
14. _____ picture in the pile shows the sea and sky. (A, An)
15. I love _____ two photographs of the sea gulls. (that, these)
16. Your picture of Janie is _____ excellent one. (a, an)
17. _____ main problem with my camera is a dirty lens! (The, A)

LEVEL C.

Write each sentence. Complete the sentence with a correct article or demonstrative adjective.

18. We visited _____ foggy beach one hundred miles from here.
19. _____ beach was rough and rocky.
20. Can you imagine _____ scene?
21. _____ photograph looks like an old post card.
22. _____ pictures are more recent.
23. Remember _____ beach in Maine?
24. _____ sea gulls ate clams on the sand.
25. I took _____ photographs of them last summer.

EXTRA PRACTICE

Three levels of practice

Mechanics: Capitalizing Proper Adjectives (page 236)

LEVEL **A.** Write each sentence. Draw a line under each proper adjective.

1. Greek statues are beautiful.
2. Italian painters were masters.
3. Iranian rugs are among the finest in the world.
4. These Peruvian blankets are very beautiful.
5. We admire Swiss watches for their accuracy.
6. North American quilts are warm and colorful.
7. My grandmother had a pair of Russian boots.
8. She cooked delicious Hungarian dishes.
9. Your mother makes wonderful Swedish pancakes.

LEVEL **B.** Write each sentence. Capitalize the proper adjective in each sentence.

10. Mrs. Lanski served polish sausage.
11. Mr. Lal brought indian curry.
12. Did you try the ethiopian bread?
13. I loved the korean rice dishes.
14. Concha cooks south american specialties.
15. You will enjoy the english pudding.
16. Please pass me the german potato salad.
17. Kerry made some irish soda bread.

LEVEL **C.** Write each sentence. Change each proper noun to a proper adjective.

18. (Japan) food is Mark's favorite.
19. Sylvia likes (Mexico) food best.
20. Most people like (Italy) food.
21. (North Africa) food is quite spicy.
22. (France) food is rich and good.
23. New York City has many (China) restaurants.
24. There is a (Portugal) restaurant in my neighborhood.
25. The grocer sells salty (Greece) olives.

EXTRA PRACTICE

GRAMMAR

Three levels of practice

Vocabulary Building: Synonyms and Antonyms (page 238)

LEVEL **A.** Write each pair of words. Then write whether they are **synonyms** or **antonyms**.

1. small–little
2. frisky–calm
3. frosty–chilly
4. untidy–neat
5. firm–hard
6. brave–courageous
7. crowded–empty
8. wild–tame
9. finished–complete

LEVEL **B.** Write each sentence. Replace each underlined word with a synonym or antonym as shown in parentheses.

10. Lily's kitchen is a <u>cheerful</u> place. (synonym)
11. The shelves hold <u>dull</u> pottery. (antonym)
12. The teakettle is always <u>cold</u>. (antonym)
13. Lily's cookies taste <u>wonderful</u>. (synonym)
14. Her <u>big</u> puppy sits by the table. (antonym)
15. A <u>pretty</u> canary sings in her cage. (synonym)
16. <u>Dark</u> curtains frame the windows. (antonym)
17. A <u>pleasant</u> smell fills the air. (synonym)

LEVEL **C.** Write each sentence. Rewrite the sentence with a synonym or antonym from the list in the box.

many
relaxing
appealing
tidy
attractive
calm
lush
colorful

18. Our living room is <u>ugly</u>. (antonym)
19. <u>Few</u> plants hang by the windows. (antonym)
20. <u>Bright</u> paintings decorate the walls. (synonym)
21. A <u>thick</u> carpet covers the floor. (synonym)
22. Visitors find the room <u>pleasant</u>. (synonym)
23. The <u>sloppy</u> room is my favorite. (antonym)
24. It is a <u>restful</u> spot. (synonym)
25. I feel <u>restless</u> in that room. (antonym)

MAINTENANCE

UNIT 1: Sentences

Sentences and Sentence Fragments (pages 2, 16) Write whether each group of words is a **sentence** or a **sentence fragment**.

1. Why do giraffes have such long necks?
2. Can eat leaves from tall trees.
3. Small animals cannot reach the high branches.
4. A definite advantage.

Subjects and Predicates (pages 6–11) Draw a line between the complete subject and the complete predicate of each sentence. Draw one line under the simple subject. Draw two lines under the simple predicate.

5. Janice hurries to the post office.
6. She passes two friends on the way.
7. The busy girl has no time for conversation.

Compound Subjects and Compound Predicates (page 12) Write each sentence. Draw one line under each compound subject. Draw two lines under each compound predicate.

8. My friends and I went to the zoo today.
9. Joshua watched and enjoyed the seals.
10. The seals swam and jumped out of the water.

Compound Sentences (page 14) Write each sentence. Write **simple sentence** or **compound sentence** next to each.

11. My family went to the desert and camped there.
12. The days were hot, but the nights were cool.
13. The desert was dry, and it never rained.
14. We brought our own water and food.

Using Context Clues (page 20) Write the correct meaning of the underlined word in each sentence. Then write the word or words you used as context clues.

15. Miguel tried to envision what his new house would look like.
    a. see b. hear
16. The metal parts of the house must be welded together.
    a. separated b. joined

UNIT 3: Nouns

What Is a Noun? (pages 76, 82) Write each sentence. Draw a line under each noun. Capitalize each proper noun.

17. The panama canal was built many years ago.
18. The canal connects the atlantic ocean and the pacific ocean.
19. The canal improves industry in the republic of panama.
20. What is a famous canal in the united states?
21. The erie canal is quite famous.

Plural Nouns (pages 78, 80) Write the plural form of each underlined noun.

22. The policeman helps the child.
23. He shows the girl the correct bus.
24. The driver waits for the person.
25. He tears the ticket in half.
26. He helps the passenger.

Singular and Plural Possessive Nouns (pages 84–89) Write each sentence. Replace the words in parentheses with a phrase that includes a possessive noun.

27. (The home of Jamie) is in the city.
28. (The jobs of her parents) are interesting.
29. (The work of Jamie) is done after school.
30. (The work of students) can help the community.

Abbreviations (page 90) Write the correct abbreviation for each word.

31. April
32. afternoon
33. Road
34. Senior
35. Corporation

Compound Words (page 92) Make compound words by matching the nouns in columns.

36.	ball	guard
37.	gang	clothes
38.	life	beach
39.	line	plank
40.	jump	way
41.	drive	rope

UNIT 5: Verbs

Main Verbs and Helping Verbs (page 148) Write each sentence. Draw one line under the main verb. Draw two lines under the helping verb.

42. We are playing baseball.
43. Marjorie is hitting the ball.
44. The ball has hit the fence.
45. She has scored a run.

MAINTENANCE

Linking Verbs (page 150) Write each sentence. Draw one line under each linking verb. Draw two lines under the word or words in the predicate to which the subject is linked.

46. Brian is ready for the race.
47. Domingo is an excellent runner.
48. Anne is a gracious winner.
49. The crowd looks excited.
50. The day seems perfect.

Verb Contractions (page 152) Write the correct contraction for the underlined words.

51. Luis <u>has not</u> seen the mountains.
52. His parents <u>have not</u> traveled very often.
53. We <u>cannot</u> believe his luck!
54. He <u>would not</u> forget his camera.
55. I <u>did not</u> see photographs from the last trip.

Verb Tenses (page 154) Change each underlined verb to the tense shown in parentheses.

56. Johan and Jim <u>watch</u> the younger children. (past)
57. The children <u>played</u> quietly. (present)
58. Louisa and Freddy <u>eat</u> dinner soon. (future)
59. Their parents <u>come</u> home at last. (past)
60. The family always <u>ate</u> dinner together. (present)

Subject-Verb Agreement (page 158) Write each sentence, using the correct present-tense form of the verb in parentheses.

61. Many birds (migrate, migrates) in the fall.
62. They (fly, flies) great distances.
63. Some birds (travel, travels) from Europe to Africa.
64. A bird (find, finds) the same place every year.
65. Naturalists (study, studies) the flight patterns of the birds.

Using Irregular Verbs (pages 162, 164) Write each sentence. Use the past-tense form of the verb in parentheses.

66. Alicia has (teach) music for many years.
67. She (go) to music school.
68. She (give) a concert last week.
69. I have (choose) the music for her recital.

UNIT 7: Adjectives

What Is an Adjective? (page 226) Write each sentence. Draw one line under each adjective. Draw two lines under the noun described by the adjective.

70. The blue heron lives in a marsh.
71. A small creek flows through our garden.
72. Tiny hummingbirds eat from the feeder.

Adjectives That Compare (page 228) Write each sentence. Complete the sentence with the correct form of the adjective.

73. Rhode Island is _____ than New Jersey. (small)
74. New York City is _____ than Scranton. (large)
75. The _____ mountain in the United States is Mt. McKinley in Alaska. (high)

Comparing with *more* and *most* (page 230) Write each sentence. Use the correct word in parentheses.

76. Teddy and Lena have the (more, most) wonderful books of all.
77. Some of the books have (more, most) illustrations than others.
78. The (more, most) beautiful book on the shelf has large color pictures.

Comparing with *good* and *bad* (page 232) Write each sentence using the correct word.

79. Juan liked the amusement park (best, better) than the beach.
80. The roller coaster ride was (worse, worst) than the Ferris wheel.
81. Kim liked the beach (better, best) than the park.
82. The (worse, worst) problem of all was the rain.

Using Articles and Demonstrative Adjectives (page 234) Write each sentence. Complete the sentence with the correct article or demonstrative adjective.

83. _____ record is better than that one. (This, That)
84. Steve has _____ excellent record collection. (a, an)
85. Linda has _____ record from 1950. (a, an)
86. _____ album is good. (Those, That)

Vocabulary Building: Synonyms and Antonyms (page 238) Match the synonyms or antonyms in the two columns. Label each pair **synonym** or **antonym**.

87.	full	foolish
88.	acquaintance	pier
89.	dock	empty
90.	wise	friend

WRITING

UNIT

8

The Granger Collection

Writing Descriptions

Read the quotation and look at the picture on the opposite page. The quotation was written by Virginia Hamilton, the author of a story you will read in this unit. How does a writer use words to make worlds?

When you describe something, you want your audience to see the same image, or picture, that you see. Using vivid adjectives will help your audience see what you see.

Focus Descriptive writing creates a clear and vivid picture of a person, place, or thing.

What would you like to describe? On the following pages you will find a story that contains vivid descriptions and some photographs of things you might like to describe. You can use the story and the photographs to find ideas for writing.

THEME: *IMAGES*

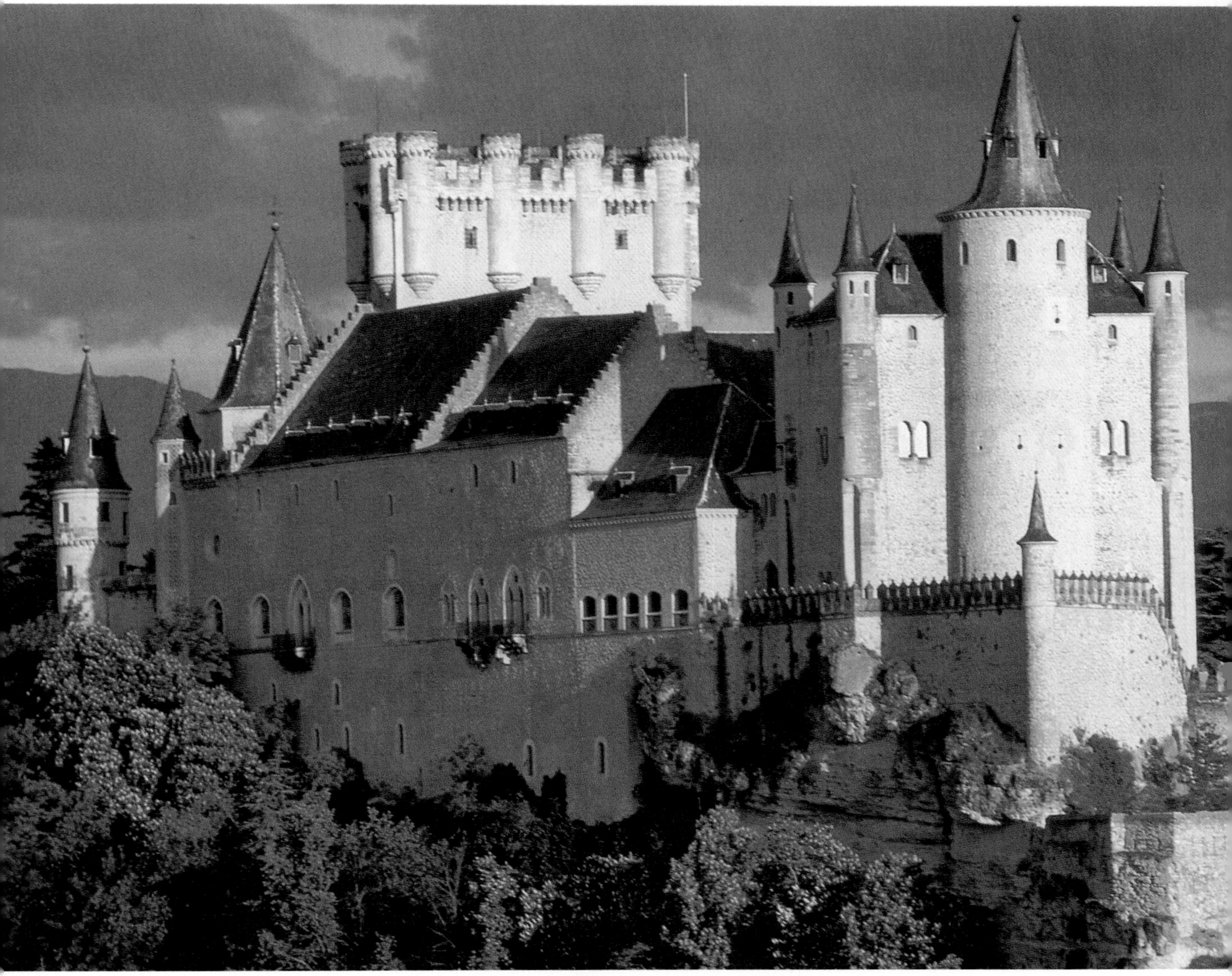

Words that make worlds are magic for me . . .
Oh, I am a believer in language and its magic
monarchy. To bind its boundless spell to me
is why I write.

—Virginia Hamilton

LITERATURE

Reading Like a Writer

AWARD WINNING SELECTION

Have you ever been amazed or delighted by something you saw? How did you describe it to other people?

Geeder has imagined many wonderful things about Zeely, a person she admires. Finally, Geeder hears the real story of Zeely's life.

As you read the selection, look for the details that the author uses to help you see Zeely as Geeder sees her.

From

Zeely

BY VIRGINIA HAMILTON

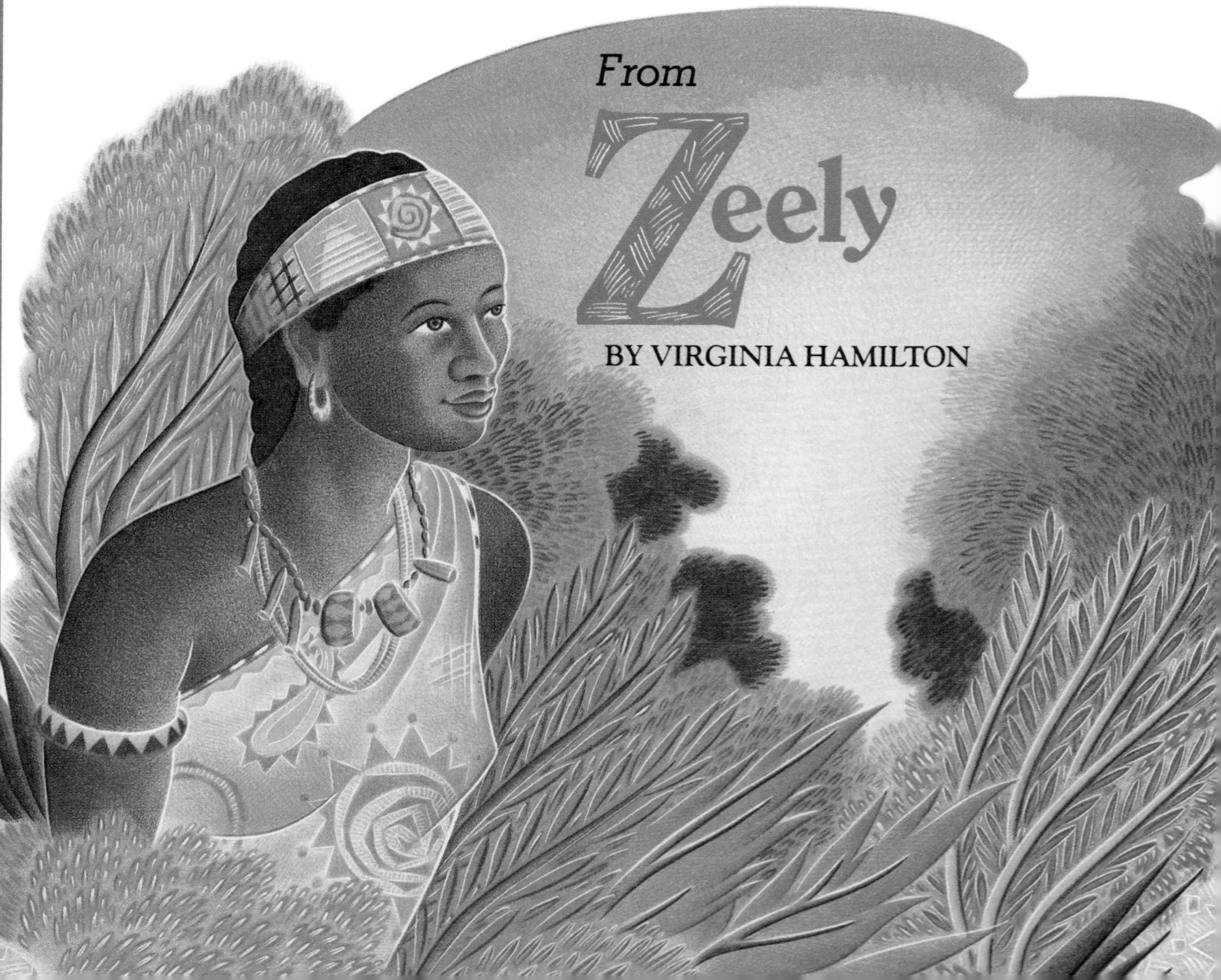

Geeder stood in amazement. Never had she seen Zeely dressed in such a way. She wore a length of varicolored silk wound around her delicate body and draped over her left shoulder. Around her head was a band of green silk, brilliant against her black hair. The long garment was beautiful and strange but the band around Zeely's hair was what held Geeder's attention. In her mind, she saw the picture of the Watutsi woman, the picture which right now she had hidden in her blouse. The Watutsi woman had worn such a headband.

The relationship between Geeder and Zeely is shown in this clear image of the two girls.

"I'm glad you've come," Zeely said. Her voice was quiet, hardly above a whisper, and yet, it was perfectly clear. She smiled, adding, "Please follow me." She turned and led the way into the forest. Geeder, still unable to speak, followed.

Zeely plunged through stinging nettles. Often, she stamped them down for Geeder or stopped to hold a bramble aside. At such times, Geeder forced herself to look up at Zeely; always, when she did so, she felt awfully small.

"Your many beads are pretty," Zeely said suddenly. "You have a lot of clothes?" She spoke as if Geeder were someone she had known for years. But her voice was halting, the way a person might speak when he hadn't had anyone to talk to for a long, long time.

Geeder was so startled by Zeely's question, her mind went empty. "Why, I don't know!" she said at last. "I've a dress to go to a party. I've got clothes for school. Mother buys them every fall and Christmas." She felt ashamed that she hadn't worn long pants instead of shorts to her meeting with Zeely.

"A girl should have clothes," Zeely said.

"Miss Zeely, I think your dress is about the most pretty one I've ever seen," Geeder said, shyly.

Zeely touched the bodice of her robe with her long fingers. Geeder could tell she was pleased by the compliment.

"I've had it a long time," Zeely said. "Twice a year, I hang it in the sun so that the colors will catch and hold the light." Very delicately, she gathered the skirt and smoothed it evenly about her feet. The colors leaped and glowed.

Geeder didn't know why they had started talking about clothes. Since they had begun to speak, she was bursting to ask Zeely about herself.

"Miss Zeely, do you come from Tallahassee?" she blurted out. "I think somebody told me you came from there."

"No," said Zeely, "we come from far to the north, from Canada."

"Canada!" Geeder said. The thought that Zeely came from such a place excited her. "I've never been there," she said. "Was it cold?"

"Where we were, it was cold," Zeely said. "It snowed and there was not much summer."

"Did you have hogs there, too?" Geeder asked. She entwined her fingers, eager to talk.

"We always have hogs," Zeely said. "We sell the best. We eat the meat of those that are left." She looked away from Geeder. "It's by them that we live."

The way Zeely spoke about the hogs made Geeder feel she had said something wrong. She grew uneasy. "Well," she said, "I just thought it was maybe Tallahassee you came from. I remember someone told me that."

"The same someone who says I am a queen?" Zeely asked. Her eyes held to Geeder's.

Geeder's hands flew to her face. "I didn't mean anything bad!" she cried. "Miss Zeely? Here!" she fumbled in her blouse and her hand shook as she gave Zeely the photograph of the Watutsi woman.

Zeely looked at the photograph. She smiled, vaguely, as though she didn't know she smiled. Finally, she gave the picture back to Geeder. She sat stiff and still. She could have been carved out of the trees, so dark was she seated there. Then, the rigid mask of her face melted, as if it were made of wax. A smile parted her lips. From deep in her throat came a warm, sweet giggle. She threw back her head and laughed and laughed. It was to Geeder a delicious, soft sound.

Notice the author's use of descriptive details that paint a picture of Zeely.

Geeder was so happy, she began to laugh, too, and got up to sit next to Zeely. All at once, they were side by side, just the way Geeder had dreamed it.

"You are very much the way I was at your age." Zeely said.

"You were like *me*?" Geeder said. "Were you just like me?"

Zeely smiled. "I mean that because you found this picture, you were able to make up a good story about me. I once made up a story about myself, too."

"Miss Zeely!" Geeder said. "I wouldn't have told a soul if I hadn't found that picture. The picture is proof!"

Carefully, Zeely ran her long fingers over her robe. "My mother's people were Watutsi people out of Africa a long time ago," she said quietly.

"Just like the lady in the picture!" Geeder said.

"Yes," said Zeely, "and I believed that through my veins ran the blood of kings and queens! So it was that my mother came to make this robe for me," Zeely said. "I had asked her many questions about her people—I talked of nothing else for quite a while. She made this robe exactly like the ones they wore." Then she added, "I put it on today because wearing it, I can be more the way I was. You may touch it, if you like."

And very gently, Geeder touched it.

Thinking Like a Reader

1. If you wanted to describe a special person or thing, what details would you select?

Write these details in your journal.

2. Which of your details best captures this person or thing? List the details.

Thinking Like a Writer

3. What images does the author use to show how Geeder pictures Zeely?
4. How do the details in the description help you to understand the characters?

Write a response in your journal.

Responding to LITERATURE

Brainstorm *Vocabulary*

In "Zeely," the author describes the scene in which Zeely and Geeder meet. She uses phrases such as "The rigid mask of her face" and "the colors leaped and glowed." Think of a person or place you know well. Write any images in your journal that come to mind. These can be words or phrases. Begin to create your personal vocabulary lists. These lists can help you when you write a description of your own of a person or place.

Talk It Over
Describe a Person

When Geeder sees Zeely in her robes and headband, she is reminded of the picture that she carries. Describe a famous person. What makes this person unusual or interesting? Think of some details. Tell a partner your description. Be sure to use clear, precise language. Then, ask your partner to guess who the person is.

Quick Write
Write an Advertisement

You have been thinking about people and places to describe. Write an advertisement for a place or product. Include details that show why the place or thing is special.

Vacation Home for Rent

Lovely four-room summer cottage in Ocean Cove, New Jersey. This neat home faces the beach. The house has a two-car garage and five acres of land. The cottage is available from July 1 – August 26.

Idea Corner
Interesting People or Places

You have already started to think about interesting people and places that you would like to describe. How could you help your reader to see a person or place as you do? In your journal make some notes about people or places you know. Use these notes when you write a description.

PICTURES SEEING LIKE A WRITER

Finding Ideas for Writing

Look at the pictures. Think about what you see.
What ideas for descriptive writing do the pictures give you?
Write your ideas in your journal.

1 GROUP WRITING: A Description

COOPERATIVE LEARNING

The **purpose** of a good description is to give the reader or **audience** a picture that is clear and vivid. What makes a picture clear and vivid?

- An Overall Impression
- Sensory Details
- Order of Details

An Overall Impression

Read the following paragraph. Notice the underlined sentence.

> One huge, snow-capped peak rose high out of the surrounding landscape. The base of the mountain joined the lower hills, which stretched as far as the eye could see. On the lower part of the mountain were larger trees, green bushes, and tall wildflowers. Scrubby trees and rough, granite boulders could be seen under the snow line. Clear, fresh water roared down from hundreds of places to streams and lakes far below. Sheer, vertical cliffs dropped thousands of feet.

The underlined sentence gives an **overall impression** or general idea of the mountain. Each detail adds to the overall impression of the scene. The description lets the reader "see" what the writer sees.

Guided Practice: Stating an Overall Impression

Work with your class to choose a place that you would like to describe. Discuss important things to include in a description. Think about the picture you wish to create. Together, write a sentence that gives a strong overall impression of that place.

Example: The old house looks worn out and tired.

Sensory Details

In a description, the writer includes many sensory details. These details appeal to a reader's five senses. **Sensory details** tell how things look, feel, taste, sound, or smell.

In the paragraph about the mountain, the sensory details help you to get an overall impression of a place. Look back at that paragraph.

- Which words help you to picture the mountain rising up from the surrounding landscape?
- Which details appeal to your sense of sight, feeling, taste, sound, or smell?

Guided Practice: Charting Sensory Details

Remember the place you have chosen to describe. Think of sensory details that describe that place. Copy the chart below. Write two or three details that appeal to each sense.

Overall Impression: The old house looks worn out and tired.

SIGHT	FEEL	TASTE	SOUND	SMELL
drab peeling paint	drafty clammy sticky	rusty water in pipes	creaks dripping faucets	dusty moldy stale

Order of Details

In a description of a place, the most logical order of details is one that maps out the picture for the reader. Each detail is arranged so that the reader is able to get a clear impression.

In the paragraph describing the mountain, the details are arranged from bottom to top. The writer has ordered the details so that a reader's eye would move from the base of the mountain up to its peaks. You can also choose to describe something from left to right, or from right to left.

Putting a Description Together

With your class, you have written a sentence that gives an overall impression of a place. You have also made a chart of sensory words or details that describe this place.

Look at your overall impression sentence and your chart of sensory words. Choose those that best fit the overall impression you wish to create.

Here are the sensory details one student selected to support the overall impression sentence that describes the old house.

The old house looked worn out and tired.

SIGHT	FEEL	TASTE	SOUND	SMELL
gloomy dark	cold clammy	rusty water in pipes	creaky dripping	stale musty

Guided Practice: Writing a Descriptive Paragraph
Write at least four detail sentences to add to your overall impression sentence. Include sensory words from your chart in these detail sentences. Remember to put your detail sentences in a logical order.

Share your description with a classmate. Ask your partner to suggest ways which will make your description clearer and more vivid.

Checklist: Descriptive Writing

When you write a descriptive paragraph, you will want to remember some points. A checklist will help to remind you of the things you will want to include in your descriptive paragraph.

Look at this checklist. You can add other points to it if you wish. Make a copy of the checklist and keep it in your writing folder. You can refer to it when you write your descriptive paragraph.

CHECKLIST

- ✓ Purpose and Audience
- ✓ Sensory Details
  - ■ Sight ______________
  - ■ Sound ______________
  - ■ Smell ______________
  - ■ Feel ______________
  - ■ Taste ______________
- ✓ Order of Details
- ______________
- ______________
- ______________
- ______________

2 THINKING AND WRITING: Classifying Sensory Details

You have seen that good descriptive writing creates a clear picture for the reader. A description appeals to a reader's senses.

A writer classifies or groups sensory details that give an overall impression of a place. Details about sight, sound, smell, taste, and touch each belong to a separate group. The writer chooses certain details to fill in the picture for the reader. Look at this page from a writer's journal. The writer plans to write a description of her favorite Mexican restaurant. On the page, many details are listed.

close to my home
fresh corn tortillas
delicious, spicy enchiladas
dark and quiet inside
fast service
convenient parking lot
soft guitar music
flowers on table

Thinking Like a Writer

- Which details do you think are important to the overall impression?

The writer should select only the details that add important information about the restaurant to her description. She can leave out the details about the parking lot and the distance of the restaurant from her home.

When you write a description, you will have to select and classify details carefully, too.

THINKING APPLICATION Classifying Sensory Details

COOPERATIVE LEARNING

Each of the writers named below is planning to write a description. Help each writer to decide which details to include. On a separate piece of paper, list the sensory details that the student should include. You may wish to discuss your thinking with other students. In your discussions, explain your choices to each other.

1. Estelle's poem will describe a frightening thunderstorm. She wants to create an overall impression that the night is dramatic and scary. Which details should she include?

deafening thunder	brilliant flashes of lightning
heavy rain	a sea gull

2. Edward's paragraph will describe an angry elephant at the zoo. He wants to create an overall impression that the animal is wild and powerful. Which details should he include?

loud, trumpeting call	stamping of huge feet
pool of water in cage	thrashing, long trunk

3. Robin's letter will describe a pleasant summer day spent at a baseball stadium. He wants to create an overall impression of a lively, happy scene. Which details should he include?

warm sunshine	green baseball field
cheering fans	peanuts cost fifty cents

4. Katherine's paragraph will describe a neighborhood street fair. She wants to create an overall impression of a happy crowd in an entertaining place. Which details should she include?

colorful booths on street	smell of barbecued food
lively, loud music	street fair is free

3 INDEPENDENT WRITING: A Description

Prewrite: Step 1

You have learned a good deal about description. Now you can choose your own topic to describe. Janet, a student your age, wanted to write a description for her classmates. She chose a topic in this way.

Choosing a Topic

1. First, she made a list of people she admired.
2. Next, she thought about describing each person.
3. Last, she decided on the person she could best describe.

my grandfather
Aunt Jane
Eleanor Roosevelt
a famous athlete
my Girl Scout leader
my teacher

Janet decided that she would most like to describe someone she knew personally. She narrowed her topic to her grandfather, and she was ready to explore her idea.

Exploring Ideas: Charting Strategy

My Grandfather

sight	sound	smell	feel	taste
white hair	snores	wood	rough	makes
blue eyes	tools	smoke	hands	maple
married				syrup
grandmother				
in 1935				

Janet thought she had some good ideas. She knew that her **purpose** was to describe her grandfather so that her **audience** could see him as she saw him.

Before she started to write, Janet recalled many details about her grandfather. She thought about the impression her grandfather made upon the people who knew him. Then, she changed some of the details on her chart.

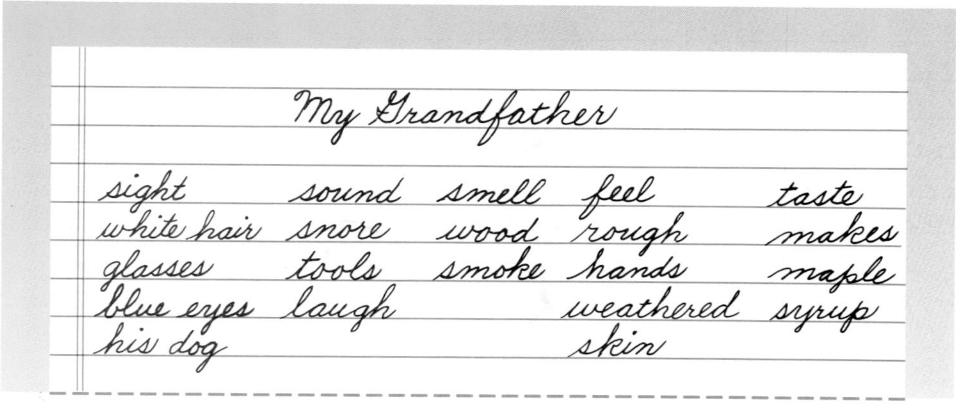
My Grandfather
sight
white hair
glasses
blue eyes
his dog
sound
snore
tools
laugh
smell
wood
smoke
feel
rough
hands
weathered
skin
taste
makes
maple
syrup

Thinking Like a Writer

- What did Janet add?
- What did she decide to leave out?
- How do these changes help to create an overall impression of her grandfather?

YOUR TURN

JOURNAL

Think of a person that you would like to describe. You might look at **Pictures** or your journal for ideas. Follow these steps.

- Make a list of people.
- Choose one whom you know well.
- Think of the overall impression this person makes.
- Think about your purpose and audience.

Make a chart of details. Remember, you can add or take away from the chart at any time.

Write a First Draft: Step 2

Janet knows what her description should include. She used a planning checklist.

Janet is now ready to write her first draft.

Janet's First Draft

My grandfather is a carpenter. He has white hair, and his eyes are bluest than the sky. He smiles a lot. His big hands are rough. He wears baggy pants. He also has big work shoes. His english sheepdog, joe, goes with him everywhere. I hear the sound of his woodworking tools when I think of him.

While Janet was writing her first draft, she did not worry about errors. She wanted to put her ideas down on paper.

Planning Checklist

- Remember purpose and audience.
- Include an overall impression.
- Use sensory words or details.
- Use a logical order of details.

YOUR TURN

Write your first draft. As you prepare to write, ask yourself these questions.

- What will my audience want to know about my subject?
- How can I best express my overall impression?

TIME-OUT You might want to take some time out before you revise. That way you will be able to revise your writing with a fresh eye.

Revise: Step 3

After she finished her first draft, Janet read it over to herself. She shared her writing with her classmate, Monica. She asked Monica to suggest ways to improve her work.

Janet then looked at her planning checklist. She noticed that she had forgotten an important point. She checked it off so that she would remember it. Janet now has a checklist to use as she revises.

I like your paragraph, but I think you should tell what impression your grandfather makes on you, before you give all the details.
Thanks. I'll add a sentence that introduces my grandfather before I describe him.

Janet made changes to her paragraph. Notice that she did not correct small errors. She knew she could fix them later.

The revisions Janet made changed her paragraph. Turn the page. Look at Janet's revised paragraph.

Revising Checklist

- ■ Remember purpose and audience.
- ✓ ■ Include an overall impression.
- ■ Use sensory details.
- ■ Use a logical order of details.

Janet's Revised Draft

is one of the most comfortable people to be around.
My grandfather is a carpenter. He has white hair,
a wise face. He His cheeks wrinkle when
and his eyes are bluest than the sky. He smiles
feel when you shake them.
a lot. His big hands are rough. He wears
and
baggy pants. He also has big work shoes.
His english sheepdog, joe, goes with him
everywhere. I hear the sound of his
and smell wood shavings
woodworking tools when I think of him.

Thinking Like a Writer

WISE WORD CHOICE

- Which sentence did Janet add?
- What sensory details did she add?
- Which sentences did she combine? How does combining sentences improve the paragraph?

YOUR TURN

Read your first draft. Make a checklist. Ask yourself these questions.

- How can I improve the overall impression I want to create?
- What details might I add to my description?
- How can I make the order of details more logical?

You may want to ask a classmate to read your paragraph and make suggestions. Then revise your paragraph.

Proofread: Step 4

Janet knew that her work would not be complete until she had proofread her paragraph. She used a proofreading checklist while she proofread.

Janet's Proofread Draft

is one of the most comfortable people to be around.
My grandfather is a carpenter. He has white hair,
a wise face. He bluer His cheeks wrinkle when
and his eyes are bluest than the sky. He smiles
feel when you shake them.
a lot. His big hands are rough. He wears
and
baggy pants. He also has big work shoes.
His english sheepdog, joe, goes with him
everywhere. I hear the sound of his
and smell wood shavings
woodworking tools when I think of him.

YOUR TURN

Proofreading Practice

Below is a paragraph that you can use to practice your proofreading skills. Find the errors. Write the paragraph correctly on a separate sheet of paper.

> My cats name is ex. Ex is short for exit. He is a large gray cat with gren eyes. his fur is thik and smooth. Ex's whiskers are long. At night he go outside and hunt for mice. He is the good hunter on my block. I like to watch him run threw tall grass.

Proofreading Checklist

- Did I indent my paragraph?
- Did I spell all words correctly?
- What punctuation errors do I need to correct?
- What capitalization errors do I need to correct?

Applying Your Proofreading Skills

Now proofread your description. Read your checklist again. Review **The Grammar Connection** and **The Mechanics Connection**. Use the proofreading marks to mark changes.

THE GRAMMAR CONNECTION

Remember these rules about adjectives.

- Add *er* to most adjectives to compare two nouns.

  This car is **newer** than that car.

- Add *est* to most adjectives to compare more than two nouns.

  The blue car is the **newest** car on the lot.
  Our house is the **oldest** one in town.

Check your descriptive paragraph. Be sure you have used adjectives of comparison correctly.

THE MECHANICS CONNECTION

Remember these rules about proper adjectives.

- A **proper adjective** is formed from a proper noun.
- A proper adjective always begins with a capital letter.

England	- - - ->	English
France	- - - ->	French
Spain	- - - ->	Spanish
America	- - - ->	American

The rugs from **Turkey** have beautiful patterns.
The **Turkish** rugs have beautiful patterns.

Check your descriptive paragraph. Have you capitalized all proper adjectives?

Proofreading Marks

- ¶ indent
- ^ add
- ℘ take out
- ≡ capital letter
- / make a small letter

Publish: Step 5

Janet shared her paragraph with her classmates. She copied her work in her best handwriting and posted it on the class bulletin board. Several of her classmates asked her about her grandfather. They wanted to know about the things her grandfather built.

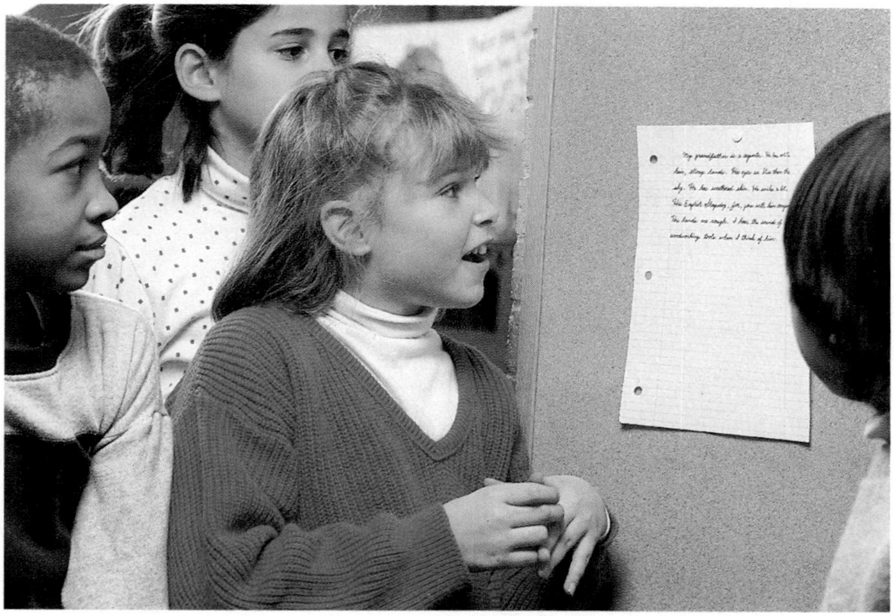

YOUR TURN

Make a final copy of your descriptive paragraph. Use your best handwriting. Think of a way to share your description. You might find some ideas in the **Sharing Suggestions** box below.

SHARING SUGGESTIONS

Read your work aloud to your classmates.	Ask an older relative or friend to read your description.	Make a tape recording of your description.

4 SPEAKING AND LISTENING: Describing a Subject

You have just written a description of a person that you know. Your description included an overall impression of the person. It also included some sensory details. Now, you can use what you know about writing a description to give a short talk. In your talk, you will tell your **overall impression** of a person, place, or thing.

First, you will want to make a note card to use for your talk. You do not have to write everything on your note card. The note card should include only the main points and some of the details. Look at this note card.

Notes Impressions of a Zebra

zebra—horse-like animal of African plains

1. Four and a half feet tall at the shoulder
2. black and white stripes
3. roams in herds in Africa
4. eats grass
5. black mane and tail
6. hunted by lions

Notice that the overall impression is listed on the note card. What other points are listed? How do the details support the overall impression? Are enough details included to give listeners a clear picture of a zebra?

When you give a talk, keep your **purpose** and **audience** in mind. These speaking guidelines will help you to focus your talk.

SPEAKING GUIDELINES: Describing a Subject

1. Remember that your **purpose** is to describe.
2. Tell an overall impression. Include sensory details. Use logical order.
3. Make a note card. Practice using your note card.
4. Look at your **audience**.
5. Speak in a clear voice. Pause briefly between sentences, and do not speak too quickly.

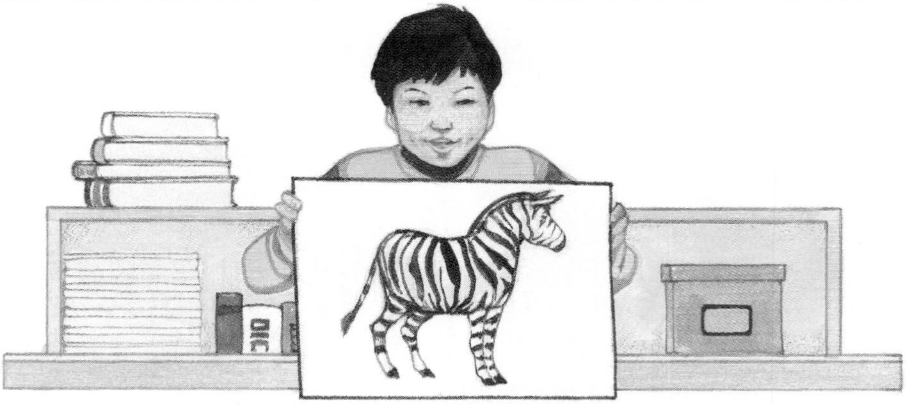

SPEAKING APPLICATION: Describing a Subject

Think of a person, place, or thing you particularly like. Prepare a note card to use to give a short talk about your subject. Use the speaking guidelines to help you prepare. Your classmates will be using the following guidelines as they listen to your description.

LISTENING GUIDELINES: Describing a Subject

1. Listen to "see" the image.
2. Listen for an overall impression.
3. Listen for sensory details.

5 WRITER'S RESOURCES: The Encyclopedia

You have written a description of a place and a person that you know. It is also possible to write a description of a place or person you have never seen. The encyclopedia is a good resource for ideas.

An **encyclopedia** is a set of books that contains information about many topics. Each book, or volume, has articles that are arranged in alphabetical order. Encyclopedia articles give information about people, places, things, and events.

Notice that the volumes are labeled with one or more letters. Each volume includes subjects beginning with that letter. For example, an article about *France* would be in volume 7. An article about *bats* would be in volume 2.

Articles on people are listed under each person's last name. An article on Amelia Earhart would be listed under *E*, in volume 6.

Every encyclopedia has an **index** that lists all the subjects included in the encyclopedia. The index in the encyclopedia above is in volume 22.

Practice

Use the encyclopedia on the opposite page. Write each name in the list below. Then, write the number of the volume that would have an article about that person or subject.

1. Albert Einstein
2. Dorothy Mary Crawfoot Hadgkin
3. Guglielmo Marconi
4. Ivan Pavlov
5. Anna Freud
6. Isaac Newton
7. Marie Curie
8. George Washington Carver
9. Galileo Galilei
10. Robert Fulton
11. Australia
12. Mt. Everest
13. electricity
14. kangaroos
15. computers
16. botany
17. volcanoes
18. ecology
19. Panama Canal
20. irrigation

Albert Einstein

WRITING APPLICATION A List

Use an encyclopedia to look up information about a famous scientist. Pay particular attention to facts about the person's achievements in his or her particular area of knowledge. You might also decide to make notes about the scientist's date and place of birth and any other interesting information you find in the encyclopedia entry. You may choose one of the scientists listed above or select another scientist. Write a list of details and facts about this person. Keep your list in your writing folder. You will use it in **The Curriculum Connection** page 286.

Writing About Science

Scientists write descriptions every day. They must describe natural things such as the weather and the habits of animals. Astronomers study the universe and describe the movement of the stars and planets, as well as the course of the sun and moon. Geologists describe how the earth was made. In fact, scientists even try to describe things that cannot be seen or heard!

Look at the world around you. Rocks, mountains, oceans, streams, plants, insects, and animals can all be studied and described. The more you carefully observe something, the more details you will find to describe. Scientists may spend years studying one particular plant or animal.

ACTIVITIES

Describe Something Think of something you know well in nature. Try to see it as clearly as you can. Then write notes about this thing. Record any details that describe its shape, size, surface, and any other qualities that help to describe it. Use sensory words and make your notes clear and vivid. When you have remembered everything you can, look carefully at the object and see what you have forgotten to record in your notes.

Describe a Famous Scientist Look at the list of things about the scientist whom you looked up in the encyclopedia. Imagine that you *are* this famous scientist. What would you want people to know about you? Write a brief description of your accomplishments in your special field of science. Be sure to organize your details in a logical order.

Respond to Literature The following selection is a scientific description of shooting stars. The author explains what is happening when a "star" races brightly across the sky. After reading the description, write a response. You might discuss the description, or write your own description of something that occurs in nature, such as a volcanic eruption or an eclipse.

Shooting Stars

from *The Reasons for Seasons*

Shooting stars or meteors are dots of dust on fire. Space is filled with particles. There are two theories about their origin. One is that they are particles left over after the birth of a planet. The other is that they are debris from a dead planet.

Whatever they are, these particles occasionally collide with the earth. Most of them are tiny, about the size of a grain of sand. They burn up when they enter the earth's upper atmosphere. Their glow is what we call a shooting star.

UNIT CHECKUP

LESSON 1 **Group Writing: Description** (page 268) Read this paragraph. On a separate sheet of paper, write the sentence that states the overall impression.

> Her eyes are black and lively, and her laugh is always loud. With one hug she can send you gasping for breath. She is always hugging somebody. Mrs. Sanchez is a big, jolly woman who makes everyone feel welcome.

LESSON 2 **Thinking: Classifying Sensory Details** (page 272) Imagine that you are going to write a description of a doctor. You wish to create the overall impression that she is hard-working, dedicated to her patients, and kind. Which of these details would you include? Write these details on a separate sheet of paper.

1. workday from 8 a.m.to 7 p.m.
2. came to Buddy's house for an emergency
3. had a salad for lunch
4. made Leslie feel unafraid
5. saw a movie last Tuesday

LESSON 3 **Writing a Description** (page 274) What does your best friend think when he or she looks at you? Write a description of yourself as you think your best friend might see you.

LESSON 4 **Speaking and Listening: Describing a Subject** (page 282) Imagine that you are about to give a short talk to your class in which you describe one of your favorite paintings or photographs. Make a note card to use during your talk.

LESSON 5 **Writer's Resources: The Encyclopedia** (page 284) Select a topic of your choice. Use an encyclopedia to find information about this topic. Write a short summary of the information that you find.

THEME PROJECT — ART REVIEW

You have now written several descriptions and learned how writers create clear and vivid pictures. There are ways to describe things other than with words. One common way is with a drawing or a painting.

Look at the painting below.

In the Park, William Merritt Chase

Before photography, people drew or painted scenes that they wished other people to see. A painting can tell a viewer about a place. At the same time, a painting or drawing can tell the viewer how the person who made it felt about his or her subject. Talk with your classmates about what you see in the painting.

Write a review of a work of art.

- Choose a picture or photograph that you admire.
- Look at your subject carefully.
- Write a description of what you see in the picture. In your review, tell your readers why they would also like this picture or photograph.

UNIT 9

Pronouns

In Unit 9 you will learn about pronouns. Pronouns can take the place of nouns. One way to avoid using the same nouns over and over in your writing is by using pronouns.

Discuss Read the poem on the opposite page. What view does the poet have about the destruction of the town?

Creative Expression The theme of this unit is *Views*. When you have a view about something, you have an opinion about it. What views, or opinions, do you have? Work with a partner. Write a few sentences that tell your opinion of something. You could write about a favorite movie, song, book, or food. Write your thoughts in your journal.

THEME: *VIEWS*

They're tearing down
a town, a town,
They'll probably take the rest.
Progress takes its toll, I'm told—
But should it take the best?

—Jud Strunk,
from "They're Tearing Down a Town"

GRAMMAR

1 WHAT IS A PRONOUN?

A pronoun is a word that takes the place of one or more nouns and the words that go with the nouns.

You can use a pronoun to avoid repeating a noun or group of words with a noun.

The pitcher was ready. **She** was ready.

	Subject Pronouns	Object Pronouns
Singular	I	me
	you	you
	he/she/it	him/her/it
Plural	we	us
	you	you
	they	them

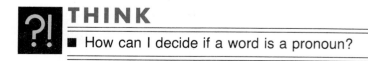

Guided Practice

Tell which word in each sentence is a pronoun.

Example: We come to the park for relaxation. *We*

1. Jim brings Dad's paper to him.
2. He always waits for the mail carrier.
3. We discuss the events of the day.
4. The neighbors join us in the park.

?! THINK

- How can I decide if a word is a pronoun?

GRAMMAR

REMEMBER

■ A **pronoun** is a word that takes the place of a noun.

More Practice

A. Write the pronoun in each sentence.

Example: We plan a picnic together. *We*

5. They appreciate the trees and flowers.
6. The Grants have picnics in the park with us.
7. Paul invited Nan and me to the picnic.
8. Mother helped prepare food with us.
9. Nan and I packed a picnic basket.
10. Nan made a special potato salad for me.
11. She cooked wonderful food for the Grants.
12. They loved the food.

B. Write each sentence. Then replace each underlined word or group of words with a pronoun.

Example: Father made a chicken sandwich.
He made a chicken sandwich.

13. Sammy thanked Mother and Nan for the chicken.
14. Mrs. Grant enjoyed the potato salad.
15. She told Nan some wonderful recipes.
16. The Grants are all good cooks.
17. Sammy made popcorn for Nan and Mrs. Grant.
18. Mr. Grant roasted peanuts for Sammy.
19. Nan and Sammy supervised the cleanup.
20. The park is a beautiful place.

Extra Practice, page 318

WRITING APPLICATION An Editorial

Suppose your town council voted to build a park in your neighborhood. Write an editorial in which you state your opinions about the project. Ask a partner to circle the pronouns in your editorial.

COOPERATIVE LEARNING

2 SUBJECT PRONOUNS

A subject tells *whom* or *what* a sentence is about. A pronoun can take the place of a noun. A **subject pronoun** takes the place of a noun that is the subject of a sentence.

Bill took a bus to the zoo. **He** took a bus to the zoo.

Subject pronouns are used after forms of the linking verb *be*. Notice the placement of **I** in the sentence below.

The winners of the contest **were** Julie and **I**.

Subject Pronouns

Singular	Plural
I	we
you	you
she/he/it	they

Guided Practice

Tell which word in each sentence is the subject pronoun.

Example: We will visit the aquarium. *We*

1. I will enjoy the trip.
2. You look forward to the day.
3. It is a new experience for many students.
4. They ask the teacher for information.

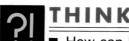

?! **THINK**

■ How can I tell if a word is a subject pronoun?

REMEMBER

- A **subject pronoun** can take the place of a noun as the subject of a sentence.

More Practice

A. Write each sentence. Draw a line under the subject pronoun in each sentence.

Example: You will enjoy the dolphins.

5. He shows the class a filmstrip.
6. We went to the aquarium on Thursday.
7. You talked about the dolphins.
8. They are intelligent animals.
9. I saw a dolphin last year.
10. He was named Albert.
11. Jan and I loved Albert.
12. We watched Albert for hours.

B. Write each sentence. Use a subject pronoun in place of the underlined word or words.

Example: Sue took photographs of the seals.
She took photographs of the seals.

13. Simon loved the dolphins and porpoises.
14. Dolphins and porpoises are similar animals.
15. Simon and I asked for a tour.
16. A seal performed funny tricks.
17. The cutest animals were the baby seals.
18. Marian loved the sea turtles.
19. Jack and I saw an octopus.
20. The octopus scared Betsey.

Extra Practice, page 319

WRITING APPLICATION A Proposal

With a partner write a proposal for a class trip that you would like to take. Tell where you wish to go, and offer suggestions for transportation. Read your proposal to your classmates.

COOPERATIVE LEARNING

GRAMMAR

3 OBJECT PRONOUNS

A subject pronoun can be the subject of a sentence. An **object pronoun** is a pronoun that can be used as the object of a verb or after words such as *to, for, with, in,* or *at.*

He plays the **flute**. He plays **it**. He carries **it** with **him**.

Object Pronouns	
Singular	**Plural**
me	us
you	you
her/him/it	them

You and *it* may be subject pronouns or object pronouns.

Guided Practice

Tell which word in each sentence is an object pronoun.

Example: Mother bought a record for us. *us*

1. The new record sounds great to me.
2. I gave them that record as a gift.
3. John saw it advertised on television.
4. Every song reminds me of the concert.

?! **THINK**

■ How can I decide whether to use a subject pronoun or an object pronoun in a sentence?

REMEMBER

- An **object pronoun** can be used as the object of an action verb or after words such as *to, for, with, in,* or *at*.

GRAMMAR

More Practice

A. Write each sentence. Draw a line under the pronoun. Then write whether the pronoun is a **subject pronoun** or an **object pronoun**.

Example: Music fascinates us. *object pronoun*

5. I watched the commercial with them.
6. The record is for you.
7. It was made at the concert.
8. You will enjoy the music.
9. The record delights me.
10. Karen told us about the violinists.
11. She likes violins the best.
12. Mother got concert tickets for us.

B. Write each sentence, using the correct pronoun from the pair in parentheses.

Example: Buy extra tickets for (they, them).
Buy extra tickets for them.

13. The concert will thrill (we, us).
14. Mother will take you and (me, I).
15. Father and (she, her) have many records.
16. She gave (he, him) a new record player.
17. Father bought records for (she, her).
18. The evening will be fun for (we, us).
19. Barbara and (I, me) are excited.
20. I talked to (she, her) about the concert.

Extra Practice, page 320

WRITING APPLICATION An Advertisement

Write an advertisement for an exciting event that will soon take place. Have a partner circle the pronouns.

4 USING *I* AND *ME* CORRECTLY

You already know that the subject pronoun **I** can replace a noun as the subject of a sentence or follow the linking verb *be*.

I won. The winner was **I**.

The object pronoun **me** can replace a noun that follows an action verb or a word such as *with*, *in*, *at*, *to*, or *for*.

Jim explained the rules to **me.**
He tells **me** about the prizes.

Sometimes a compound subject or a compound object contains the pronoun *I* or *me*. To help you figure out whether to use *I* or *me* in a compound, leave out the other word.

Bill and I entered the contest.
I entered the contest.
The rehearsals were hard for **him and me**.
The rehearsals were hard for **me**.

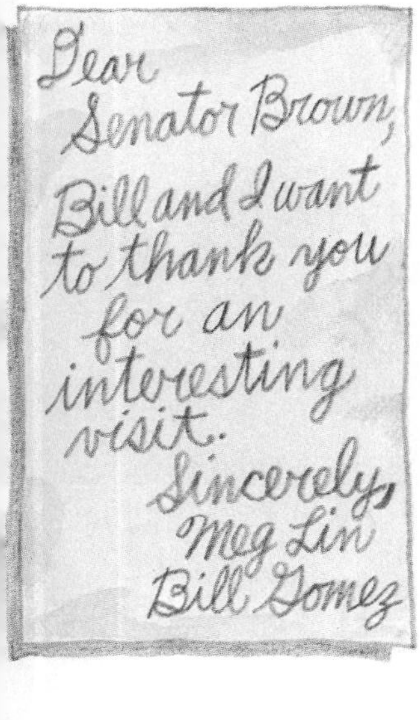
Dear
Senator Brown,
Bill and I want
to thank you
for an
interesting
visit.
Sincerely,
Meg Lin
Bill Gomez

Notice that in the sentences above, the pronouns *I* and *me* follow the other pronoun or noun in the compound. When you use *I* or *me* with nouns or other pronouns, you name yourself last.

Guided Practice

Tell the pronoun that completes each sentence correctly.

Example: The plane trip was exciting for Bill and (I, me).
me

1. The winners of the contest were he and (I, me).
2. The senator welcomed Bill and (I, me).
3. Bill and (I, me) thanked him warmly.
4. The senator took Bill and (I, me) on a tour.
5. Bill and (I, me) learned about government.

?! **THINK**

■ How can I decide whether to use *I* or *me* in a sentence?

REMEMBER

- Use **I** as the subject of a sentence or after the linking verb *be*.
- Use **me** after action verbs or after a word such as *with, in, at, to,* or *for*.

More Practice

Write each sentence. Complete the sentence correctly with **I** or **me**.

Example: You and _____ loved the tour.
You and I loved the tour.

6. The tour was thrilling for Bill and _____.
7. He and _____ learned about Washington, D.C.
8. The guide walked along with him and _____.
9. He took other tourists and _____ around the White House.
10. Bill and _____ had discussed the city.
11. The happiest visitors were he and _____.
12. My friends and _____ saw the Smithsonian.
13. That museum was interesting to the other tourists and _____.
14. _____ toured the White House with my class.
15. The monitors were Kate and _____.
16. Badges were given to Bill and _____.
17. John and _____ had a wonderful time.
18. Washington was very impressive to Bill and _____.
19. My friend and _____ shook hands with a guard.
20. At night, Tim and _____ were tired but happy.

Extra Practice, page 321

WRITING APPLICATION An Article

Write an article about a place you have visited with a friend or relative. What did you do there? Whom did you meet? Describe some of the experiences you shared with your companion. Exchange articles with a partner. Check for the correct use of *I* and *me* in each other's writing.

5 POSSESSIVE PRONOUNS

A **possessive pronoun** is a pronoun that shows *who* or *what* owns something. A possessive pronoun can take the place of a possessive noun. Sometimes possessive pronouns come before a noun.

Some possessive pronouns can stand by themselves. They can replace nouns in a sentence.

Possessive Pronouns

Possessive Pronouns with Nouns		**Possessive Pronouns That Stand Alone**	
my	*My* book is good.	mine	The desk is *mine*.
your	*Your* kitten is tiny.	yours	*Yours* is gray.
his	*His* dog is brown.	his	The dog is *his*.
her	*Her* train is late.	hers	The ticket is *hers*.
its	*Its* purpose is clear.	its	*Its* is clear.
our	*Our* house is quiet.	ours	*Ours* is noisy.
your	Where is *your* friend?	yours	Where is *yours*?
their	*Their* trip was fun.	theirs	*Theirs* was fun.

Guided Practice

Tell which word in each sentence is a possessive pronoun.

Example: Several books about space are on my desk. *my*

1. Our space program is Martin's favorite topic.
2. His ambition is to explore outer space.
3. The model spaceship is mine.
4. Space travel is my destiny.
5. Mars is ours!

?! THINK

■ How can I use possessive pronouns correctly?

REMEMBER

- The pronouns *my*, *your*, *his*, *her*, *its*, *our*, and *their* come before nouns.
- The pronouns *mine*, *yours*, *his*, *hers*, *its*, *ours*, and *theirs* can stand alone.

GRAMMAR

More Practice

A. Write each sentence, using the correct possessive pronoun from the pair in parentheses.

Example: Molly designed (her, hers) space suit.
Molly designed her space suit.

6. Joel and Kim built (their, theirs) spaceship.
7. The idea for the spaceship was (my, mine).
8. We used (my, mine) bicycle for spare parts.
9. They asked (their, theirs) father for nails.
10. I brought (my, mine) telescope.
11. We each had (our, ours) favorite star.
12. Which one is (your, yours)?

B. Write each sentence. Replace the underlined word or words with the correct possessive pronoun.

Example: <u>Donald's</u> drawing shows the rings of Saturn.
His drawing shows the rings of Saturn.

13. <u>Jill's</u> favorite planet is Mars.
14. Pluto is <u>Eddie's</u>.
15. <u>Mars's</u> nickname is "the red planet."
16. The teacher praised <u>Sam and Pete's</u> project.
17. <u>Maria and Yolanda's</u> was wonderful, too.
18. The class admired <u>the one belonging to me</u>.
19. I liked <u>Molly's</u>.
20. The best poster was <u>Ted and Ann's</u>.

Extra Practice, page 322

WRITING APPLICATION A Description

Write a description of your favorite planet. Have a partner circle the possessive pronouns in your writing.

GRAMMAR

6 USING POSSESSIVE PRONOUNS

As you know, a possessive pronoun shows *who* or *what* owns something. Possessive pronouns never have an apostrophe (').

Remember, some possessive pronouns come before nouns. Possessive pronouns can also replace a noun.

Your bat is broken. **Yours** is broken.

Notice that a possessive pronoun can show ownership of one or more person, place, or thing.

Our game is tomorrow. **Ours** is Saturday.
Theirs are Sunday, Tuesday, and Thursday.

Guided Practice

Tell which possessive pronoun completes each sentence correctly.

Example: We show each other (our, ours) games. *our*

1. It is time for (our, ours) demonstration.
2. The tennis racket is (her, hers).
3. Sheila and Rene brought (their, theirs) from home.
4. Pete does not use (their, theirs) rackets.
5. He prefers (our, ours).

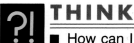

?! **THINK**

- How can I use a possessive pronoun to show ownership?

REMEMBER

- Possessive pronouns can come before nouns or stand alone.
- Possessive pronouns can show ownership of one or more person, place, or thing.

GRAMMAR

More Practice

Write each sentence. Choose the possessive pronoun from the pair in parentheses that completes each sentence correctly.

Example: Mark traded his racket for (my, mine).
Mark traded his racket for mine.

6. You explained the rules of (your, yours) game.
7. Betty explains the rules of (her, hers).
8. Sheila and Mark demonstrate (their, theirs) skills.
9. (Your, Yours) game is difficult.
10. That football is (our, ours).
11. The one in the locker is (your, yours).
12. I described (my, mine) favorite sport.
13. (Our, Ours) jungle gym is fun.
14. Sue and Dave practice (their, theirs) gymnastics.
15. You explain (your, yours) favorite stunts.
16. Lorna shares (her, hers) dance routine with us.
17. Sandy and Paul practice (their, theirs) all day.
18. I demonstrate (my, mine).
19. What will (your, yours) be?
20. (Our, Ours) is fun for everyone.

Extra Practice, page 323

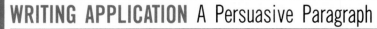

WRITING APPLICATION A Persuasive Paragraph

Write a paragraph that persuades your classmates to learn your favorite game. Write at least three reasons why this is your favorite game. Exchange paragraphs with a classmate. Have your partner underline the possessive pronouns in your paragraph.

7 PRONOUN CONTRACTIONS

A **contraction** is a shortened form of two words. Subject pronouns can be combined with some verbs to form contractions.

Some Common Contractions with Pronouns

Pronoun + Verb	Contraction	Pronoun + Verb	Contraction
I am	I'm	I have	I've
you are	you're	you have	you've
she is	she's	she has	she's
he is	he's	he has	he's
it is	it's	it has	it's
we are	we're	we have	we've
they are	they're	they have	they've
I will	I'll	I had	I'd
you will	you'll	you had	you'd
he will	he'll	he had	he'd
she will	she'll	she had	she'd
it will	it'll	it had	it'd

Guided Practice

Tell the contraction for each pair of words.

Example: I am *I'm*

1. they have
2. I will
3. she is
4. you will
5. we are

?! **THINK**

■ Where do I use an apostrophe in a contraction?

REMEMBER

- An **apostrophe** is used in place of the letter or letters that have been left out to form a contraction.

More Practice

A. Write the words from which the contraction in each sentence is formed.

Example: They're cooking a big meal for the holiday.
They're *They are*

6. We're having a holiday dinner with Grandma.
7. It's a festive occasion.
8. I'm looking forward to it.
9. She'll have a big turkey and trimmings.
10. She's inviting many people.
11. You'll eat two or three helpings.
12. I'll eat three or four!

B. Write the contraction for the underlined words in each sentence.

Example: I have bought some flowers for Grandma. *I've*

13. He is bringing the apples.
14. She will make a pie.
15. It will be delicious.
16. I am excited about the dinner.
17. She is an expert cook.
18. She will put the flowers on the table.
19. I will tie a ribbon around them.
20. They are my holiday present to her.

Extra Practice, Practice Plus, pages 324-326

WRITING APPLICATION An Invitation

Write an invitation to a friend for a holiday meal. Be sure to include the date, time, and place of the occasion. Your invitation will be informal, so feel free to use contractions. Circle the contractions.

GRAMMAR

8 USING *WE* AND *US* WITH NOUNS

You can use **we** and **us** with nouns to make your meaning clear. Remember that the subject pronoun *we* can be used with a noun or after forms of the verb *be*.

We students study journalism.
The editors of the paper are **we** students.

The object pronoun *us* can be used after action verbs or after words such as *to*, *for*, *with*, or *at*.

The teacher asked **us** writers for some ideas.
The principal gave the credit to **us** journalists.

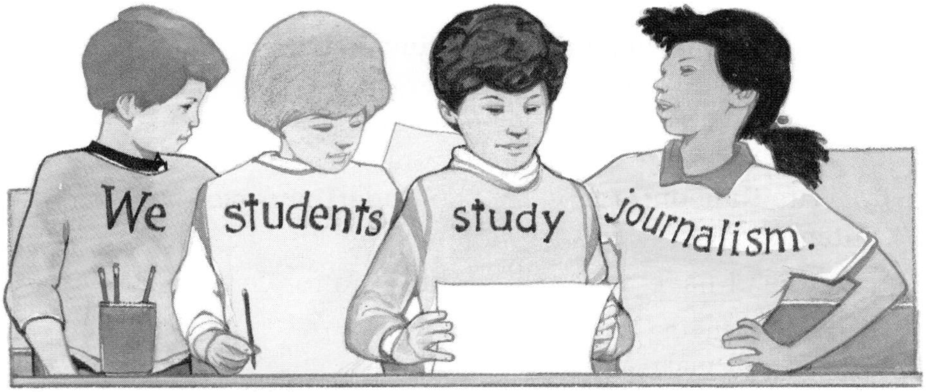

Guided Practice

Tell whether *we* or *us* completes each sentence correctly.

Example: Newspapers are important to (us, we) citizens.
us

1. (We, Us) students read the newspapers.
2. The papers tell the problems of (we, us) people.
3. (Us, We) fifth graders started a newspaper.
4. The project is fun for (we, us) journalists.
5. It teaches (we, us) students about events at school.

THINK

■ How can I decide whether to use *we* or *us* with nouns?

REMEMBER

- Use **we** with nouns after linking verbs.
- Use **us** with nouns after action verbs or prepositions.

More Practice

Write each sentence, using the correct word from the pair in parentheses.

Example: The teacher suggested a project for (we, us) writers. *The teacher suggested a project for us writers.*

6. (We, Us) students plan our articles carefully.
7. It is hard work for (we, us) writers.
8. (We, Us) journalists cover important events.
9. (We, Us) writers interview people.
10. Students speak to (we, us) journalists.
11. (We, Us) writers ask serious questions.
12. Many issues concern (we, us) students.
13. (We, Us) students need more typewriters.
14. Typewriters help (we, us) writers meet deadlines.
15. (We, Us) journalists use notebooks, too.
16. Some of (we, us) writers carry tape recorders.
17. (We, Us) artists make sketches for the paper.
18. Editors are grateful to (we, us) illustrators.
19. (We, Us) artists work closely with writers.
20. (We, Us) readers support the newpapers.

Extra Practice, page 327

WRITING APPLICATION A Statement of Opinion

Write a paragraph or a persuasive article that states your opinion of class parties. Include at least four reasons that support your position. Exchange your work with a partner. Circle **we** and **us** in each other's writing. Read aloud your partner's statement of opinion. Then discuss what makes the writing persuasive.

9 MECHANICS: More Comma Rules

Sometimes you name the person to whom you are speaking in a sentence. This is called a **noun in direct address**.

Clara, which holiday trip did you prefer?
I know, **Clara**, that you love the ocean.

➡ Use a comma or commas to set off a noun in direct address from the rest of the sentence.

You can begin a sentence with a word such as *well*, *oh*, *no*, or *yes*. These words are called **introductory words**.

Well, Cape Cod is lovely. **Yes**, I agree.

➡ Use a comma after an introductory word.

You may also use an introductory word and a noun in direct address in the same sentence.

Well, Clara, tell me more about the trip.

Guided Practice

Tell where to add a comma or commas in each sentence.

Example: Oh where are your photos? *comma after Oh*

1. You have a picture Terence of the beach at Truro.
2. Well this is a photograph of our hotel.
3. I stayed there last month Terence.
4. Oh Clara that is a coincidence!

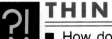

?! THINK

- How do I use commas to set off a noun in direct address or an introductory word?

REMEMBER

- Use a **comma** after an introductory word.
- Use a comma or commas to set off a noun in direct address.

More Practice

Write each sentence. Add a comma or commas where they are needed.

Example: Clara I had a wonderful trip. *Clara, I had a wonderful trip.*

5. Terence do you prefer lake or ocean beaches?
6. Well I loved our trip to Lake Charles.
7. Where is the lake Terence?
8. It is in Louisiana Clara.
9. Oh isn't the weather hot in Louisiana?
10. Yes Clara but I enjoy hot weather.
11. Terence what did you do there?
12. Well I swam in and boated on the lake.
13. Oh I cannot swim well yet Terence.
14. Have you taken lessons Clara?
15. No but I may sign up for a course soon.
16. Clara why do you prefer the ocean?
17. I like the breezes Terence on the shore.
18. Yes but the lake shore has shady trees.
19. Well is there a good breeze from the lake?
20. No I guess the ocean beach is cooler.

Extra Practice, page 328

WRITING APPLICATION A Dialogue

Write a dialogue that might take place between yourself and a friend about vacations. Your dialogue might contain interesting facts about places you have visited. Include nouns in direct address and introductory words in your dialogue. Have a partner circle the commas in your dialogue. Read aloud each other's dialogues.

GRAMMAR

10 VOCABULARY BUILDING: Prefixes

There are different ways to change the meaning of a word. One way to change the meaning of a word is to add other word parts to the base word. A **prefix** is a word part added to the beginning of a base word. A prefix changes the meaning of the word to which it is added.

Some Common Prefixes

Prefix	Meaning
re	again, back
un	not, the opposite of
dis	not, the opposite of
mis	bad or wrong, badly or wrongly
im	not, without, in, into
in	not, without, in, into
il, ir	not, without
non	not, the opposite of, without
pre	before, in preparation for
post	after, later

Guided Practice

Identify the prefix and give the meaning of each word below.

Example: unhappy *un* *not happy, sad*

1. refund
2. imperfect
3. misuse
4. nonsense
5. illogical

?! THINK

■ How can I figure out the meaning of a word which contains a prefix?

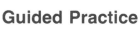

REMEMBER

- A **prefix** is a word part added to the beginning of a base word.
- A prefix changes the meaning of the base word to which it is added.

More Practice

Write each underlined word. Draw a line under the prefix and write the meaning of the word.

Example: The weather became unpleasant.
unpleasant *not pleasant*

6. On a boat trip, one must take every precaution.
7. We make sure our old boat is refinished.
8. We are unafraid of hard work.
9. Some sailors are inconsiderate.
10. They misjudge the dangers of the sea.
11. We review our maps and charts.
12. A lost crew is most unfortunate.
13. This boat is a postwar model.
14. Eric considers the boat unsinkable.
15. Our captain firmly disagrees.
16. In choppy water we rethink our voyage.
17. On the high seas, our engine is irreplaceable.
18. High speeds become impossible.
19. We cannot refuel at sea, either.
20. The captain returns the boat to the shore.

Extra Practice, page 329

WRITING APPLICATION A Report

Write a report on a trip you have taken or planned to take. Describe in detail what you found interesting and enjoyable about the trip. In your report, include some of the prefixes you have learned. When you have finished, exchange reports with a partner. Underline the prefixes in each other's writing.

GRAMMAR AND WRITING CONNECTION

Using Pronouns Correctly

You know that there are many ways to make your writing clear and precise. You can use pronouns to refer to nouns to avoid unnecessary repetition. You will want to be sure that the pronoun you choose refers clearly to the noun that comes before it.

Look at the sentence below.

I read books about careers, and **it** is interesting.

You may have trouble understanding to which word *it* refers. Now look at another sentence.

I read an interesting book about careers, and **it** contained important information.

The word *it* in the second part of the sentence refers correctly to the word *book*.

Working Together

COOPERATIVE LEARNING

With your class, discuss how to use pronouns correctly. Supply the correct pronoun in place of each incorrect pronoun in the sentences below.

Example: The children ran toward its parents.
The children ran toward their parents.

1. A bird landed on their perch.
2. The policeman found the little girl and brought us home.
3. Maria saw Andy and told them the news.
4. Andy met his friends and spoke to it about the little girl.
5. Andy's friends knew the little girl and its parents.

Revising Sentences

Kelly wrote these sentences about careers. Help Kelly to make her sentences correct. Be sure that in each revised sentence, the pronoun refers clearly to the noun that comes before it.

6. I chose the book because they was good.
7. The author explains their research.
8. The author knows a great deal about their subject.
9. Some careers require that students complete his work.
10. Students can understand the job market if he tries.
11. The markets are huge; it include many jobs.
12. People should write more books on this subject; he will sell many copies.
13. The book said that students should explore many types of jobs; he will be successful.
14. Students talked about his ideas.
15. My father and Jim told me about his new plans, too.

WRITER AT WORK

Brainstorm to think of a career or job that interests you. Write a paragraph that persuades other students to learn more about this job or career. When you have finished, check your writing carefully to be sure each pronoun refers correctly to the noun that comes before it.

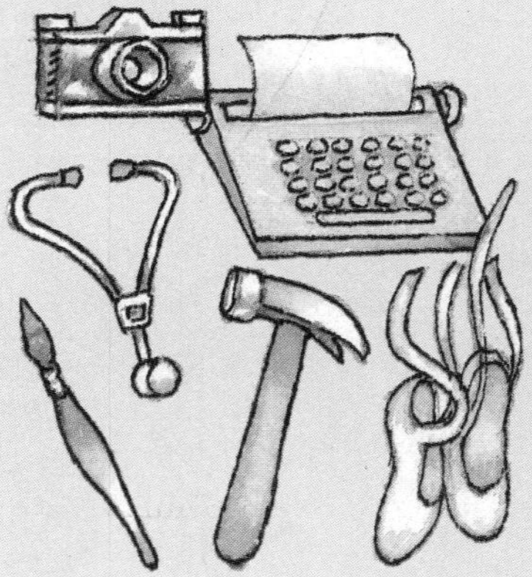

UNIT CHECKUP

LESSON 1 **What Is a Pronoun?** (page 292) Write each sentence. Underline each pronoun.

1. Paul asks his friend for help.
2. She is a good history student.
3. The girl studies with him.
4. They prepare for a test.
5. The teacher is pleased with them.

LESSONS 2-3 **Subject Pronouns and Object Pronouns** (pages 294–297) Write each sentence. Draw a line under each pronoun and write whether it is a subject or an object pronoun.

6. The game was a thrill for me.
7. Dad gave us a ride home.
8. He stopped at a restaurant.
9. We had a delicious meal.
10. The biggest eater was I!

LESSON 4 **Using *I* and *me* Correctly** (page 298) Write each sentence. Complete the sentence with **I** or **me**.

11. Math is a hard subject for _____.
12. _____ must study harder.
13. The teacher gave _____ extra help.
14. Tom and _____ passed the test.
15. The highest scorers were Dana and _____.

LESSONS 5-6 **Possessive Pronouns** (pages 300–303) Write each sentence using the correct possessive pronoun.

16. Wayne goes to (our, ours) dentist.
17. (My, Mine) checkup was good.
18. Julie takes care of (her, hers) teeth.
19. We must take care of (our, ours).
20. (Their, Theirs) teeth are strong.

LESSON 7

Pronoun Contractions (page 304). Form a contraction from each pair of words. Write the contraction.

21. We are
22. It is
23. He has
24. She will
25. I am

LESSON 8

Using *we* and *us* with Nouns (page 306) Write each sentence. Complete the sentence correctly with **we** or **us**. Remember to capitalize the first word of a sentence.

26. _____ tourists like to travel.
27. It is work for _____ salespeople.
28. Bicycles are used by _____ mail carriers.
29. _____ firefighters have trucks.
30. The slowest are _____ walkers.

LESSON 9

Mechanics: More Comma Rules (page 308) Write each sentence. Add commas where they are needed.

31. Nancy I read your report on water pollution.
32. Well I agree with your arguments.
33. Yes Jeffrey pollution is a serious problem.
34. We all depend on our water system Nancy.
35. I read your report Jeffrey on pollution.

LESSON 10

Vocabulary Building: Prefixes (page 310) Write the meaning of each underlined word with a prefix.

36. Laziness is unacceptable here.
37. Injustice is also frowned upon.
38. He was treated with disrespect.
39. Do not be impatient with us.
40. You will not be misunderstood.

41-45.

Writing Application: Comma Usage (page 308) The following letter contains 5 errors with commas. Rewrite the paragraph correctly.

Barbara I have considered your problem carefully. Yes you should make a weekly budget. Your allowance Barbara should cover your needs. Well sometimes you may require some extra money.

ENRICHMENT

TELEPHONE

Play this game with your classmates. One student begins a story with a sentence using a pronoun. The next student continues the story by adding a sentence that tells to whom or what the pronoun refers. Keep playing until the story comes to a satisfying end.

QUAKER QUOTES

The Quakers use different pronouns than we do. For *you*, they substitute *thee* and *thou*, and for *your* and *yours*, they use *thy* and *thine*. Rewrite these sentences as a Quaker might say them.

I'd like to thank you.
Your help was appreciated.
I'd like to help you with yours.

ILLEGAL EAGLES

Words with prefixes often lend themselves to puns. For example, *illegal* can also mean a sick bird ("ill eagle"). Have a "prefix pun" contest in your class for the best prefix puns and illustrations. Use your dictionary to look up more words that contain prefixes.

LIFE STORIES

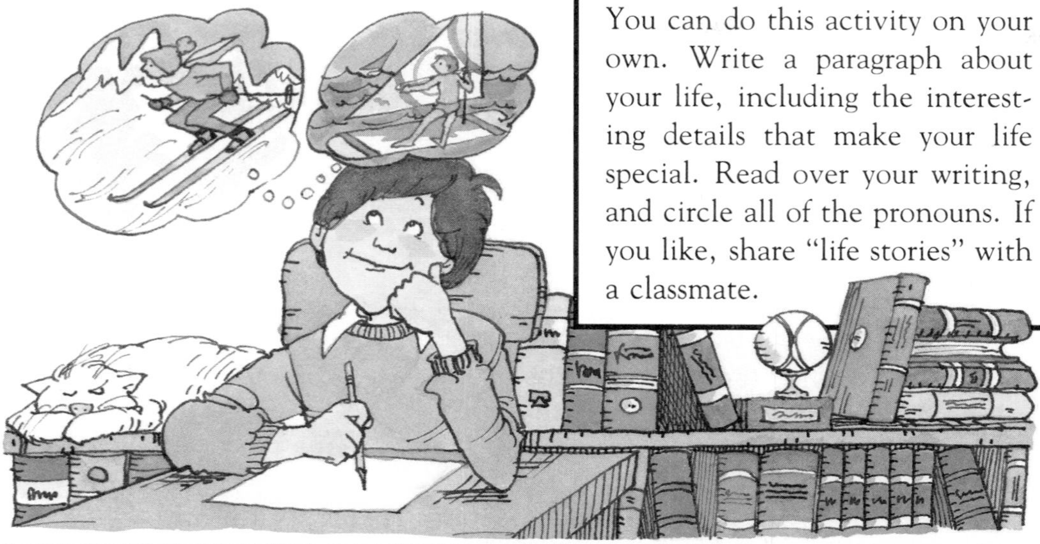

You can do this activity on your own. Write a paragraph about your life, including the interesting details that make your life special. Read over your writing, and circle all of the pronouns. If you like, share "life stories" with a classmate.

Debate Team

Play this game with two teams. Write down some topics for debate, and vote on the one you like best. Start the debate. As you argue for or against an idea, use some words with prefixes to make your point. For instance, if one debater says, "It is fair to hold secret school elections," you might answer, "It is unfair to hold secret school elections." Have the teacher or another student keep track of the number of words with prefixes each debater uses.

EXTRA PRACTICE

Three levels of practice

What Is a Pronoun? (Page 292)

LEVEL **A.** Write each sentence. Draw a line under the pronoun.

1. Sue and I go to the beach often.
2. She and Tim play a game together.
3. They throw a football back and forth.
4. It sails over Jeff's head.
5. He looks up in surprise.
6. The beach is beautiful to us.
7. We enjoy the water and the cool breeze.
8. You love this sunny weather.
9. Mother tells me about the beaches in Spain.

LEVEL **B.** Write each sentence. Draw a line under each pronoun. Then, write whether the pronoun is a **subject pronoun** or an **object pronoun.**

10. I pass a bowl of fruit to Grandmother.
11. She sits in a lawn chair.
12. The girls wave to her.
13. She speaks to Grandfather.
14. Grandmother gives him a pair of sunglasses.
15. He reads the newspaper slowly each day.
16. Janet and Kate brought books with them.
17. They read until the sun goes down.

LEVEL **C.** Write each sentence using a correct pronoun.

18. The children's grandmother supervises ______.
19. ______ lost a towel somewhere on the beach.
20. Dana buys ______ a snack from the vendor.
21. Janet and ______ compare books with one another.
22. ______ are both about horses.
23. ______ enjoyed this day at the beach.
24. ______ should come to the beach next time.
25. You would have fun with ______.

EXTRA PRACTICE

Three levels of practice

Subject Pronouns (page 294)

LEVEL **A.** Write each sentence. Draw a line under each subject pronoun.

1. I am excited about the contest results.
2. We look forward to the prize.
3. The winners were Sara and I.
4. We went to the circus.
5. I liked the clowns best.
6. She ate too much popcorn.
7. She and I met the ringmaster.
8. We wrote a report for the class.
9. It was about the experience at the circus.

LEVEL **B.** Write each sentence. Replace the underlined word or words with the correct subject pronoun.

10. Jill bought some souvenirs.
11. The acrobats were graceful.
12. The circus is a thrilling place.
13. Tito and Frank fed peanuts to the elephants.
14. A man applauded wildly.
15. Mrs. Henderson was especially impressed.
16. Sara and I had never seen so many animals.
17. Sara is saving money for another visit to the show.

LEVEL **C.** Write each sentence. Complete the sentence with a correct subject pronoun.

18. ______ preferred the acrobats to the animals.
19. ______ took a picture of the lions.
20. ______ were amazed by the elephants.
21. ______ was an exciting show.
22. ______ had the best time!
23. When can ______ go again?
24. Jill and ______ bought posters of the event.
25. ______ and ______ loved the clowns.

EXTRA PRACTICE

Three levels of practice

Object Pronouns (page 296)

LEVEL A. Write each sentence. Draw a line under the object pronoun.

1. Airplanes have made life easier for us.
2. On Grandma's birthday the family visits her.
3. Father carries some gifts with him.
4. The flight attendant brought me a magazine.
5. Travel is a thrill for me.
6. This row has a seat for you.
7. Share this magazine with her.
8. Father brought a newspaper with him.
9. Mother gave him a book, too.

LEVEL B. Write each sentence, replacing the underlined word or words with the correct pronoun.

10. The flight seemed pleasant to <u>Father and June</u>.
11. The seat was too small for <u>Uncle Dave</u>.
12. June and Denise slept during <u>the flight</u>.
13. I like to fly with <u>Mother</u>.
14. I played cards with <u>Uncle Dave and Father</u>.
15. I traded seats with <u>Father</u>.
16. Father told <u>Uncle Dave</u> about an article in the newspaper.
17. Mother covered <u>June</u> with a blanket.

LEVEL C. Write each sentence. Draw a line under the pronoun. Then, write whether the pronoun is a **subject pronoun** or an **object pronoun**.

18. Dad explained flight patterns to us.
19. He has experience as a pilot.
20. We have never been afraid of airplanes.
21. The journey is a treat for me.
22. The pilot gave us a tour of the plane.
23. Mother and I enjoyed the movie.
24. The trip was a little long for her.
25. The first passengers off the plane were she and I.

EXTRA PRACTICE

Three levels of practice

Using *I* and *me* Correctly (page 298)

LEVEL **A.** Write each sentence, using the correct pronoun.

1. Terry and (I, me) joined the school newspaper.
2. It was a great opportunity for Terry and (I, me).
3. The first writers were he and (I, me).
4. The editor sent a photographer with Terry and (I, me).
5. Terry and (I, me) finished our stories.
6. The editor congratulated Terry and (I, me).
7. The artist and (I, me) worked together.
8. She and (I, me) designed the newspaper.
9. The principal gave an award to her and (I, me).

LEVEL **B.** Write each sentence. Complete each sentence with **I** or **me.**

10. My father bought a typewriter for _____.
11. _____ always type my articles.
12. The research is hard work for _____.
13. The author of the article was _____.
14. The football coach encouraged _____.
15. _____ had written a story about the team.
16. The coach praised _____.
17. The happiest writer was _____.

LEVEL **C.** Write each sentence, using the correct words from the pair in parentheses.

18. The sports writers were (Charles and I, I and Charles).
19. A new assignment was given to (Sue and me, me and Sue).
20. (I, me) believe in responsible journalism.
21. Honesty is important to (I, me).
22. The editor gave (I, me) an exciting assignment.
23. (Cora and I, I and Cora) were working together again!
24. This is a challenge for (you and I, you and me).
25. (Charles and I, Charles and me) will work with Cora today.

EXTRA PRACTICE

Three levels of practice

Possessive Pronouns (page 300)

LEVEL **A.** Write each sentence. Draw a line under the possessive pronoun.

1. Our school is really special.
2. The best teachers are mine.
3. Their classes are always interesting.
4. My music class is wonderful.
5. Georgette also likes hers.
6. Her teacher is from Peru.
7. Your new teacher arrives today.
8. Yours will be an exciting week.
9. Our first music class is today.

LEVEL **B.** Write each sentence, using the correct possessive pronoun from the pair in parentheses.

10. Debra and Joan wrote a story about (their, theirs) class.
11. The article in the paper is (their, theirs).
12. The photograph is (my, mine).
13. I will write (my, mine) own article.
14. It will describe (our, ours) school.
15. I will interview my friends and (your, yours).
16. The editor gave the article (her, hers) approval.
17. (Hers, Her) is a demanding position.

LEVEL **C.** Write each sentence. Replace the underlined word or words with the correct possessive pronoun.

18. <u>Mary's</u> favorite class is chemistry.
19. The longest paper is <u>Frank's</u>.
20. <u>The one I did</u> was the best experiment.
21. The teacher appreciates <u>Mary and Frank's</u> work.
22. <u>John's</u> favorite science is biology.
23. <u>We students'</u> most interesting hours are spent in school.
24. Gail works all afternoon on <u>Gail's</u> project.
25. <u>Gail's</u> is the most complicated experiment of all.

EXTRA PRACTICE

GRAMMAR

Three levels of practice

Using Possessive Pronouns (page 302)

LEVEL **A.** Write each sentence. Draw a line under the possessive pronoun.

1. Our car broke down in the mountains.
2. Ours is an old car.
3. Mr. Charles opened his door.
4. Roberta and Sara opened their windows.
5. Roberta took this photograph with her camera.
6. It shows my surprise at the beautiful view.
7. Sara and I could not believe our eyes.
8. Mine were wide open with delight!
9. Roberta and Sara said the same about theirs.

LEVEL **B.** Write each sentence. Use a possessive pronoun in place of each underlined group of words.

10. These are <u>the binoculars belonging to me.</u>
11. The picture shows <u>the expression belonging to you.</u>
12. Nadine loves <u>Nadine's</u> new hobby.
13. This photograph was taken with <u>the camera belonging to her</u>.
14. <u>The snapshots belonging to them</u> are the clearest.
15. Fred can see <u>the house belonging to him.</u>
16. <u>Fred's</u> is a big house with a slate roof.
17. The house is two miles north of <u>Nadine's.</u>

LEVEL **C.** Write each sentence. Complete each sentence with a correct possessive pronoun.

18. _____ sister describes the beautiful waterfall.
19. _____ friends admire the photographs of the trip.
20. Donna expresses _____ surprise.
21. Donna's parents took _____ vacation in those mountains.
22. Brett shows Sara _____ post card.
23. Mr. Charles sent it from _____ trip.
24. _____ was a wonderful vacation.
25. Wanda is saving money for _____.

EXTRA PRACTICE

Three levels of practice

Pronoun Contractions (page 304)

LEVEL A. Write the contraction for each pair of words.

1. they are
2. I am
3. we would
4. you have
5. she is
6. he will
7. you had
8. they had
9. we will

LEVEL B. Write each sentence. Draw a line under the contraction. Write the words from which the contraction is formed. Remember to capitalize the first word of a sentence.

10. You can tell it's springtime.
11. She's wearing a new dress.
12. We're having a picnic.
13. I'll tell the other students.
14. You've chosen a pretty park.
15. We'll enjoy the day.
16. You've brought your sister.
17. She's an excellent athlete.

LEVEL C. Write each sentence. Form a contraction from the underlined words.

18. <u>You had</u> invited a friend to the picnic.
19. <u>He will</u> be there with his baseball glove.
20. <u>It is</u> time for a celebration.
21. <u>You have</u> made a cake!
22. <u>They will</u> really appreciate this.
23. <u>We would</u> like some cake, too.
24. <u>You are</u> ready for the meal.
25. <u>We have</u> planned a perfect day.

PRACTICE + PLUS

GRAMMAR

Three levels of additional practice for a difficult skill

Pronoun Contractions (page 304)

LEVEL **A.** Write each sentence. Draw a line under the contraction in the sentence. Write the words from which the contraction is formed.

1. We'll exchange books today.
2. We've both read our books already.
3. I've enjoyed the adventure story.
4. You'd like it, too.
5. We've gotten familiar with the characters.
6. They've become just like real friends.
7. You'll love the hero.
8. She's the bravest girl in the story.
9. I'm certain about that!
10. She'd proved herself courageous many times.
11. I've great admiration for that character.
12. You'd lent some good books to my brother.
13. He's told me about several of them.
14. I'll give two other books to you.
15. They'll surprise and delight you.
16. We'd all read many books this year.
17. Now, we've borrowed more books from the library.
18. It's just a short walk from the school.

LEVEL **B.** Write each sentence. Form a contraction from the underlined words in the sentence.

19. You had described this character to me.
20. We have met this hero in other novels by the same author.
21. He had written several other adventure stories.
22. They have all been wonderful books.
23. I had discussed the plots with my friends.
24. They will tell you about the other books, too.
25. You will find this story fascinating.
26. I would not spoil the suspense for you.
27. You would never forgive me!

PRACTICE + PLUS

28. <u>We are</u> both due for some excitement.
29. <u>I am</u> planning to read your book, too.
30. <u>I have</u> respect for your opinions about books.
31. <u>You had</u> told me your list of favorite authors.
32. <u>We have</u> some of the books at home.
33. <u>They have</u> interesting plots and characters.
34. <u>We would</u> have enough books for the whole summer.

LEVEL **C.** Write each sentence. Complete the sentence correctly with a contraction that makes sense.

35. ______ collected a wonderful set of mystery novels.
36. ______ enjoy a visit to your private library.
37. ______ received many books from your father.
38. ______ been a mystery fan for a long time.
39. ______ shared your collection with friends.
40. ______ built their own book collections, too.
41. ______ a fascinating hobby for anyone.
42. Now, ______ all bought dozens of novels.
43. ______ also developed an interest in biographies.
44. ______ chosen nonfiction books about fascinating people.
45. ______ studied the lives of some famous artists.
46. ______ often been more interesting than characters in fiction.
47. ______ traded mystery novels and biographies this week.
48. ______ tell me your opinion of the biographies.
49. ______ tell you my thoughts about the mystery books.
50. ______ learn about every type of book.

EXTRA PRACTICE

GRAMMAR

Three levels of practice

Using *we* and *us* with Nouns (page 306)

LEVEL **A.** Write each sentence. Draw a line under the pronoun. Write whether it is a **subject pronoun** or an **object pronoun**.

1. We children love this new pet.
2. The cat is a treat for us animal lovers.
3. We Smiths disagreed at first.
4. We boys wanted a dog.
5. Mother agreed with us girls.
6. The winners were we Smiths.
7. The cat is a good companion for us children.
8. We vacationers bring the cat in the car.
9. The cat sits quietly with us passengers.

LEVEL **B.** Write each sentence, using the correct pronoun.

10. (We, Us) girls named the cat Sam.
11. The name seemed silly to (we, us) boys.
12. The boys finally agreed with (we, us) girls.
13. (We, Us) children also got a turtle.
14. The turtle was given to (we, us) Smiths by Jeff.
15. (We, Us) Smiths now have enough pets.
16. Mother gives chores to (we, us) children.
17. (We, Us) pet fans have many responsibilities!

LEVEL **C.** Write each sentence. Complete each sentence with **we** or **us**.

18. _____ students study the turtle.
19. The cat is fed by _____ girls.
20. The turtle's bowl is cleaned by _____ boys.
21. _____ children take good care of our pets.
22. Turtles are interesting to _____ scientists.
23. _____ children are quite content.
24. Animals are a fascinating topic for _____ researchers.
25. _____ girls write a composition about the cat.

EXTRA PRACTICE

Three levels of practice

Mechanics: More Comma Rules (page 308)

LEVEL **A.** Write each sentence. Draw one line under each comma that sets off an introductory word. Draw two lines under each comma that sets off a noun in direct address.

1. Mom, where are you going now?
2. Oh, I am going out to the garden.
3. I must do some work in this sunny weather, Glenn.
4. Let me help you, Mom.
5. Yes, there is quite a bit of work for us.
6. Glenn, do you have a pair of old gloves?
7. Well, yes, I have my painting gloves here.
8. Oh, Glenn, the weather forecaster predicts rain!
9. No, he forecast rain for tomorrow, Mom.

LEVEL **B.** Write each sentence. Add commas where they are needed.

10. Denise what are your plans for today?
11. Well I must shop for a new jacket this morning.
12. Sylvia can you go with me?
13. Oh yes I am free all day.
14. I heard Denise about a sale at our favorite store.
15. Yes Sylvia I saw the advertisement in the newspaper.
16. Do you like long coats Denise?
17. No I need a short jacket for the cold weather.

LEVEL **C.** Write each sentence. Complete each sentence with an introductory word or a noun in direct address.

18. _____ please come downtown with me now.
19. We should volunteer for Clean Park Day _____.
20. _____ do we sign up this week?
21. _____ _____ we must do it today.
22. Clean Park Day is important for the neighborhood _____.
23. _____ people of all ages participate in the work.
24. _____ I worked in the park last year _____.
25. _____ we all achieved beautiful results.

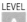

EXTRA PRACTICE

GRAMMAR

Three levels of practice

Vocabulary Building: Prefixes (page 310)

LEVEL **A.** Draw a line under each prefix in the words below.

1. disjointed
2. misplace
3. illegible
4. incredible
5. irrational
6. precaution
7. nonsense
8. unsuitable
9. postscript

LEVEL **B.** Write each underlined word. Find the correct definition of the word in a dictionary.

10. Researchers deal with common misconceptions each day.
11. Old ideas often fall into disfavor in later years.
12. Postoperative care is important for patients.
13. Ideas about health are reviewed regularly.
14. Old-fashioned theories were often irrational.
15. Scientists exchange information unselfishly.
16. New theories are unveiled at yearly conferences.
17. The age and background of a scientist are unimportant.

LEVEL **C.** Write a definition for the underlined word in each sentence. You may use a dictionary, if necessary.

18. One researcher can disbelieve the ideas of another.
19. The contributions of many scientists are irreplaceable.
20. Some speeches are unremarkable.
21. Strange ideas are not illegal!
22. The listeners must not prejudge the speakers.
23. All input should be welcome at the conference.
24. Immature ideas need time for growth.
25. Scientists often reevaluate their work.

WRITING

UNIT 10

Writing Persuasive Paragraphs

Read the quotation and look at the picture on the opposite page. The quotation was written by Marjorie Weinman Sharmat, the author of a story you will read in this unit. Why might the author have wanted to be a detective or a lion tamer? What is your opinion?

When you write to persuade, you will want to present facts to support your opinion. You will want to persuade your audience to feel the way that you feel.

Focus Persuasive writing encourages the audience to share in the writer's beliefs.

What would be a good topic for persuasive writing? You can use the story and the photographs that follow to find ideas for writing.

THEME: *VIEWS*

My earliest ambition was to become a writer or a detective or a lion tamer.

—Marjorie Weinman Sharmat

LITERATURE

Reading Like a Writer

Think about an idea that excites or interests you. How might you try to interest someone else in this idea?

Maggie and Thad are both excited about running for class president, but neither is sure how to make a good campaign speech.

As you read the selection, look for the ways Maggie and Thad try to gain the confidence of their classmates. Look for words and phrases that show what the author thinks of the candidates' speeches.

From

Maggie Marmelstein ★★★★★★★ for ★★★★★★★ President

by Marjorie Weinman Sharmat

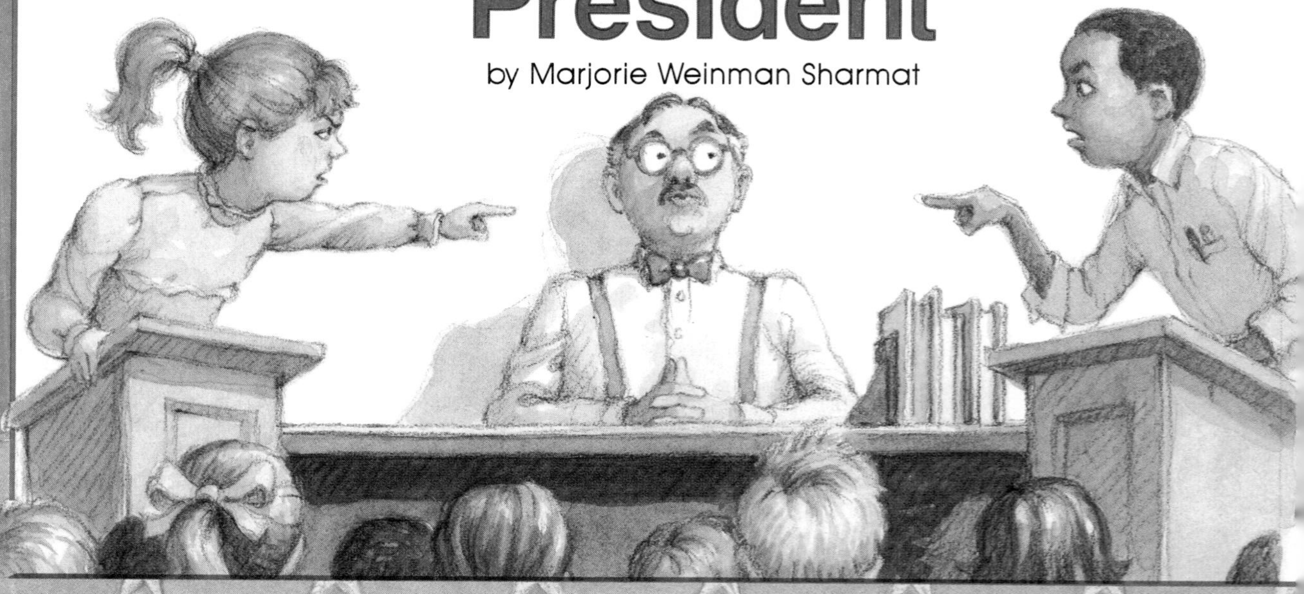

Mr. Krickleman rose and said, "Members of the sixth grade, this afternoon we will hear a debate between the two candidates for the office of class president: Maggie Marmelstein and Thad Smith. They will be introduced by their campaign managers: Noah Moore for Maggie and Henry Emery for Thad."

Suddenly Ralph and Jody stood up. Ralph was holding his guitar, which he had just taken out of its case. He stuck a collapsible cowboy hat, which he had swiftly removed from his pocket and opened, onto his head. He started to play and sing:

Notice that Ralph's song is supposed to convince the sixth-graders that Maggie can help them solve their problems.

Well, I'm walkin' down a lonely road,
And I'm cryin' in a dream,
And I'm needin' help with problems,
And I think of Marmelstein.

'Cause I'm tired of walkin' lonely,
And I'm tired of cryin', too.
So I'm askin' Maggie Marmelstein
To see what she can do.

Henry got up from his chair, almost knocking it over. "I object!" he said. "This is a debate, not a musical show. I know at least six people who can sing and dance for Thad Smith. And do imitations, too, and one can juggle three Frisbees at a time and one can play songs with a spoon and a glass. And I want equal time for them to do their thing for Thad Smith."

Mr. Krickleman spoke. "Henry is right to object. However, since the song did not deal with any issues, it won't affect the debate. But, just to be completely fair, after the debate anyone wishing to perform in behalf of Thad Smith is entitled to three minutes. Now, will the campaign managers please introduce their candidates. Henry, as long as you are on your feet, you may go first."

Henry walked to the center of the stage. "Thad Smith is," he said.

There was a long pause.

"Is Thad Smith," Henry continued. "And who is Thad Smith? He's a great guy. The first time I ever saw this great guy, I said to myself, 'This is a great guy.' Everything about him right away was great. All great. All right away. And when somebody is a great guy, what else can I say about him except one word: president. When I look at Thad, this great guy, I think President Smith. *President* Thad Smith. That sounds right to me. Doesn't that sound right to you?"

A few kids in the audience yelled at the same time, "Right!" "Wrong!" "Right!" "Wrong!"

Henry went on. "I now introduce a great guy, our future president, Thad Smith!"

There was some applause and whistling.

Thad stood up, waved and sat down.

Noah got up and walked to the center of the stage.

This is a good example of persuasive language. The speaker draws the audience to his side.

"My fellow sixth graders," he said, "this election is not a popularity contest. The president of the sixth grade should be chosen on the basis of what *she*—or he—can do for the sixth grade. Is everybody in the sixth grade happy?"

"NO!" some kids shouted.

"Could life be better in the sixth grade? Do we need changes? Can we improve the way things are done?"

"Yes, yes, yes!" cried the audience.

"The sixth grade needs help," said Noah. "And my candidate, Maggie Marmelstein, will help the sixth grade. And here she is—my candidate and yours—Maggie Marmelstein!"

There was some applause and whistling. Maggie couldn't tell whether there was more or less than for Thad.

Maggie stood up, waved and sat down.

Mr. Krickleman said, "We will now flip a coin to see which candidate speaks first." He held up a nickel. "Heads or tails?" he asked.

"Heads," said Maggie and Thad.

Everyone laughed and clapped.

Noah said, "My candidate is willing to speak first or second. It's the words and not their order that's important."

Thad stood up. "I'll let Maggie go first or second."

"No special favors," said Maggie, "I can win on my own."

Mr. Krickleman said, "Will one of you please start the debate."

Maggie stood up. "I should be president because I'll be a better president than Thad Smith, who sometimes isn't very good at all, especially in his **WRITTEN WORK**."

What do you think of Maggie's choice and ordering of reasons? Is this information persuasive?

"Please be careful of character assassination, Maggie," said Mr. Krickleman. "Thad, would you care to comment on your written work as it pertains to the presidency?"

"Yes, I would care to comment on that," said Thad. "On that very thing, my written work. In that very way that you mentioned. Yes, I would. Well, my written work is, um, splendiferous."

"What's that?" said someone in the audience. "Wow!"

"Big words. I don't use big words," said Maggie. "Why, I've got a campaign manager, Noah, who knows more big words than every kid in this room put together. But I wouldn't borrow any big words, because a presidential candidate shouldn't be a borrower of words or anything."

Thad spoke. "Well, all I borrow are pencils, and money for the ice-cream machine. I'll be a good president."

"Why?" asked Mr. Krickleman. "Discuss the issues, please."

"So will I," said Maggie.

"Issues, issues," said Mr. Krickleman.

"I'll be better than you," said Maggie.

"No, I'll be better than you," said Thad.

"**ISSUES! ISSUES!**" called Mr. Krickleman..

"I will be a fair and honest president," said Maggie.

"I will be a fair and honest president," said Thad.

"Details, details," called Mr. Krickleman.

Mr. Krickleman wants the candidates to state some facts. Do you think he has been impressed by this debate?

Thinking Like a Reader

1. Why does Mr. Krickleman keep interrupting the debate?
2. If you were in this class, would you be persuaded by the reasons offered by the candidates?

Write your responses in your journal.

Thinking Like a Writer

3. What does the author think of the arguments or reasons that Maggie and Thad present to their classmates in order to win votes?
4. Which reasons are convincing? Write a list of these reasons.

Responding to

LITERATURE

Brainstorm *Vocabulary*

In "Maggie Marmelstein for President," the author uses specific words about politics to show the mood of the campaign. Some examples are *candidate, campaign manager, debate, issues,* and *president.* Think of some topics that excite you. Begin to create your personal vocabulary lists, using words and phrases that tell about things in which you are interested. Use these words and phrases in your writing.

Talk It Over
You, the Candidate

When you want to persuade someone about an idea, you must offer specific reasons. These reasons should support your opinion, or idea. With a partner, imagine that you are running for the office of class president. Tell your partner three reasons why you would make a good president. Use language that would convince an audience to feel as you do. Then, let your partner play the role of candidate.

Quick Write *Write a Speech*

You have been thinking about persuasive language, or how to convince others that your ideas are worthwhile. Suppose that you had been asked to give a one-minute speech about something that is important to you and your classmates. How could you best use this time to create a strong response on the part of your listeners? Write a sentence that tells your opinion of this important issue. Then, write three reasons to support your opinion.

Idea Corner *Your Views*

You have been thinking about ideas that are important to you. How might you persuade someone to accept your views on a topic? What types of facts and opinions can you list in support of your ideas? In your journal make some notes about your views and the reasons that support them. Try to think of words and phrases that could make an audience see a topic from your point of view. Use these notes when you write a persuasive paragraph.

PICTURES — SEEING LIKE A WRITER

Finding Ideas for Writing

Look at the pictures. Think about what you see.
What ideas for persuasive writing do the pictures give you?
Write your ideas in your journal.

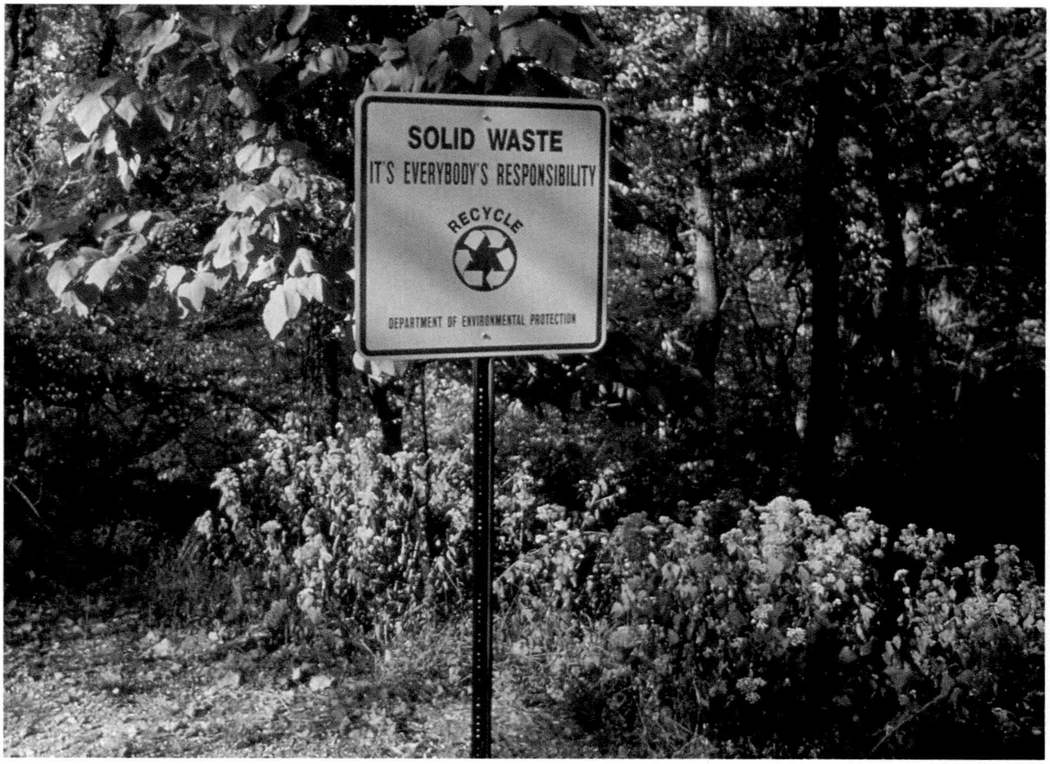
SOLID WASTE
IT'S EVERYBODY'S RESPONSIBILITY
RECYCLE
DEPARTMENT OF ENVIRONMENTAL PROTECTION

WRITING TOGETHER

1 GROUP WRITING: Persuasive Paragraphs

COOPERATIVE LEARNING

Good persuasive writing makes a reader think or feel the way the writer thinks or feels. How does a writer persuade a reader?

- Persuasive Language
- Logical Order
- Facts and Opinions

Persuasive Language

Read the following paragraph.

> Families ought to take vacations together. A family trip brings everyone closer together. It can be both fun and educational. Trips to the state parks or to national monuments can be inexpensive and convenient. It is important to relax sometimes by taking a break from school or work.

The writer begins with a topic sentence that states an opinion. Then she chooses specific words to persuade the reader to agree with her. These words show that the writer believes strongly in her ideas. Each of the underlined words and phrases above would probably appeal to a reader, because most people enjoy having fun and taking trips to the countryside.

Guided Practice: Using Persuasive Language

Work with your class to write a topic sentence that tells an opinion about an idea or issue. Then, list reasons that support the topic sentence.

Example: You should not return library books late.

lateness a bad habit	have to pay for overdue books
unfair to others	lose the right to borrow books

Logical Order

In a persuasive paragraph, the topic sentence usually states an opinion. The topic sentence is followed by reasons that support the opinion. It is usually best to state the most important reason *first*.

In the paragraph you read, the writer states that family vacations bring the family closer together. She places this reason right after her topic sentence, because it is the most important point. Look back at the paragraph.

- What other reasons does she list?
- How do these reasons support her main idea?

Guided Practice: Listing and Ordering Reasons

Recall the topic sentence you wrote with your class. Check the list of reasons you made to support your topic sentence. With the class, decide on the best order for those reasons.

Facts and Opinions

Look at the paragraph on page 340 again. Notice that the first sentence in the paragraph states an **opinion**. A **statement of opinion** tells what the speaker or writer believes. The writer supports her topic sentence with detail sentences. Some sentences give opinions and others state facts. A **statement of fact** can be proved or checked. A statement of opinion cannot be proved or checked. A writer may use both kinds of statements in a persuasive paragraph.

Guided Practice: Facts and Opinions

With your class, read and discuss the statements listed below. Work together to decide on three reasons to *agree* with each statement. Then, decide on three reasons to *disagree* with each statement. When you have completed your lists, label each reason **fact** or **opinion.**

Loud radio-playing should not be allowed in public.
People who love animals do not like other people.
It is best to exercise in the mornings.

WRITING TOGETHER

Putting a Persuasive Paragraph Together

With your class you have written a topic sentence that states an opinion about a topic or issue. You have listed supporting reasons and have decided on a good order for your reasons.

Think about your topic sentence. Then look at your list of supporting reasons. Decide which reasons to include in your persuasive paragraph.

Here is how one student chose. Read the topic sentence. Look at the reasons that are checked.

Students should read books on their own.

✓ learn new ideas

won't get bored

✓ books can be fun and exciting

might get extra credit

✓ good habit to get into

Guided Practice: Writing a Persuasive Paragraph

Write three or four detail sentences that support your topic sentence. In your detail sentences, include reasons from your list. Use persuasive language to present your reasons strongly. Write the topic sentence and the detail sentences in paragraph form. End your paragraph with a sentence that sums up your argument or opinion.

Read your persuasive paragraph to your class. Ask the class to suggest ways to make your paragraph more convincing.

Checklist: Persuasive Writing

When you write to persuade, you will want to keep some points in mind. A checklist will help you remember important points to include.

Look at this checklist. Some points need to be added. Make a copy of the checklist and complete it. Keep the copy in your writing folder. You can use it when you write your persuasive paragraph.

CHECKLIST

- ✔ Purpose and Audience
- ✔ Persuasive Language
- ✔ Order of Reasons
- ■ *Reason 1:* ________________
- ■ *Reason 2:* ___________
- ■ *Reason 3:* ___________
- ■ ________________
- ■ ________________

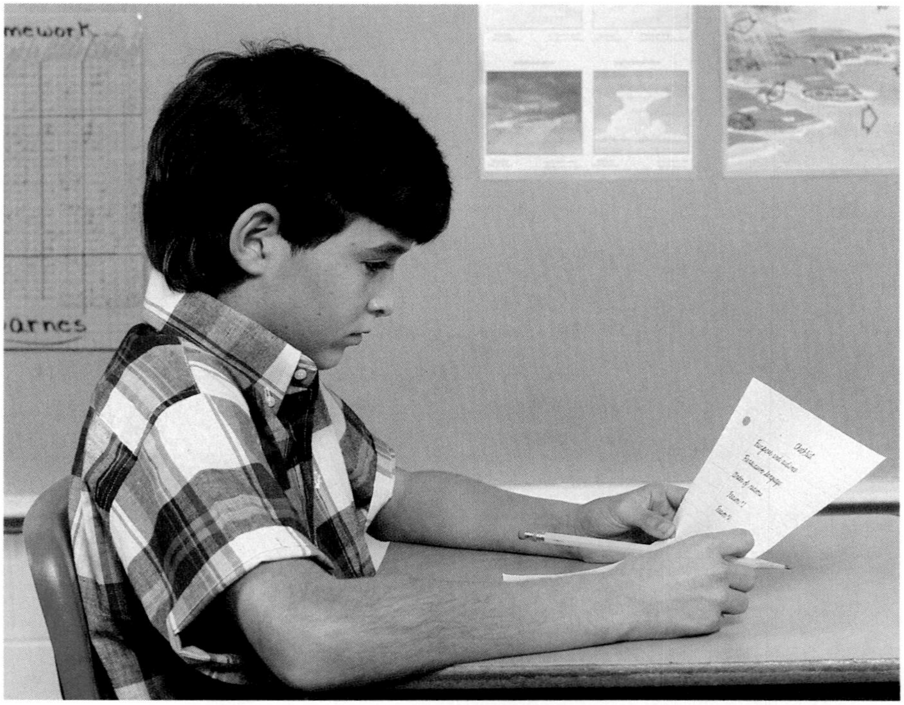

2 THINKING AND WRITING: Telling Facts and Opinions Apart

In persuasive writing, you present one side of an argument. You use facts and opinions to support your ideas. To make a convincing argument, it helps if you know the difference between a fact and an opinion. Remember, a fact can be proved. An opinion cannot be proved.

Look at this page from a writer's journal. The writer plans to write a persuasive paragraph in favor of forming study groups in her class.

1. Study groups can help students to learn.
2. The sixth graders have formed study groups.
3. Students of all ages form study groups.
4. I am good at math and could help others.
5. Peter got an "A" on his last English quiz.
6. Peter could help other students, too.
7. We fifth graders should form a study group.
8. We have several tests next week.

Thinking Like a Writer

■ Which of these reasons are facts? Which are opinions?

When you write to persuade, you must decide which facts and opinions make the most convincing reasons for your argument.

THINKING APPLICATION Facts and Opinions

COOPERATIVE LEARNING

Each of the writers named below is planning to write a persuasive paragraph. Help each writer to decide which **facts** and **opinions** to include. Write each reason listed below on a separate piece of paper. Then, write whether it is a fact or an opinion. Remember to consider whether or not the statement could be proved. If there is too much doubt in your mind about a statement, it is probably an opinion. You might wish to discuss your thinking with other students. In your discussion, explain your reasons to each other.

1. Margie wants to persuade her cousin to come to summer camp with her. Which reasons are convincing? Which are facts, and which are opinions?

Four of our friends are going.

Camp Sunnyvale is in New Hampshire.

I think you would like tennis.

You would be bored in the city.

2. Saul wants to persuade his father to purchase a computer. Which reasons are convincing? Which are facts, and which are opinions?

There is a sale on computers this week.

I need one for homework.

Mom could store her work on it, too.

It would help my grades.

3. Georgia wants to persuade her friend to enter a talent contest with her. Which reasons are convincing? Which are facts, and which are opinions?

You and I are great dancers.

We were in last year's contest.

I know we would win.

The entry fee is only $5.00.

4. Chuck wants to persuade his mother to let him take swimming lessons. Which reasons are convincing? Which are facts, and which are opinions?

I'll still have time for homework.

The lessons are twice a week.

Trips to the beach and lake will be safer if I swim well.

The lessons cost fifteen dollars a week.

3 INDEPENDENT WRITING: Persuasive Paragraphs

Prewrite: Step 1

You have learned some important ideas about persuasive writing. Now you are ready to choose a topic of your own. Gina, a student your age, wanted to persuade her classmates to participate in an activity which she believed was important. She chose a topic in this way.

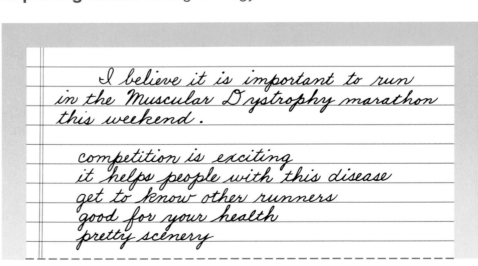

Choosing a Topic

1. First, she made a list of topics.
2. Next, she thought about ways to present each topic.
3. Last, she decided on the best topic.

Learning to play a flute
Joining school clubs
Running a race
Saving money

Gina liked the third topic on her list best. She narrowed her topic to running in a marathon.

Next, Gina explored her topic by making a list.

Exploring Ideas: Listing Strategy

I believe it is important to run in the Muscular Dystrophy marathon this weekend.

competition is exciting
it helps people with this disease
get to know other runners
good for your health
pretty scenery

Gina knew she had some excellent reasons. She knew that her **purpose** for writing was to persuade her **audience** to run in a marathon for a good cause.

Before beginning to write, Gina read over her list and considered each of her reasons carefully. At this point, she made some changes on the list.

it helps people with this disease
good for your health
competition is exciting
get to know other runners
makes you feel good because you helped

Thinking Like a Writer

- Which reason did she add?
- Which reason did she leave out?
- Why do you think she made these changes?

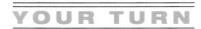

YOUR TURN

JOURNAL

Think of a topic about which you have a strong opinion. Use **Pictures** or your journal for ideas. Follow these steps.

- Make a list of topics you believe are important.
- Choose one about which you would enjoy writing.
- Narrow your topic if you think it is too broad.
- Think of some facts and opinions about this topic.
- Think about your purpose and audience.

Make a list. Remember, you can add to or take away from the list at any time.

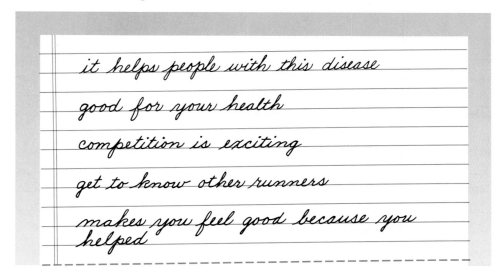

Write a First Draft: Step 2

Gina knows what her persuasive paragraph should include. She used a planning checklist.

Gina is now ready to write her first draft.

Gina's First Draft

I believe its important to run in the Muscular Dystrophy marathon this wekend. Running is good for your health. The cause is a worthy one. You will feel good that you did it. You also get to meet other runners. Events like this allow you to compete against your friends, too, but all in good fun. Its going to be a great race.

While Gina was writing her first draft, she did not worry about errors. She wanted to get her ideas down on paper.

Planning Checklist

- Remember purpose and audience.
- Use persuasive language.
- Write reasons in order of importance.
- Include facts and opinions.

YOUR TURN

Write your first draft. As you prepare to write, ask yourself:

- What do I want to persuade my audience to believe?
- How can I persuade my audience to agree with my idea?

TIME-OUT You might want to take some time out before you revise. That way you will be able to revise your writing with a fresh eye.

Revise: Step 3

After she finished her first draft, Gina read it over to herself. Then she shared her writing with a classmate. She asked Teresa to suggest ways she could improve her work.

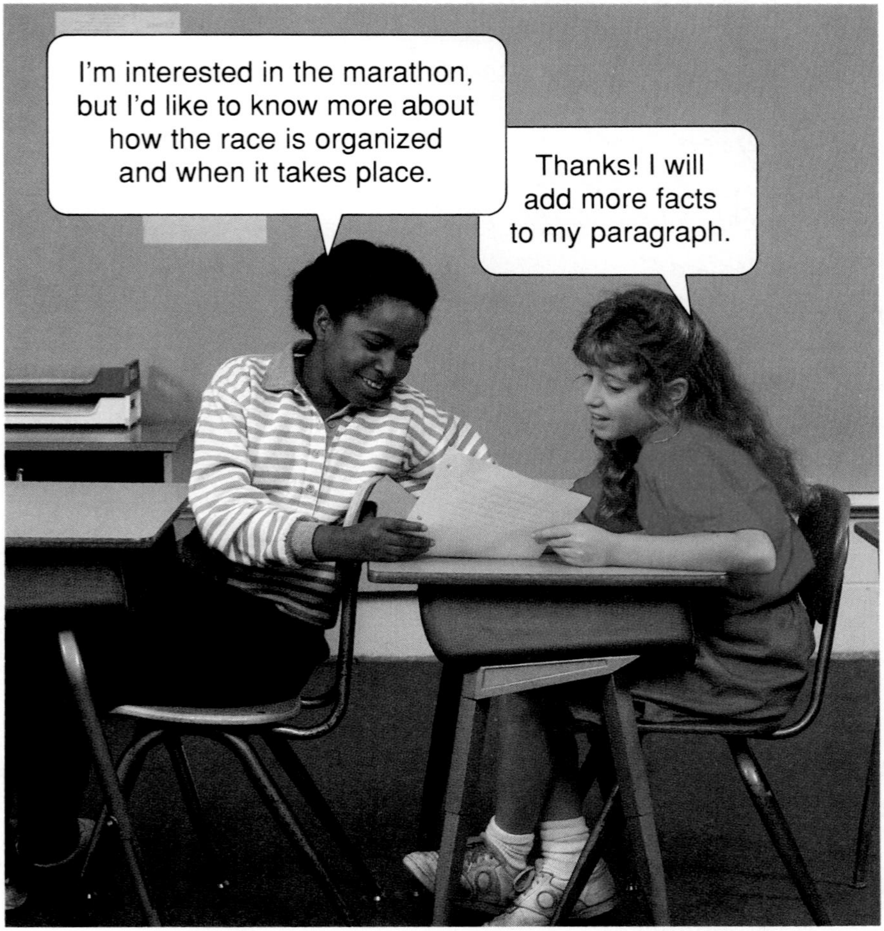

I'm interested in the marathon, but I'd like to know more about how the race is organized and when it takes place.
Thanks! I will add more facts to my paragraph.

Gina then looked back at her planning checklist. She noticed that she had forgotten one point. She checked it off so that she would remember it when she revised. Gina now has a checklist to use as she revises.

Gina made changes to her paragraph. Notice that she did not correct small errors. She knew she could fix them later.

The revisions Gina made changed her paragraph. Turn the page. Look at Gina's revised draft.

Revising Checklist

- ■ Remember purpose and audience.
- ■ Use persuasive language.
- ■ Write reasons in order of importance.
- ✓ ■ Include facts and opinions.

Gina's Revised Draft

I believe its important to run in the
Muscular Dystrophy marathon this wekend.
and
Running is good for your health. The cause is
The race begins at two p.m. on Saturday.
a worthy one. ~~You will feel good that you did~~
Each sponsor pays twenty-five cents for every mile
~~it. You also get to meet other runners.~~ Events
a runner completes.
like this allow you to compete against
your friends, ~~too,~~ but all in good fun.
Its going to be a great race.

Thinking Like a Writer

WISE WORD CHOICE

- What facts did Gina add?
- How did Gina change the order of her reasons? How does the new order improve the paragraph?
- Which sentences did Gina combine? What do you think of these changes?

YOUR TURN

Read your first draft. Make a checklist. Ask yourself these questions.

- How can I make my paragraph more persuasive?
- How can I improve the order of my supporting reasons?
- How can I make facts and opinions support one another?

Proofread: Step 4

Gina knew her work was not complete until she proofread her paragraph. She used a proofreading checklist while she proofread.

Part of Gina's Proofread Draft

weekend
Muscular Dystrophy marathon this wekend.
and
Running is good for your health. The cause is
The race begins at two p.m. on Saturday.
a worthy one. ~~You will feel good that you did~~
Each sponsor pays twenty-five cents for every mile
~~it. You also get to meet other runners.~~ Events
a runner completes.
like this allow you to compete against
your friends, ~~too~~, but all in good fun.
It's going to be a great race.

YOUR TURN

Proofreading Practice

Below is a paragraph that you can use to practice your proofreading skills. Find the errors. Write the paragraph correctly on a separate sheet of paper.

Its always a good idea to eat at Mo's. Mo is the best cook for miles around and its famous from Alabama to Tennessee. Her cornbread and biskits are delicious Whatever you do, don't miss Mo's as you drive through Upton County.

Proofreading Checklist

- Did I indent my paragraph?
- Did I spell all words correctly?
- What punctuation errors do I need to correct?
- What capitalization errors do I need to correct?

Applying Your Proofreading Skills

Now proofread your persuasive paragraph. Read your checklist again. Review **The Grammar Connection** and **The Mechanics Connection**. Use the proofreading marks to mark changes.

THE GRAMMAR CONNECTION

Remember these rules about pronouns.

- A *pronoun* should follow closely the noun that it replaces.
- Make sure each pronoun refers directly to the noun it replaces.

The **librarian** gave a lecture.
She discussed the card catalog.
Give the notebook to the **boy**.
Give the notebook to **him**.

THE MECHANICS CONNECTION

Remember these rules about using apostrophes.

- An *apostrophe* replaces one or more letters in a contraction.
- In a *contraction* of a subject pronoun and a verb, the letters are always dropped from the verb.

I would enjoy a vacation.
I'd enjoy a vacation.
He has shown me a map of Canada.
He's shown me a map of Canada.

Proofreading Marks
¶ indent
∧ add
take out
≡ capital letter
/ lower-case letter

Publish: Step 5

Gina copied her paragraph in her best handwriting and read it at a school assembly. After the assembly, Gina's classmates told her how much they had enjoyed her ideas. Many of them asked her how they could sign up to run in the next marathon.

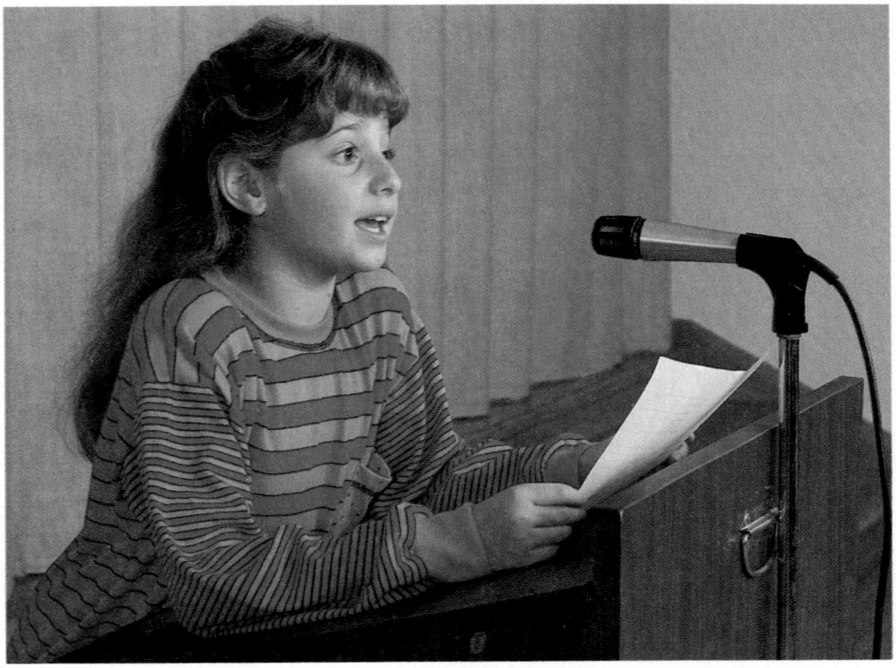

YOUR TURN

Make a final copy of your persuasive paragraph. Write as neatly as you can. Think of a way to share your work. Some ideas are given in the **Sharing Suggestions** box below.

SHARING SUGGESTIONS

Read your work at a school function.	Submit your paragraph to the school newspaper.	Send your paragraph to a pen pal.

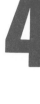

WRITING

EXTENSION

4 SPEAKING AND LISTENING: Listening for Point of View and Bias

When you write to persuade, your purpose is to make your audience behave in a particular way. People who write advertisements for television, radio, and newspapers write to persuade. Advertisements use a combination of persuasive language, facts, and opinions. They are meant to convince people to buy a certain product or to accept a **point of view** or **bias**.

Read these statements from an advertisement for an imaginary candidate named Frank Bardin.

1. Frank Bardin is the best man for the job.
2. Vote for Frank Bardin, the people's choice.
3. Frank Bardin stands for honest government.

The statements above may look like *facts*, but they are really *opinions*. They could not be proved true or false. For instance, statement #2 uses the phrase, *the people's choice*. The writer has used a persuasive device called a **loaded word** or **loaded phrase**. Voters like to feel that they are in agreement with many other people. The writers want their audience to believe that most people are voting for the same candidate, Frank Bardin.

If you listen carefully to advertisements, speeches, or arguments, you can tell the difference between facts and opinions. You can figure out the speaker's point of view or bias, and make your own decisions.

- How can listening for another person's point of view or bias help me to make my own decisions?
- How can I make judgments about the truth or accuracy of the advertisements I hear and read?

Careful attention to speeches can help you to understand a politician's bias. Careful attention to advertisements may help you to tell if the product in question could actually be of use to you.

LISTENING GUIDELINES: Persuasion

1. Remember that the speaker's purpose is to persuade.
2. Listen for statements of opinion and loaded words.
3. Listen for statements that sound like facts but cannot be proved.

Listen as your teacher or a classmate reads these advertisements.

CRAZY DAVE'S STEREOS
has the best prices in town.

We have special discounts for seniors and students.
IF YOU CAN FIND A BETTER DEAL,
WE WILL REFUND YOUR MONEY!

PLASTIC SOUND
HAS DEALS THAT CANNOT BE BELIEVED!
WE'LL STAND ON OUR HEADS TO GET YOUR BUSINESS.
DON'T BE A SQUARE, AND GO TO THE COMPETITION.

- Which advertisement makes use of facts rather than opinions and loaded words?

SPEAKING APPLICATION A Statement of Opinion

Think of two products, one of which you like very much. Work with a partner. Describe the two products to your partner. Ask your partner to listen for your point of view. Have him or her try to figure out which product you prefer.

5 WRITER'S RESOURCES: Graphs, Tables, and Maps

In this unit, you have found some resources for persuasive writing. Some possible resources for finding facts are **graphs**, **tables**, and **maps**.

Rock Star Magazine wants to persuade companies to place their advertisements in this magazine. They mail out brochures containing graphs, tables, and maps, to show who reads the magazine. A **graph** compares information.

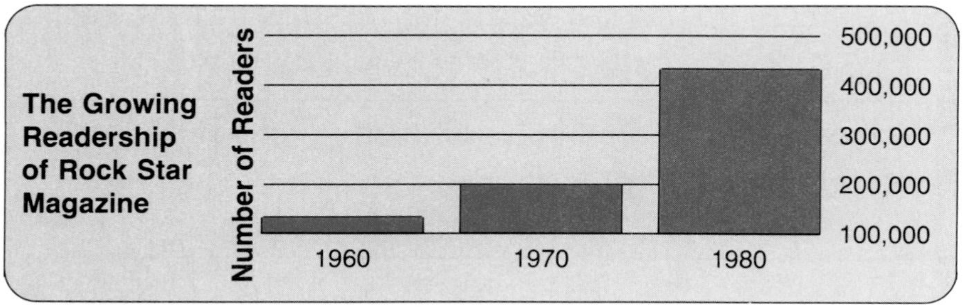

This bar graph shows advertisers that the audience of *Rock Star Magazine* has been growing steadily larger.

To read the bar graph, look at the captions on the right side and at the bottom. The right side shows the number of readers in each year. The bottom shows the dates being compared.

A **table** can also help you to see and compare information. This table shows the type of products readers of various age groups buy. The facts might persuade manufacturers of these products to advertise in *Rock Star Magazine*.

	What Rock Star Magazine's Readers Buy		
	product:		
age group:	cars	stereos	vacations
over 50	6%	3%	7%
30-50	21%	7%	20%
20-30	10%	12%	7%

Maps give facts, too. They can show advertisers in different parts of the country where their audience lives.

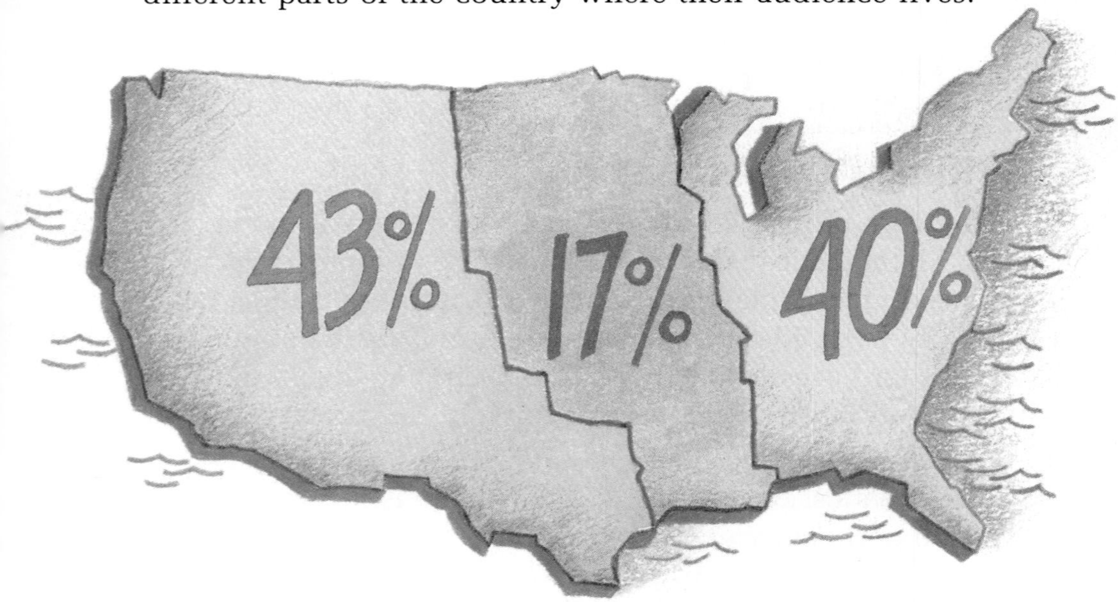

This map could convince a manufacturer in Connecticut to advertise in *Rock Star Magazine*.

Practice

Use the graph, table, and map from this lesson to answer the following questions.

1. By how many readers did the circulation of *Rock Star Magazine* increase from 1970 to 1980?
2. Of the products shown, what do *Rock Star Magazine* readers from the ages of 20 to 30 spend the most money on?
3. Advertising in *Rock Star Magazine* would be most effective for advertisers in what part of the country?

WRITING APPLICATION A List

Find a graph, table, or map in your math book. List five facts that you learned from the resource you found. Save the list in your writing folder. You will use it in **The Curriculum Connection** on page 358.

Writing About Math

The work of mathematicians applies to many areas of our lives. Mathematics is used in fields such as finance, mapmaking, city-planning, and architecture, as well as in our daily lives. Mathematicians are always developing new theories and uses for mathematics. Each new theory or application must be proved with facts and figures.

Graphs, tables, and maps are all created through the use of mathematics. Numbers and their relationships are used to prove points of view and also to disprove them. Without an understanding of basic mathematical relationships, we would find graphs, tables, and maps useless.

ACTIVITIES

Summarize Facts Use the list of facts you wrote from the graph, table, or map in your math book. Write a paragraph that tells what you learned from the resource.

Use Charts and Graphs Read each of the theories or opinions below. Think of a way to look for numbers that might support it. For example, for theory 1, you might make a graph which shows the distance above sea-level for New York City over each of the last ten years.

Theory 1: New York City is sinking into the ocean.
Theory 2: Girls are smarter than boys.
Theory 3: Eating hamburgers makes you live longer.

Respond to Literature You use mathematics every day. Whether you pay two dollars for a magazine, or use higher mathematics in science, you are using a system that has its

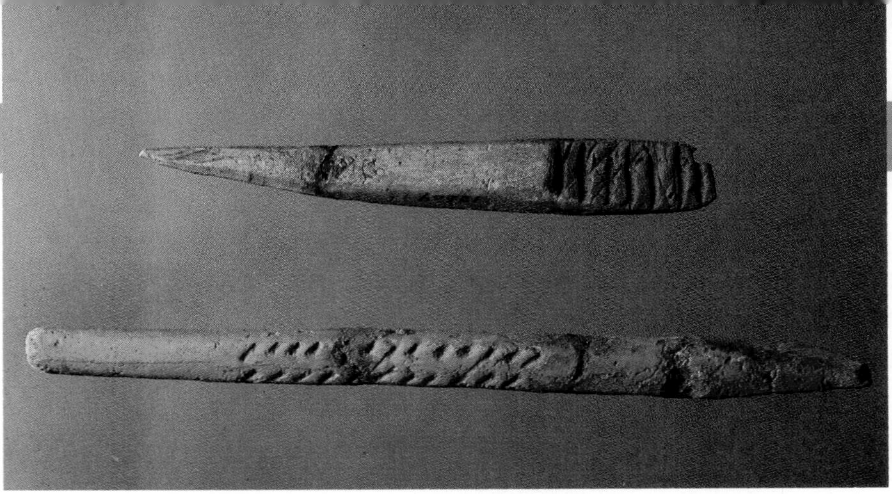

roots in ancient history. Read the selection below, then write a response. You might write about some of the ways in which you use mathematics in your daily life. When you have finished, share your writing with your class. Discuss the different ways that mathematics works for each of you.

Counting and Numbers
from *The Penguin Book of the Physical World*

No one knows when man first began to use language or when he first began to count. But primitive men probably matched the things they wanted to count against something else, such as notches in a stick, or pebbles, or knots tied on a cord. As each day passed, for instance, a pebble could be added to a pile. We say now that there is a one-to-one correspondence between the things we count and the things we count them with.

The next step in the development of counting was to use names for numbers. A group of objects could be counted by saying or thinking the names: for instance, we say one, two, three as we count. In the same way it is convenient to use symbols for writing numbers. The ancient Egyptians simply made upright marks from right to left on their papyrus. One was |, two was ||, and so on.

UNIT CHECKUP

LESSON 1

Group Writing: Persuasive Paragraphs (page 340)
Write five persuasive sentences that could support one of the topic sentences below.

Littering is a bad habit.
Public transportation should be free.

LESSON 2

Thinking: Telling Facts and Opinions Apart (page 344)
Write each sentence. Label each one *fact* or *opinion*.

1. Tacos are good for you.
2. Beef is more expensive than jello.
3. Fish and meat contain protein.
4. Eating candy is wrong.
5. Babies like fresh fruit.

LESSON 3

Writing a Persuasive Paragraph (page 346)
Suppose that you are working on the drama committee for your school. Write an article for the school paper that will get people excited about a school play.

LESSON 4

Speaking and Listening: Point of View and Bias (page 354)
Imagine that you will take part in a debate on the question "Should people be allowed to play their radios at the beach?" Write at least three reasons that support your point of view.

LESSON 5

Writer's Resources: Graphs, Tables, and Maps (page 356)
Use library resources to find these facts. Tell whether you found each fact in a graph, table, or map.

1. the difference in size between Texas and Rhode Island
2. the major export of Chile
3. the population of Detroit, Michigan, in 1975
4. the average amount of rainfall in Seattle, Washington, each year

THEME PROJECT A CLASS MAGAZINE

Think about the magazines that you enjoy reading. Magazines give information and present opinions. Journalists who write for magazines are free to look at different sides of issues and report on interesting topics. Though the magazine as a whole may have a point of view, each writer is expressing his or her own ideas and observations about a topic. How do you think that magazine editors choose the topics for the articles in their magazines? What do you think would be some interesting topics or issues for articles?

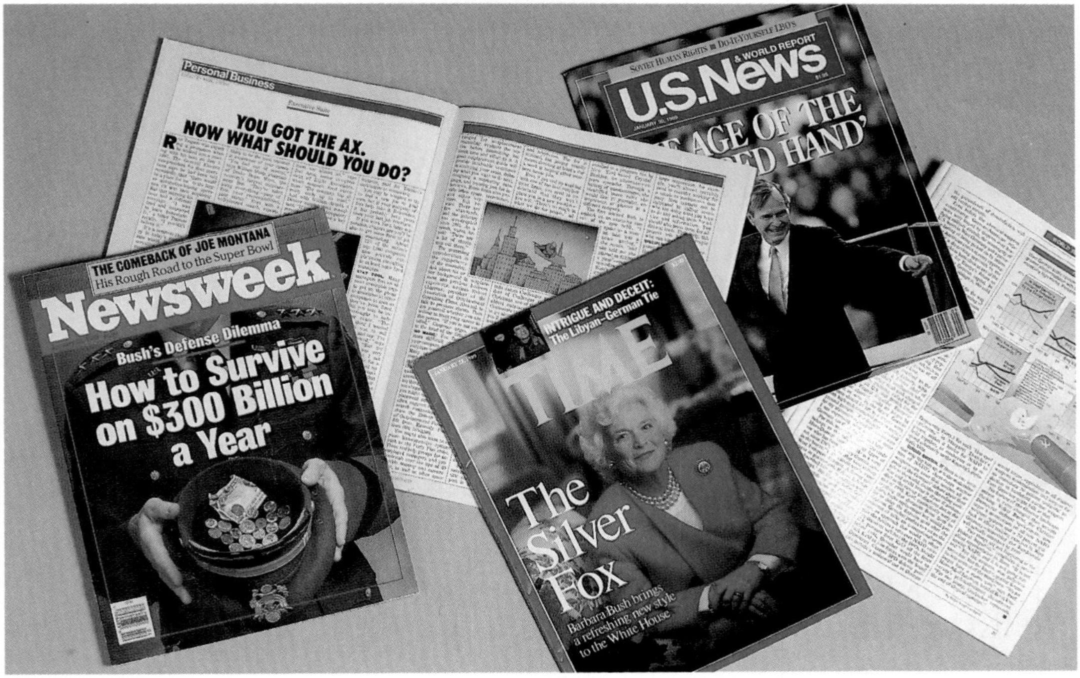

Work with your class to create a magazine.

- As a class, discuss the point of view of the magazine and decide what kinds of topics it should include.
- Choose topics that you think would interest other students in your school.
- When you are finished, share your magazine with the rest of the school.

GRAMMAR

UNIT 11

Adverbs

In this unit you will learn about adverbs. Adverbs tell more about verbs. Adverbs can help to make your writing more lively and precise.

Discuss Read the poem on the opposite page. What kinds of adventures does the poet describe?

Creative Expression The unit theme is *Adventures*. Where would you go if you could go anywhere in the world? Write a list of all the places you would explore. Write your list in your journal.

JOURNAL

THEME: *ADVENTURES*

When you put me up on the Elephant's back,
I'll go round the world and never come back.
I will travel for miles away from home
To London, Paris, Vienna, and Rome.

—William Jay Smith, from "Elephant"

GRAMMAR

1 WHAT IS AN ADVERB?

An adverb is a word that tells more about a verb.

You have learned that an adjective describes a noun or pronoun. An **adverb** is a word that describes a verb. Adverbs tell *how*, *when*, or *where* an action happened.

How: The guide **slowly** explains the rules.
When: The tour begins **immediately**.
Where: The entrance lies **here**.

Notice that many adverbs end in *ly*.

Common Adverbs

How	When	Where
quickly	yesterday	outside
together	often	there
gracefully	last	below
softly	always	above
hard	next	near
happily	then	ahead
deeply	finally	forward

Guided Practice

Tell the adverb that describes each underlined verb.

Example: Finally, the tour of the caves starts. *Finally*

1. The rowboats creak slightly.
2. The stream winds gracefully around the caves.
3. We always enjoy a boat ride.
4. The guides row smoothly.
5. The boats move forward.

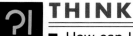

?! THINK

■ How can I recognize an adverb in a sentence?

REMEMBER

- An **adverb** is a word that tells more about a verb.
- An adverb tells *how, when,* or *where.*

More Practice

A. Write each sentence. Write whether the underlined adverb answers the question *how*, *when*, or *where*.

Example: Marvin sits <u>calmly</u> in the boat. *how*

6. Grace read a guidebook <u>yesterday</u>.
7. She whispers <u>often</u> to Marvin.
8. Marvin looks <u>happily</u> at the cavern.
9. He grasps his camera <u>suddenly</u>.
10. Marvin <u>quickly</u> points at the bats.
11. They hang <u>together</u> from their perches.
12. Marvin gazes <u>above</u> him.

B. Write each sentence. Draw two lines under the adverb that describes the underlined verb.

Example: Water <u>pours</u> <u>loudly</u> from the rocks.

13. The guides <u>tie</u> the boats firmly to a post.
14. Grace <u>looks</u> eagerly at the stream.
15. The stream <u>runs</u> deeply in this cavern.
16. It <u>rushes</u> outside to the sea.
17. The guides <u>walk</u> ahead.
18. The other students <u>follow</u> behind.
19. Marvin <u>steps</u> quickly toward the waterfall.
20. He <u>takes</u> another photograph there.

Extra Practice, page 384

WRITING APPLICATION A Narrative

Imagine that you are an explorer. Write a short narrative or story about your discovery of a secret cave. How did you find it? What did it look like? Underline the adverbs in your narrative.

2 USING ADVERBS TO COMPARE

You know that adjectives can compare two or more people, places, or things. Adverbs can compare two or more actions. Study the chart below.

Comparing with Adverbs		
1. Most short adverbs add *er* or *est* to the adverb.	lowly lowlier lowliest	hard harder hardest
2. Most adverbs of two or more syllables use *more* or *most* with the adverb.	eagerly more eagerly most eagerly	cleverly more cleverly most cleverly

Guided Practice

Tell the correct form of the adverb to compare two actions and three or more actions.

Example: slowly *more slowly* *most slowly*

1. softly
2. cheerfully
3. late
4. quickly
5. soon

?! THINK

■ How can I use adverbs when I compare two or more actions?

REMEMBER

- To compare two actions, use *er* or *more*.
- To compare three or more actions, use *est* or *most*.

More Practice

A. Write each sentence. Complete the sentence with the correct form of the adverb in parentheses.

Example: Marco Polo dealt with the Chinese _____ than others. (successfully)
Marco Polo dealt with the Chinese more successfully than others.

6. Marco Polo traveled _____ to China than we travel today. (slowly)
7. The trip took _____ than he imagined. (long)
8. The Kublai Khan greeted him _____ than he had greeted others. (kindly)
9. The Chinese people lived the _____ of any people in the world. (gracefully)
10. Of all the visitors, Marco Polo learned the customs the _____. (fast)
11. Many strangers handled chopsticks _____ than he did. (awkwardly)
12. He wrote the Chinese alphabet _____ than other students did. (skillfully)
13. He spoke _____ than some Chinese children. (easily)
14. The Khan treated him _____ of all the visitors. (graciously)
15. He returned to Europe _____ than he had left. (triumphantly)

Extra Practice, page 385

WRITING APPLICATION A Letter

Imagine that you have traveled to an unfamiliar country. Write a letter comparing the place to your own country. Underline the adverbs.

3 ADVERBS BEFORE ADJECTIVES AND OTHER ADVERBS

Adverbs describe or tell more about verbs. Adverbs can also tell more about adjectives or other adverbs.

Adverb Before an Adjective:
The weather seems **terribly** hot.

Adverb Before an Adverb:
The man drove **very** far.

Sometimes it is hard to tell the difference between an adverb and an adjective. Remember, an adjective describes a noun or a pronoun.

The **grateful** man thanked us. **Adjective**
The man thanked us **gratefully**. **Adverb**

Study the chart below.

Adverbs That Describe Adjectives and Other Adverbs

almost	fairly	quite	slightly	terribly	too
completely	hardly	really	so	very	

Guided Practice

Tell the adverb that describes each underlined adverb or adjective.

Example: We flew in a really big balloon. *really*

1. The day was slightly windy.
2. The preparation was almost over.
3. The crew was so tired.
4. Lulu was quite cheerful.
5. We had worked very hard.

?! **THINK**

- How can I use adverbs to describe other adverbs or adjectives?

REMEMBER

■ **Adverbs** can describe verbs, adjectives, or other adverbs.

More Practice

A. Write each sentence. Draw two lines under the adverb that describes each underlined word.

Example: The crew arrived slightly late.

6. The fire was quite hot.
7. The balloon seemed completely full of air.
8. We were almost ready for the trip.
9. The departure was very sudden.
10. We soared so high into the sky!
11. George looked down fairly often.
12. He was clearly excited about the voyage.

B. Write each sentence. Write whether the underlined adverb describes an adjective or another adverb.

Example: George was fairly comfortable. *adjective*

13. We soared so rapidly in the air.
14. The flight was very smooth.
15. We flew joyfully together.
16. In fact, the ascent seemed too rapid!
17. Quite suddenly, Joe began the descent.
18. The balloon landed fairly fast.
19. It was hardly late in the day.
20. The trip had ended so quickly!

Extra Practice, page 386

GRAMMAR

WRITING APPLICATION A Journal Entry

COOPERATIVE LEARNING

Imagine that you were on a balloon trip that took off from your neighborhood. What might happen on the trip? Write a journal entry about the trip. When you have finished, have a partner read your journal entry. Ask him or her to circle the adverbs.

4 FORMING ADVERBS FROM ADJECTIVES

Many adverbs are formed by adding *ly* or *ily* to the adjective form of the word.

Columbus was a **curious** man. **Adjective**
Columbus looked **curiously** at the island. **Adverb**

When forming adverbs from words ending with a consonant and *y*, change the *y* to *i* and add *ly*.

The crew was **weary**.
They stared **wearily** at the ocean.

Good is an adjective.

➡ Use *good* before a noun or after a linking verb.

Well can be either an adjective or an adverb. *Well* is an adjective when it means "healthy."

➡ Use *well* as an adverb to describe a verb.

The trip began **well**. **Adverb**
The captain is **well**. **Adjective**

Sometimes it is difficult to tell whether a word is an adjective or an adverb. Remember, adverbs tell more about verbs.

Guided Practice

Tell the word that completes each sentence correctly.

Example: The Arawaks lived _____ on their island. (good, well) *well*

1. Tall ships _____ sailed into the harbor. (slow, slowly)
2. The Arawaks greeted the Spaniards _____. (wary, warily)
3. The Arawaks stood _____ on the shore. (peaceful, peacefully)
4. The Spaniards _____ renamed the land Puerto Rico. (immediate, immediately)
5. The voyage (final, finally) ended.

?! THINK

■ How can I form an adverb from an adjective?

REMEMBER

- Form some adverbs by adding *ly* to the adjective form of the word.
- Form adverbs from words ending with a consonant and *y* by changing the *y* to *i* and adding *ly*.

GRAMMAR

More Practice

Write each sentence, using the adverb form of the adjective in parentheses.

Example: The Spanish troops acted (forceful).
The Spanish troops acted forcefully.

6. Columbus climbed (weary) from his ship.
7. The sailors cheered (proud) for their captain.
8. They (quick) planned their next move.
9. The Arawaks hunted (brave).
10. Ponce de Leon (easy) conquered the Arawaks.
11. Large plantations were (rapid) introduced.
12. Ships arrived from Spain (regular).
13. The Puerto Ricans (slow) became American citizens.
14. Sugar grows (easy) on the island.
15. Some islanders (strong) want American citizenship.
16. Others (clear) want independence.
17. The governor speaks (forceful) on the television.
18. The islanders listen (careful) to their choices.
19. Some (loud) proclaim their desire for independence.
20. Some (eager) choose United States citizenship.

Extra Practice, Practice Plus pages 387-388

WRITING APPLICATION A Story

Imagine that you discover an island. Write a story about life on your island. What foods and shelter does the island provide? Does anyone else live there? Include some adverbs in your story to make your writing lively and precise. Exchange stories with a classmate. Underline the adverbs in each other's stories.

GRAMMAR

5 NEGATIVES

You have learned to form a contraction with a verb and the word *not*. These contractions are called **negatives**. The adverbs *no* and *not* are negatives. Study the sentences below.

Kathy **doesn't** like cold weather.
She **never** goes to the frozen tundra.

Using more than one negative in a sentence is usually incorrect.

Incorrect: We don't visit nobody.
Correct: We visit nobody.
Correct: We don't visit anybody.

Common Negatives				
nobody	not	nothing	nowhere	no one
aren't	doesn't	haven't	wouldn't	never

Guided Practice

Tell the negative word in each sentence.

Example: The tundra wouldn't be bearable without warm clothing. *wouldn't*

1. Tony can't wait for the departure.
2. We have never been north of Minnesota.
3. Nobody is afraid of the cold.
4. We won't forget our equipment.
5. We go nowhere without it.

?! **THINK**

■ How can I recognize a negative in a sentence?

REMEMBER

- A **negative** is a word that means *no* or *not*.
- Use only one negative in a sentence.

More Practice

A. Write each sentence. Underline the negative word.

Example: Polar bears aren't afraid of cold weather.

6. The subsoil on the tundra never warms.
7. There are no trees on the tundra.
8. We won't see much vegetation on this trip.
9. The forests don't grow here.
10. The moose don't approach strangers.
11. No one has seen a reindeer.
12. Nothing frightens a polar bear.

B. Write each sentence correctly. Use only one negative in each sentence.

Example: You can't never get warm here.
You can't ever get warm here.

13. No musk oxen never leave the tundra.
14. We never see no birds.
15. Haven't you not seen an Arctic hare?
16. This Arctic fox isn't no bigger than a dog.
17. None of the walruses have no tusks.
18. A walrus doesn't eat nothing but shellfish.
19. The wolverine hasn't got no pups.
20. No roses never grow in the tundra.

Extra Practice, page 389

WRITING APPLICATION A Report

Imagine that you have gone on an expedition to a foreign land. You have seen a strange and wonderful animal. Write a report about the animal. Underline the negative words in your report.

G R A M M A R

6 MECHANICS: Using Quotation Marks

When you write dialogue, or conversation, you record the speaker's exact words in a **direct quotation.** The punctuation marks that set off the direct quotation from the rest of the sentence are called **quotation marks** (" "). The first word of each sentence in a quotation is always capitalized.

➡ Use a comma before the quotation when the speaker's name comes first.

Julie asked, "What is it?"

➡ Use a comma, a question mark, or an exclamation mark to end the quotation when the speaker's name comes last.

"It's an incredible invention!" cried Marvin.

➡ Use a period after the speaker's name.

➡ Use commas to separate the name from the quotation when a quotation is interrupted by the speaker's name.

"I believe," said Julie, "you are correct."

When there are two sentences in the quotation, a period follows the name.

"Yes," replied Marvin. "It is an airplane."

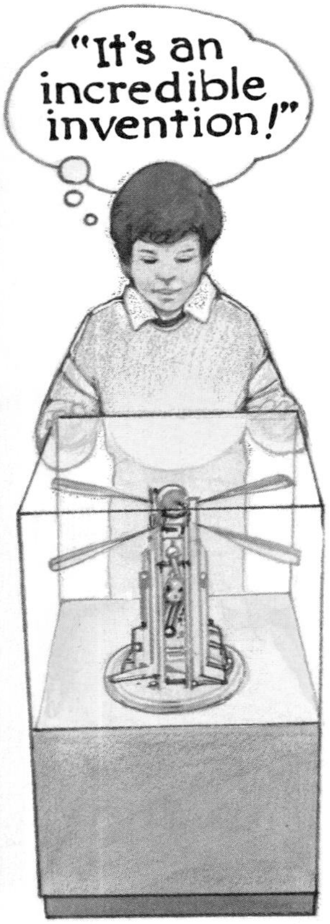

Guided Practice

Tell which part of each sentence is a direct quotation.

Example: "I am curious," said Julie. *I am curious*

1. Julie asked, "Did this machine ever fly?"
2. "No, it never did," replied Marvin.
3. "I've never seen anything like this!" Julie exclaimed.
4. "It was drawn in the 1400's," Marvin said.

?! THINK

■ How do I punctuate a direct quotation in a sentence?

REMEMBER

- **Direct quotations** are set off from the rest of the sentence by **quotation marks** and end punctuation marks.

More Practice

Write each sentence. Be sure to use punctuation marks and capital letters correctly.

Example: Look at this page said Marvin.
"Look at this page," said Marvin.

5. Julie wondered who was the designer?
6. Leonardo da Vinci designed this, Marvin told Julie.
7. I never knew that! Julie exclaimed.
8. Marvin added, Yes, and he also painted the Mona Lisa.
9. Was he an artist? Julie asked.
10. Yes, he had many talents, said Marvin.
11. Do artists design airplanes? asked Julie.
12. Marvin said, The first pilots were bicycle repairmen.
13. That's the first powered flying machine Marvin said.
14. Julie replied it doesn't look very sturdy.
15. It only flew a few hundred feet Marvin said.
16. Julie asked where was that?
17. It happened at Kitty Hawk Marvin answered.
18. I have been there Julie said.
19. Marvin asked did you see the monument?
20. We drove past it she said.

Extra Practice, page 390.

WRITING APPLICATION A Dialogue

Imagine that you were at Kitty Hawk for the Wright brothers' first flight. Write a dialogue between you and Orville and Wilbur Wright, the inventors of the airplane. What would you ask the Wright brothers? What do you think they might have said? Make sure you punctuate and capitalize your sentences correctly.

7 VOCABULARY BUILDING: Suffixes

A **suffix** is a word part added to the end of a base word. A suffix changes the meaning of the base word to which it is added. It may also change the part of speech of the base word to which it is added.

Suffix	Meaning of Suffix
ful	full of
able, ible	capable or worthy of being
ness	quality, condition or state of being
less	without, that does not
ment	the act, state, quality, or result of
less	without, that does not
ation, ition	the act, state of being, or result of
ward	in the direction of
ly	in a _____ way
er, or	one who _____, something that _____
ist	one who does or makes
an, ian	one who believes in, one who was born or lives in, one who is skilled in _____
y	full of, somewhat, like

Guided Practice

Identify the suffix and give the meaning of the word. Use a dictionary to help you define any base word that you do not yet know.

Example: senator *or* *a member of the senate*

1. determination
2. aimless
3. enjoyment
4. flexible
5. artist

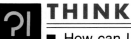

?! THINK

■ How can I figure out the meaning of a word with a suffix?

REMEMBER

- A **suffix** changes the meaning of the base word to which it is added.

More Practice

A. Write each sentence. Draw a line under the word with the suffix.

Example: The hero looked forward to the adventure.

6. I read the new book with wonderment.
7. The hero of the story was very thoughtful.
8. He was penniless as a child.
9. The character's mother had a sudden realization.
10. She was the boy's closest relation.
11. Regardless, she sent him on an adventure.
12. His first months alone were joyless.

B. Write each sentence. Change each underlined base word by adding the correct suffix.

Example: The people were fear of the dragon.
The people were fearful of the dragon.

13. The king could not hide his bewilder.
14. The country was in a horror condition.
15. The dragon was a destroy.
16. Each week he caused destruct.
17. A stranger in town suggested his plan calm.
18. The dragon was just a complain.
19. To the dragon's amaze, the boy dampened his fiery breath.
20. The smoke dragon did no more damage!

Extra Practice, page 391

WRITING APPLICATION A Fable

COOPERATIVE LEARNING

A fable is a very short story with a message about how to behave in a particular situation. Fables teach the difference between wisdom and foolishness. Write your own fable. Have a partner underline the suffixes.

GRAMMAR AND WRITING CONNECTION

Combining Sentences

There are words that show the relationship between ideas and events. They can show *why* or *when* an event or experience happens. Words like *when*, *since*, *because*, *until*, *after*, and *before* show a relationship between two or more sentences.

We were happy. The rain had stopped.
We were happy **because** the rain had stopped.

Dad waited. The roads became safe.
Dad waited **until** the roads became safe.

Notice that in the first sentence, the word **because** gives a reason, or shows *why* something happened. In the second sentence, the word **until** shows *when* something happened. In both sentences, the joining word makes the writer's meaning clear.

Combining the sentences makes the writing flow more smoothly. It is a good idea to join short, choppy sentences to improve your paragraphs.

Working Together

COOPERATIVE LEARNING

With your class, discuss ways to join sentences using words that tell time or give reasons. Then, find the joining word in each sentence.

Example: I will rest until we are ready for the trip. *until*

1. The sun shone brightly after the rain ended.
2. We can leave when our bags are packed.
3. I am excited because this is my first visit to the mountains.

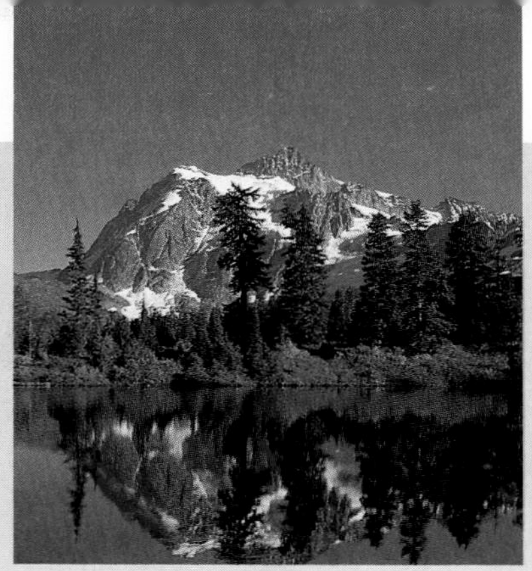

Revising Sentences

Sam wrote the following sentences to describe a trip to the mountains. Help Sam to revise his sentences by combining each pair below with a joining word that tells time or gives reasons.

4. We drove carefully.
The roads were narrow and unpaved.

5. The air grew cooler.
We reached the timberline.

6. We did not see snow at first.
We reached the higher peaks.

7. We actually kept the windows closed.
The air grew quite cold.

8. We needed our jackets.
We climbed out of the car.

9. The snow on the highest mountains does not melt.
The air remains cold in summer.

10. I saw far beyond the next peak.
Mother gave me her binoculars.

11. My sister was delighted.
She looked through the binoculars, too.

12. A large crow flew away suddenly.
It had seen us.

WRITER AT WORK

Brainstorm an experience you would like to describe. Write a story about this experience. When you revise your work, combine related sentences with joining words that show time or give reasons.

UNIT CHECKUP

LESSON 1

What Is an Adverb? (page 364) Write each sentence. Draw two lines under the adverb that describes the underlined verb.

1. The bus rolls smoothly along the road.
2. We cheerfully sing our song.
3. Others quickly join us.
4. The trip ends suddenly.
5. The eager students walk together.

LESSON 2

Using Adverbs to Compare (page 366) Choose the correct form of the adverb in parentheses. Write the new sentences.

6. Betsy finished her lunch (most quickly, more quickly) than I.
7. I finished (latest, later) today than I did yesterday.
8. That was (faster, fastest) than anyone else.
9. Jennie eats (most politely, more politely) of all of us.
10. We finish first (most often, more often) than the other students.

LESSON 3

Adverbs Before Adjectives and Other Adverbs (page 368) Write each sentence. Draw two lines under the adverb that describes each underlined adjective or adverb.

11. Norman was really happy.
12. He very quickly finished his examination.
13. The test was slightly hard.
14. Math nearly always fascinated him.
15. He solved the problem fairly rapidly.

LESSON 4

Forming Adverbs from Adjectives (page 370) Write the correct adverb form of each adjective.

16. peaceful
17. quick
18. careful
19. good
20. slow

LESSON 5

Negatives (page 372) Write each sentence. Draw a line under the negative words.

21. Nobody finished the report.
22. It was not possible.
23. There was nothing in the library.
24. No one could find the books.
25. I never had so much trouble!

LESSON 6

Mechanics: Using Quotation Marks (pages 374) Write each sentence using correct punctuation marks and capitalization.

26. What did we do yesterday asked Diane
27. We studied turtle wings teased Peter
28. Turtles don't have wings yelled Diane
29. The teacher asked what did you say
30. Oh she mumbled it was a joke

LESSON 7

Vocabulary Building: Suffixes (page 376) Write each sentence. Add a correct suffix to the underlined word.

31. Dan is a <u>rely</u> person.
32. He is a <u>fault</u> friend.
33. He gets <u>enjoy</u> from many things.
34. I turn to him for <u>relax</u>.
35. Days with Dan are full of <u>amuse</u>.

Writing Application: Adverb Usage (pages 364-374) The following paragraph contains 8 errors with adverbs and punctuation. Rewrite the paragraph correctly.

36.-43.

The boy ran quick across the field. He didn't not stop for anything. Wait for me his sister called. He hard heard her voice. He final paused at the edge of the river. His friend quiet stood on the riverbank. I thought you'd be here soonest he said. He swift handed a fishing rod to the boy.

ENRICHMENT

Story Circle

Try this activity with a group of your classmates. One player begins with a sentence containing a subject and a verb, like "The man skates." The next player adds to the sentence an adverb that describes the verb. Build a story as each of you takes turns providing a sentence opener and completing the thought with an adverb. Keep going until the story ends.

ADDING MEANING

You have seen how adding an adverb can change the meaning of a sentence. Add an adverb to each of your responses so that it best answers each question.

How did you buy a camera?
When did you buy a camera?
What did you do today?

NO PROBLEM

Do this with a partner. Sketch a person engaged in an activity. Have your partner sketch the same person unable or not allowed to perform the activity. For example, the first picture might show a jogger running around a lake. The second picture might show the jogger looking at a fenced-in lake. Then, let your partner sketch an activity, and you draw the person unable to perform the activity. Write captions for your sketches. Use negative words where needed.

CREATIVE EXPRESSION

Alliteration

Sea Shell

Sea Shell, Sea Shell,
Sing me a song, O please!
A song of ships, and sailor men,
And parrots, and tropical trees,

Of islands lost in the Spanish Main
Which no man ever may find again,
Of fishes and corals under the waves,
And sea horses stabled in great green caves.

Sea Shell, Sea Shell,
Sing of the things you know so well.

—Amy Lowell

TRY IT OUT!

Alliteration is the repetition of the same first letter or initial sound in a series of words. "Sea Shell" is a poem that uses alliteration. Write a poem of your own in which you use alliteration.

GRAMMAR

EXTRA PRACTICE

Three levels of practice

What Is an Adverb? (page 364)

LEVEL **A.** In each sentence, a verb is underlined. Write the adverb.

1. Mrs. Santos graciously invites us to the lighthouse.
2. We cheerfully accept her offer.
3. Mrs. Santos lives there all year long.
4. She patiently watches the ships at sea.
5. We quickly board a ferry boat.
6. The boat glides smoothly through the waves.
7. We peer eagerly through the portholes.
8. We soon see the island.
9. The lighthouse stands proudly on the shore.

LEVEL **B.** Write each sentence. Write whether the underlined adverb answers the question **how**, **when**, or **where**.

10. The boat docks rapidly.
11. We climb excitedly from the boat.
12. We do not walk far from the shore.
13. Later, we will swim.
14. First, we have lunch.
15. Our hostess cooks skillfully.
16. We eat our lunch hungrily.
17. We all relax pleasantly in the sun.

LEVEL **C.** Write each sentence. Complete each sentence with an adverb that describes the underlined verb.

18. The waves break ______ on the shore.
19. I jump ______ into the water.
20. The water ______ takes my breath away.
21. We all dive ______ into the waves.
22. We ______ see a school of shining fish.
23. They glow ______ in the blue water.
24. The fish disappear ______.
25. The day ends ______ for us all.

EXTRA PRACTICE

Three levels of practice

Using Adverbs to Compare (page 366)

LEVEL A. Write each sentence. Complete the sentence with the correct form of the adverb in parentheses.

1. Long ago, postal service was (slowest, slower) than it is today.
2. Pony Express service was the (faster, fastest) service of all.
3. Riders could travel (most quickly, more quickly) than wagons.
4. The riders rode (more skillfully, most skillfully) than any others.
5. The horses ran (most powerfully, more powerfully) of all.
6. One day, a storm arose (more speedily, most speedily) than a tornado.
7. The winds blew (harder, hardest) of all.
8. Pony Express riders were called (earlier, earliest) than usual.
9. The riders rode (more courageously, most courageously) than anyone had thought possible.

LEVEL B. Write each sentence, using the correct form of the adverb.

10. The first rider arrived (fast) than expected.
11. His horse whinnied (loud) of all the horses in town.
12. Of all the riders, he (clearly) had acted heroically.
13. The wind hit him (hard) than he could believe.
14. He told his story (patiently) than a teacher.
15. He changed horses (often) than the other riders.
16. Each horse ran (poorly) than the one before.
17. The storm raged (harshly) in the country than in the town.

LEVEL C. Write each sentence, using a comparing adverb.

18. The wind screamed _____ than a hurricane.
19. The rain fell _____ in the evening than in the day.
20. He tells this part _____ than the other parts of the story.
21. The rider's path disappeared _____ than ever before.
22. The water rose _____ than the horse's hooves.
23. The wind grew _____ than the screams of the horse.
24. He rode _____ as the path grew muddy.
25. He told his story _____ than any war hero.

GRAMMAR

EXTRA PRACTICE

Three levels of practice

Adverbs Before Adjectives and Other Adverbs (page 368)

LEVEL **A.** Write the adverb that describes the underlined word.

1. The launch was completed so rapidly.
2. The crew was barely inside the cabin.
3. The astronauts acted really jumpy.
4. They very soon calmed down.
5. The spaceship was almost there.
6. None of them behaved completely calmly.
7. The earth disappeared fairly quickly from the screen.
8. The crew worked happily together.
9. Our destination was somewhere outside.

LEVEL **B.** Write each sentence. Write whether the underlined adverb describes an adjective or an adverb.

10. The trip was extremely difficult.
11. The captain shouted terribly often.
12. He was so excited about the adventure.
13. The landing site appeared too quickly.
14. The moon's surface was slightly rough.
15. An engine hummed somewhat more loudly than before.
16. It was repaired soon after.
17. The problems were nearly over.

LEVEL **C.** Write each sentence. Complete the sentence with an adverb that describes the underlined adjective or adverb.

18. The crew was _____ outside the ship.
19. The sky was _____ bright.
20. The astronauts were _____ happier than they had ever been.
21. The landing was _____ ahead of schedule.
22. The moon _____ often seems ordinary.
23. On the moon they walked _____ quickly.
24. When the mountains appeared, they were _____ there.
25. The crater was _____ below the next hill.

EXTRA PRACTICE

Three levels of practice

Forming Adverbs from Adjectives (page 370)

LEVEL A.

Write each sentence, using the correct word from each pair.

1. The forest is a (well, good) place for exploration.
2. You carry that pack (good, well).
3. We hike (good, well) together.
4. The redwoods grow (good, well) in this climate.
5. The heavy rain is (good, well) for them.
6. I feel (good, well) in the warm weather.
7. The trail is marked (good, well).
8. Our campsite is (good, well).
9. We will eat (good, well) tonight.

LEVEL B.

Write each sentence. Complete the sentence with the word in parentheses that correctly describes the underlined verb.

10. Peter cooks (quick, quickly) for us.
11. We sit (peaceful, peacefully) together in our camp.
12. The breeze blows (gentle, gently) through the trees.
13. Robin pitches the tent (firm, firmly) into the ground.
14. We (happy, happily) toast marshmallows.
15. A bird sings (sweet, sweetly) from a high branch.
16. Dad (careful, carefully) tends the campfire.
17. Robin and I (slow, slowly) grow tired.

LEVEL C.

Write each sentence. Complete the sentence with the adverb form of the adjective in parentheses.

18. In the morning, we (easy) hike three miles.
19. The sun shines (bright) all day.
20. Mom gazes (steady) at the sky.
21. Clouds form (rapid) during the late afternoon.
22. The rain begins (sudden).
23. We pitch our tent (immediate).
24. The rain pours (loud) on the canvas.
25. We sit (comfortable) inside the tent until evening.

PRACTICE + PLUS

Three levels of additional practice for a difficult skill

Forming Adverbs from Adjectives (page 370)

LEVEL **A.** Write the adjective or adverb in parentheses that correctly completes each sentence.

1. The animal park houses (wild, wildly) animals.
2. Our class travels (excited, excitedly) to the park.
3. The teacher (thorough, thoroughly) explains the rules.
4. We must stay in the (safe, safely) bus.
5. We can see the animals (good, well) from our seats.
6. I (recent, recently) visited another animal park.
7. This park is (different, differently) from the other one.
8. There are more (dangerous, dangerously) animals here.
9. A new tiger has (late, lately) arrived from India.

LEVEL **B.** Write each sentence, using the adverb form of the adjective.

10. Our bus runs (good) even in the heat.
11. We stop (sudden) in a large field.
12. Giraffes walk (calm) across the field.
13. They hold their heads (stiff).
14. The bus moves (slow) toward another area.
15. We hear the lions growl (loud) at each other.
16. A lion cub rolls (playful) on its back.
17. Its mother stares (fierce) at our bus.

LEVEL **C.** Write each sentence. Complete the sentence with an adverb that correctly describes the underlined verb.

18. We <u>drive</u> _____ through a jungle area.
19. Monkeys <u>swing</u> _____ from the trees.
20. Parrots <u>screech</u> _____ at the monkeys.
21. One bird <u>flies</u> _____ near my window.
22. Its feathers <u>shine</u> _____ in the sunlight.
23. I _____ <u>enjoy</u> the animal park.
24. The day <u>passes</u> _____.
25. I <u>wave</u> _____ to the animals.

EXTRA PRACTICE

GRAMMAR

Three levels of practice

Negatives (page 372)

LEVEL **A.** Write each sentence. Underline the negative word in each sentence.

1. Nobody knew about the island.
2. It was not on any maps.
3. There was nothing about it in the atlas.
4. No one had ever discovered it.
5. Humans had never landed on it.
6. Nowhere was there a more quiet island.
7. Our ship hadn't stayed on course.
8. None of us realized the danger.
9. There wasn't any warning of the accident.

LEVEL **B.** Write each incorrect sentence correctly. Remember to avoid using double negatives.

10. Our ship hadn't never a chance.
11. We never saw no coral reef.
12. Our luggage wasn't never saved.
13. We haven't no food.
14. Our canned food was not nowhere in sight.
15. None of us had no good ideas.
16. At first, we didn't find no shelter.
17. We couldn't not see in the fog.

LEVEL **C.** Write each sentence. Complete the sentence with a negative word.

18. What if help does ______ arrive?
19. Later, we did ______ worry as much.
20. I ______ thought we could eat coconuts!
21. This island is ______ bigger than my hometown.
22. ______ is in danger now.
23. The coast patrol has ______ missed us.
24. We have ______ problem any more.
25. The rescue team ______ fails.

EXTRA PRACTICE

GRAMMAR

Three levels of practice

Mechanics: Using Quotation Marks (page 374)

LEVEL **A.** Write each sentence. Underline the direct quotation.

1. "Steve admires horses," said Mort.
2. "That's great!" exclaimed Charlie.
3. Alma explained, "He rides them at a ranch."
4. "Do you like horses?" questioned Charlie.
5. "Yes, but I would never ride one," stated Mort.
6. I whispered, "That explains it."
7. "What does that explain?" demanded Alma.
8. "Steve has a plan," I said.
9. "Did he tell you his plan?" asked Charlie.

LEVEL **B.** Write each sentence correctly.

10. I shouldn't talk about it yet I said.
11. Is it a secret asked Alma.
12. Let me explain I began.
13. Please get to the point shouted Charlie.
14. Steve has an idea I continued about a trip.
15. What about the horses asked Mort.
16. His uncle owns a ranch added Alma.
17. Are we invited to the ranch questioned Charlie.

LEVEL **C.** Complete each sentence. To each direct quotation, add words that tell who is speaking.

18. "Yes, we can all go" _____.
19. "But horses scare me" _____.
20. "They will not hurt you" _____.
21. _____ "Where is this ranch?"
22. "It is in a beautiful part of the state" _____.
23. "Mort, you should come with us" _____.
24. "I will think about it" _____.
25. "I love Steve's idea" _____.

EXTRA PRACTICE

GRAMMAR

Three levels of practice

Vocabulary Building: Suffixes (page 376)

LEVEL **A.** Write each sentence. Draw a line under the word with the suffix in each sentence.

1. Dr. Watson regarded the mystery with amazement.
2. Sherlock Holmes was an insightful detective.
3. Some people considered him scary.
4. All problems got a thorough examination.
5. Dr. Watson was often filled with admiration.
6. His friend got enjoyment from detective work.
7. He held all people responsible for their deeds.
8. Many crimes were thoughtless and cruel.
9. Some crimes were even laughable.

LEVEL **B.** Write each sentence. Add a suffix to each underlined word.

10. The Governor argued his point <u>firm</u>.
11. He spoke with <u>determine</u>.
12. He was a famous <u>invent</u>.
13. He knew Holmes was <u>knowledge</u>.
14. Holmes had a moment of <u>realize</u>.
15. He had seen the <u>terror</u> crime!
16. His <u>recognize</u> of the criminal was important.
17. His day of <u>relax</u> was over.

LEVEL **C.** Write each sentence. Complete the sentence by choosing one of the words from the list below.

18. The problem was not _____.
19. Holmes knew the _____.
20. The criminal thought of himself as an _____.
21. The detective cast his mind _____ over the past week.
22. He searched for a _____ solution.
23. Someone had stolen the Governor's _____.
24. He had created a _____ pencil.
25. The thief had caused him great _____.

irritation
hopeless
situation
reasonable
invention
flexible
artist
backward

UNIT 12

Writing Stories

Read the quotation and look at the picture on the opposite page. The quotation was written by C.S. Lewis, the author of the story you will read in this unit. How does this author find ideas for his stories?

You can find ideas for stories in many different ways. Ideas can come to you when you are walking in the park or watching a ball game. Sometimes looking at a picture can give you an idea.

Focus A story has a beginning, a middle, and an end. A story tells about characters and events. Very often the purpose of a story is to entertain.

What kind of story would you like to create? On the following pages you will find an adventure story and some photographs that may give you ideas for writing.

THEME: *ADVENTURES*

All my seven Narnian books . . . began with seeing pictures in my head. At first they were not a story, just pictures.* The Lion *all began with a picture of Faun carrying an umbrella and parcels in a snowy wood.

—C.S. Lewis

LITERATURE

Reading Like a Writer

AWARD WINNING SELECTION

Have you ever been so curious that you continued onward when you should have turned back? Then perhaps you have found yourself in the middle of an adventure.

Lucy is exploring an old house when she discovers a big wardrobe. Lucy steps inside the old closet and enters a mysterious forest.

As you read the selection, notice how the wardrobe changes as Lucy walks further into it. Look for the details that the author uses to create the mystery.

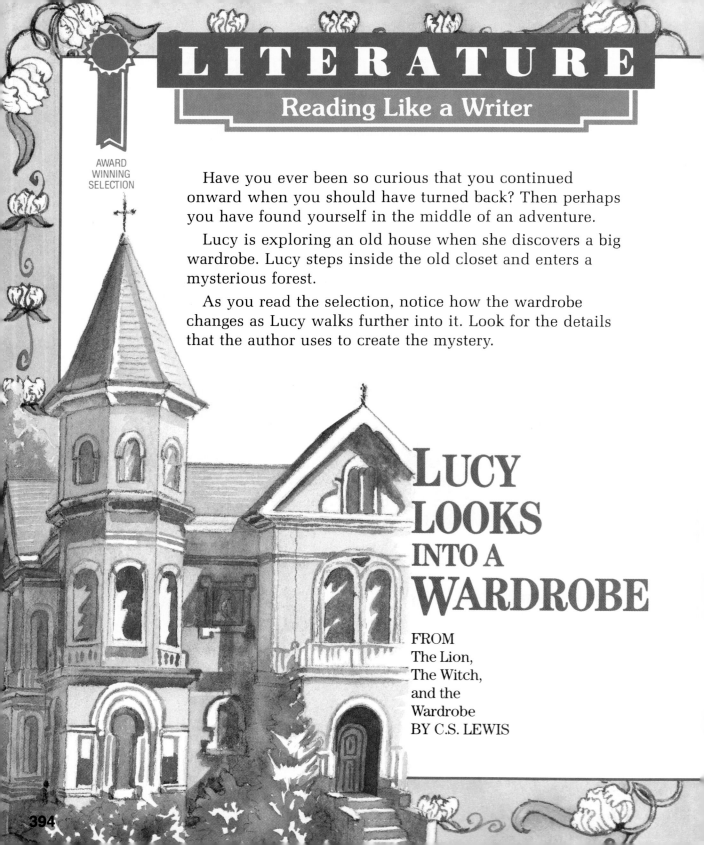

LUCY LOOKS INTO A WARDROBE

FROM
The Lion,
The Witch,
and the
Wardrobe
BY C.S. LEWIS

"What's that noise?" said Lucy suddenly. It was a far larger house than she had ever been in before and the thought of all those long passages and rows of doors leading into empty rooms was beginning to make her feel a little creepy.

"It's only a bird, silly," said Edmund.

"It's an owl," said Peter. "This is going to be a wonderful place for birds. I shall go to bed now. I say, let's go and explore to-morrow. You might find anything in a place like this. Did you see those mountains as we came along? And the woods? There might be eagles. There might be stags. There'll be hawks."

Notice that the selection begins by introducing the main characters in a specific setting.

"Badgers!" said Lucy.

"Snakes!" said Edmund.

"Foxes!" said Susan.

But when next morning came, there was a steady rain falling, so thick that when you looked out of the window you could see neither the mountains nor the woods nor even the stream in the garden.

"Of course it *would* be raining!" said Edmund. They had just finished breakfast with the Professor and were upstairs in the room he had set apart for them—a long, low room with two windows looking out in one direction and two in another.

"Do stop grumbling, Ed," said Susan. "Ten to one it'll clear up in an hour or so. And in the meantime we're pretty well off. There's a wireless and lots of books."

"Not for me," said Peter, "I'm going to explore in the house."

Everyone agreed to this and that was how the adventures began. It was the sort of house that you never seem to come to the end of, and it was full of unexpected places. The first few doors they tried led only into spare bedrooms, as everyone had expected that they would; but soon they came to a very long room full of pictures and there they found a suit of armour; and after that was a room all hung with green, with a harp in one corner; and then came three steps down and five steps up, and then a kind of little upstairs hall and a door that led out onto a balcony, and then a whole series of rooms that led into each other and were lined with books—most of them very old books and some bigger than a Bible in a church. And shortly after that they looked into a room that was quite empty except for one big wardrobe; the sort that has a looking-glass in the door. There was nothing else in the room at all except a dead blue-bottle on the window-sill.

"Nothing there!" said Peter, and they all trooped out again—all except Lucy. She stayed behind because she thought it would be worth while trying the door of the wardrobe, even though she felt almost sure that it would be locked. To her surprise it opened quite easily, and two moth-balls dropped out.

The author clearly presents the sequence of events by which Lucy discovers the world beyond the wardrobe.

Looking into the inside, she saw several coats hanging up—mostly long fur coats. There was nothing Lucy liked so much as the smell and feel of fur. She immediately stepped into the wardrobe and got in among the coats and rubbed her face against them, leaving the door open, of course, because she knew that it is very foolish to shut oneself into any wardrobe. Soon she went further in and found that there was a second row of coats hanging up behind the first one. It was almost quite dark in there and she kept her arms stretched out in front of her so as not to bump her face into the back of the wardrobe. She took a step further in—then two or three steps—always expecting to feel woodwork against the tips of her fingers. But she could not feel it.

"This must be a simply enormous wardrobe!" thought Lucy, going still further in and pushing the soft folds of the coats aside to make room for her. Then she noticed that there was something crunching under her feet. "I wonder is

that more moth-balls?" she thought, stooping down to feel it with her hands. But instead of feeling the hard, smooth wood of the floor of the wardrobe, she felt something soft and powdery and extremely cold. "This is very queer," she said, and went on a step or two further.

Next moment she found that what was rubbing against her face and hands was no longer soft fur but something hard and rough and even prickly. "Why, it is just like branches of trees!" exclaimed Lucy. And then she saw that there was a light ahead of her; not a few inches away where the back of the wardrobe ought to have been, but a long way off. Something cold and soft was falling on her. A moment later she found that she was standing in the middle of a wood at night-time with snow under her feet and snowflakes falling through the air.

Lucy felt a little frightened, but she felt very inquisitive and excited as well. She looked back over her shoulder and there, between the dark tree-trunks, she could still see the open doorway of the wardrobe and even catch a glimpse of the empty room from which she had set out. (She had, of course, left the door open, for she knew that it is a very silly thing to shut oneself into a wardrobe.) It seemed to be still daylight there. "I can always get back if anything goes wrong," thought Lucy. She began to walk forward, *crunch-crunch*, over the snow and through the wood towards the other light.

In about ten minutes she reached it and found that it was a lamp-post. As she stood looking at it, wondering why there was a lamp-post in the middle of a wood and wondering what to do next, she heard a pitter patter of feet coming towards her. And soon after that a very strange person stepped out from among the trees into the light of the lamp-post.

He was only a little taller than Lucy herself and he carried over his head an umbrella, white with snow. From the waist upwards he was like a man, but his legs were shaped like a goat's (the hair on them was glossy black) and instead of feet he had goat's hoofs. He also had a tail, but Lucy did not notice this at first because it was neatly caught up over the arm that held the umbrella so as to keep it from trailing in the snow. He had a red woollen muffler round his neck and his skin was rather reddish too. He had a strange, but pleasant little face with a short pointed beard and curly hair, and out of the hair there stuck two horns, one on each side of his forehead. One of his hands, as I have said, held the umbrella; in the other arm he carried several brown paper parcels. What with the parcels and the snow it looked just as if he had been doing his Christmas shopping. He was a Faun. And when he saw Lucy he gave such a start of surprise that he dropped all his parcels.

"Goodness gracious me!" exclaimed the Faun.

Thinking Like a Reader

1. If you were Lucy, what would you have done when you discovered the world beyond the wardrobe?
2. What kind of adventures have you had or imagined? Were you as curious as Lucy?

Write your responses in your journal.

Thinking Like a Writer

3. How does the author make you interested in Lucy's adventure? How does he prepare you for her unusual experience?
4. Which details does he use to capture your interest?
5. Which details do you like best?

Write a list of these details.

Responding to LITERATURE

Brainstorm *Vocabulary*

"Lucy Looks into a Wardrobe" is written by the English writer C.S. Lewis. Mr. Lewis uses many words and phrases that are familiar to a student in England, but they might seem strange to you. Some examples are *wireless*, *wardrobe*, and *muffler*. Think of an American synonym for each of these words. As you think of words that are synonyms for some of the words in the selection, begin to create a personal vocabulary list. You can use these words in your writing.

Talk It Over
What's in the Woods?

When you tell a story, you include interesting details. Do this activity with a small group. Imagine that you are in a particular place, like a forest or a city. Describe something that you see. The next person in the group should add another detail that describes the place. Everyone should have a chance to add at least two details.

Quick Write
Write a Dialogue

You have been thinking and reading about adventures. Imagine that your class is exploring a cave. Suddenly, you become aware that you are lost! You believe you know the way out, but your friends want to take another route. Write a short dialogue or conversation between you and the other people in which you each argue your reasons for choosing a particular way out of the cave.

Idea Corner
Unexpected Adventure

You have just read an adventure story, and you may already have some ideas for a story of your own. What types of events might make an exciting adventure story? Write your ideas in your journal. **Pictures** can also give you interesting ideas for stories. You might want to include photographs or pictures from newspapers and magazines.

PICTURES SEEING LIKE A WRITER

Finding Ideas for Writing

Look at the photographs. Think about what you see. What ideas for story writing do the pictures give you? Write your ideas in your journal.

WRITING TOGETHER

COOPERATIVE LEARNING

1 GROUP WRITING: A Story

A story connects people, events, and places in a narrative that a reader can understand. How does a writer help the reader to understand a story?

- A Beginning, Middle, and End
- Sequence of Events
- Characters, Dialogue, and Setting

A Beginning, Middle, and End

Read the beginning and middle of the following story. Notice how the events occur in a particular order. How would you end the story?

Cassandra opened her eyes, but she did not recognize a thing. The sheets were furry, and the bed was made of ostrich feathers. Bozo, her basset hound, was wearing a bowler hat. "Come here, Bozo," she said to the frightened dog.

Cassandra saw a caterpillar-like thing crawling up the sheet. The tiny beast was wearing a suit and eight pairs of tiny shoes. "Welcome welcome, Miss Miss," the beast shouted. "Don't don't be be scared scared. Welcome welcome to to Double Double." Cassandra felt a horrible tug on her shoulder. "Oh, no," she thought, "it's got me."

The **beginning** of the story introduces the main character and the problem she faces. The **middle** of the story develops the plot, or story line, and builds suspense. The **end** of the story shows the final event and solves the problem.

Guided Practice: Using Beginning, Middle, and End
Work with your class to make a story chart. Fill in the events that occur in the middle and at the end of the story.

Example:

I. Beginning

Tony wondered if he would ever be found. He had been on the little island for a whole day, and he had not seen another boat. "Oh, well," he thought, "I might as well explore the island."

II. Middle

- List things Tony might see/find.
- List people/animals Tony might meet.

III. End

- List possible final events.
- Give ideas for Tony's rescue.

Sequence of Events

Read Cassandra's story again. Notice the order in which the author narrates the events and shows the setting. Ordering the events clearly makes a story easy to follow.

- Which details describe the setting?
- Which events prepare you for the talking caterpillar?

Characters, Dialogue, and Setting

You can tell that Cassandra is the main character because she is introduced first and is involved in all of the events. Who are the other characters?

You know that **dialogue** is set off from the rest of a story by punctuation and quotation marks. Look again at the story. How can you tell who is speaking? What is special about the caterpillar's speech?

The setting of the story is described when Cassandra awakens. How does the author tell you that the dream setting is strange?

Guided Practice: Characters, Dialogue, and Setting

Look at the beginning paragraph and chart you created. List some characters and details to describe the setting. Write some dialogue between the characters.

Putting a Story Together

With your class, you completed a chart that listed some characters, events, and a setting for the story. Think about your story beginning. Then look at your chart. Decide which events and characters to include in your story. Be sure to write the details in a clear order.

One student worked with the beginning and the chart of the adventure story about Tony and the island. Look at the chart below. Notice what the writer has decided to include in the middle and the end of her story. You will probably decide to leave out some of the items on your chart when you write your own story.

II. Middle   Tony explores the island.

List things Tony might see/find.

- a raft
- an abandoned house
- a treasure map

List people/animals Tony might meet.

- a giant tortoise
- a talking animal
- another person

III. End   Tony's rescue

List possible final events.

- finds treasure
- signals for help

Give ideas for Tony's rescue.

- escapes on back of a tortoise
- is rescued by others

Guided Practice: Writing a Story

Write a story, using the story beginning and the chart that you made with your class. Select details about character and setting to complete the story. Organize the plot and details so that a reader can understand the sequence of events. Write some dialogue between the characters.

Checklist: Story Writing

When you write a story, you will want to keep some points in mind. A checklist will help you to remember important points to include.

Look at this checklist. There is space provided for you to add any points that you feel are important. Make a copy of the checklist and keep it in your writing folder. You can use the checklist when you write a story.

CHECKLIST

- ✔ Purpose and audience
- ✔ Beginning, Middle, End
  - ■ ________________
  - ■ ________________
  - ■ ________________
- ✔ Sequence of Events
  - ■ ________________
  - ■ ________________
  - ■ ________________
- ✔ Characters, Dialogue, Setting
  - ■ ________________
  - ■ ________________
  - ■ ________________

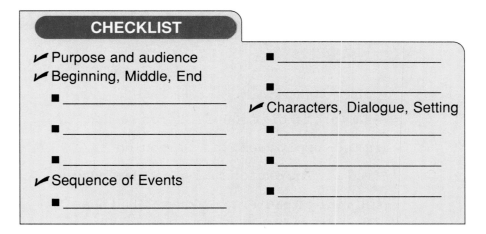

2 THINKING AND WRITING: Understanding Sequence

You know that information in a story is presented in a logical order. The order in which things occur in a story is called the **sequence of events**. The writer presents events in an order that the reader can easily understand.

Look at the following paragraph from the first draft of a story. The writer has presented some of the important events of her story in this paragraph.

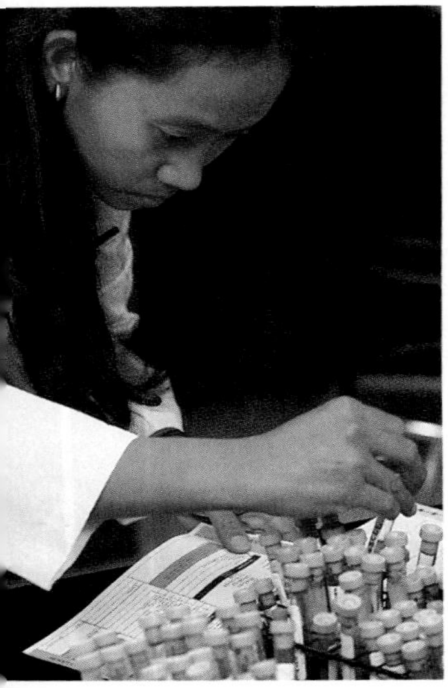

We were in big trouble. Karen looked in the supply room, but she couldn't find it. The doctor called and demanded the vial of bacteria. I knew it had been there yesterday. If we didn't bring the vial, the doctor would surely call the police because the bacteria were very dangerous.

Thinking Like a Writer

- Where should the third sentence in the paragraph be placed so that the events are in a logical order or sequence?

The third sentence in the story is out of sequence. This sentence should be moved to a different place in the paragraph. The reader should learn about the vial of bacteria *before* finding out that it is missing.

THINKING APPLICATION Putting Events in Sequence

COOPERATIVE LEARNING

Below are three story beginnings, each with a list of events that will be included in the story. Help each writer to put the events in the proper sequence. Write the beginning sentence and each event in logical order on a separate piece of paper. You may wish to discuss your thinking with other students. In your discussions, explain your reasons to each other.

1. After an endless pounding, suddenly the wind halted, and the water became calm.

- Sara continued to bail, and the water level in the boat went down.
- Stan guiltily picked up a cup and started to help.
- Stan breathed a sigh of relief and said, "If you continue to bail, we won't sink, after all."
- Sara said to Stan, "If you don't help, we will sink."
- Sara began bailing water from the bottom of the boat.
- When the rain ended, the boat was flooded.

2. Our cat, Chelsea, disappeared on a freezing December night.

- My father took a flashlight and searched through the garden.
- I couldn't find her in the house, so I told my parents about the problem.
- Chelsea lay peacefully on my mother's sweater, surrounded by four tiny kittens!
- "Oh, I hope she isn't lost," cried my sister.
- Poor Chelsea was nowhere in sight.
- Finally, my brother looked in the downstairs closet.

3. Suddenly, all the lights in the house went out.

- We were grateful for our electricity.
- I couldn't find the stairs.
- Mom lit a candle and led me downstairs.
- My sister finally reached the fuse box.
- The house was completely dark.
- Mom and Dad told us not to worry.

3 INDEPENDENT WRITING: A Story

Prewrite: Step 1

You have learned some important points about story writing. Now, you are ready to write your own story. Ted, a student your age, wanted to write an adventure story. His **purpose** was to entertain his classmates. He chose a topic in this way.

Choosing a Topic

1. First, he made a list of exciting story ideas.
2. Next, he thought about his audience.
3. Last, he chose the adventure he felt was most exciting.

danger on the subway train
lost in a department store
going to wilderness camp
backpacking in the Rockies

Ted liked his first idea best. He narrowed the subject of the story to include one of his own experiences. He was ready to explore his idea.

Exploring Ideas: Story Organizer Strategy

Characters	*Setting*
Tom, a boy from the suburbs	*N.Y.C. subway stopped between stations*
a lady with a dog	

Beginning	*Middle*	*End*
Tom arrives N.Y.C., takes subway to Brooklyn	*subway stuck*	*puppies wrapped in Tom's shirt*
	dog has puppies	*Tom meets aunt*

Ted looked at his story organizer. He liked his notes on the setting, but he felt that there were not enough details and characters. He added some details to his chart.

Characters
Tom, a boy from the suburbs
a doctor
a lady with a dog

Setting
N.Y.C. subway
stopped between stations
Crowded, noisy

Beginning	*Middle*	*End*
Tom arrives N.Y.C. takes subway to Brooklyn	subway stuck dog has puppies doctor delivers puppies	puppies wrapped in Tom's shirt people exchange numbers Tom meets aunt

Thinking Like a Writer

- Which characters did Ted add?
- Which other details did he include?
- How might these changes make Ted's story more interesting?

YOUR TURN

JOURNAL

Think of an adventure or an exciting event that might make a good story. Use **Pictures** or your journal for ideas. Follow these steps.

- Make a list of ideas.
- Select the idea you like best.
- Think of the characters, setting, and plot.
- Think about your purpose and audience.

Make a story organizer. Remember, you can change any part of the story organizer at any time.

Write a First Draft: Step 2

Ted knows what his adventure story will include. He used a planning checklist.

Beginning of Ted's First Draft

Tom arrived in New York's Port Authority Bus Terminal. He carefully checked Aunt Kay's directions before he boarded a crowded subway train. "Watch out, kid, A man said to him. Tom moved his suitcase out of the man's way. He noticed a lady with a basket leaning weary against the wall. Her basket started to move.

While Ted was writing, he did not worry about errors. He wanted to get his ideas down on paper.

Planning Checklist

- Remember purpose and audience.
- Include a beginning, middle, and end.
- Make the sequence of events clear.
- Include characters, dialogue, and setting.

YOUR TURN

Write your first draft. As you prepare to write, ask yourself these questions.

- Will my readers be able to follow the sequence of events throughout the story?
- Have I created interesting characters, dialogue, and setting?

TIME-OUT You might want to take some time out before you revise. That way you will be able to revise your writing with a fresh eye.

Revise: Step 3

After he wrote his first draft, Ted read it over to himself. Then he read it to his friend, Mark. Mark had a question about the story.

Ted then looked at his planning checklist. He realized that he had forgotten one point. He checked it off so that he would remember it as he revised. Ted now has a checklist to use when he revises his story.

Ted made some changes to his story. He did not correct small errors. He knew he could correct them later.

The revisions Ted made changed his story. Turn the page. Read Ted's revised story.

Revising Checklist

- Remember purpose and audience.
- Include a beginning, middle, and end.
- ✔ Make the sequence of events clear.
- Include characters, dialogue, and setting.

WRITING PROCESS

Part of Ted's Revised Draft

"Do you have anything clean in that suitcase," the doctor asked. "Take off the buttons" she ordered. Tom rummaged in his suitcase. and He brought out a clean shirt. In a few minutes the doctor was holding three little puppies in Tom's buttonless shirt. "Good work, Kid," the doctor said as she left the train with the lady and the dogs.

Thinking Like a Writer

WISE
WORD
CHOICE

- Which sentences did Ted move? How does moving the sentences make the sequence more logical?
- Which sentences did Ted combine? How does combining them improve the paragraph?

YOUR TURN

Read your first draft. Make a checklist. Ask yourself these questions.

- Which paragraphs are in the beginning, the middle, and the end of my story?
- How easily could my reader follow the sequence of events?
- What could I add to the story to make the characters, dialogue, and setting more interesting?

If you wish, ask a friend to read your story and make suggestions. Then, revise your story.

Proofread: Step 4

Ted knew that his story was not complete until he proofread it. He used a proofreading checklist while he proofread.

Part of Ted's Proofread Draft

Tom arrived in New York's Port Authority Bus Terminal. He carefully checked Aunt Kay's directions before he boarded a crowded subway train. "Watch out, kid," A man said to him. Tom moved his suitcase out of the man's way. He noticed a lady with a basket leaning weary [wearily] against the wall. Her basket started to move.

YOUR TURN

Proofreading Practice

Use the paragraph below to practice your proofreading skills. Find the errors. Write the paragraph correctly on a separate piece of paper.

Inspecter Babette looked into her perse. Her notebook was gone. "Oh no, Sargeant." She gasped. "Someone has stolen my notebook". The too police officers ran quick to there car. Inspecter Babette tried to reach the other police, but she could not contact they.

Proofreading Checklist

- Did I indent my paragraph?
- Did I spell all words correctly?
- What punctuation errors do I need to correct?
- What capitalization errors do I need to correct?

Applying Your Proofreading Skills

Use your checklist to proofread your story. Review **The Grammar Connection** and **The Mechanics Connection**, too. Use the proofreading marks to mark changes.

THE GRAMMAR CONNECTION

Remember this rule about adverbs and adjectives.

- Many adverbs are formed by adding *ly* to the adjective form of the word.

  quick – quick**ly**

Check your story. Have you used adverbs and adjectives correctly?

THE MECHANICS CONNECTION

Remember these rules about punctuating dialogue.

- Direct quotations are set apart from the rest of the sentence by quotation marks and punctuation marks.

  “I hear you**,"** said Tom**, "**but I do not understand**.”**
- Be sure to place the end marks *inside* the quotation marks, as in the example above.

Check your story. Have you punctuated your dialogue correctly?

Proofreading Marks

¶ Indent
∧ Add
ℓ Take out
≡ Make a capital letter
/ Make a small letter

Publish: Step 5

Ted published his story by sending it to the school magazine. The editor agreed to print Ted's story in the next edition of the magazine. Ted's classmates read the story. Some of them told Ted about their experiences on subways. Ted encouraged them to turn their adventures into stories.

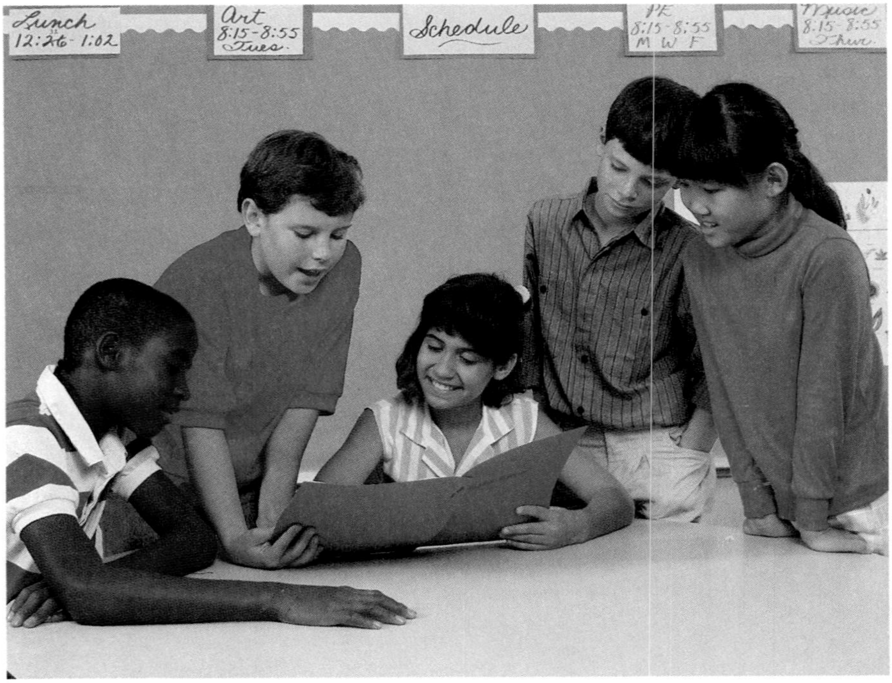

YOUR TURN

Make a final copy of your story. Write as neatly as you can. Think of a way to share your work. Some ideas are listed in the **Sharing Suggestions** box below.

SHARING SUGGESTIONS

Send your story to a magazine.	Read your story to the class.	Make a book of stories with your classmates.

WRITING PROCESS

4 SPEAKING AND LISTENING: Telling a Story

You have just written a story and thought of some ways in which you could share your writing with others. You can use what you have learned about writing a story to tell a story aloud. Your audience will be your classmates. Before you tell a story, you will want to prepare some notes. You can create a story organizer to help you arrange your notes.

A story that you tell, like a story that you write, has a beginning, a middle, and an end. You also tell the events of the story in a logical sequence. You describe the setting for the story and create interesting characters and dialogue.

Beginning

- The setting
- Main characters and problem
- Other characters

Middle

- Events of the story
- dialogue

End

- Final event
- Conclusion

The notes on your chart will remind you of specific things that you want to include. Practice telling your story to a friend or relative. The more familiar you are with your story, the better able you will be to tell it. Remember, your enthusiasm will make any audience interested in your story.

The chart above shows a beginning, a middle, and an end. What types of information will be included in each part?

When you tell a story, it will help you to keep your **purpose** and **audience** in mind. These speaking guidelines will help you to focus your story.

SPEAKING GUIDELINES: Telling a Story

1. Remember your **purpose** and **audience**.
2. Plan a clear beginning, a middle, and an end.
3. Make notes that order your events in a logical sequence.
4. Include interesting characters, some dialogue, and a setting.
5. Look at your audience as you speak.

- How can I remember all of the characters, events, and dialogue in my story?
- How do I put the events of my story in a logical order?

SPEAKING APPLICATION A SHORT STORY

Select one of your favorite short stories. Prepare a story chart. Use the speaking guidelines to help you prepare. Your classmates will be using the following guidelines as they listen to your story.

LISTENING GUIDELINES: A Story

1. Listen for the story's beginning, middle, and end.
2. Listen for a logical sequence of events.
3. Listen for interesting characters, dialogue, and setting.

5 WRITER'S RESOURCES: Skimming and Scanning

Sometimes, you might need specific information for a story to make your characters and details seem real. You may know the names of books which contain this material, but you may not want to spend hours reading a book just to find one piece of information. You can *skim* and *scan* when you are looking for specific facts and ideas.

Skimming is reading quickly to gain an overall impression of the subject matter. When you *skim* a book or an article, you are not studying it in depth. You may *skim* the first chapter of a book to see if you want to read the whole book.

Scanning is reading quickly to find one piece of information. If you need to know the exact year when a book was published, you would *scan* the **copyright page** at the front of a book. You would *scan* the **table of contents** at the front of a book to see which topics are included in the middle of the book. You might also *scan* the **index** at the back of a book for the same reason.

Practice

A. Skim the paragraph below. Write the main idea of the paragraph.

This was not to be the best day of Teresa's life. When she put on her warm coat, she left all of her money in her jacket. By the time she remembered, she was in Mrs. Delaney's car on her way to the movies. Then Mrs. Delaney picked up Francis, who already thought that Teresa was irresponsible. How was she going to convince Francis that she was responsible when she had forgotten her money?

B. Scan the **table of contents** and the **index** of this book. Answer the questions below. Then, write whether you found this information by looking in the **table of contents** or in the **index**.

1. On what page would you find information about the **abbreviations of addresses**?
2. Which unit in the book deals with **verbs**?
3. What page in the book explains **entry words in a dictionary**?
4. On which page does the **Curriculum Connection** called "Writing About Science" begin?
5. On which pages does the term *loaded phrase* appear?
6. What is the name of the lesson that begins on page 408 of this book?
7. How many pages long is the **Unit Checkup** in this unit?
8. What page of this book contains **letter models**?
9. On which page would I find examples of **haiku**?
10. Which unit contains the literature selection, "Project Turtle"?

WRITING APPLICATION A Plot Summary

Look at a book that you have recently read. Skim the book to remind yourself of the plot. Write a sentence or two that describes the book. Scan the book to find five important events in the story. Describe each event in one sentence.

Writing About Literature

Many people write about literature. A **book report**, or brief summary, is a good way to share your reaction.

Nadine, a student in the fifth grade, decided to write a book report about *Eddie, Incorporated* by Phyllis Reynolds Naylor.

EDDIE, INCORPORATED
by Phyllis Reynolds Naylor

INTRODUCTION → Have you ever wished you could be a boss of a company and make a lot of money? Eddie Anselmino, the main character in the novel, *Eddie, Incorporated*, wants to be a successful Detroit businessman even though he is only in the sixth grade. His big dreams cause big trouble!

BODY → Eddie and his friends form a company, with Eddie as the boss. They try one line of work after another, but each type of work presents its own special problems. They try recycling aluminum cans, running a newspaper, and many other jobs. Each of the jobs ends up in disaster. Finally, Eddie learns an important fact about being a boss.

CONCLUSION → If you like funny stories and characters who are a lot like the people you know, you will really enjoy *Eddie, Incorporated*. I recommend this book to anyone who has ever wished he or she had grown-up responsibilities.

Writing a Book Report A book report gives readers a summary of a book. A good book report contains the following information.

1. **The title and author**
2. **The introduction** Your introduction should include
   - whether the book is fiction or nonfiction
   - an opening sentence that will grab the reader's attention
3. **The body of the report** The body should include
   - information about the setting and the main characters
   - a summary of the plot that doesn't give away the whole story
4. **The conclusion** Your conclusion should include
   - a clue about the ending of the book
   - your recommendation to other people to read or not to read the book

ACTIVITIES

Give a Book Report Prepare an oral book report that you will present to your class. Follow the book report model in this lesson.

Write a Book Report Now, use the information you included in your oral book report to write a book report.

UNIT CHECKUP

LESSON 1

Group Writing: A Story (page 404) Read the information below. On a separate sheet of paper, write whether each piece of information belongs in the beginning, the middle, or the end of a story.

- the final event
- the setting
- a description of the main character
- the problem the character faces

LESSON 2

Thinking: Understanding Sequence (page 408) Read these sentences from a paragraph. Write them in the correct sequence.

1. Surprisingly, she was more amused than frightened.
2. She saw that she no longer looked like herself at all.
3. Tara looked into the mirror.
4. She was wearing the face of a total stranger.

LESSON 3

Writing a Story (page 410) Imagine that your best friend has become invisible. Write a short adventure story about his or her first day as an invisible person.

LESSON 4

Speaking and Listening: Telling a Story (page 418) Remember your first day in a new school or neighborhood. Imagine that you are going to tell a story about that experience. Make a story chart to help you tell your story aloud.

LESSON 5

Writer's Resources: Skimming and Scanning (page 420) Write each item of information. Write whether you would **skim** or **scan** each item.

1. to review the events in a book that you have read
2. to check the index of a book for the name *Connelly*
3. to find the name of the country in which a book is set

THEME PROJECT Book of Stories

You have been reading and writing about adventures. You have learned that an adventure can happen in a special place, such as an island, or in an ordinary place, such as a street corner. An adventure can happen to a special person or to anyone at all.

A photograph or picture can be the inspiration for an adventure story. Look at the photograph below.

From this simple photograph, a writer could tell a story that begins on a street corner and ends in a hot-air balloon.

Work with a small group of classmates to create a book of stories.

- Bring in pictures from magazines. Select the picture that might inspire the best story.
- Brainstorm for characters, problem, setting, and events. Write a story about what you see in the pictures.
- When all the stories are completed, work with your classmates to make a story collection. Include your photographs as illustrations for the book of stories.

UNIT 13

Prepositions, Conjunctions, and Interjections

In this unit you will learn about prepositions, conjunctions, and interjections. These important words can help you to join related ideas and add variety to your sentences.

Discuss Read the poem on the opposite page. Why do you think the poet encourages the reader to open the door?

Creative Expression The unit theme is *Investigations*. You can investigate, or try to find information about, all sorts of things. What is something that you would like to know more about? Write a few sentences that tell what you would like to investigate. Write your sentences in your journal.

THEME: *INVESTIGATIONS*

Go and open the door.
Maybe outside there's
a tree, or a wood,
a garden,
or a magic city.

—Miroslav Holub,
from "The Door"

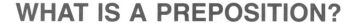

GRAMMAR

1 WHAT IS A PREPOSITION?

A preposition is a word that relates a noun or pronoun to another word in a sentence.

In your sentences, you often use words such as *to, for, at,* and *with*. These words are **prepositions**.

Prepositions show relationships between other words. When you write, you carefully choose the preposition that best fits your meaning.

The mystery stories are **in** the library.
Sir Arthur Conan Doyle wrote **during** the 1800s.

The **object of the preposition** is the noun or pronoun that follows a preposition.

I gave my favorite book to **Jeremy.**
I gave my favorite book to **him**.

Common Prepositions

about	among	down	inside	out	under
above	around	during	into	outside	until
across	at	except	near	over	up
after	behind	for	of	past	with
against	beside	from	off	through	within
along	by	in	on	to	without

Guided Practice

Tell the preposition in each sentence.

Example: Detection was easy for Holmes. *for*

1. Doyle wrote about Sherlock Holmes.
2. Doyle studied medicine for a time.
3. After medical school, he became a writer.
4. He wrote his mysteries from experience.
5. Medical knowledge is important to a detective.

?! **THINK**

■ How can I recognize a preposition and its object?

REMEMBER

- A **preposition** relates a noun or pronoun to another word in a sentence.
- The **object of a preposition** is the noun or pronoun that follows the preposition.

More Practice

Write each sentence. Draw a line under the preposition. Draw two lines under the object of the preposition.

Example: The sleuth was on a difficult assignment.

6. Sherlock Holmes was created by Doyle.
7. Holmes was the most popular character in England.
8. His popularity traveled across the Atlantic.
9. Dr. Watson was a companion to Holmes.
10. He helped with many cases.
11. Holmes was very wary among criminals.
12. Many mysteries were solved by the brilliant detective.
13. Sherlock Holmes stories are popular in my school.
14. Students find them in the library.
15. The mysteries are stacked by the reference books.
16. Most mysteries are solved after sundown.
17. The solution does not come until the end.
18. Finally, the criminal is under arrest.
19. The reader can guess between different outcomes.
20. The clues are always within the story.

Extra Practice, page 448

WRITING APPLICATION A Case Report

Imagine that you are on the scene when Sherlock Holmes solves a case. Create a scene that includes witnesses, criminals, and an intriguing problem for Holmes to solve. Write a report about the case, including information on how the case was solved and who was involved. When you have finished, underline the prepositions in your case report.

GRAMMAR

2 PREPOSITIONAL PHRASES

You know how to identify a preposition and its object. A **prepositional phrase** is a group of words that begins with a preposition and ends with a noun or pronoun. This noun or pronoun is called the object of the preposition.

The Curies were a family **of French scientists**.

For several generations, the Curies researched scientific questions.

Marie Curie, **with her family**, studied radium.

Notice that a prepositional phrase can be at the beginning, middle, or end of a sentence.

Guided Practice

Tell the prepositional phrases in each sentence.

Example: Important research took place in Europe.
in Europe

1. During the last century, little was known about radiation.
2. Many scientists did not believe in radiation.
3. Science changed with the discovery of radium.
4. By 1900, everyone believed in radioactivity.
5. The world changed for scientists and everyone else.

?! **THINK**

- How can I decide if a group of words is a prepositional phrase?

REMEMBER

- A **prepositional phrase** begins with a preposition and ends with a noun or pronoun.
- The noun or pronoun that follows the preposition is the **object of the preposition.**

More Practice

Write each sentence. Draw a line under each prepositional phrase. Draw two lines under each object of the preposition.

Example: The Curies worked on their research.

6. Marie Curie looked for radioactive elements.
7. Her discoveries were of radium and polonium.
8. Uranium was found within pitchblende.
9. Marie Curie was married to Pierre Curie.
10. Their daughter was influenced by them.
11. Following in their footsteps, she won a Nobel Prize.
12. With her husband, Irene Curie studied chemistry.
13. Scientists around the world read Marie's reports.
14. Across the ocean, scientists worked with radium.
15. They experimented within their laboratories.
16. Marie and Pierre talked about their experiments.
17. They worked for scientific progress.
18. Unfortunately, Marie had become sick from radium.
19. Working with uranium was not without risk.
20. Marie Curie received a Nobel Prize for the discoveries of radium and polonium.

Extra Practice, page 449

The Granger Collection

Marie Curie

WRITING APPLICATION A Biography

Research the life of a famous scientist. Use your information to write a brief biography of the scientist. Include information about the scientist's important discoveries in his or her particular field of research. Have a partner underline the prepositional phrases in your report.

3 OBJECT PRONOUNS IN PREPOSITIONAL PHRASES

As you know, the object of a preposition is the noun or pronoun that follows the preposition.

Cats are very special pets for **us**.
I found a cat and played with **her**.

When the object of a preposition is a pronoun, as in the sentences above, use an **object pronoun**.

Object Pronouns	me him it us you her them

To be sure you have used pronouns correctly in a compound object, leave out the other object in the compound and check the pronoun alone.

Many breeds appeal to **Dan and me**.
Many breeds appeal to **me**.

Guided Practice

Tell which words in the sentence are the prepositional phrase. Then, tell which pronoun is the object of the preposition.

Example: Pets provide company for us.
for us   prepositional phrase
us   object of the preposition

1. Cats share certain traits with us.
2. Teresa read her report to her family and me.
3. She wrote about cats and us human beings.
4. The teacher gave a good grade to her.
5. Teresa illustrated her report for him.

?! THINK

- How can I decide on the object pronoun to use in a prepositional phrase?

GRAMMAR

REMEMBER

- Use object pronouns *me*, *you*, *him*, *her*, *it*, *us*, and *them* as objects in prepositional phrases.

More Practice

A. Write each sentence. Draw one line under the prepositional phrase. Draw two lines under the object pronoun.

Example: The report explained animals to us.

6. The cat's nose gives important information to him.
7. Cats' eyes do not give as much data to them.
8. Total darkness poses problems for them.
9. My cat cannot always see the food dish below her.
10. She sometimes needs help from me.
11. I leave a light on for her.
12. The cats often jump on Teresa and me.
13. They are good company for my sister and me.

B. Complete each sentence with the correct pronoun.

Example: Teresa shared some ideas with (I, me).
Teresa shared some ideas with me.

14. Teresa's cats sat down beside (I, me).
15. The cats sniffed at (we, us).
16. My parents had brought the dog with (they, them).
17. My father kept the dog near (he, him).
18. He had carried a leash for (she, her).
19. Teresa spoke to (we, us) about animal research.
20. Teresa stroked the gray cat next to (she, her).

Extra Practice, **Practice Plus**, pages 450-451

WRITING APPLICATION A Summary

Research several facts about an animal and write a short summary. Work with a small group of classmates, and circle object pronouns in prepositional phrases in each summary.

COOPERATIVE LEARNING

GRAMMAR

4 WHAT IS A CONJUNCTION?

A conjunction is a word that joins words or groups of words.

You know that the words *and*, *but*, and *or* can join related subjects or predicates. These words are called **conjunctions**. Conjunctions can also join two sentences to form a compound sentence.

➡ Use *and* to join word groups, subjects, or predicates together.

Louis Leakey **and** his wife Mary worked in Africa.

➡ Use *but* to show contrast.

Anthropologists study human beginnings, **but** archaeologists study the past.

➡ Use *or* to show choice.

Were they anthropologists **or** archaeologists?

Conjunctions can also connect other words in a sentence.

The Leakeys worked eagerly **but** carefully.
Field researchers work alone **or** in teams.
They uncover fossils **and** human possessions.

Louis Leakey

Guided Practice

Tell the conjunction in each sentence.

Example: The Leakeys were famous at home and abroad. *and*

1. Louis Leakey was born in Kenya, but Mary Leakey was born in England.
2. Tools or weapons can help us learn about a society.
3. Fossils in Asia and Africa tell about life long ago.
4. Archaeologists work slowly and patiently on digs.
5. A dig might unearth some pottery or a building.

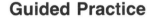

?! **THINK**

■ How do I decide which conjunction to use in a sentence?

REMEMBER

- Use *and* to join, *but* to show contrast, and *or* to show choice.

More Practice

Complete each sentence with the correct conjunction.

Example: I will study either history (and, <u>or</u>) anthropology.

6. The people (and, or) homes of long ago interest me.
7. Fossils look dull, (but, or) they are valuable.
8. This fossil might be a fish (or, but) a mollusk.
9. You find arrowheads in caves (and, but) forests.
10. Mohawk (and, or) Onondaga tribes lived together here.
11. Did Native Americans (or, and) Europeans make these masks?
12. They look old, (but, and) they might be recent.
13. Did the first people come from Africa (and, or) did they come from Asia?
14. I know about history since 1800, (and, but) I know little about earlier times.
15. I have books on American (and, or) world history.
16. Our school library has many books, (or, but) the town library has a bigger collection.
17. Books by the Leakeys (or, but) Ruth Benedict are good.
18. I have nearly finished my report, (and, but) I will need one more day of work.
19. I write my final copy neatly (and, or) quickly.
20. We have learned many new ideas (and, or) facts.

Extra Practice, page 452

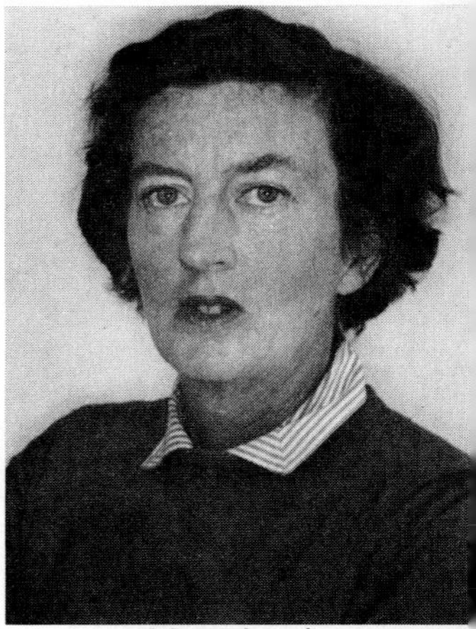

Mary Leakey

WRITING APPLICATION A Brief History

Write a short history of the area in which you live. Research some facts of your neighborhood, town, or state. You might include information about the area's famous people, buildings, or geography. Circle the conjunctions.

GRAMMAR

5 WHAT IS AN INTERJECTION?

An interjection is a word or group of words that expresses strong feeling.

You have learned how to use commas with introductory words. Sometimes these introductory words show strong feeling or call special attention to a statement. These words are called **interjections**.

➡ Use a comma to set off a mild interjection from the rest of the sentence.

My, this is a lovely day.

➡ Use an exclamation mark to set off a strong interjection from the rest of the sentence.

Hurray! We're having a tour of the restaurant.

When an exclamation mark sets off the interjection, the next word of the sentence begins with a capital letter.

Guided Practice

Tell which word is an interjection in each sentence.

Example: Wow! I love this restaurant! *Wow*

1. Oh! We have waited for this tour for weeks.
2. Well, restaurants are busy places.
3. Oops! Be quiet in the dining area.
4. Hey! Follow the teacher quickly.
5. Goodness, the kitchen is huge!

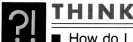

?! **THINK**

■ How do I use an interjection in a sentence?

REMEMBER

- Use a comma or an exclamation mark to set off an interjection.

GRAMMAR

More Practice

A. Write each sentence. Draw a line under the interjection in the sentence.

Example: Gee, I wish it were time for lunch!

6. Wow! Something smells delicious in here!
7. Look, the cook is making a stew.
8. Oh! He wears a tall white hat.
9. Gee, I am getting hungry!
10. My, he uses many different spices.
11. Yes! That stew will taste wonderful!
12. Hurray! He will let us taste some dishes.

B. Write and punctuate each sentence correctly.

Example: Oh there is a huge rack of spices
Oh, there is a huge rack of spices!

13. Goodness the cook likes spicy food.
14. Wow his recipes all use garlic and pepper.
15. Aha here is his supply cabinet.
16. Ssh we will disturb his work.
17. Oh he says we can look in the refrigerator.
18. Ah do you see all those kettles and pans?
19. Gee he can cook huge amounts of food at once.
20. Whew it's terribly hot near the stove!

Extra Practice, page 453

WRITING APPLICATION A Dialogue

Write a dialogue between you and other people during a class trip. Where did your class go? Whom or what did you see? Use interjections to make the dialogue lively. Act out the dialogue with your classmates while other students point out the interjections.

COOPERATIVE LEARNING

GRAMMAR

6 MECHANICS: Capitalizing Titles

There are special rules for capitalizing words in titles. The first and last words in a title are always capitalized. Important words in the title should be capitalized. Most prepositions, conjunctions, and articles are not capitalized.

When you write some titles, you underline them to show that they are written in *italics*.

Time magazine contains many photographs.

A new edition of Treasure Island is in the library.

Other titles are set off by quotation marks.

I read an article called "Summer Fun in the City."

"The Road Not Taken" is my favorite poem.

Underlined Titles	*Titles in Quotation Marks*
books	poems
newspapers	short stories
magazines	songs
movies	articles
	book chapters

Guided Practice

Tell how you would write each title.

Example: the silver chair (book)
The Silver Chair

1. children's times (magazine)
2. black beauty (movie)
3. a wrinkle in time (book)
4. the chicago tribune (newspaper)
5. paul revere's ride (poem)

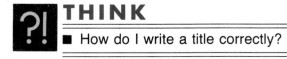

?! **THINK**

■ How do I write a title correctly?

REMEMBER

- Capitalize the first, last, and all important words in a title.
- Set off titles by underlining them or by putting them in quotation marks.

GRAMMAR

More Practice

A. Write each title correctly, using the proper punctuation and capitalization.

Example: a special day (story) *"A Special Day"*

6. sleeping beauty (story)
7. lucy looks into a wardrobe (book chapter)
8. the san francisco chronicle (newspaper)
9. casey at the bat (poem)
10. german legends (book)
11. superman (movie)
12. little literature (magazine)

B. Write and punctuate each sentence correctly.

Example: I read the poem titled Two People.
I read the poem titled "Two People."

13. We read Sleeping Beauty aloud.
14. The movie called Robinson Crusoe scared us.
15. I have a book called German Legends.
16. Treasure Mountain is a book of folk tales.
17. We know the words to the song, Dreams.
18. The Earth Is Sore is a Native American poem.
19. We read an article called Poems for Students.
20. The book, The Crane Wife, was recommended by a writer for The Chicago Tribune.

Extra Practice, page 454

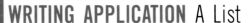

WRITING APPLICATION A List

Make a list of your favorite stories, books, movies, and poems. When your list is complete, have a partner check to see that you have punctuated and capitalized titles correctly.

7 VOCABULARY BUILDING: How Language Changes

You may have noticed that people in different regions or parts of the country refer to the same objects by different names. If you buy a sandwich on a long, narrow loaf of bread in Maryland, you might ask for a *hoagie*. If you buy the same kind of sandwich in California, you might ask for a *grinder*. The same sandwich is also called a *poorboy*, *wedgie*, *sub*, and *hero*.

Language can also change over a period of time. The bus you take to school would have been called an *autobus* seventy-five years ago. Words, like clothing styles, change.

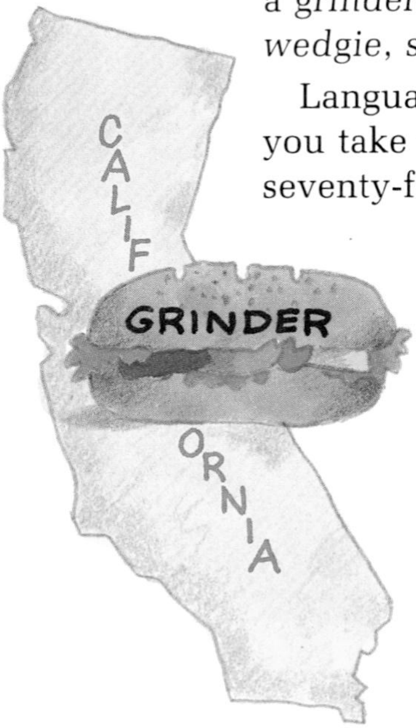

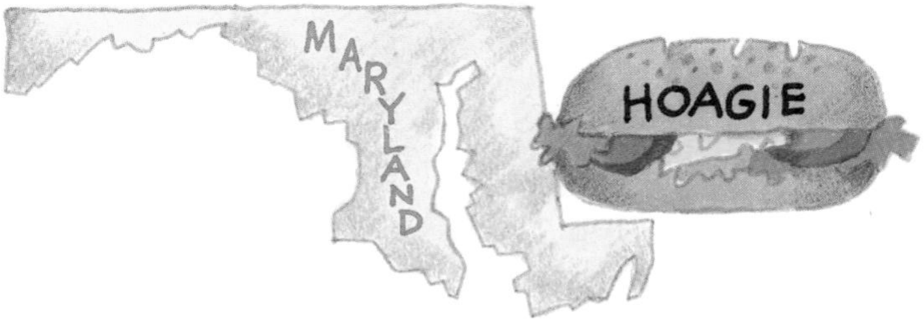

Guided Practice

Tell the familiar word from each pair. Your answer will depend on where you live.

1. seesaw/teeter-totter
2. bucket/pail
3. bathrobe/dressing gown
4. sofa/couch
5. bag/suitcase

?! THINK

■ In what ways can language change or vary?

REMEMBER

- Objects can have different names in different regions.

More Practice

A. Look at each object. Write the word that describes the object in your region.

6. a. notebook b. binder c. tablet

7. a. snap beans b. string beans c. green beans

8. a. skillet b. frying pan c. spider pan

9. a. jeans b. dungarees c. denims

10. a. pier b. landing c. wharf

B. Write each sentence. Complete each sentence with the word that is used in your region.

11. A cold, fizzy drink is a (pop, soda, cola).
12. You comb your hair while looking in a (looking glass, mirror).
13. On cold winter nights, use a (quilt, comforter).
14. The lowest floor of a house is usually the (basement, cellar).
15. The long space that connects the rooms in a house is called a (corridor, hall).
16. On cold days, wear a (ski jacket, parka).
17. For a sore throat, try a (cough drop, lozenge).
18. Keep warm in a woolen (sweater, pullover).
19. (Dinner, supper) is served between 5 and 7 o'clock at night.
20. Carry the groceries home from the store in a paper (bag, sack).

Extra Practice, page 455

WRITING APPLICATION A Report

Report on some words a stranger would encounter in your area. Share your work with a classmate.

GRAMMAR AND WRITING CONNECTION

Expanding Sentences

You know that a prepositional phrase adds information to a sentence. You can add more than one prepositional phrase to a sentence to make the meaning of a sentence clear and precise.

Look at the sentences below.

I went **to the animal shelter.**
I went **with my classmates to the animal shelter**.
On Tuesday I went **with my classmates to the animal shelter**.

Each prepositional phrase above adds a particular detail. The meaning of each sentence is different because of the prepositional phrases it includes.

Working Together

COOPERATIVE LEARNING

With your class, discuss how to add more than one prepositional phrase to a sentence to make your meaning clear. Then, add two prepositional phrases to each sentence.

Example: One dog looked sad.
The face of one dog looked sad for a moment.

1. A volunteer gave us a tour.
2. We saw many homeless pets.
3. I felt sorry.
4. There were many cages.
5. The animals waited.

Revising Sentences

Pete has written these sentences for a paragraph about his visit to an animal shelter. Help Pete to make his sentences more detailed by adding two prepositional phrases to each short sentence.

6. There were dogs and cats.
7. The cages were clean.
8. The animals looked lonely.
9. The volunteers love animals.
10. We walked around.
11. I wanted a pet.
12. I will come back.
13. Mom promised me a pet.
14. I would like a puppy.
15. I saw a picture.
16. Pets need love.
17. Many animals are abandoned.
18. They need our help.
19. Would you like a pet?
20. Visit an animal shelter.

WRITER AT WORK

Brainstorm to think of a place you have visited that impressed you. Write a paragraph in which you report on what you recall about the place. When you have finished, check your paragraph to see if you have made your writing more detailed by including prepositional phrases.

UNIT CHECKUP

LESSON 1 **What Is a Preposition?** (page 428) Write each sentence. Underline the preposition.

1. The discovery was in the scientist's grasp.
2. He had worked through the day.
3. His assistant worked beside him.
4. They finished their project during the night.
5. They danced happily around the laboratory.

LESSON 2 **Prepositional Phrases** (page 430) Write each sentence. Draw one line under the prepositional phrase. Draw two lines under the object of the preposition.

6. The assembly was held inside the old gym.
7. Important news was announced by me.
8. Students learned about the new cafeteria.
9. The school would have another lunchroom for us.
10. The new room would be near the old cafeteria.

LESSON 3 **Object Pronouns in Prepositional Phrases** (page 432) Write each sentence, using the correct pronoun.

11. The student had his dog beside (he, him).
12. The teacher smiled sadly at (they, them).
13. The boy asked a question of (she, her).
14. "The dog can't stay," she said to (he, him).
15. "He will wait for (I, me)," said the boy.

LESSON 4 **What Is a Conjunction?** (page 434) Write each sentence. Draw one line under the conjunction. Draw two lines under the words or groups of words that the conjunction joins.

16. The fifth and sixth graders are having a picnic.
17. Larry or I will find the best spot.
18. I like the park, but Larry prefers the beach.
19. The beach might be windy or cold in May.
20. Let's call the Commissioner of Parks and Grounds.

LESSON 5

What Is an Interjection? (page 436) Rewrite and punctuate each sentence correctly.

21. Eureka I have found it
22. Hurrah this is a wonderful discovery
23. Why that is nothing new
24. Hey what do you mean
25. Well others have made the same discovery

LESSON 6

Mechanics: Capitalizing Titles (page 438) Write each title correctly.

26. mary's big day (story)
27. math today and tomorrow (book)
28. the high school gazette (newspaper)
29. i love jelly (poem)
30. school times (magazine)

LESSON 7

Vocabulary Building: How Language Changes (page 440) Write the familiar word that describes the object.

31.	a. faucet	b. spigot	c. tap
32.	a. dragonfly	b. spindle	c. darning needle
33.	a. pancakes	b. griddlecakes	c. hot cakes
34.	a. parcel	b. package	c. bundle
35.	a. soda	b. pop	c. soft drink

36.-40.

Writing Application: Prepositions, Conjunctions, and Interjections Usage (pages 428-436) The following paragraph contains 5 errors of usage with prepositions, conjunctions, and interjections. Rewrite the paragraph correctly.

I arrived of the store with my mother and Jenny. Jenny or I both bought new summer clothing. "Hey You girls look wonderful in those dresses," said our Mom. We paid to the purchases and found a restaurant in the mall. Then we waited for our mother after a few moments as she shopped for a jacket.

ENRICHMENT

WHERE AM I?

Play this game with a small group. Sit in a circle. One player asks the question, "Where am I?" The second player answers with a sentence that includes a prepositional phrase, such as "in a tree." The next player adds a second prepositional phrase, creating "in a tree behind the house." Each person in the group adds a prepositional phrase to the sentence until all the players run out of ideas.

NAME GAME

Some words that you use come from a person's name. The word *sandwich*, for example, comes from the Earl of Sandwich. The Earl did not like to stop for lunch. He ordered his servant to bring him some thick slices of beef between two pieces of toasted bread. From this event, the word sandwich was born. Here are some more words that come from a person's name:

pants boycott leotard spoonerism

Look up the words in a dictionary or encyclopedia to find their meanings and origins. Use each word in a sentence.

CAT MOVES

Draw a comic strip that includes a cat. Under each drawing, write a prepositional phrase that describes what the cat is doing. You might, for example, draw a house with a cat sitting *on the roof*.

CREATIVE EXPRESSION

Personification

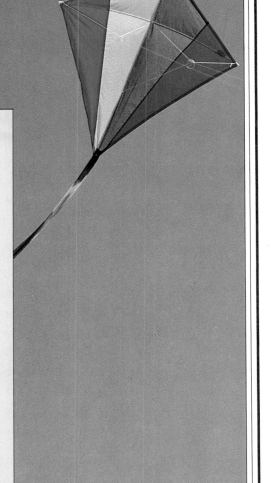

The Wind

I saw you toss the kites on high
And blow the birds about the sky;
And all around I heard you pass,
Like ladies' skirts across the grass—
O wind, a-blowing all day long,
O wind, that sings so loud a song!

I saw the different things you did,
But always you yourself you hid.
I felt you push, I heard you call,
I could not see yourself at all—
O wind, a-blowing all day long,
O wind, that sings so loud a song!

O you that are so strong and cold,
O blower, are you young or old?
Are you a beast of field and tree,
Or just a stronger child than me?
O wind, a-blowing all day long,
O wind, that sings so loud a song!

—Robert Louis Stevenson

TRY IT OUT!

"The Wind" is a poem in which a child speaks to the wind as though it were a person. **Personification** gives human traits to something other than a person. Write a poem in which you use personification.

EXTRA PRACTICE

Three levels of practice

What Is a Preposition? (page 428)

LEVEL **A.** Write each sentence. Draw a line under the preposition.

1. A Dutch inventor held two lenses in his hands.
2. He looked through both of them.
3. The inventor was peering at something.
4. The lenses were placed inside a tube.
5. The invention was similar to a microscope.
6. A microscope helps us look at tiny things.
7. The lenses are necessary for magnification.
8. The inventor leaned against his chair.
9. He breathed a great sigh of relief.

LEVEL **B.** Write each sentence. Draw one line under the preposition. Draw two lines under the object of the preposition.

10. We were talking about balloons.
11. Hot air from a flame lifted the first balloons.
12. The inventors learned by accident.
13. A shirt was drying over a fire.
14. Smoke rose above the fire.
15. The shirt sailed into the air.
16. The inventors put their idea into action.
17. They created a passenger balloon through experimentation.

LEVEL **C.** Add a preposition to each group of words to form a sentence that makes sense. Write the new sentence.

18. Bicycles traveled roads.
19. They bounced the hard and bumpy ground.
20. Boys and girls would fall the bicycles.
21. A man named Dunlop put air rubber tires.
22. People thought they were riding air.
23. Later, a similar type of tire was used automobiles.
24. Tires come different widths.
25. Balloon tires are used children's bicycles.

EXTRA PRACTICE

Three levels of practice

Prepositional Phrases (page 430)

LEVEL **A.** Write each sentence. Underline each prepositional phrase.

1. Benjamin Banneker lived during the eighteenth century.
2. He was a black man in a slave society.
3. He was a mathematician and a surveyor for the city.
4. He was also an astronomer of great talent.
5. American scientists had all been white until then.
6. Banneker's contributions to almanacs were very important.
7. They were about the location of the planets.
8. Banneker sent Thomas Jefferson a copy of his first almanac.
9. He also sent a letter about the anti-slavery movement.

LEVEL **B.** Write each sentence. Draw a line under the prepositional phrase. Draw two lines under the object of the preposition.

10. John James Audubon drew pictures of wild birds.
11. Few people know that Audubon was born in Haiti.
12. The artist studied the animals around him.
13. These drawings tell us much about many North American birds.
14. He worked with a Scottish naturalist.
15. They traveled through many states together.
16. Audubon had a deep love of nature.
17. The Audubon Society was founded in his honor.

LEVEL **C.** Add a preposition to each group of words to make a prepositional phrase that correctly completes the sentence. Write the new sentence.

18. Casimir Funk came _____ the United States.
19. He wrote a paper _____ vitamins and diseases.
20. His papers were also _____ hormones.
21. People gained knowledge _____ his research.
22. Funk explored many fields _____ science.
23. No one had investigated vitamins _____ Funk.
24. The role of vitamins _____ the human body is important.
25. Funk's research caused changes _____ medical science.

EXTRA PRACTICE

Three levels of practice

Object Pronouns in Prepositional Phrases (page 432)

LEVEL **A.** Write each sentence. Draw a line under the object pronoun in each sentence.

1. Miss Marple brought a clue to us.
2. She carried a magnifying glass with her.
3. A handkerchief had initials sewn on it.
4. One of them was torn.
5. Miss Marple placed the handkerchief before us.
6. She had information about it.
7. She explained her idea to me.
8. I had several questions for her.
9. She spoke intelligently to us.

LEVEL **B.** Write each sentence, using the correct pronoun.

10. Miss Marple looked at the people beside (she, her).
11. She gazed thoughtfully at (they, them).
12. The detective arrived and she spoke to (he, him).
13. I was the most confused one of (we, us).
14. The detective paid a compliment to (I, me).
15. Miss Marple spoke highly of (he, him).
16. The thief would be caught by (we, us).
17. The handkerchief had been torn by (he, him).

LEVEL **C.** Write each sentence. Complete the sentence with an object pronoun that makes sense.

18. Jenny thought the mystery was about ______.
19. Leonard believed the culprit was near ______.
20. Miss Marple said the fuss was over ______.
21. Her anger was directed at ______.
22. The clues were beside ______.
23. I had taken my notebook with ______.
24. Miss Marple read my article to ______.
25. The newspapers would have no information without ______.

PRACTICE + PLUS

GRAMMAR

Three levels of additional practice for a difficult skill

Object Pronouns in Prepositional Phrases (page 432)

LEVEL **A.** Write each sentence. Draw a line under the object pronoun in each sentence.

1. Holidays are observed by us.
2. For me, the best part is the feast.
3. With you, I will plan a wonderful meal.
4. Don't start the preparations without me!
5. We'll visit the market near you.
6. The grocer will save a turkey for us.
7. I will bring a list with me.
8. Sit down beside me.
9. Explain that recipe to us.

LEVEL **B.** Write each sentence, using the correct pronoun from the pair in parentheses.

10. Joan has shared some recipes with (I, me).
11. We've gotten many good tips from (she, her).
12. I hold the list before (I, me).
13. Mom will bring money with (she, her).
14. Dad will follow after (we, us).
15. We can load the car for (he, him).
16. Mom sits beside (we, us).
17. She keeps her purse near (she, her).

LEVEL **C.** Write each sentence, using an object pronoun.

18. This recipe was written by ______.
19. The meal will taste delicious to ______.
20. I will take some vegetables for ______.
21. Please share this turkey with ______.
22. Will you sit beside ______?
23. Mom places a platter near ______.
24. She tells Aunt Dora about ______.
25. You were the biggest help to ______.

EXTRA PRACTICE

Three levels of practice

What Is a Conjunction? (page 434)

LEVEL A. Write each sentence. Draw a line under the conjunction.

1. Find the meaning and pronunciation of the word.
2. You may use the dictionary, but try other reference books, too.
3. Dictionaries and thesauruses help define words.
4. A thesaurus gives synonyms and antonyms for words.
5. Should I use the dictionary or the thesaurus?
6. The dictionary has a pronunciation key, but the thesaurus does not.
7. Look at the first or second definition of a word in your dictionary.
8. The same word might be a noun and a verb.
9. Read every definition, but do not get confused.

LEVEL B. Write each sentence. Draw a line under the conjunction. Draw two lines under the words or phrases that the conjunction joins.

10. Try the school or public library.
11. You must find articles and graphs.
12. Librarians and scientists have something in common.
13. They research and explore sources of information.
14. Our library is good, but Smithtown's is better.
15. Go to Smithtown next Friday or Saturday.
16. Take the bus or the train.
17. You can take some books home, but others cannot leave the library.

LEVEL C. Write each sentence. Complete the sentence with the correct conjunction from the pair in parentheses.

18. Are you reading a book, (and, or) writing a paper?
19. I scanned that book, (and, but) it had no information.
20. The librarian (and, or) I searched the shelves together.
21. Will you check those books out (and, or) read them here?
22. I cannot read (and, or) take notes at the same time.
23. My last paper was good, (or, but) this one must be better.
24. This book is interesting, (and, but) the words are difficult.
25. I read part of your report, (and, but) I haven't finished yet.

EXTRA PRACTICE

GRAMMAR

Three levels of practice

What Is an Interjection? (page 436)

LEVEL **A.** Write each sentence. Draw a line under the interjection.

1. Wow! This barn is dark!
2. Well, should we go inside?
3. Gee, let's wait for Alonzo.
4. Ah! Is he so brave?
5. Hush! I hear footsteps!
6. No, that is only the wind.
7. Hey! Where are you?
8. Oops, I dropped the flashlight!
9. Help! I can't find it!

LEVEL **B.** Write each sentence correctly, using commas and exclamation marks where they are needed. Be sure to use capital letters correctly.

10. Yikes who turned out the lights
11. Oh no I can't see a thing
12. Well what should we do now
13. Oh here is my flashlight
14. Goodness this barn is scary
15. Yes can we leave soon
16. Hey don't be so nervous
17. Heavens is that a monster

LEVEL **C.** Write each sentence. Complete the sentence with an interjection. Be sure to punctuate and capitalize correctly.

18. ______ have you ever seen anything like this?
19. ______ where is the door?
20. ______ who suggested this idea, anyway?
21. ______ even Alonzo is scared!
22. ______ shall we tell anyone about this?
23. ______ they would never believe us.
24. ______ there is the exit!
25. ______ we're safe at last!

GRAMMAR

EXTRA PRACTICE

Three levels of practice

Mechanics: Capitalizing Titles (page 438)

LEVEL A. Write each title correctly. Underline or use quotation marks.

1. to build a fire (story)
2. tales of the arctic (book)
3. the anchorage news (newspaper)
4. white desert (poem)
5. blues in the alaska night (song)
6. nanook of the north (movie)
7. how it all began (book chapter)
8. the tundra quarterly (magazine)
9. ice-fishing made simple (article)

LEVEL B. Write each sentence correctly.

10. The magazine, Science, has an article about igloos.
11. Everyone sang alaska, my alaska very loudly.
12. The teacher had us read the chapter called morning.
13. We thought terror from the north was a silly movie.
14. How to tame sled dogs was the best article.
15. Animals of the tundra is a wonderful book.
16. The bear is one of my favorite stories.
17. The post is a newspaper with accurate sports information.

LEVEL C. Add a title to each group of words to make a complete sentence. Write the new sentence.

18. The company made a film called ______.
19. It is based on the book, ______.
20. My paper, ______, is about logging.
21. I submitted it to ______ as an article.
22. It was printed with the title, ______.
23. Randy's poem is called ______.
24. The magazine, ______, published her work.
25. The poem will be reprinted in a book of students' writing called ______.

EXTRA PRACTICE

GRAMMAR

Three levels of practice

Vocabulary Building: How Language Changes (page 440)

LEVEL A. Write the familiar word that describes the object.

1. a. carnival	b. festival	c. fair
2. a. movie	b. film	c. flick
3. a. peanuts	b. goobers	c. goober peas
4. a. shed	b. shack	c. lean-to
5. a. sneaker	b. running shoe	c. tennis shoe
6. a. hero	b. grinder	c. sub
7. a. thongs	b. flipflops	c. beach sandals
8. a. seltzer	b. soda	c. fizz
9. a. porridge	b. oatmeal	c. hot cereal

LEVEL B. Complete each sentence with the familiar word from the box.

10. The gardener turned on the ______.
11. I ate ______ at the picnic.
12. A bright ______ flew over the meadow.
13. I ordered a vanilla ______ at the ice cream shop.
14. Sherri devoured a strawberry ______.
15. I wore my ______ during the cold weather.
16. Do you like ______ baked or roasted?
17. Can you play the ______?

10. a. faucet b. spigot c. tap
11. a. corn on the cob b. roasting ears
12. a. darning needle b. dragonfly c. spindle
13. a. milk shake b. frappe
14. a. ice cream soda b. float
15. a. parka b. ski jacket
16. a. potatoes b. spuds
17. a. harmonica b. mouth organ

LEVEL C. Use each of the regional words below to complete the following sentences.

18. Instead of a suit, the man wore ______.
19. He carried his things away in a ______.
20. He thought the detective would never ______ him.
21. The detective finished his breakfast of ______.
22. He sat on the ______ for an hour.
23. He suddenly threw some clothes in a ______.
24. He drove toward the local ______.
25. He found the man eating ______ under a tree.

nab tote dungarees johnnycakes veranda satchel filberts swimming hole

MAINTENANCE

UNIT 1: Sentences

Sentences (pages 2, 4) Label each sentence correctly as **declarative**, **interrogative**, **imperative**, or **exclamatory**. If a group of words is not a sentence, label it **fragment**.

1. That was a wonderful show!
2. Were the tigers terribly fierce?
3. Tell me about them.
4. Tigers in their cages.
5. Yesterday the circus.

Subjects and Predicates (pages 6-13) Write each sentence. Draw one line under the simple subject and two lines under the simple predicate. Draw a line between the complete subject and the complete predicate.

6. Strange plants grow in jungles.
7. Myra will travel to the Amazon.
8. She knows a great deal about plants.
9. The tour guide will give her more information.

Compound Sentences/ Correcting Sentence Fragments (pages 14, 16) Combine each group of words into a complete sentence. Label each compound sentence **compound**.

10. Living things eat. Because they are hungry.
11. We feel hungry. When our bodies need energy.
12. Sometimes I get hungry. But I don't eat.
13. After a few hours. I feel extremely tired.

Using Context Clues (page 20) Choose the correct meaning for each underlined word. Then, write the word or words you used as context clues.

14. The air is so humid it almost drips.
    a. wet b. dry
15. In some cities people inhale dirty air.
    a. breathe b. drink
16. Air pollution can damage our health and cause illness in people and animals.
    a. harm b. help
17. New laws can curb the spread of pollution and control further damage to the environment.
    a. further b. limit

UNIT 3: Nouns

Singular and Plural Possessive Nouns (pages 84-89) Write the possessive form of each noun.

18. mice
19. lady
20. fox
21. class
22. fish

Compound Words (page 92) Make compound words with the words in the columns.

23.	ear	road
24.	key	walk
25.	rail	fighter
26.	side	hole
27.	fire	muffs

UNIT 5: Verbs

Action Verbs and Direct Objects (pages 144, 146) Write each sentence. Draw one line under the action verb. Draw two lines under the direct object.

28. A man waved his hand at a cabdriver.
29. The driver stopped the taxicab.
30. The passenger held a map.
31. The passenger soon reached his destination.

Main Verbs and Helping Verbs (page 148) Write each sentence. Draw one line under the main verb. Draw two lines under the helping verb.

32. The horses have eaten the hay.
33. Now they are running wildly.
34. One horse has jumped over the stream.
35. A pony was chasing a mare.

Linking Verbs (page 150) Write the linking verb in each sentence.

36. The weather seemed fine this morning.
37. Now, the sky looks overcast and cloudy.
38. I am not disappointed, though.
39. This cool weather feels comfortable to me.

Contractions (page 152) Write the contraction for the underlined words in each sentence.

40. Michael does not know Cynthia well.
41. She was not in his class last year.
42. I will eat lunch with them today.
43. They have saved me a place at our favorite table in the school cafeteria.

MAINTENANCE

Verb Tenses (pages 154, 156) Write each sentence. Complete the sentence with the correct tense of the verb in parentheses.

44. I (walk, will walk) to the fair tomorrow with my sister and brother.

45. Yesterday, I (promise, promised) my little sister a treat.

46. Now she (looked, looks) tall enough for the donkey rides around the fairgrounds.

47. We always (enjoy, will enjoy) the fair and the exciting rides.

Subject-Verb Agreement (page 158) Write each sentence. Complete the sentence with the correct form of the verb in parentheses.

48. Exercise (is, are) good for everyone.

49. An active person (feel, feels) healthy.

50. I (jump, jumps) rope every day.

51. We each (choose, chooses) our favorite exercise routine for the sports demonstration.

Using Irregular Verbs (pages 162, 164) Write the correct past tense of each verb. Then, write the correct past tense with the helping verb.

52. come	**56.** sing
53. give	**57.** teach
54. take	**58.** know
55. run	**59.** see

Using the Comma (page 166) Write each sentence, using commas where they are needed.

60. The dark dense mysterious forest is alive tonight.

61. Owls rodents and insects are awake.

62. The moon stars and lake all shine brightly.

63. The bats fly an owl hoots and a cat prowls.

Homophones (page 168) Write each sentence, using the correct word in parentheses.

64. Tonight Robert will eat (meat, meet) and potatoes.

65. He will watch a (miner, minor) league baseball game.

66. Then he will fish in the (creak, creek).

67. Now he makes (doe, dough) for biscuits.

UNIT 7: Adjectives

What Is an Adjective? (page 226) Write each sentence. Draw a line under each adjective.

68. The loud thunder crashed.

69. Bright lightning flashed in the sky.

70. After the terrible storm, the sky cleared.

71. A beautiful rainbow appeared.

Comparing with Adjectives (pages 226–233) Write each sentence. Complete the sentence with the correct word.

72. The Golden Gate Bridge is the (longer, longest) bridge I have ever seen.

73. The traffic is (heavier, heaviest) today than yesterday.

74. There are (more, most) cars than ever on the roads today.

75. The (better, best) hours of all for a drive are in the early afternoon.

76. Accidents are a (worse, worst) problem than traffic jams.

Using Articles and Demonstrative Adjectives (page 234) Write each sentence using the correct word in parentheses.

77. (A, An) rodeo came to town.

78. (A, The) event attracted many people.

79. Marie said, "(This, That) horse over there is beautiful."

80. Michael replied, "(This, That) horse near us is my favorite."

Capitalizing Proper Adjectives (page 236) Write the proper adjective that is formed from each proper noun below.

81. India

82. Canada

83. Italy

84. Germany

85. America

UNIT 9: Pronouns

What Is a Pronoun? (page 292) Write each sentence. Draw a line under the pronoun. Then, write whether it is a **subject** or an **object** pronoun.

86. John watches the children and makes lunch for them.

87. They play football, catch, and tag in the garden until noon.

88. We play soccer with Sue for an hour.

89. John explains the important rules to us.

MAINTENANCE

I* and *me*, *we* and *us (pages 298, 306) Write each sentence using the correct word in parentheses.

90. Sharon threw the ball to (I, me).

91. (We, Us) play baseball every Saturday.

92. Sports are fun for Sharon and (I, me).

93. (I, Me) have organized a game for our class.

Possessive Pronouns (pages 300, 302) Write the possessive pronoun in each sentence.

94. Julie sent a card to her grandparents.

95. Julie had visited their beach house.

96. Its rooms were cool and airy.

97. Theirs is a lovely home.

98. Julie's brother will spend his vacation there, too.

UNIT 11: Adverbs

What Is an Adverb? (page 364) Write the adverb in each sentence.

99. The sun shone brightly.

100. I quickly dove into the pool.

101. Jan and I swim well.

102. I will dive again.

Using Adverbs to Compare (page 366) Write each sentence. Use the correct form of the adverb.

103. I ran (faster, fastest) than you.

104. The storm arose (more quickly, most quickly) than we had expected.

105. Jamie pitched the tent (more speedily, most speedily) of all the campers.

106. Our new tent remained (drier, driest) than our old one.

Adjective or Adverb? (page 370) Write each sentence. Write **adjective** or **adverb** above the underlined word.

107. The <u>local</u> bus stops nearby.

108. It travels <u>slowly</u> up Elm Road.

109. Mr. Lee is a <u>careful</u> driver.

110. He speaks <u>politely</u> to us.

Negatives (page 372) Write each sentence. Draw a line under the negative word.

111. Divers never work alone.

112. Nobody takes foolish risks.

113. I do not swim by myself.

114. Take no foolish risks.

Using Quotation Marks (page 374) Write each sentence, using correct punctuation and capitalization.

115. Lou said let's go to the store.

116. Which store do you like asked Lil.

117. The discount store has nice socks replied Lou.

118. I need new socks too said Lil.

Suffixes (page 376) Write each sentence. Add a correct suffix to each underlined word.

119. The old house looked <u>cheer</u>.

120. Quick <u>act</u> was needed!

121. The poor <u>art</u> required our help.

122. We were <u>response</u> for the repairs.

123. The elderly man thanked us for our <u>charity</u> work.

UNIT 13: Prepositions, Conjunctions, and Interjections

Prepositions and Prepositional Phrases (pages 428, 430) Write the prepositional phrase in each sentence. Draw a line under the preposition.

124. There are beautiful objects on the shelves.

125. Lovely glass bottles shine under the light.

126. A china dog sits near a glass owl.

127. Watercolor paintings hang above the cabinet.

Object Pronouns in Prepositional Phrases (page 432) Write each sentence, using the correct pronoun.

128. Three hawks flew over (I, me).

129. My dog barked at (they, them).

130. Dad talked to (we, us).

131. A small hawk landed near (he, him).

Conjunctions (page 434) Write each conjunction.

132. Take a train or a bus home.

133. Cora and I will meet you.

134. Sandy cannot come, but Danny will be there.

Interjections (page 436) Write the interjection in each sentence.

135. Oh! What is that noise?

136. Well, it is just the wind.

137. Hey, close that door.

Capitalizing Titles (page 438) Write each title correctly.

138. Sleeping beauty (movie)

139. the time machine (book)

140. hiawatha (poem)

WRITING

UNIT 14

Writing Research Reports

Look at the picture and read the quotation on the opposite page. The quotation was written by George Ancona, who wrote the article that you will read in this unit. Why do you think curiosity is important to a writer?

When you write a research report, you need to conduct an investigation. You will want to find and organize information for your audience.

Focus A research report provides information about a specific subject. The purpose of a research report is to inform.

What topic would you like to investigate and then write a report about? The article and the photographs in this unit may give you some ideas.

THEME: *INVESTIGATIONS*

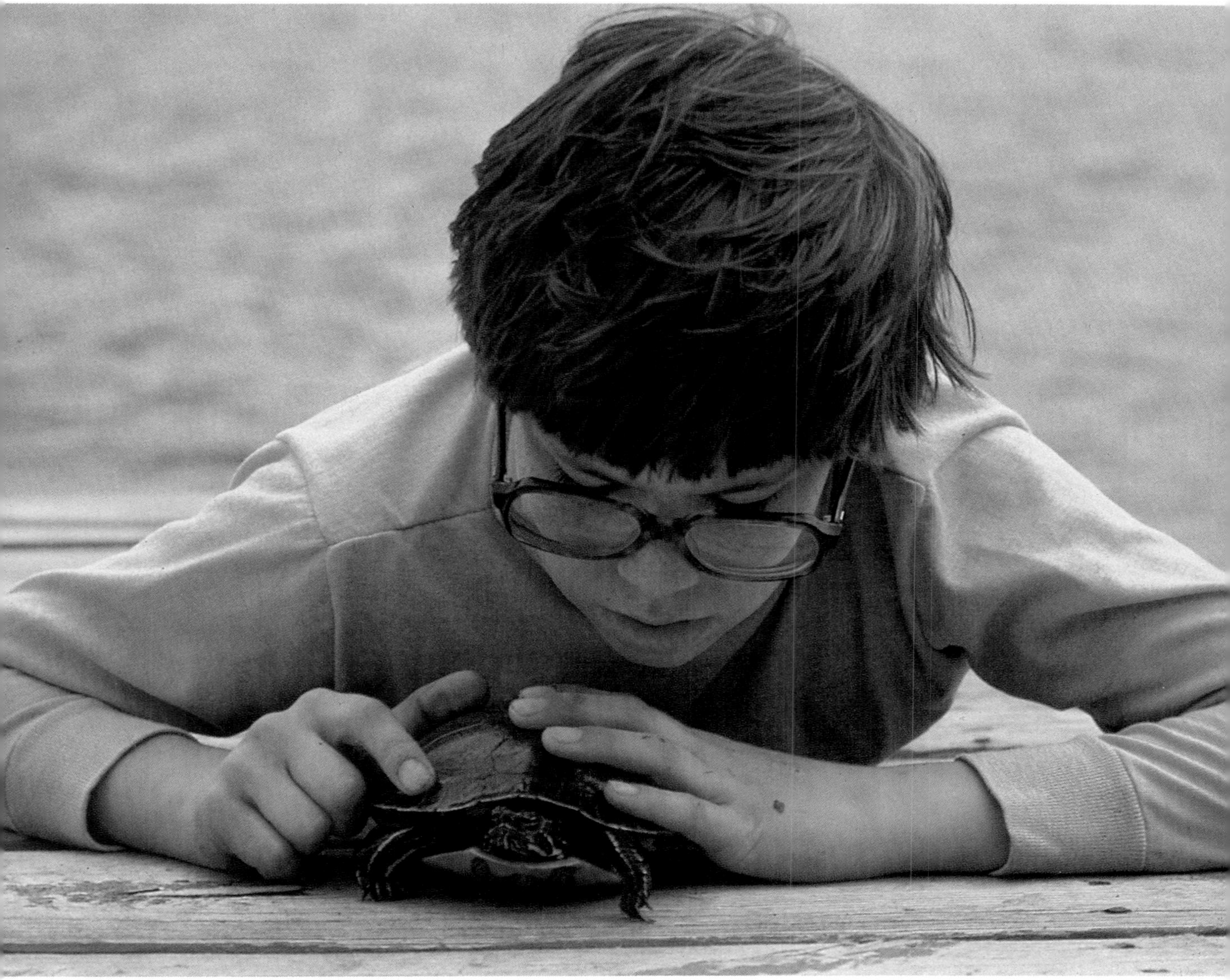

Curiosity is the biggest element in my work. . . . I love to find myself in strange places, meeting people, getting to know them and learning about them.

—George Ancona

LITERATURE

Reading Like a Writer

AWARD WINNING SELECTION

Think about the world outdoors. What types of living things do you find there?

Julio and Neca work for TAMAR, a project that studies sea turtles. TAMAR members hope that their work will help to save these endangered animals from extinction.

As you read the selection, notice how the author uses interesting facts in his report on TAMAR and the turtles.

PROJECT TURTLE

FROM **TURTLE WATCH** *by George Ancona*

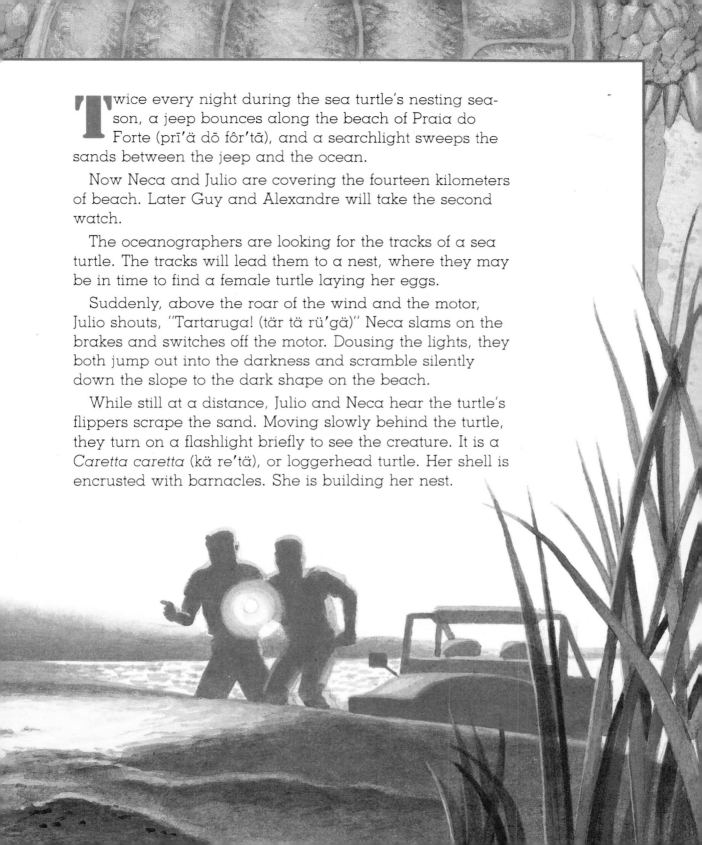

Twice every night during the sea turtle's nesting season, a jeep bounces along the beach of Praia do Forte (prī′ä dō fôr′tā), and a searchlight sweeps the sands between the jeep and the ocean.

Now Neca and Julio are covering the fourteen kilometers of beach. Later Guy and Alexandre will take the second watch.

The oceanographers are looking for the tracks of a sea turtle. The tracks will lead them to a nest, where they may be in time to find a female turtle laying her eggs.

Suddenly, above the roar of the wind and the motor, Julio shouts, "Tartaruga! (tär tä rü′gä)" Neca slams on the brakes and switches off the motor. Dousing the lights, they both jump out into the darkness and scramble silently down the slope to the dark shape on the beach.

While still at a distance, Julio and Neca hear the turtle's flippers scrape the sand. Moving slowly behind the turtle, they turn on a flashlight briefly to see the creature. It is a *Caretta caretta* (kä re′tä), or loggerhead turtle. Her shell is encrusted with barnacles. She is building her nest.

The turtle has just finished digging her bed, or body pit, a slight depression in the sand in which she now rests her bulk. She is building her nest above the high-water mark, since saltwater would kill the eggs.

Neca and Julio watch as the turtle begins to dig out the egg cavity. Using her rear flippers, she scoops out a hole in the moist sand. In dry sand, the cavity would collapse.

Notice the author's use of detail in showing how the turtle buries her eggs.

The turtle raises the front of her body as she works, enabling her to dig a deeper hole. She lifts each flipper full of sand vertically so that she will not disturb the wall of the hole. By now the cavity is about sixteen inches deep. Finally, the turtle widens the bottom of the hole.

Julio scrapes away some sand beneath the loggerhead to reveal the egg chamber. The cavity completed, the turtle releases a thick liquid from the cloaca (klō ä'kä), an opening located slightly in front of her tail. This mucous will protect the eggs as they fall and fill the nest.

Now the turtle's body begins to contract, and the first egg drops into the cavity. As the contractions continue, eggs begin to fall at a faster rate. In about twenty minutes, the turtle has laid from one hundred to one hundred and fifty eggs. The eggs are about the size of a Ping-Pong ball, not hard but leathery and flexible.

While the turtle is laying her eggs, she seems to be in a trance. She is not disturbed by the camera or by the flashlight that Julio uses from time to time.

Julio moves in to attach a metal tag to the turtle's right front flipper and to measure her shell. The tag carries a number and a request that anyone finding the turtle advise TAMAR of the tag number, the location of the sighting, and the dimension of the shell. From now on, whenever this turtle is seen nesting, scientists will be informed and will learn more about the habits of sea turtles.

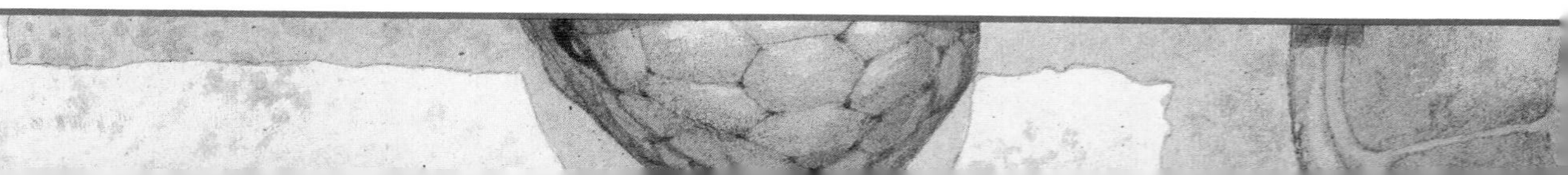

Using her rear flippers, the loggerhead now begins to bury the eggs. She gathers sand from the side of the bed and sweeps it into the egg cavity until the hole has been filled. Then she moves forward and uses her front flippers to fill in the entire bed. Almost an hour has passed since Neca and Julio first sighted the turtle. The turtle seems awake now and aware of her surroundings. Breathing heavily, tired from her efforts, she turns around and begins her return to the ocean. The tracks she leaves parallel those she made when she emerged from the sea. When she reaches the water, she hesitates, lifts her head, then plunges into the waves and disappears.

Neca and Julio know that the turtle will be back. They have learned from the tags on other turtles that she will return to this beach to lay eggs as many as three times each nesting season, which lasts from September through March.

Neca and Julio have followed the turtle to the ocean. Now they go back to the nest for the eggs. If they were to leave them, the eggs might be dug up by other people, or by wild dogs or other animals. With a thin stick, Neca and Julio prod the nest to locate the egg cavity. Once they feel a soft spot, they start to dig with their hands. Soon the eggs are uncovered.

The author outlines the steps by which Julio and Neca dig up and transfer the eggs to a protected nest.

Making sure the eggs remain at the angle at which they found them, Neca and Julio count the eggs and put them inside a Styrofoam cooler. Julio packs them in moist sand to protect them during the trip back home. Then Neca measures the depth of the egg cavity.

Back at the jeep, Julio makes note of the number assigned to the turtle, its species, the size of its shell, the depth of its nest, and the number of eggs found inside.

Then the scientists return to their base and carefully transfer the eggs to a new nest. They bury the eggs at the same depth at which they found them. There the eggs will be protected from the heat while they incubate for about fifty days.

Thinking Like a Reader

1. Would you enjoy working on a project like the one described in the selection? Why or why not?
2. On what projects have you worked? How might you report on one of these projects?

Write your responses in your journal.

Thinking Like a Writer

3. What information does the author give you about TAMAR and the work of Julio and Neca with the turtles?
4. Which facts and details does he use to report on his topic?
5. Which facts do you find most interesting?

Write a list of these facts.

Responding to LITERATURE

Brainstorm *Vocabulary*

In "Project Turtle," the author tells about a process. Each step of the process must take place at a particular time. He uses time-order words and phrases to show the passing of time. Some examples are *now*, *by now*, *finally*, *while*, and *in about twenty minutes*. In your journal, write any time-order words that come to mind. Begin to create a personal vocabulary list. You can use some of these words when you write a report.

Talk It Over *A Process*

In the selection you read, the author reports on the process by which Julio and Neca work with the turtles. He includes specific details that show the reader exactly how each step is performed. Think of a process with which you are familiar. Outline the steps of this process to a partner. Make the steps of your outline clear for your partner. Then, listen as your partner tells you about a process. Check to be sure you can understand the steps your partner outlines for you.

Quick Write *Write a Proposal*

Before a project gets started, money must be found to support the work. Often, scientists write proposals describing the work they wish to do. People who give money to scientists read many proposals. They choose the ones they think are best.

Write a proposal that tells your idea for a nature study. Explain why it is a good idea to give money for this work. You may want to tell why you are the best person to do the study, or why this study is so important to science.

Idea Corner

Reporting on Nature

You have already started to think about a process in nature. What would you include in a report on this process? In your journal make some notes about facts and details you observe when studying a process found in nature. You can include sketches or photos of the steps of the process. Use these notes when you write a report.

PICTURES SEEING LIKE A WRITER

Finding Ideas for Writing

Look at the photographs. Think about what you see.
What ideas for report writing do the photographs give you?
Write your ideas in your journal.

Abercrombie & Kent
A&K
KXS 629

1 GROUP WRITING: A Research Report

The **purpose** of a research report is to give a reader information about a specific topic. How does a writer prepare to write a report?

- Finding Information/Note Taking
- Outlining
- Introduction/Body/Conclusion

Finding Information/Note Taking

Roy went to the library to find information about smog. He read an encyclopedia article and a magazine article. He took these notes on his reading.

kind of air pollution   smoke + fog = smog
Two kinds of coal and fuel oil, car emissions
problems: hurts eyes and lungs,
damages metal
worst cases: Mexico City and Denver
possible solutions: lawsuits, emission control
Environmental Protection Agency

The notes Roy took contain important facts that will help him when he organizes his report. In a report, facts and details give the reader an understanding of the topic.

Guided Practice: Taking Notes

With your class, choose a topic from the list that follows, or think of one on which you all agree. Go to the library with your class and find an article or encyclopedia entry on this topic. Read the article and take careful notes on specific facts.

pesticides   acid rain   endangered species

Outlining

In an outline, the writer lists points in the order in which they will be discussed. Each numbered point will become a paragraph. In the outline, important points of the topic are indicated by a roman numeral.

Smog

I. Introduction
- **A.** Definition
- **B.** Kinds of smog
- **C.** Problems and solutions

II. Problems
- **A.** Health hazards
- **B.** Destruction of materials

III. Solutions
- **A.** EPA and control of smog
- **B.** Emission controls

IV. Conclusion
- **A.** Summary
- **B.** Other Solutions

- How many paragraphs will be in this report?
- Which are the important points in the outline?

Guided Practice: Making an Outline

Using your notes, make an outline for a four-paragraph report. Follow the model above.

Introduction/Body/Conclusion

The main idea of a report is stated in the **introduction**. The **body** of the report contains specific information that supports and develops this main idea. The **conclusion** summarizes the points and adds an opinion about the topic. Look back at Roy's outline.

- Which information belongs in the introduction, the body, and the conclusion?

Putting a Research Report Together

With your classmates you researched to find some information on a topic. You took notes on your reading and organized the notes into an outline.

Think about the main idea of your report. Then, look at the outline you made. Which points would help your reader to understand the main idea of your report? Include those points. Leave out any information that would not help to make your report clear. Read this outline.

Earthquakes

I. Introduction
- **A.** Causes of earthquakes
- **B.** Predictions
- **C.** Problems and solutions

II. Problems
- **A.** Loss of lives
- **B.** Destruction of land and property

III. Solutions
- **A.** Long-term predictions
- **B.** Short-term predictions

IV. Conclusion
- **A.** Summary
- **B.** Other preventive measures

Guided Practice: Writing a Research Report

Use your notes and outline to write a report. Include information that will help you to present your main idea clearly into paragraph form. Organize your report into a logical introduction, body, and conclusion.

Share your report with a classmate. Ask your partner whether you have presented your main idea with enough facts and details to make the topic understandable.

Checklist: Report Writing

When you write a research report, a checklist will remind you of the things you will want to include in your report.

Look at this checklist. It will help you to start writing your report into fully-developed paragraphs. Some points need to be added. Make a copy of the checklist and complete it. Keep a copy of it in your writing folder.

CHECKLIST

- ✓ Purpose and audience
- ✓ Finding information/notetaking
- ✓ Outlining
- ✓ Introduction/Body/Conclusion
- ✓ Label subheads
- ■ ______________
- ■ ______________
- ■ ______________

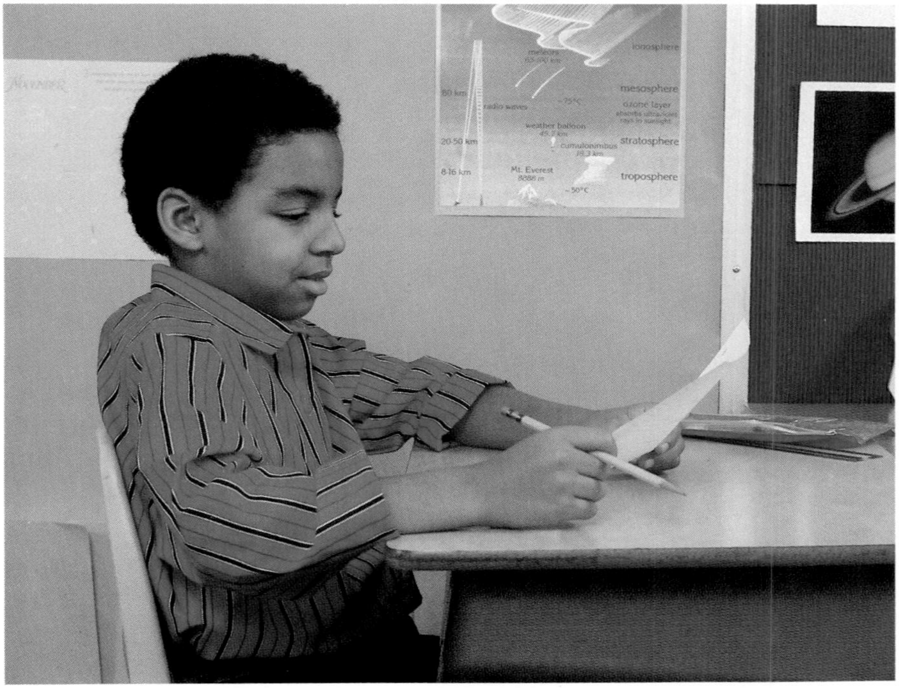

2 THINKING AND WRITING: Summarizing

You have learned that a research report presents information on a subject. Each paragraph in a report contains facts and details. The last paragraph, or conclusion, summarizes the information and makes a final point.

When you take notes for your research report, you summarize the information you read. You *paraphrase*, or state in your own words, the important points. A **summary** briefly tells the main idea of a piece of writing.

Reread this passage from the selection "Project Turtle." Then, read one student's summary.

> Making sure the eggs remain at the angle at which they found them, Neca and Julio count the eggs and put them inside a Styrofoam cooler. Julio packs them in moist sand to protect them during the trip back home. Then Neca measures the depth of the egg cavity.
>
> Back at the jeep, Julio makes note of the number assigned to the turtle, its species, the size of its shell, the depth of its nest, and the number of eggs found inside.

Student's Summary

Julio and Neca pack the turtle eggs carefully inside a Styrofoam container. The scientists make careful records concerning the turtle, its nest, and the number of her eggs. Then they take the eggs back to their workplace and put the eggs in a new nest just like the first one.

Thinking Like a Writer

- Which main ideas did the writer want her readers to understand? Which details did she leave out?

When you summarize your report in your conclusion, do not repeat everything you just wrote. Choose the most important point. This is your chance to offer the reader your final thoughts on the topic of the report.

THINKING APPLICATION Summarizing Information

COOPERATIVE LEARNING

Suppose that you have your own radio news program. Decide which information your audience would need to know from the news article below. On a separate piece of paper, write a three-sentence summary of the article for your broadcast.

October 12, 1990. The investigation continues into the cause of a three-alarm fire at Long Row Mall last Tuesday. Fire fighters had ruled out arson until a witness stepped forward. Jack Flora of 10 Winter Road was parked in the lot to the east of the mall late last night when four youths ran by. Moments later, flames were reported by the janitor in Tidy Homes Hardware, Karen Reeves. By the time fire fighters reached the mall, Tidy Homes and its two nearest neighbors, Tot Togs and HairPower, were engulfed in flames. Captain Turnbull of the Teeburg Police says that he is working "hand in hand" with Chief Phyre. They are asking all citizens with any knowledge of the crime to call 444-3300.

WRITING PROCESS

3 INDEPENDENT WRITING: A Research Report

Prewrite: Step 1

You have seen how research reports present information on a specific topic. Now, you can write a report of your own. Mae, a student your age, wanted to write about a topic which would interest the members of her science club. She chose a topic in this way.

Choosing a Topic

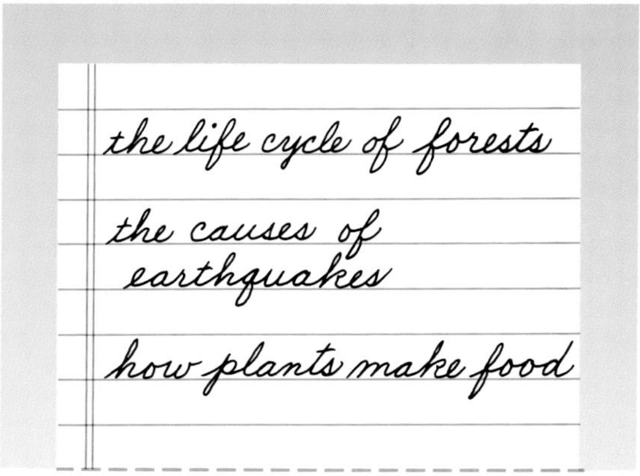

1. First, Mae thought about topics she had read about in her science textbook.
2. Next, she started a list of interesting topics for further research.
3. Last, Mae chose the topic she thought she could research easily in the school library.

Mae thought she could best research how plants make food. She discovered that plants use nitrogen to make protein. Once she had narrowed her topic to the nitrogen cycle, she was ready to explore her idea.

Exploring Ideas: Outlining Strategy

Mae used an outline to organize her notes. Notice that Mae's outline clearly shows how her information will be divided into an introduction, a body, and a conclusion.

Mae can now use the numbered parts of her outline to help her organize her report into clear paragraphs.

Before she actually wrote her report, Mae decided it was important to review her outline carefully. She added information to her outline and changed the order of points.

The Nitrogen Cycle

I Introduction
  A. Definition
  B. Relationship to plants

II Movement from soil to plants
  A. Nitrogen-fixing bacteria
  B. Plant protein

~~III~~ IV Conclusion
  A. Summary
  B. The cycle of life

III Movement from plants to soil
  A. Animal protein
  B. Decay

Thinking Like a Writer

- What did Mae add to her outline?
- Why did she add these points?

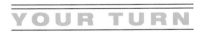

YOUR TURN

JOURNAL

Choose a topic which you would like to investigate. Use **Pictures** or your journal for ideas. Follow these steps.

- Choose a topic that interests you.
- Find information about the topic in the library.
- Narrow the topic if it is too broad.
- Think about your purpose and audience.

Using your notes, make an outline. Remember, you can change any part of your outline later.

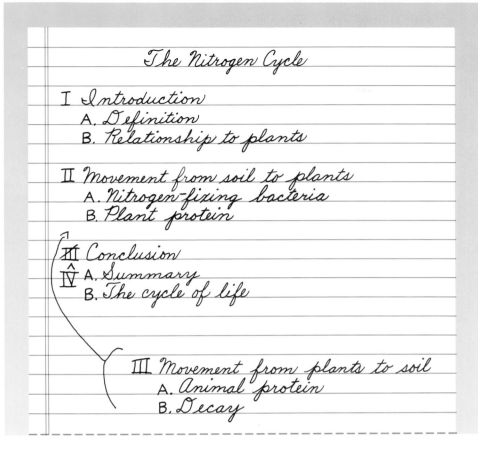

Write a First Draft: Step 2

Mae knows what to include in a report. She has made a planning checklist. Mae is ready to write her first draft.

Mae's First Draft

In an artical in Science magazine, Dr Edward Li calls nitrogen ''the stuff of life.'' This gas is found in the air, in the ground, and in all living things. Its movement is called the nitrogen cycle. Nitrogen is important for we.

Nitrogen moves from soil to plants. Bacteria found in certain plants make the gas into something plants can use. Plants convert this to protein.

Nitrogen moves back to the soil. Animals eat plants and convert plant protein to animal protein. As animals and plants die and decay, nitrogen moves back to the soil.

The movement of nitrogen is a basic part of life.

As Mae wrote, she did not worry about errors. She wanted to put her ideas down on paper.

Planning Checklist
- Remember purpose and audience.
- Find information and take notes.
- Outline points clearly.
- Include an introduction, body, and conclusion.

YOUR TURN

Write your first draft. As you prepare to write, ask yourself these questions.

- What will my audience need to know?
- How can I interest my audience in these facts?

TIME-OUT You might want to take some time out before you revise. That way you will be able to revise your writing with a fresh eye.

Revise: Step 3

After she finished her first draft, Mae read it over to herself. Then she shared her report with a classmate, Sandy. She asked Sandy to suggest ways she could improve her report.

Your facts are clear, but your report just seems to end all of a sudden.
You're right. I will write a better conclusion.

Mae then looked back at her planning checklist. She realized that she had forgotten one point. She checked it off so that she would remember it when she revised. Mae now has a checklist to use as she revises her report.

Mae made changes to her report. She did not correct small errors. She knew she could fix them later.

The revisions Mae made changed her report. Turn the page. Look at Mae's revised draft.

Revising Checklist
- ■ Remember purpose and audience.
- ■ Find information and take notes.
- ■ Outline points clearly.
- ✓ ■ Include an introduction, body, and conclusion.

WRITING PROCESS

Part of Mae's Revised Draft

nitrogen "the stuff of life." This gas is found in the air, in the ground, and in all living things. Its movement is called the nitrogen cycle. Nitrogen is important for we.

Nitrogen moves from soil to plants. Bacteria found in certain plants, like peas and beans, make the gas into something plants can use~~.~~ and ~~Plants~~ convert ~~this~~ to protein.

Nitrogen moves back to the soil. Animals eat plants and convert plant protein to animal protein. As animals and plants die and decay, nitrogen moves back to the soil.

The movement of nitrogen is a basic part of life. If it weren't for nitrogen, we would not exist. It has a cycle that involves people, plants, animals, and the earth.

Thinking Like a Writer

WISE WORD CHOICE

- Which sentences did Mae combine? How does combining them improve her writing?
- What sentences did Mae add? How do these added sentences make her conclusion clearer?

YOUR TURN

Read your first draft. Ask yourself these questions.

- Does my report contain enough information to be clear?
- Do my paragraphs follow the order of points in my outline?
- Does my report have an introduction, a body, and a conclusion?

If you wish, ask a friend to read your report and make suggestions. Then, revise your report.

Proofread: Step 4

Mae knew that her work was not complete until she proofread her report. She used a proofreading checklist while she proofread.

Part of Mae's Proofread Draft

The Nitrogen Cycle

In an ~~artical~~ article in Science magazine, Dr. Edward Li calls nitrogen "the stuff of life." This gas is found in the air, in the ground, and in all living things. Its movement is called the nitrogen cycle. Nitrogen is important for ~~we~~ us.

Nitrogen moves from soil to plants. Bacteria found in certain plants, like peas and beans, make the gas into something plants can use ~~.~~ and ~~Plants~~ convert ~~this~~ to protein.

YOUR TURN

Proofreading Practice

Below is a paragraph that you can use to practice your proofreading skills. Find the errors. Write the paragraph correctly on a separate sheet of paper.

How Kiley Canyon Was Made

A thousand years ago, kiley river was just a streem. Snow melted each spring and fed the trickel. People watched as it grew in size until it became a river to wide for they to cross. Later, the sandstone streembedd was worn away over the coarse of many years. The river widened and deepened, carving out a canyun.

Proofreading Checklist

- Did I indent my paragraphs?
- Did I spell all words correctly?
- What punctuation errors do I need to correct?
- What capitalization errors do I need to correct?

WRITING PROCESS

Applying Your Proofreading Skills

Now proofread your research report. Read your checklist once again. Review **The Grammar Connection** and **The Mechanics Connection**, too. Use the proofreading marks to mark changes.

THE GRAMMAR CONNECTION

Remember this rule about prepositional phrases.

- Use object pronouns as objects in prepositional phrases.

  The joke is **on me**. I laughed **at her and him**.

Check your report. Have you used object pronouns correctly?

THE MECHANICS CONNECTION

Remember these rules about titles.

- Capitalize the first letter of each important word in a title.
- Underline titles of books, newspapers, and magazines to show that they should be italicized.
- Put quotation marks around the titles of short stories, songs, articles, book chapters, and most poems.

  I read the poem, "The Wind," in The Collected Verse of Robert Louis Stevenson.

  The article, "Our Beaches," in The Local Banner was excellent.

Check your report. Have you written all titles correctly?

Proofreading Marks

- ¶ Indent
- ∧ Add
- Take out
- ≡ Make a capital letter
- / Make a small letter

Publish: Step 5

Mae shared her report by reading it aloud to her class. She showed a diagram of the nitrogen cycle and pointed to the diagram as she read. Her classmates said the diagram helped them to understand the cycle.

YOUR TURN

Make a neat final copy of your research report. Think of a way to share your work. Some ideas are given in the **Sharing Suggestions** box below.

SHARING SUGGESTIONS

Illustrate your report and make a cover for it. Keep it in the classroom library.

Make a science magazine with your class. Include your reports and diagrams or pictures.

Read your report aloud to a friend or relative.

4 SPEAKING AND LISTENING: Giving an Oral Report

You have just written a research report. Your report presented your ideas about a topic, which you supported with facts and details. Now you can use what you know about writing reports to give an oral report.

First, you will want to make an outline for your oral report. The outline should include your topic and the main points you plan to discuss. Look at the outline below.

Lemmings

I Introduction
  A. Small rodents
  B. Strange migration

II Facts about lemmings
  A. Live in Arctic
  B. Live in groups

III Migration of lemmings
  A. Caused by overpopulation
  B. Some drown when they reach the sea

IV Conclusion
  A. Summary
  B. What we can learn about overpopulation

Notice that the information contained in the outline shows the main points that the student's talk will include. How does the outline show how the points are ordered?

When you give an oral report, it will help you to keep your **purpose** and **audience** in mind. These speaking guidelines will help you to focus your oral report.

SPEAKING GUIDELINES: An Oral Report

1. Remember your **purpose** and **audience**.
2. Make an outline. Practice using the outline.
3. Make sure your outline has an introduction, a body, and a conclusion.
4. Look at your listeners and speak in a strong, clear voice.
5. Prepare to answer questions when you finish.

- What is the main idea of my oral report?
- Does my information support this main idea?

SPEAKING APPLICATION An Oral Report

Think of a topic that would make an interesting oral report. Prepare an outline to use as you organize the information in your report. Use the speaking guidelines to help you prepare. Your classmates will be using the following guidelines as they listen to your report.

LISTENING GUIDELINES: An Oral Report

1. Listen for the main idea of the report.
2. Listen for a clear introduction, body, and conclusion.
3. Listen for interesting facts and details.

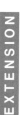

5 WRITER'S RESOURCES: The Atlas and the Almanac

In this unit you have researched information in order to prepare written and oral reports. You have learned that it is important to find accurate facts and details. Two useful resources for the writer are the atlas and the almanac.

An **atlas** is a book of maps. Some atlases have tables of the population, climate, and size of the countries of the world.

Imagine that you are a researcher. You are about to travel to Venezuela to study an unusual bird. You will write a report on your findings. First, you want to learn something about the area you will visit. You would use an atlas to find a map of Venezuela.

This map shows the countries that border Venezuela. You can see where the main river flows and what the capital city is.

Imagine that you will be exploring along the Orinoco River. You might wonder how the river compares in length to other rivers you have explored. You would look up *rivers* in an **almanac**. Here is part of a table you might find in an almanac.

World Rivers — Length in Miles

River	Length	River	Length
Niger	2,590	Ohio	975
Nile	4,145	Orinoco	1,600
Oder	567		

From this table you can see that the Orinoco is much longer than the Ohio River, but less than half the length of the Nile.

Almanacs contain many kinds of information. New almanacs are published every year. They contain facts about population, current events and history, people, sports, and many other things.

Practice

A researcher must find the answers to many questions. Write **atlas** or **almanac** to tell where you can find the answer to each of the following questions.

1. Is Angel Falls the highest waterfall anywhere?
2. What islands lie off the coast of Venezuela?
3. Does Venezuela export oil?
4. How much United States aid is sent to Venezuela each year?
5. Do Brazil and Venezuela share a border?
6. Do I cross Cuba when I fly to Venezuela from the United States?
7. What is the average income of a Venezuelan?
8. When did Europeans discover the Orinoco?
9. In what direction does the Orinoco flow?
10. Does the Equator run through Venezuela?

WRITING APPLICATION Questions

Imagine that you are about to travel to some country or place that interests you. Write ten questions about the place you choose. Then use an atlas and an almanac to answer the questions. Keep this information in your writing folder. You might wish to create a record of interesting facts for your own use.

THE CURRICULUM CONNECTION

Writing About Computers

Today, computers aid us in everything we do, from getting a weather forecast to finding a book in the library. Many professional writers use computers. There are also people who write about computers and explain their uses.

ACTIVITIES

Computer Diary Watch for computers as you go through your day. Record everything you do that involves a computer. Remember that some watches and calculators have computers in them. Share your diary with others.

Summarize a Flow Chart People who write software often begin by making a flow chart. Many computers work on a simple "yes-no" system. Read this flow chart. Write a three-sentence summary telling what the flow chart shows.

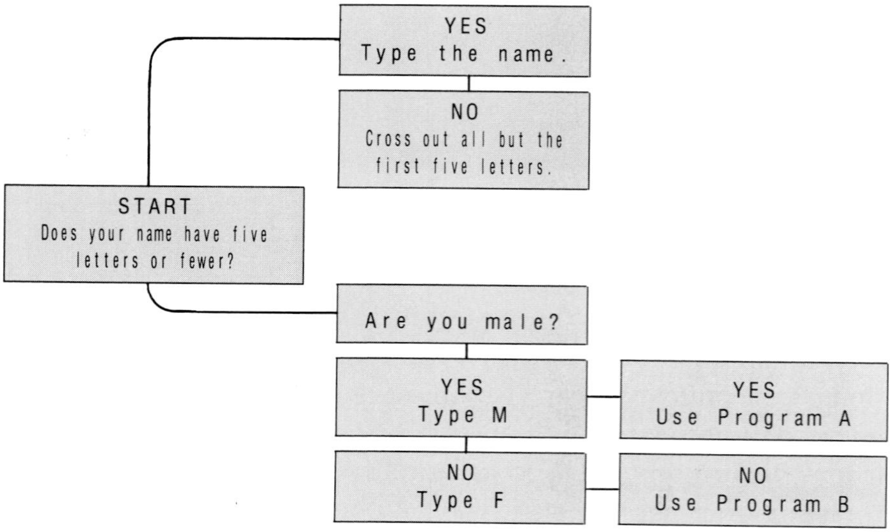

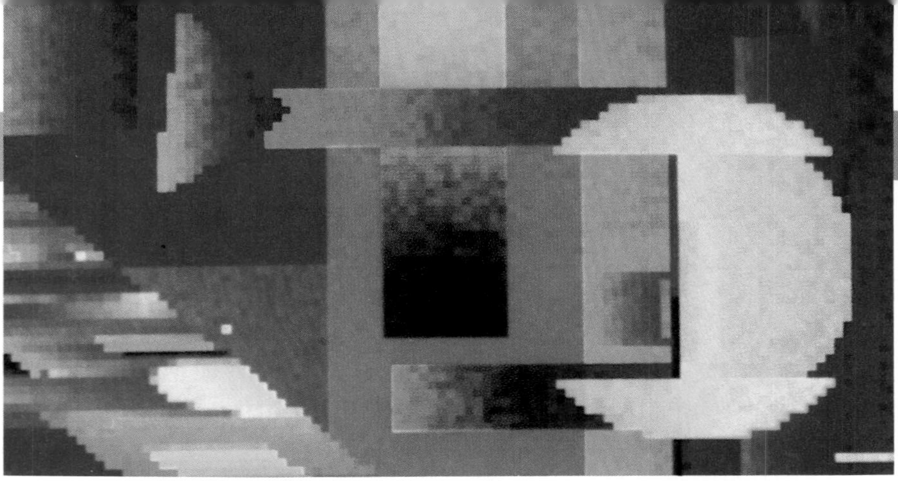

Respond to Literature Computers have some artistic and entertaining uses. The following selection reports on ways that computers can reproduce pictures. After you read the selection, work with a partner to brainstorm for some uses of computer art. Make a list of your ideas.

from Pixels and Patterns

In some shopping malls, you can find people who will take your picture with a TV camera and reproduce the image with a printer on paper or a tee shirt. If you or your school has access to equipment like this, here is an opportunity to explore the principles of TV imaging, digitizing, and the ability of people to recognize a picture when its detail has been reduced. How is the image from the TV camera converted into picture elements, or pixels? How are light values assigned? How are these values converted into a printed image?

Computer art has practical applications as well, beyond those suggested so far. The designing of quilts, needlepoint, and weaving frequently requires that the artist draw out the pattern and then modify and often redraw it, sometimes many times. Computer programs can produce these patterns on the screen and then perhaps reproduce them on paper later. Such programs would allow the artist to make a small change at the keyboard and see the results instantly.

UNIT CHECKUP

LESSON 1 **Group Writing: Finding Information and Note Taking** (page 472) Turn to page 491 and reread the selection from *Pixels and Patterns.* Take notes on the paragraph as though you were going to write a report about computers.

LESSON 2 **Thinking: Summarizing** (page 476) Write a two-sentence summary of this news report.

Port Moresby Three American and two French explorers have settled in a village in the interior of New Guinea in hopes of learning more about the people there. The tribe is so remote that the explorers are believed to be the first visitors they have ever had. Reports from the explorers indicate that the villagers rely on stone and wooden tools and have no written language. A film crew tried to reach the village but was unable to pass through the jungle.

LESSON 3 **Writing a Research Report** (page 478) Imagine that you are a travel agent. You have been asked to write part of a brochure about island vacation spots. Choose any island you think might be interesting. Find information, take notes, and make an outline. Write a four-paragraph report about the island for your brochure.

LESSON 4 **Speaking and Listening: An Oral Report** (page 486) Imagine that you will give an oral report on a topic of your choice. Write a topic sentence and three facts that support this sentence.

LESSON 5 **Writer's Resources: The Atlas and the Almanac** (page 488) Write **atlas** or **almanac** to tell where you could find the answers to these questions.

1. What countries border the Persian Gulf?
2. Who is the American ambassador to China?
3. Through which states do the Rocky Mountains run?

THEME PROJECT — Data Chart

You have been reading about investigations of many kinds. In art, science, literature, and in everyday life, there are fascinating topics for investigation.

Whether you are a detective or a scientist, you follow a series of steps in an investigation. First, you pose a question to which you do not have an answer. You may make some guesses about what the answer is. Finally, you must collect facts, or data, to prove or disprove your guesses. You might do this by observing, simply by looking around and noticing clues. Or, you might set up an experiment and look at the results.

Think of some topics which interest you. Work with a small group of your classmates.

- Begin by brainstorming for some ideas.
- Collect data, or information, on a topic and summarize what the information means.
- After you have collected your data, write it in the form of a chart.
- With your classmates, summarize the results of the data.

WRITER'S REFERENCE

Writer's Reference

CONTENTS

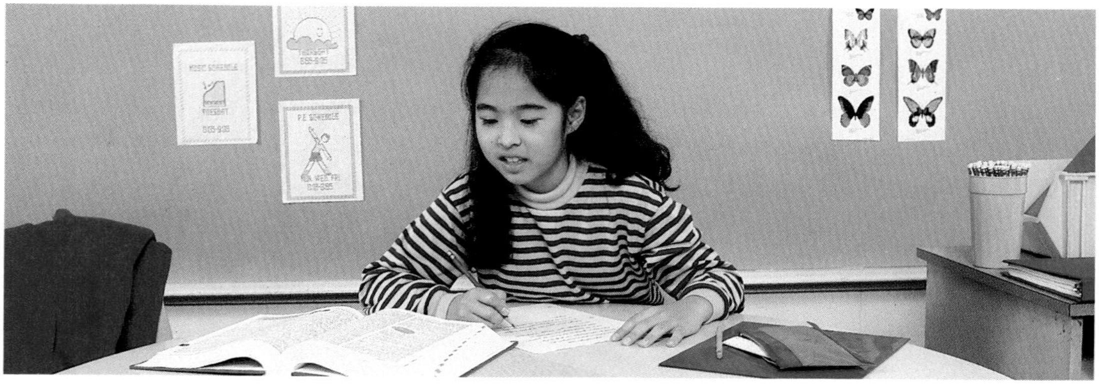

LANGUAGE STUDY HANDBOOK

GRAMMAR

Sentences

A **sentence** is a group of words that expresses a complete thought. A sentence contains a subject and a predicate.

An Asian cook/prepared the meal.
subject **predicate**

The **subject** tells whom or what the sentence is about. The subject may be one word or more than one word.

Sam skates well. **Sam and Donna** skate well.

The **predicate** tells what the subject does or is. The predicate contains the **verb**, which may be one word or more than one word.

Cathy **walked** with Jean. The girls **were walking** for hours.

There are four kinds of sentences. Notice the end punctuation of each sentence type.

I collect stamps**.** (statement—ends with a period)
How do you get them**?** (question—ends with a question mark)
Ask me questions**.** (command—ends with a period)
I love my hobby**!** (exclamation—ends with an exclamation mark)

A **run-on sentence** joins together two or more sentences incorrectly. Often, they should be written separately.

I went to the grocery store and on the way there I saw my friend on the other side of the street I called to her and she waved to me.

Divide a run-on sentence into several sentences.

I went to the grocery store. On the way there, I saw my friend on the other side of the street. I called to her, and she waved to me.

A **sentence fragment** is incomplete.

HANDBOOK

Add a subject or a predicate to complete a sentence fragment.

The river water rushed past me.

The river water.	(fragment—no predicate)
Rushed past me.	(fragment—no subject)

Nouns

A **noun** is a word that names a person, place, thing, or idea.

student farm book democracy

A **singular noun** names one person, place, thing, or idea.

girl store jar skill

A **plural** noun names more than one person, place, thing, or idea. Add **s** to most singular nouns to make them plural.

girls stores jars skills

If a singular noun ends in **s**, **z**, **x**, **sh**, or **ch**, add **es** to form the plural.

glass—glasses waltz—waltzes fox—foxes brush—brushes lunch—lunches

If a singular noun ends in a vowel and **y**, add **s**.

toy—toys boy—boys

If a singular noun ends in a consonant and **y**, change the **y** to **i**, and add **es**.

country—countries lily—lilies

If a singular noun ends in **f** or **fe**, change the **f** to **v**, and add **es** to some nouns. Add **s** to other nouns.

wife—wives cliff—cliffs

If a singular noun ends in a vowel and **o**, add **s**.

stereo—stereos video—videos

If a singular noun ends in a consonant and **o**, add **s** or **es**.

silo—silos hero—heroes

Some nouns are **irregular nouns**. You must memorize the plurals of irregular nouns.

deer—deer ox—oxen foot—feet

A **plural possessive noun** shows what more than one person or thing owns. If a plural noun ends in **s**, an **apostrophe** is added to form the plural possessive.

horses' hooves the girls' team

If a plural noun does not end in **s**, **'s** is added to form the plural possessive.

children**'s** stories men**'s** hats

A **possessive noun** is a noun that shows ownership.

A **singular possessive noun** shows what one person or thing owns. Usually, **'s** is added to singular nouns to form a singular possessive.

Sandy**'s** painting the cat**'s** paw

Verbs

A **verb** expresses action or tells what something is or is like.

count counted is was

The **time** expressed by a verb is called its **tense**.

Present tense expresses action that is happening now.

I **close** the door. (present)

Past tense expresses action that has already happened.

I **closed** the door. (past)

Future tense expresses action that has not yet happened.

I **will close** the door. (future)

Most verbs add **d** or **ed** to form their past tense.

dance—danced work—worked

An **irregular** verb does not add **d** or **ed** to form its past tense.

Present	**Past**	**Past with has, have, had**
go	went	gone
fly	flew	flown
break	broke	broken
ride	rode	ridden
throw	threw	thrown

HANDBOOK

Adjectives

An **adjective** is a word that describes a noun. An adjective tells **what kind** or **how many**.

red dress　　**small** cup　　**long** hair　　**six** elephants

Articles

A, **an**, and **the** are special adjectives called **articles**.

Use **a** before a singular noun beginning with a consonant. Use **an** before a singular noun beginning with a vowel. Use **the** before plural nouns and before singular nouns that name a particular person, place, or thing.

a rock on **a** beach　**an** answer to your question　**the** pages of **the** book

Pronouns

A **pronoun** is a word that takes the place of one or more nouns and the words that go with the nouns.

Subject pronouns are used in the subject part of sentences. Subject pronouns are also used after forms of the linking verb *be*.

Subject pronouns: I, you, he, she, it, we, they

Object pronouns are used after verbs and after words such as *into*, *of*, *with*, and *to*.

Object Pronouns: me, you, him, her, it, us, them

Possessive pronouns show who or what owns something.

Possessive Pronouns: my, mine, your, yours, his, her, hers, its, our, ours, their, theirs

Adverbs

An **adverb** is a word that tells more about a verb. An adverb tells **how**, **where**, or **when**.

She runs **quickly**.	(how)
He ran **downhill**.	(where)
They will leave **later**.	(when)

To make an adjective into an adverb, add **ly**.

polite—polite**ly**　　rude—rude**ly**

Prepositions

A **preposition** is a word that relates a noun or pronoun to another word in a sentence.

Pat saw a parrot **at** the zoo.
It sat **on** a branch.

A **prepositional phrase** is a group of words that begins with a preposition and ends with a noun or pronoun.

Pat saw a parrot **at the zoo.**
The parrot perched **near her**.

The noun or pronoun that follows a preposition is called the **object of the preposition**.

The parrot flew around the **cage.**
The bird looked happy to **me.**

When the object of a preposition is a pronoun, use an object pronoun: *me*, *you*, *him*, *her*, *it*, *us*, or *them*.

Pat told Janet about **Robert.**
Pat told Janet about **him.**

MECHANICS

Punctuation

End Punctuation

Use **end punctuation** to end a sentence.

A **period** (.) ends a **statement** or a **command.**
A **question mark** (?) ends a **question.**
An **exclamation mark** (!) ends an **exclamation.**

I have a cold.	(statement)
Take your medicine.	(command)
Will I get well?	(question)
I finally feel better!	(exclamation)

HANDBOOK

Periods

Use a **period** to show the end of an abbreviation and with initials.

Apr. Sat. Dr. St. Co. Sally K. Ride

Lyndon B. Johnson

Colons

Use a **colon** to separate hours and minutes in time.

3:25 7:15 4:30

Use a **colon** after the greeting of a business letter.

Dear Sir: Dear Mr. Lee:

Commas

Use a **comma** between the names of cities and states.

Bangor, Maine Houston, Texas

Use a **comma** between the day and the year in dates.

December 7, 1941 July 20, 1969

Use a **comma** to separate words in a series.

Joan's dress is blue, green, and yellow.

Use two commas to set off an **appositive**, a group of words that tells more about the subject.

Joe, a good student, enjoys science class.

Use a **comma** after introductory words or phrases in a sentence.

Yes, I enjoyed the meal you cooked.

Use a **comma** with nouns in direct address.

Jane, are you hungry?

Use **commas** to set off a direct quotation in a sentence.

"Do you know," she asked, "what time it is?"

Use a **comma** before *and*, *but*, or *or* in a compound sentence.

I love winter, but Pat enjoys fall.
The weather is cold, and it is windy.
Mike will buy a copy of his favorite book, or he will borrow it.

Apostrophes

Use **apostrophes (')** in contractions to show where letters are missing.

won't　　they'll

Use **apostrophes** with nouns to show possession. Add **'s** to singular nouns or plural nouns that do not end in **s**.

Mary**'s** cat　　Joe**'s** house　　women**'s** suits

Add an ' alone to plural nouns ending in **s**.

jars' tops　　coats' collars

Hyphens

Use a **hyphen** to connect two words to form compound words, or to join syllables of a word that have been separated.

half-hour　　drive-in

Quotation Marks

Put **quotation marks** before and after a direct quotation. Do **not** use quotation marks unless you use the speaker's exact words.

"I do not want any potatoes," said Paul.
Paul said that he did not want any potatoes.

Put **quotation marks** before and after the title of a short story, a song, a poem, or a chapter title.

"Cinderella"　　"America the Beautiful"

Underlining

Underline the titles of books, newspapers, magazines, and movies.

<u>Black Beauty</u>　　<u>The New York Times</u>

Capitalization

Capitalize the names of specific persons, pets, places, or things.

Abraham Lincoln　　Spot　　Maine　　Jefferson Memorial

Capitalize initials.

John F. Kennedy　　Franklin D. Roosevelt

HANDBOOK

HANDBOOK

Capitalize titles of respect when they are part of a specific name.

President Eisenhower   Doctor Jonas Salk

Always capitalize the first-person pronoun **I**.

Capitalize the first, last, and all important words in the title of a book, newspaper, song, poem, play, short story, or movie.

<u>Julie of the Wolves</u>
"The Elves and the Shoemaker"
"Jingle Bells"

Capitalize family names if they refer to specific people.

I told Father about my project.
The mother penguin protected her chick.

Capitalize the days of the week and the months of the year.

Sunday   Wednesday   May   November

Capitalize the names of holidays and religious days.

Valentine's Day   Memorial Day   Easter

Capitalize the names of specific cities, states, countries, continents, rivers, oceans, and other geographic locations.

Tacoma   Oregon   Spain   Europe
Hudson River   Atlantic Ocean   Niagara Falls

Capitalize the names of streets and avenues.

Main Street   Third Avenue

Capitalize the titles of specific clubs, organizations, and companies.

Explorers' Club
Federal Bureau of Investigation
General Foods Corporation

Capitalize proper adjectives.

German   Mexican   Vietnamese   Egyptian

Capitalize the first word in a sentence. Capitalize the first word in a quotation.

She asked, "Where does Mickey think he is going?"

Capitalize all the words in the greeting of a letter.

Dear Sir:

Capitalize only the first word in a letter's closing.

Yours truly,

Capitalize the first word of each main topic and subtopic in an outline. Put a period after each Roman numeral and capital letter in an outline.

I. Types of mammals
  A. Land mammals
  B. Sea mammals

Abbreviations

Capitalize and put a period after abbreviations used in titles of respect.

Sen. Mrs. Prof.

Capitalize and put a period after abbreviations of addresses.

Rd. Ave. Pl.

Capitalize and put a period after abbreviations for days and months.

Thurs. Sun. Sept. Dec.

Use the **United States Postal Service** abbreviations for state names. Notice that each abbreviation consists of two capital letters. No period follows these abbreviations.

AL (Alabama)	LA (Louisiana)	OH (Ohio)
AK (Alaska)	ME (Maine)	OK (Oklahoma)
AZ (Arizona)	MD (Maryland)	OR (Oregon)
AR (Arkansas)	MA (Massachusetts)	PA (Pennsylvania)
CA (California)	MI (Michigan)	RI (Rhode Island)
CO (Colorado)	MN (Minnesota)	SC (South Carolina)
CT (Connecticut)	MS (Mississippi)	SD (South Dakota)
DE (Delaware)	MO (Missouri)	TN (Tennessee)
FL (Florida)	MT (Montana)	TX (Texas)
GA (Georgia)	NE (Nebraska)	UT (Utah)
HI (Hawaii)	NV (Nevada)	VT (Vermont)
ID (Idaho)	NH (New Hampshire)	VA (Virginia)
IL (Illinois)	NJ (New Jersey)	WA (Washington)
IN (Indiana)	NM (New Mexico)	WV (West Virginia)
IA (Iowa)	NY (New York)	WI (Wisconsin)
KS (Kansas)	NC (North Carolina)	WY (Wyoming)
KY (Kentucky)	ND (North Dakota)	

USAGE

Verbs

Avoid changing from one tense to another in a sentence.

The doorbell **rang**, and Lori **runs** to answer it.
(incorrect: past to present)
The doorbell **rang**, and Lori **ran** to answer it.
(correct: both past)

Subjects and verbs must **agree** in **number**. If a subject is singular, the verb must be singular as well. If a subject is plural, the verb must be plural as well.

The **dog scratches** its ear. (singular subject and verb)
The **dogs scratch** their ears. (plural subject and verb)

Adjectives

If an adjective compares two nouns, the adjective usually ends in **er**.

Saturday was a **colder** day than Friday.
You need a **heavier** sweater than that blue one.

If an adjective compares more than two nouns, the adjective usually ends in **est.**

The **loudest** thunderclap of all frightened Sparky. He is the **youngest** of our three cats.

Some adjectives use **more** and **most** to show comparison. Use **more** to compare two nouns.

Sparky is **more** frightened than Ginger.

Use **most** to compare more than two nouns.

The **most** adventurous of the cats is Pepper.

Do not combine **er** with the word **more**.
Do not combine **est** with the word **most.**

Li is **quieter** than his sister. (correct)
Li is **more quieter** than his sister. (incorrect)
In fact, Li is the **quietest** person in his whole family. (correct)
In fact, Li is the **most quietest** person in his whole family. (incorrect)

Pronouns

Use a **subject pronoun** as the subject of a sentence.

> **We** entered the bicycle race.
> **He** was the winner.

Use an **object pronoun** after a verb and after words such as *to*, *with*, *for*, and *at*.

> Mr. Stewart drove **us** home.
> Please take a walk with **me**.

The pronouns **I** and **me** are **personal pronouns.** When you use **I** or **me** with another pronoun or a noun, always put the personal pronoun last.

> She and **I** hurried to school.
> The teacher returned the papers to José and **me**.

The pronouns **we** and **us** have their own rules, too. Use **we** with a noun that is a subject or that follows a linking verb.

> **We** singers practice daily.
> The best cellists are **we**.

Use **us** with a noun that follows an action verb or that follows a preposition such as **to**, **for**, **with**, or **at**.

> The conductor praised **us** musicians.
> The praise was meant for **us**.

Every pronoun refers to a noun. A pronoun must agree with the noun to which it refers.

> Lisa bought the **toy** and handed **it** to the baby.
> The **puppies** wagged **their** tails.

Double Negatives

Negatives are words that mean **no**.

Some examples of negatives are **no**, **never**, **none**, **not**, and **nothing**. Use only one negative in a sentence.

> I **never** saw **any**. (correct: single negative)
> I **never** saw **none**. (incorrect: double negative)

Troublesome Words

Some words or word pairs are easy to confuse.

Good and **bad** are adjectives. They describe nouns.

This is a **good** movie. That is a **bad** joke.

Well and **badly** are adverbs. They tell more about verbs.

They sing **well**. She dances **badly**.

Use **well** when talking about health.

Chris felt **well** yesterday.

When you use **good** and **bad** to compare, you must change their forms. Use **better** or **worse** to compare two items. Use **best** or **worst** to compare three or more items.

Breakfast today was **better** than breakfast yesterday.
Maybe breakfast tomorrow will be the **best** of the week.

Its is a possessive pronoun. Do not use an apostrophe with a possessive pronoun. **It's** is a contraction meaning "it is."

The squirrel buried **its** acorn.
Jay thinks **it's** the prettiest tree in the park.

Your is a possessive pronoun meaning "belonging to you."

Is that **your** jacket?

You're is a contraction meaning "you are."

You're going to leave at noon.

Their is a possessive pronoun meaning "belonging to them."

My grandparents have a telephone in **their** kitchen.

There is an adverb that tells "where."

I left my keys on the table over **there**.

They're is a contraction meaning "they are."

They're coming to see us soon.

Two is a number. **Too** means "also" or "very." **To** is a direction word meaning "toward."

William has **two** pets named Fred, **too**! Her rabbit hops **too** quickly.
They went **to** the park on different days.

THESAURUS FOR WRITING

What Is a Thesaurus?

A **thesaurus** is a reference book that can be very useful in your writing. It provides synonyms for many common words. **Synonyms** are words that mean almost the same thing.

The thesaurus can help you choose more interesting words and more exact words to use in your writing. For example, read this sentence.

Diane **looked** at her sister.

Looked is not a very interesting word, and it says very little about Diane. If you check the word *look* in the thesaurus, you will find these words: *glance, peer, stare*. Using one of these words would make your sentence more interesting and more precise.

Using the Thesaurus

The words in a thesaurus are listed in alphabetical order. If the word is listed in the thesaurus, you will find an entry. For example, if you looked up the word *right*, you would find this **main entry**.

	Part of Speech (→ *adj.*)
Entry word →	**right** *adj.* free from error; true. ← **Definition**
Example Sentence →	Her answers are always *right*.
Synonym →	**accurate** without errors or mistakes. The witness gave an *accurate* description of the thief.
Synonym →	**correct** agreeing with fact or truth. Is this the *correct* way to put this together?
Synonym →	**exact** very accurate; completely correct. The *exact* number of votes is still in question.
Antonym →	wrong, mistaken

The word *right* is called an **entry word**. The information that follows is called the **entry**.

Cross-references. In some cases you will find cross-references. For example, if you look up the word *small*, you will find this cross-reference: "*See* little." This means that you should look up the word *little*; the word *small* will be listed under *little*.

agree/big

A

agree *v.* to say "yes"; to have the same opinion; to be in harmony. Jan and Ted couldn't *agree* on what movie to see.
concur to have the same opinion. The members of the jury *concurred* that the witness was lying.
consent to give permission or approval. Will your mother *consent* to your going on the field trip?

allow *See* let.

angry *adj.* feeling or showing anger. When Lenny gets *angry*, he refuses to speak to anyone.
enraged filled with rage; angry beyond control. *Enraged* by her friend's note, Maria ripped it into a thousand tiny pieces.
furious extremely angry. Your brother will be *furious* when he finds out you ruined his bike.

answer *v.* to give a spoken or written response. I wonder whether Celia is ever going to *answer* my letter.
reply to say in response. If he insults you, don't *reply*; just walk away.
respond to give an answer. James did not *respond* to my question.
antonyms: ask, inquire

ask *v.* to put a question to. Let's *ask* that man for directions.
inquire to seek information by asking questions. Tom called the store to *inquire* about the sale.
question to try to get information (from someone). Bill's mother *questioned* him about where he had been.
antonyms: *See* answer.

awful *adj.* causing fear, dread, or awe. The tree made an *awful* noise when it fell.
dreadful causing great fear. Lydia is still in shock from her *dreadful* experience.
terrible causing terror or awe. Jason received some *terrible* news.

B

beautiful *adj.* full of beauty; having qualities that are pleasing. What a *beautiful* dog!
attractive appealing or pleasing but not in an exceptional way. They have an *attractive* house.
gorgeous extremely beautiful or richly colored. What a *gorgeous* rose garden!
lovely beautiful in a comforting way. Ben has a *lovely* voice.
antonyms: ugly, hideous, unattractive

big *adj.* of great size. Do you have any *big* boxes?
enormous much greater than the usual size. There is an *enormous* spider in the bathtub.

huge extremely big. That *huge* man is a football player.
large of great size; big. Paula seldom has such a *large* lunch.
antonyms: *See* little.

brave *adj.* willing to face danger; without fear. A person has to be *brave* to work with wild lions.
bold showing courage; fearless. Although Kevin acted *bold*, he was really very nervous.
courageous having courage. The pioneers who settled this country were *courageous* people.
daring willing to take risks. The audience gasped at the circus performer's *daring* feat.
antonyms: afraid, fearful.

break *v.* to come apart; to separate into pieces. These glass animals *break* easily.
crack to break without fully separating. Put the egg in the water slowly, or the shell will *crack*.
fracture to break or split a bone. Juan *fractured* his ankle and had to leave the game.
shatter to break suddenly into many pieces. If you drop that vase, it will *shatter*.

bright *adj.* filled with light; shining. Is that light *bright* enough to read by?
brilliant shining or sparkling with light. The king's crown was decorated with *brilliant* gems.
shiny shining; bright. Her blue coat has *shiny* silver buttons.
antonyms: dark, dull

C

clean *adj.* without dirt or stain. Be sure your hands are *clean* before you handle these pictures.
immaculate perfectly clean. For his first day at school, George put on an *immaculate* white shirt and a tie.
pure free from contamination. Is your well water *pure*?
spotless extremely clean. By the time the guests arrived, the house was *spotless*.
antonyms: dirty, filthy, messy

cold *adj.* having a low temperature; lacking warmth or heat. There is *cold* water in the refrigerator.
chilly uncomfortably cool. I put on a sweater because I was *chilly*.
icy very cold. The room felt *icy* because the furnace had been shut off.
antonyms: *See* hot.

collect *v.* to gather or bring (things) together. Sara and Louis both *collected* stamps.
assemble to gather or bring together, especially people. The marching band *assembled* in front of the town hall.

collect (continued)
compile to collect and put together (information), as in a list or report. They *compiled* a list of the mayor's supporters.
gather to bring together in one place or group. All the campers *gathered* around the campfire.

cook *v.* to prepare food for eating, using heat. Dad will *cook* dinner.
bake to cook in an oven. Alice put the bread in the oven to *bake*.
broil to cook by exposing to a flame or another source of intense heat. We're going to *broil* the hamburgers over charcoal.
roast to cook with very little moisture, in an oven or over an open fire. The directions said to *roast* the turkey for five hours.

cry *v.* to shed tears. The last scene of the movie was so sad that it made me *cry*.
sob to cry with short gasps. The lost child *sobbed* until his parents found him.
weep to show grief, joy, or other strong emotions by crying. The letter from her mother made Sofia *weep* with homesickness.
antonyms: *See* laugh.

D

do *v.* to carry out. Some days I can't *do* anything right.
execute to complete, often when told to do so; to put into effect. The job of the President is to *execute* the laws of Congress.
perform to carry out to completion. The acrobats will now *perform* a triple back flip.

dry *adj.* not wet; free of moisture. Is the paint *dry* yet?
arid dry as a result of having little rainfall. Nothing grows here because the land is so *arid*.
parched dried out by heat. The lotion felt good on my *parched* skin.
antonyms: *See* wet.

E

easy *adj.* requiring little mental or physical effort; not difficult. The math problems were so *easy* that Sheila did them in no time.
facile not hard to do or achieve; done easily and quickly. There is no *facile* solution to the problem of acid rain.
simple not complicated. The kit came with *simple* directions that were easy to follow.
antonyms: hard, difficult

F

far *adj.* a long way off; not near. The house is too *far* to see from here.
distant extremely far. Many sailors went to sea so they could visit *distant* lands.
remote faraway, in an out-of-the-way place. It took us three days to

climb to the *remote* mountain village.
antonyms: near, close

fast *adj.* moving or done with speed. A *fast* typist can type more than 100 words per minute.
quick done in a very short time. She gave a *quick* response.
rapid with great speed, often in a continuing way. Jeff kept walking at a *rapid* pace.
swift moving with great speed, often said of animals or people. A *swift* runner was sent to warn the nearby villages.
antonym: slow

funny *adj.* causing laughter. I heard a *funny* story on the radio.
amusing causing smiles of enjoyment or laughter. Harriet found the monkeys very *amusing*.
comical causing laughter through actions. The baby made all kinds of *comical* faces.
hilarious very funny and usually noisy. *Hilarious* laughter came from the party next door.

G

get *v.* to go for and return with. Did you *get* the package at the post office?
acquire to come into possession of through effort. How did she *acquire* so much money?
obtain to get as one's own, often with some difficulty. First, you'll have to *obtain* a parade permit.

give *v.* to turn over possession or control of; to make a present of. I want to *give* you this book.
confer to give as an honor. The college will *confer* an honorary degree upon the guest speaker.
contribute to give or supply in common with others. We are asking you to *contribute* $3.00.
grant to give in response to a request. *Grant* me this favor, and I promise never to ask again.
present to give in a formal way, usually something of value. Miss Kingsley *presented* a check for $5,000 to the Disaster Fund.
antonyms: *See* take.

good *adj.* above average in quality. He wanted a *good* meal.
excellent extremely good. This is an *excellent* book.
fair somewhat good; slightly better than average. He was a *fair* musician but a very good composer.
fine of high quality; very good. *Fine* jewelry is usually expensive.
antonyms: bad, poor
See also great.

great *adj.* of unusual quality or ability. Picasso was a *great* artist.
remarkable having unusual qualities. The actors did a *remarkable* job.

great (continued)
superb of greater quality than most. That was a *superb* dinner.
See also good.

H

happy *adj.* having, showing, or bringing pleasure. Their visit made Mrs. Johnson very *happy*.
glad feeling or expressing joy or pleasure. We are so *glad* you were able to join us.
joyful very happy; filled with joy. A wedding is a *joyful* occasion.
merry happy and cheerful. Suzanne is such a *merry* person that she cheered me up right away.
pleased satisfied or content. Was he *pleased* with his presents?
antonyms: *See* sad.

hard *adj.* not easy to do or deal with. These problems are *hard*.
difficult hard to do; requiring effort. The hikers planned a *difficult* climb.
tough difficult to do, often in a physical sense. We had a *tough* time finding all our lost sheep.
antonym: easy

help *v.* to provide with support; to be of service to. Mom will *help* me with my homework.
aid to give help to (someone in trouble). The Red Cross *aided* the flood victims.
assist to help, often in a cooperative way. The whole class will *assist* with the project.

high *adj.* located or extending a great distance above the ground. The eagle nested on a *high* cliff.
lofty very high; of grand or inspiring height. Above the valley rose a range of *lofty* mountain peaks.
tall having a height greater than average but with a relatively narrow width. Over the years, the pine trees grew to be very *tall*.
towering of great or imposing height. The city's *towering* buildings made Luis feel small.
antonyms: low, short

hot *adj.* having a high temperature; having much heat. This pan is *hot*.
fiery as hot as fire; burning. Inside the volcano's crater was a *fiery* pool of lava.
scalding hot enough to burn, often said of liquids. I got a bad burn from some *scalding* water.
scorching intensely hot, enough to cause burning or drying. Few plants can survive the *scorching* desert sun.
torrid extremely hot, often said of weather. The pool was crowded during last week's *torrid* weather.
antonyms: *See* cold.

hurt *v.* to cause pain or damage. I fell out of bed and *hurt* myself.

harm to do damage to. An early frost will *harm* the crops.
injure to cause physical damage. Warm up before you exercise, or you might *injure* yourself.

I

interesting *adj.* arousing or holding interest or attention. Mr. Wu gave an *interesting* talk.
captivating capturing and holding the attention by beauty or excellence. The tourists found the village a *captivating* place.
fascinating causing and holding the interest through a special quality or charm. I just read a *fascinating* book about the history of the space program.
inspiring having a rousing effect; arousing interest. Her *inspiring* example gave courage to others.
antonyms: dull, boring

L

large *See* big.

laugh *v.* to make the sounds and facial movements that show amusement. They sang songs to make the baby *laugh*.
chuckle to laugh softly, especially to oneself. The thought of Jo's surprise made Kim *chuckle*.
giggle to laugh in a silly, high-pitched, or nervous way. The two friends *giggled* over their joke.
guffaw to laugh loudly. When Rick *guffawed*, everyone looked to see what was so funny.
antonyms: *See* cry.

let *v.* to give permission to. Will Kyle *let* me borrow his bike?
allow to grant permission to or for, usually in relation to rules. Talking is not *allowed* in the library.
permit to allow to do something. The club members decided to *permit* him to join.
antonyms: deny, refuse, forbid

like *v.* to take pleasure in (something); to feel affection for (someone). They *like* cats.
admire to have affection and respect for (someone). All the team members *admire* their coach.
enjoy to take pleasure in (something). They *enjoy* playing chess together.
love to like (something) a lot; to feel great affection for (someone). The children *love* that old mutt.
antonyms: dislike, hate

little *adj.* small in size; not big. Inside the cage were two big monkeys and one *little* one.
small not large. Violets are *small* flowers.
tiny extremely small. A watch has many *tiny* parts.
wee very small. The dollhouse kitchen had some *wee* dishes.
antonyms: *See* big.

look *v.* to see with one's eyes. *Look* at what I found!
glance to look quickly. The spy *glanced* over his shoulder to make sure he wasn't being followed.
peer to look closely. We *peered* through the window of the shop.
stare to look at for a long time with eyes wide open. Mac *stared* at me as though I were crazy.
See also see.

loud *adj.* having a strong sound. The band was playing *loud* music.
deafening loud enough to make one deaf. The exciting goal brought *deafening* cheers from the fans.

noisy full of sounds, often unpleasant. Their apartment is located above a *noisy* street.

antonyms: *See* quiet.

M

mad *See* angry.

many *adj.* consisting of a large number. Jenna has *many* friends.
numerous a great many. I have *numerous* chores to get done today.
plenty (of) enough, or more than enough, suggesting a large number. There is *plenty* of food for lunch.
several more than a few but less than many. Harold checked out *several* books about mountain climbing from the library.
antonym: few

mean *adj.* lacking in kindness or understanding. Maya felt bad about being *mean* to her sister.
nasty resulting from hate. The villain wore a *nasty* sneer.
selfish concerned only about oneself. Pattie is so *selfish* that she never shares anything.
spiteful filled with ill feelings toward others. It's best to leave Dan alone when he's feeling *spiteful*.
antonyms: *See* nice.

N

neat *adj.* clean and orderly. Her homework is always very *neat*.
tidy neat and clean, often said of a place. We raked the yard to make it look *tidy*.
well-groomed carefully dressed and groomed. You should be *well-groomed* when you apply for a job.
antonyms: messy, untidy, sloppy

new *adj.* having just come into being, use, or possession. They are building a *new* house.
fresh new or seeming new and unaffected by time or use. We put a *fresh* coat of paint on the old kitchen table.
modern having to do with the present time; up-to-date. Technology is important in *modern* American life.
recent referring to a time just before the present. Critics have praised her most *recent* book.

antonym: old

nice *adj.* agreeable or pleasing. Her parents are extremely *nice.*
gentle mild and kindly in manner. Grandpa's *gentle* words made Lisa feel much better.
kind gentle and friendly; good-hearted. It is *kind* of you to offer to help.
pleasant agreeable; giving pleasure to. Georgia and Scott are always such *pleasant* company.
sweet having or marked by agreeable or pleasing qualities. He wrote a *sweet* thank-you note.
antonyms: *See* mean.

O

often *adv.* many times; again and again. James is *often* late.
frequently happening again and again. The two families get together *frequently.*
regularly happening at fixed times. It is a good idea to exercise *regularly.*
antonyms: seldom, rarely

old *adj.* having lived or existed for a long time. The *old* car broke down.
aged having grown old. Our *aged* dog sleeps most of the time.
ancient of great age; very old; of times long past. We visited the ruins of an *ancient* city.
antonym: young; *see also* new.

P

plain *adj.* not distinguished from others in any way. The meal was *plain* but hearty.
common average or standard; not distinguished. Measles are a *common* childhood illness.
ordinary plain; average; everyday. Super Food is just an *ordinary* grocery store.
antonym: special
See also unusual.

proud *adj.* having a sense of one's own worth, usually in a positive way. He was *proud* of his family's background.
conceited having too high an opinion of oneself, in a negative way. Being popular has made Gary *conceited.*
haughty having or showing much pride in oneself. The actress is too *haughty* to sign autographs.
vain overly concerned with or proud of oneself. José is *vain* about his looks.
antonym: humble

Q

quiet *adj.* with little or no noise. The woods were *quiet* tonight.
calm free of excitement or strong feeling; quiet. Sue remained *calm* as she waited to be rescued.
peaceful calm; undisturbed. He spent a *peaceful* morning fishing.

quiet (continued)
silent completely quiet; without noise. The room was *silent* after the principal's announcement.
still without sound; silent. The house was *still* and dark.
antonyms: loud, noisy

R

ready *adj.* fit for use or action. Is your costume *ready*?
prepared ready or fit for a particular purpose. We were not *prepared* for our cousins' visit.
set ready or prepared to do something. Everything was *set* for the picnic.

really *adv.* in fact. Was your dad *really* in the Olympics?
actually in fact; really. Grandpa says he's 100 years old, but he's *actually* only 70.
indeed really; truly. The person you met was *indeed* my sister.
truly in fact; really. Their garden was *truly* spectacular.

right *adj.* free from error; true. Her answers are always *right*.
accurate without errors or mistakes. The witness gave an *accurate* description of the thief.
correct agreeing with fact or truth. Is this the *correct* way to put it together?
exact very accurate; completely correct. Get *exact* change for the bus.
antonyms: wrong, mistaken

rude *adj.* not polite; ill-mannered. *Rude* people never say thank you.
discourteous without good manners. It is *discourteous* to keep people waiting.
impolite not showing good manners. Randy's *impolite* remarks made Mr. Parsons angry.
antonyms: polite, courteous

run *v.* to go quickly on foot. Milo can *run* very fast.
dash to go very fast; to run with sudden speed. Lou *dashed* to the telephone to report the accident.
race to run very fast; to run in competition with. Sharon *raced* Mitch to the corner.
scurry to move hurriedly. Mr. Flynn *scurried* about town, trying to get all his errands done.
sprint to run at top speed for a short distance. Janet *sprinted* after the departing bus.

S

sad *adj.* feeling or showing unhappiness or sorrow. I know you're *sad* that they moved away.
downcast low in spirits; sad. Ollie was *downcast* about the rain.
miserable extremely unhappy. Peg was *miserable* until she made some friends in her new school.
antonyms: *See* happy.

same *adj.* being just like something else in kind, quantity, or degree. They both gave the *same* answer.
alike similar, showing a resemblance. All three of the kittens look *alike.*
equal the same in size, amount, quality, or value. Each child got an *equal* share of the cake.
identical the same in every detail. The chair is *identical* to the one in the museum.
antonym: different

say *v.* to make known or express in words. Candidates always *say* they will be fair and honest.
declare to make known publicly or formally. The umpire *declared* that the game was canceled.
pronounce to say formally or officially that something is so. The jury *pronounced* him guilty.
speak to express an idea, a fact, or a feeling. Dr. Garcia will *speak* to the class about health habits.
state to express or explain fully in words. Mr. Jones *stated* his plan.
talk to express ideas or information by means of speech; to speak. We often *talk* about sports.
See also tell.

scared *adj.* afraid; alarmed. "I'm not *scared* of ghosts," he said.
afraid feeling fear, often in a continuing way or for a long time. Nick is *afraid* to fly in a plane.
fearful filled with fear. The child is *fearful* of strangers.
frightened scared suddenly or for a short time. They were *frightened* until the storm ended.
terrified extremely scared; filled with terror. I've always been *terrified* of dogs.

see *v.* to receive information, impressions, etc., through use of the eyes. She could *see* the river from her window.
observe to notice. Did you *observe* anyone leaving by the back door tonight?
perceive to become aware of through the sight or other senses. I *perceive* that you are unhappy.
view to see or look at, usually for some purpose. Hundreds of people visited the gallery to *view* the artist's work.
See also look.

shy *adj.* uncomfortable in the presence of others. Van was too *shy* to ask Angie to dance.
bashful easily embarrassed; very shy. Don't be *bashful*—come in!
timid showing a lack of courage; easily frightened. Deer are *timid* animals.
antonym: bold

sick *adj.* having poor health. Tom was *sick*, but now he is well.
ill not healthy; sick. He was so *ill* that he could not eat.

sick (continued)
unwell not feeling well. You should lie down if you are *unwell.*
antonyms: well, healthy

small *See* little.

smart *adj.* intelligent; bright; having learned much. There are many *smart* students in her class.
clever mentally sharp; quick-witted. He gave a *clever* answer.
intelligent able to learn, understand, and reason. Dolphins seem to be *intelligent* animals.
shrewd clever or sharp in practical matters. The woman's *shrewd* decisions have made her a success.
wise able to know or judge what is right, good, or true, often describing a person with good sense rather than one who knows a lot of facts. In this folk tale, a boy is guided by a *wise* woman.
antonym: stupid

smile *v.* to show a smile, in a happy or friendly way. Our neighbor *smiled* and waved.
beam to smile joyfully. Dan *beamed* when he received the award.
grin to smile broadly with great happiness or amusement. Walter *grinned* when he saw the picture.
smirk to smile in a silly or self-satisfied way. Nina *smirked* foolishly.
antonyms: frown, scowl

strange *adj.* differing from the usual or the ordinary. We heard a *strange* noise in the basement.
odd not ordinary. Jo has an *odd* pet.
weird strange or odd, in a frightening or mysterious way. Kids say the *weird* house is haunted.
See also unusual.

strong *adj.* having great strength or physical power. It took four *strong* men to move the piano.
muscular having well-developed muscles; strong. That shirt makes you look *muscular.*
powerful having great strength, influence, or authority. Their new car has a *powerful* engine.
antonym: weak

sure *adj.* firmly believing in something. I'm *sure* I'll have a good time once I get there.
certain free from doubt; very sure. Roy was *certain* he had left the key on the counter.
confident firmly trusting; sure of oneself or of another. Wendy is *confident* of winning the prize.
definite positive or certain. They have not made any *definite* plans.
antonyms: doubtful, unsure

surprised *adj.* feeling sudden wonder. He was *surprised* at how cold it was outside.
amazed overwhelmed with wonder or surprise. Daria was *amazed*

to learn her father had once been in the circus.
astonished greatly surprised; shocked. Everyone was *astonished* to see Mrs. Buford at the meeting.
astounded greatly surprised; stunned. The judges were *astounded* by the gymnast's performance.

T

take *v.* to get into one's hands or possession; to obtain. May I *take* this book?
grab to take roughly or rudely. Brian *grabbed* the phone and said, "What do you want?"
seize to take suddenly and by force. The rebel army *seized* the tower.
snatch to take suddenly and quickly, often in secret. He *snatched* the letter when she wasn't looking.
antonyms: *See* give.

talk *See* say.

tell *v.* to put or express in written or spoken words. May I *tell* you an interesting story?
announce to state or make known publicly. The principal will *announce* a new school program at the assembly.
narrate to tell about events, especially a story. Mr. Bell will *narrate* "Peter and the Wolf."
relate to tell or report events or details. Each boy *related* his side of the argument.
See also say.

thin *adj.* not fat. His father has always been rather *thin.*
lean with little or no fat but often strong. She has the *lean*, healthy look of a runner.
slim thin, in a good or healthy way. Exercise is important if you want to stay *slim.*
antonyms: fat, plump, chubby

think *v.* to have in mind as an opinion or attitude. What do you *think* of our new math teacher?
believe to accept as true or real. The police did not *believe* the man's story.
consider to regard; to believe. We *consider* her one of the family.

U

unusual *adj.* not usual, common, or ordinary. Jon writes *unusual* stories.
extraordinary very unusual; beyond the ordinary. Monica is an artist of *extraordinary* talent.
rare seldom happening, seen, or found. Some *rare* plants are protected by law.
uncommon rare or unusual. Such a heavy rain is *uncommon* for July.
See also strange.

antonyms: common, usual; *see also* plain.

upset *adj.* feeling uneasy; distressed. Ben is *upset* about the math test.
anxious uneasy about or fearful of what may happen. The family is *anxious* about Grandma's health.
concerned troubled or worried. We are *concerned* about the flood.
worried uneasy or troubled about something. Gene was *worried* that he would not finish in time.
antonym: calm

V

very *adv.* to a great extent. The basketball player was *very* tall.
considerably to a large or an important degree. It will be *considerably* colder tomorrow.
extremely greatly or intensely. May Ling is an *extremely* talented musician.
somewhat a little, to some extent. We are *somewhat* tired today.

W

walk *v.* to move or travel on foot. She takes the bus, but we *walk*.
march to walk with regular steps. The band will *march* in the parade.
stride to walk with long steps, usually with a purpose. Just *stride* right in and tell him.

want *v.* to have a desire or wish for. Craig *wanted* to see you.
crave to want badly, often in an uncontrollable way. I crave pie.
desire to have a strong wish for. The group *desired* a leader.
wish to have a longing or strong need for. I *wish* I were taller.
yearn to feel a strong and deep desire. The boy *yearned* for rest.

wet *adj.* covered or soaked with water or another liquid. Be careful—the floor is *wet*.
damp slightly wet. The clothes in the dryer were still *damp*.
moist slightly wet; damp. The grass was *moist* from the dew.
sopping extremely wet; dripping. Linda took off her *sopping* shoes.
antonyms: *See* dry.

whole *adj.* made up of the entire amount, quantity, or number. How could you eat a *whole* melon?
complete having all its parts. Make sure the kit is *complete*.
entire whole; having all its parts. The *entire* week was rainy.
total whole, full, or entire, often referring to numbers. The *total* bill was $14.27.
stroll to walk in a relaxed or leisurely manner. Why don't we *stroll* around the block?

LETTER MODELS

You can use these models to help you when you write.

Friendly Letter

3400 Broadway Dobbs Ferry, NY 10522 July 3, 19—	**HEADING**
Dear Jennifer,	**GREETING**
How is summer camp? My sister and I are going to Maine this year for August. I like summer in our town, though, too. There's so much to do, now that I'm babysitting for my baby brother. Write back and tell me all about camp.	**BODY**
Your friend,	**CLOSING**
Leslie	**SIGNATURE**

Thank-You Note

88 Monterey Street Pittsburgh, PA 15212 January 1, 19—	**HEADING**
Dear Aunt Jean,	**GREETING**
I love the sweater you sent me! Everyone says this shade of blue goes with my eyes. It also goes with my favorite skirt. It's just the kind of sweater I love, and I can't wait to wear it next month when you come for a visit. Thank you so much. See you in February.	**BODY**
Love,	**CLOSING**
Katie	**SIGNATURE**

Write the receiver's name, address, and zip code on the front of the envelope. Write your name and address in the upper lefthand corner.

SPELLING STRATEGIES

In your writing, it is very important to spell every word correctly. Otherwise, the meaning of what you write may not be clear. Follow the steps below to help improve your spelling.

1. Learn some basic spelling rules.
2. Learn to spell some commonly misspelled words.
3. Learn to spell words by syllables.
4. Check your work carefully when you have finished writing.
5. Use a dictionary to check your spelling.

Spelling Rules

Here are some rules to help you spell certain kinds of words correctly.

Words with *ie* and *ei* Spell the word with ***ie*** when the sound is ***ē***, except after ***c***.

Sound is *ē*: brief, relieve, yield, piece
Except after ***c***: deceive, ceiling, conceive

Spell the word with ***ei*** when the sound is not ***ē***, especially if the sound is ***ā***.

Sound is *ā*: neigh, weight, eighty, sleigh

There are some exceptions to this rule.

Exceptions: either, seize, weird, friend

Adding *s* and *es* In most cases, **s** can be added to a noun without changing the spelling.

Examples: frog + s = frogs   band + s = bands

If the word ends in ***ch***, ***s***, ***sh***, ***x***, or ***z***, add ***es***.

Examples: bush/bushes   loss/losses
witch/witches   mix/mixes

Changing *f* to *v* For most words ending in ***f*** or ***fe***, change the ***f*** to ***v*** when adding ***s*** or ***es***.

loaf/loaves   elf/elves   wife/wives

There are some exceptions to this rule.

Exceptions: roof/roofs   chief/chiefs

Words ending in *o*

For most words that end in ***o*** following a vowel, add ***s*** to form the plural.

Examples: rodeo + s = rodeos patio + s = patios

For most words that end in ***o*** following a consonant, add ***es***.

Examples: hero + es = heroes tomato + es = tomatoes halo + es = haloes echo + es = echoes

Irregular nouns

Some words become plural in irregular ways.

Examples: ox/oxen child/children mouse/mice tooth/teeth goose/geese

Some words stay the same when singular or plural.

Examples: fish/fish sheep/sheep

Adding *es, ed, ing, er* and *est*

If the word ends in a consonant and ***y***, change the ***y*** to ***i*** before any ending that does not begin with ***i***.

Examples: lady ladies bury buried

However, for most words that end in a vowel and ***y***, keep the ***y*** when adding an ending.

Examples: employ employed stay staying

In most cases, if a one-syllable word ends in one vowel and one consonant, double the consonant when adding an ending that begins with a vowel.

Examples: grab grabbed glad gladder hop hopping slim slimmest

For most two-syllable words ending in one vowel and one consonant, double the consonant only if the accent is on the second syllable.

Examples: refer referred begin beginning

If the word ends in a silent ***e***, drop the ***e*** when adding an ending that begins with a vowel.

Examples: cute cuter love loving bare barest raise raised

SPELLING STRATEGIES

Adding prefixes and suffixes When a prefix is added to a word, the spelling of the word stays the same.

Examples: pre + heat = preheat
mis + understand = misunderstand

When a suffix is added to a word, the spelling of the word may change. If the word ends in silent ***e***, drop the ***e*** when adding a suffix that begins with a vowel.

Examples: wobble + y = wobbly
machine + ist = machinist

However, for most words ending in silent ***e***, keep the ***e*** when adding a suffix that begins with a consonant.

Examples: care + ful = careful
measure + less = measureless

When adding the suffix ***ness*** or ***ly***, the spelling of the word usually does not change.

Examples: like + ness = likeness
near + ly = nearly

However, if the word ends in ***y*** and has more than one syllable, change the ***y*** to ***i***.

Examples: ready + ness = readiness
merry + ly = merrily

Homophones

Homophones are often misspelled. Knowing the meanings of homophones will help you choose and spell them correctly. Use your dictionary to check the definition of any homophone about which you are unsure.

Examples:	cent	sent	hair	hare
	real	reel	scene	seen

Contractions and Possessives Use an apostrophe in a contraction.

Examples: he + is = he's was + not = wasn't

Do not use an apostrophe with a possessive pronoun.

Examples:	hers	ours	yours
	its	theirs	his

OVERVIEW OF THE WRITING PROCESS

In this book you have learned that writing is a process. When you write, you follow certain steps. Sometimes you move back and forth between steps, but basically you proceed from the beginning to the end of the process.

Prewrite

- Decide on a purpose and an audience for your writing.
- Choose a topic that would be suitable for your purpose and audience.
- Explore ideas about your topic. You could brainstorm, make a cluster, or make a list.
- Narrow your topic if it is too broad to cover effectively.

Write a First Draft

- Use your prewriting ideas to write your draft.
- Do not worry too much about making errors. Your goal is to get your ideas on paper.

Revise

- Read your draft. Share it with a partner to get some suggestions.
- Ask yourself these questions about your draft.
  What else will my audience want to know? What details can I add?
  How can I make my purpose clearer?
  How can I make my writing easier to understand?
  How can I improve the organization of my writing?

Proofread

- Read your revised draft.
- Ask yourself these questions about your revised draft.
  Have I followed correct paragraph form?
  Have I used complete sentences?
  Have I used capitalization and punctuation correctly?
  Have I spelled all words correctly?

Publish

- Make a clean copy of your revised and proofread draft.
- Share your writing with the audience for whom you wrote it.

STUDY STRATEGIES

Studying is an important part of learning. These Study Tips will help you to study effectively.

General Study Guides

1. Plan your time carefully.
2. Keep a list of assignments.
3. Decide how much time to spend on each task.
4. Find a quiet, comfortable place to work.
5. Keep study materials handy.

Helpful Study Methods

There are many different ways to study. Two methods, 'SQ3R' and PROTO, are described below.

SQ3R The name stands for the five steps you should follow when you read a unit or a chapter.

1. **Survey** the selection to find out what it is about.
2. Think of **Questions** to help you understand the selection.
3. **Read** the material, look for answers to the questions you made up, and look for important points in what you read.
4. **Record** the important points and answers to the questions by writing them down.
5. **Review** the selection and the notes you have written.

PROTO The name stands for the five steps you should follow when you study all kinds of material.

1. **Preview**. First, preview the material to identify the general idea. Look at the title of the selection. Look at the major headings.
2. **Read**. Second, read the material. Read each part carefully, review the headings, and find the most important points.
3. **Organize**. After you have read the material once, figure out how the most important points should be organized. Important information may be organized by sequential order, classification, cause-effect, or comparison-contrast.

4. **Take Notes**. Use the method of organization to take notes. Write down the important points in what you have read. You may want to write down each major idea or title, and then write notes under each idea. Or you may want to use an outline, a picture, or a time line.
5. **Overview**. Finally, read through your notes and the list of important ideas again to form an overview or a summary of what you have read.

The PROTO Method can help you to study just about any kind of material. Here are some additional skills that will help you to use the PROTO Method.

Special Study Tips

Follow Directions Carefully

1. Identify the steps you should follow.
2. Ask questions about steps you do not understand.
3. Follow directions step by step.

Set a Purpose for Studying

1. Before you begin studying, identify the purpose of your work.
2. Your goal might be to find out why something happened or to compare two similar events or people.
3. Use the directions to help you identify your purpose.
4. Stick to your purpose as you work.

Outline Your Material

1. Make an outline of what you are studying.
2. Organize your outline according to the important points.

Map Your Material

1. Use a diagram or picture to outline what you are studying.
2. You might use a map, a time line, or a flow chart to indicate what information is important and how it is organized.

Memorize Your Material

1. **Speak and write**. First, say it out loud. Then, write it down.
2. **Classify ideas**. Think of a way to classify information you want to remember. For example, you might list important events in time order, in alphabetical order, or in groups.

3. **Invent memory joggers**. A "memory jogger" might be a word or a funny sentence that helps you to remember things. For example, the six states of New England are: Maine, New Hampshire, Vermont, Massachusetts, Rhode Island, and Connecticut. You could remember these states by making up a name or a silly sentence, such as: "*M*any *N*ew *V*olunteers *M*ake *R*esidents *C*omfortable." The first letter of each word in the sentence is the first letter in the name of a state.
4. **Repeat** things as many times as you can to help you remember them.

Taking Tests

Taking tests is an important part of your schoolwork. You can use many of the study skills you have learned to make test-taking easier.

1. **Preview the test**. Look through the test quickly to see what it covers and how long it is.
2. **Plan your time**. Your teacher will tell you how much time you have to finish the test. Decide how much time to spend on each part of the test. Some parts may take longer than others. Reading stories, for example, will usually take longer than answering vocabulary questions. Keep track of the time as you work.
3. **Follow directions**. Listen to any directions your teacher gives you. Then read the test directions carefully before you begin the test. As you work through the test, read any directions you see at the beginning of each new section.
4. **Read questions carefully**. Read each test question carefully. Figure out exactly what the question means. Use key words to figure out what kind of answer is required. (Key words might include "why," "when," "who," "because," "after," and "what.") Then, decide on your answer.
5. **Do easy questions first**. Work through the test and finish every question for which you know the answer. Leave the difficult questions for last. Then, go back and work on each difficult question.
6. **Mark your answers carefully**. If you are taking a multiple-choice test, fill in only one bubble for each question and fill it in completely. If you are writing your answers, write each one clearly and neatly.
7. **Check your work**. When you have answered all the questions, use the time you have left to go back and check your work.

SENTENCE STRUCTURE: Diagraming Guide

A sentence diagram shows how the words in the sentence go together. The diagram begins by putting the most important words in the sentence on a line called a **base line**. You will learn how to diagram the most important words first. You will learn how to diagram other words in later lessons.

Simple Subject and Simple Predicate (pages 8-11)

The simple subject is the main word or words in the complete subject. The simple predicate is the main word or words in the complete predicate. An up-and-down line separates the simple subject and the simple predicate on the base line. Find the simple subject and the simple predicate in this sentence.

The class studied the planets.

Look at the diagram below. You can see how the simple subject and simple predicate are diagramed.

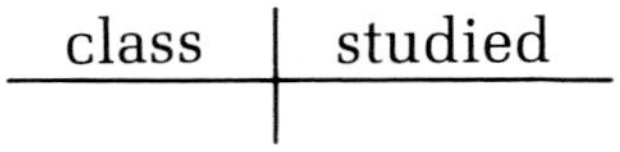

Sometimes the simple subject is not given. This subject is *you* understood. This kind of subject is found in imperative sentences.

Learn the nine planets.

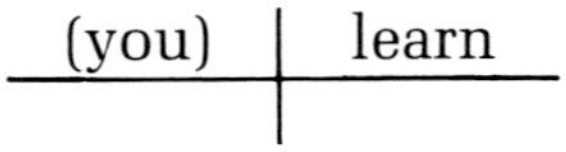

Practice Make a sentence diagram of the simple subject and predicate in each sentence.

1. Planets circle the Sun.
2. The Earth completes an orbit in one year.
3. Mercury lies closest to the Sun.
4. Pluto has the longest orbit.
5. Many moons surround some planets.

Compound Subjects (pages 12-13)

A compound subject is two or more subjects with the same predicate. The simple subjects are joined by *and* or *or*. Each of the subjects appears on a separate line in the sentence diagram. The word *and* or *or* is written on a dotted up-and-down line connecting the compound subjects.

Read this sentence. Find the two words that make up the compound subject.

Authors and poets tell about folk heroes.

Look at the diagram. See how the compound subject is diagramed.

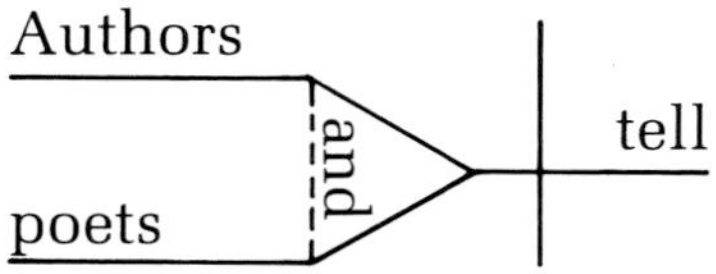

Some compound subjects contain more than two words. Find the compound subject in this sentence.

Pecos Bill, Paul Bunyan, and John Henry have their own tales.

Look at the diagram of this sentence. See how *and* is placed in the compound subject.

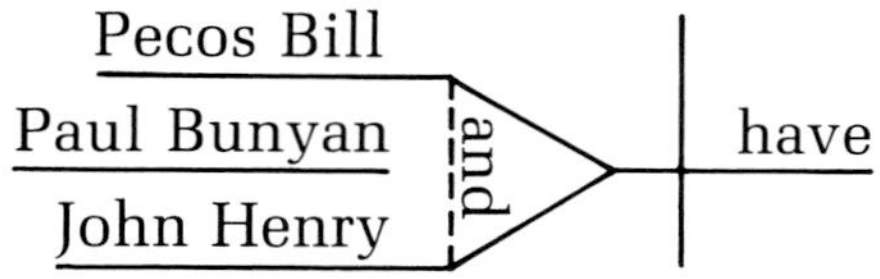

Practice Diagram the compound subject and the simple predicate in each sentence.

1. Engineers, steelworkers, and sailors also have folk heroes.
2. Joe Magarac and Stormalong became popular heroes.
3. Paul Bunyan and Babe, the Blue Ox, appeal to many.
4. Sourdough Sam and several other giants worked for Paul Bunyan.
5. Books, movies, and songs tell of these legends.

Compound Predicates (pages 12-13)

A compound predicate is two or more simple predicates with the same subject. The predicates are joined by *and* or *or*. Each part of a compound predicate appears on a separate line in a diagram. The word *and* or *or* is written on a dotted up-and-down line that connects the parts of the compound predicate.

Read this sentence. Which words form the compound predicate?

The students read and talked about the Pilgrims.

Study this diagram of the compound predicate.

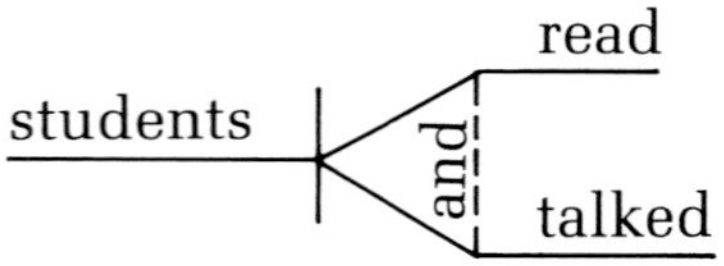

A sentence may contain both a compound subject and a compound predicate.

The leaders and the people planned and made a decision.

Study the sentence diagram. Notice where each *and* appears.

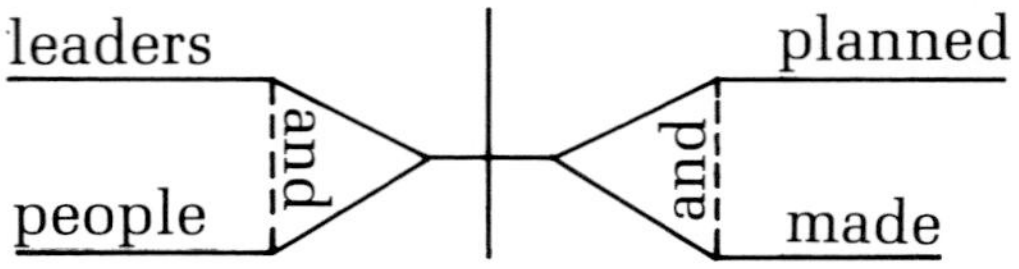

Practice Diagram the subjects and the predicates in each sentence.

1. The Pilgrims left England and sailed to America.
2. The crew and the passengers had a difficult trip.
3. The waves and the wind rocked and shook the ship.
4. My friends and I read and study about the Pilgrims.
5. I planned and built a model of the *Mayflower.*

DIAGRAMING GUIDE

Direct Objects (pages 146-147)

A direct object is a noun or pronoun in the predicate that receives the action of the verb. A direct object is diagramed on the base line after the subject and the predicate. The direct object is separated from the verb by an up-and-down line.

Read this sentence and identify the direct object.

My club made posters.

Look at the sentence diagram below. Notice that the line separating the verb and the direct object does not go below the base line.

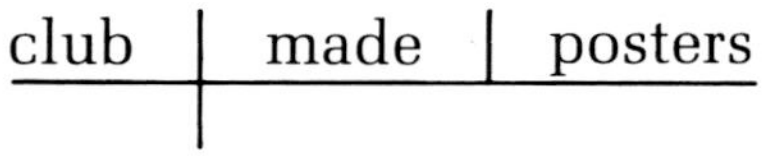

A verb can have more than one direct object. Find the compound direct object in this sentence.

We used paint and photographs.

See how a compound direct object is diagramed.

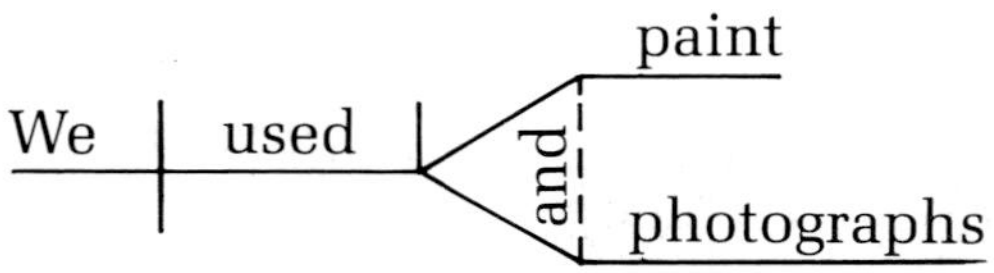

Practice Diagram only the subjects, the predicates, and the direct objects in each sentence.

1. Our club designed health education posters.
2. We encourage good nutrition and exercise.
3. Our pamphlets list many rules.
4. People study our posters and pamphlets.
5. Our members give intelligent speeches.

Linking Verbs (pages 150-151)

A linking verb joins the subject of a sentence to a noun or an adjective in the predicate. In a sentence diagram, a slanting line separates the linking verb from the noun or adjective in the predicate.

My favorite sport is baseball.

See how this sentence is diagramed. Find the word that names or describes the subject in the sentence diagram.

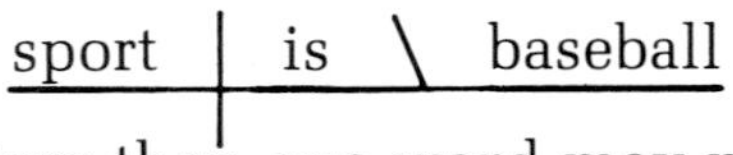

More than one word may name or describe a subject.

Baseball games are exciting and entertaining.

See how the compound parts are diagramed.

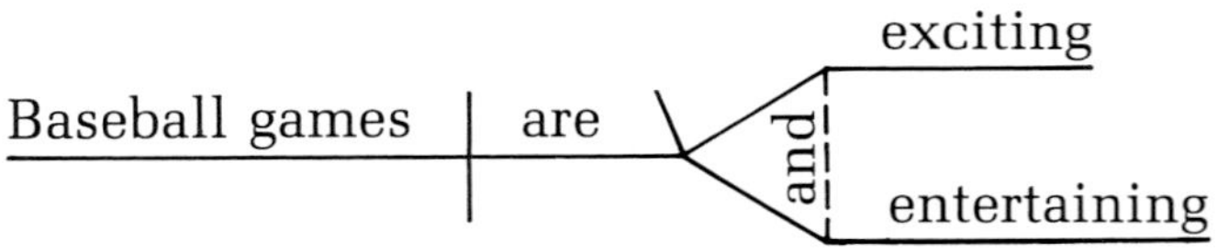

Practice Diagram each linking verb and the two parts of the sentence that it joins.

1. Baseball seems very American.
2. Many people are loyal fans.
3. The games appear complicated and interesting.
4. My favorite players are pitchers.
5. The pitcher is a most important player.

Adjectives (pages 226-235)

Adjectives, including the articles *a*, *an*, and *the*, are diagramed on a slanting line below the noun they describe.

Find the adjectives in this sentence.

The class wrote the first few poems.

Notice how the adjectives are diagramed. Remember that the words *a*, *an*, and *the* are special adjectives called **articles**.

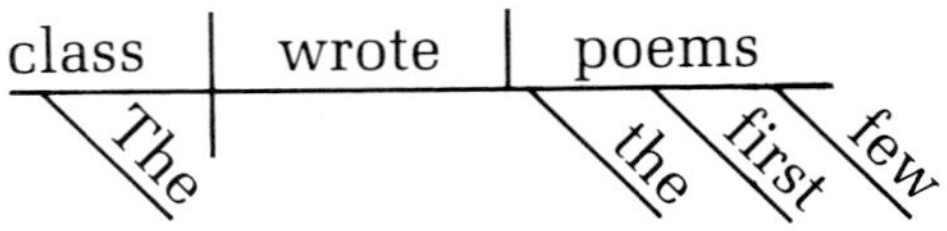

Sometimes adjectives appear in a series. Find the series of adjectives in this sentence.

A poem uses many colorful and exciting words.

See how the word *and* is written with the adjectives in a series.

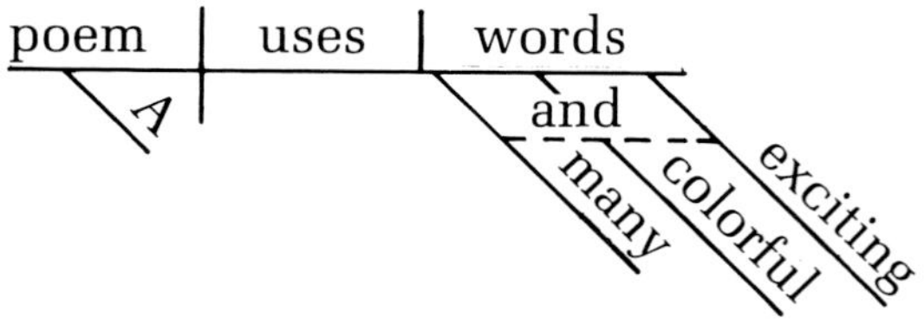

Practice Diagram every word in these sentences.

1. One poem described a large, round, and yellow ball.
2. The yellow ball was the bright summer sun.
3. A short poem seems easy.
4. A longer poem takes patient, hard work.
5. The teacher read the best new poems.

Adverbs (pages 364-371)

Adverbs, like adjectives, are placed on slanting lines below the words they describe.

Find the adverb and the word it describes in this sentence.

A talented child sang beautifully.

Look at the diagram of the sentence.

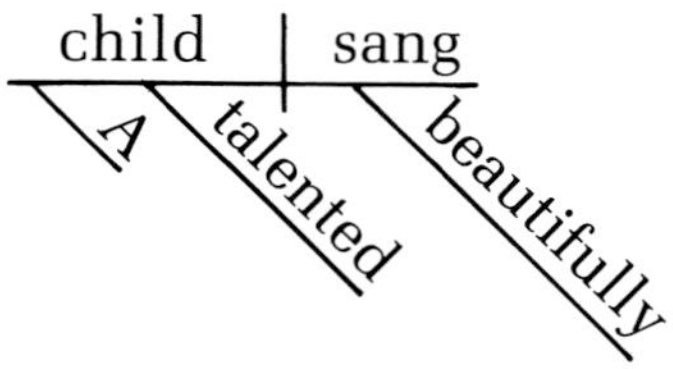

Notice that an adverb does not always appear next to the word it describes. Where is the adverb in the sentence below?

Later, the girl played the violin.

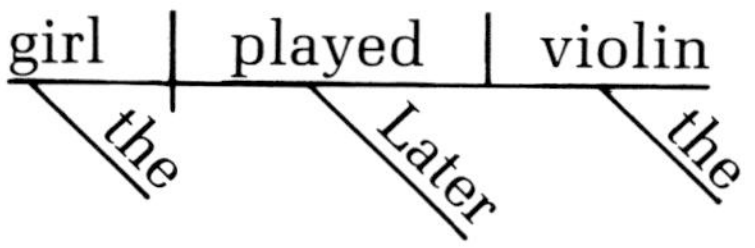

Read this sentence. Notice that an adverb describes another adverb.

The thoughtful student talks very quietly.

Study the sentence diagram.

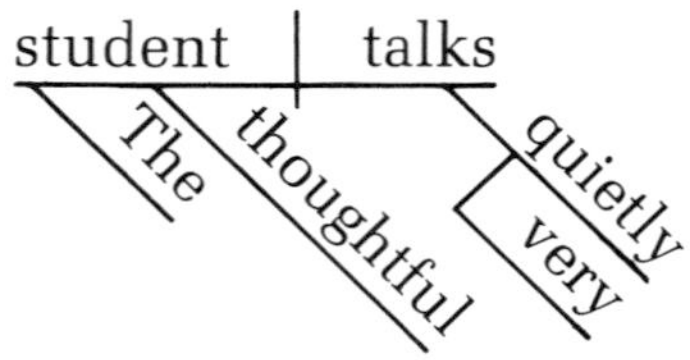

Practice Diagram every word in these sentences.

1. Every student does very fine work.
2. A few kind students help the teacher often.
3. Some people complete homework very quickly.
4. The good student works carefully and seriously.
5. An excellent student studies often and wisely.

Prepositional Phrases (pages 428-431)

In a sentence diagram, a prepositional phrase is written on a slanting line below the word it describes. The object of the preposition is written on a connecting line. The words that describe the object of the preposition are written on slanting lines below it.

Read this sentence. Find the prepositional phrase. What word does it describe?

The girl in the red velvet dress is class president.

See how the sentence is diagramed. Find the prepositional phrase in the diagram.

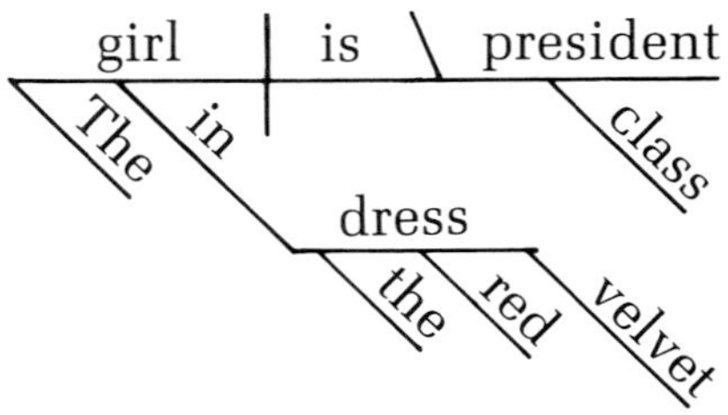

Practice Diagram every word in these sentences.

1. The boy with red hair campaigned very carefully.
2. He and the winner gave speeches from their seats.
3. The people in this room thought very carefully.
4. We voted in a special booth.
5. The winner of the election is a very happy girl.

Compound Sentences (pages 14-15)

A compound sentence contains two or more simple sentences joined by *and*, *or*, or *but*. Diagram each sentence in a compound sentence separately. Write the connecting word *or*, *and*, or *but* on a line between the two sentences. Draw a dotted line connecting this word to each sentence.

Read this sentence. Find the two sentences that make up the compound sentence.

Football is a great game, but I prefer soccer.

See how the compound sentence is diagramed.

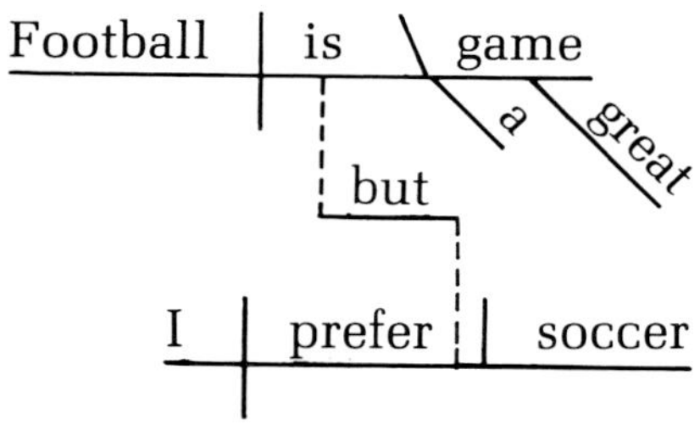

Practice Diagram every word in these compound sentences.

1. Football is very slow, and I like fast games.
2. The game is exciting, or I go home.
3. Soccer is fun, but it takes great skill.
4. I practice often, and I play in school games.
5. The boy in the red shorts plays a hard game, but he is a very polite player.

DIAGRAMING GUIDE

GLOSSARY

OF WRITING, GRAMMAR, AND LITERARY TERMS

WRITING TERMS

audience	the reader or readers for whom a composition is written
detail sentences	sentences that tell more about the main idea of a paragraph
first draft	the first version of a composition, in which the writer gets his or her basic ideas down on paper
main-idea sentence	the sentence that states the overall point of a paragraph
overall impression	the general idea or feeling expressed in a description
personal narrative	a piece of writing in which the writer tells about something that has happened in his or her life
prewriting	the stage in the writing process in which the writer chooses a topic, explores ideas, gathers information, and organizes his or her material before writing a first draft
prewriting strategies	particular ways of gathering, exploring, planning, and organizing ideas before writing the first draft of a composition

• **charting** a way to gather ideas under different headings—especially useful in comparing and contrasting

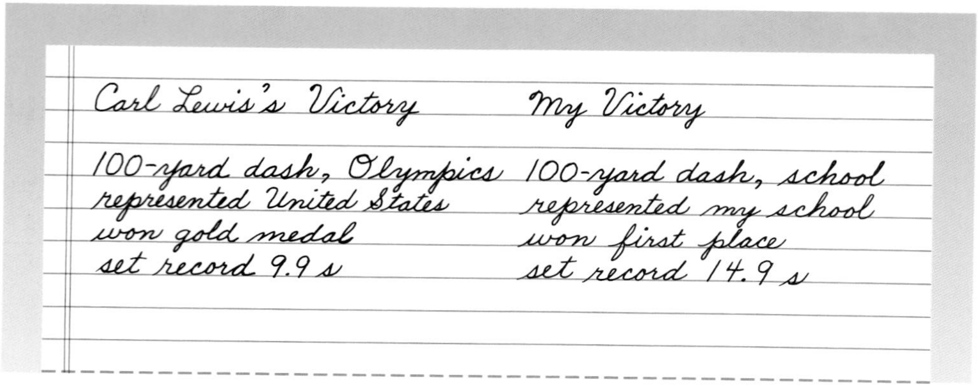
Carl Lewis's Victory
My Victory
100-yard dash, Olympics
represented United States
won gold medal
set record 9.9 s
100-yard dash, school
represented my school
won first place
set record 14.9 s

• **clustering** a way to explore ideas by gathering details related to the writing topic

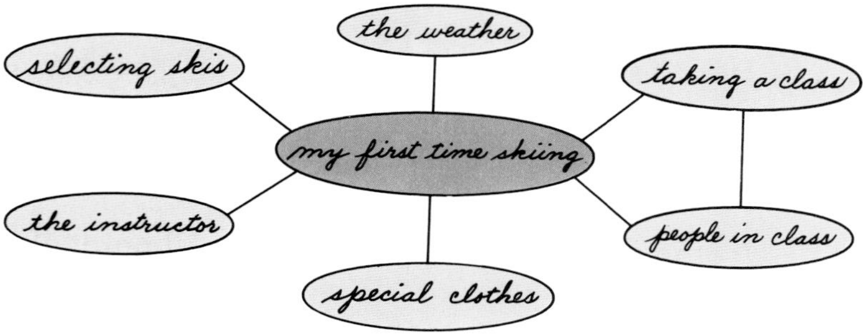

• **flow chart** a way to organize the steps when writing instructions

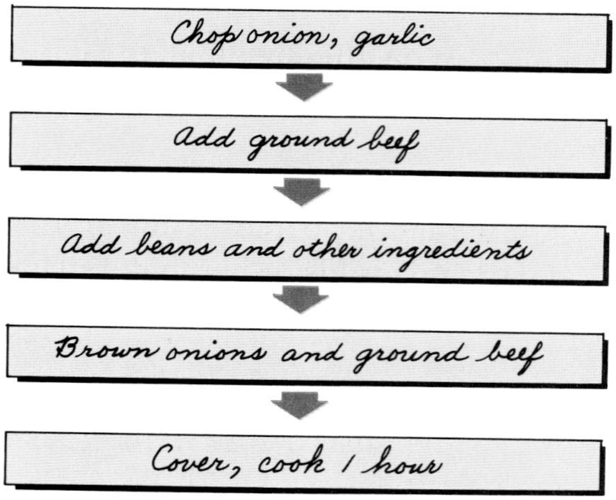
Chop onion, garlic
Add ground beef
Add beans and other ingredients
Brown onions and ground beef
Cover, cook 1 hour

- **listing** a way to gather supporting reasons and details—especially useful in persuasive writing

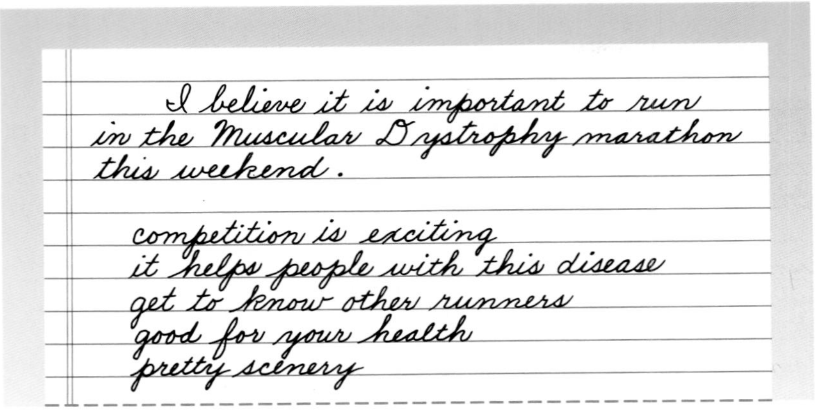
I believe it is important to run in the Muscular Dystrophy marathon this weekend.

competition is exciting
it helps people with this disease
get to know other runners
good for your health
pretty scenery

- **outline** a way to organize topic-related ideas in the order in which they will be discussed—especially useful in drafting a research report

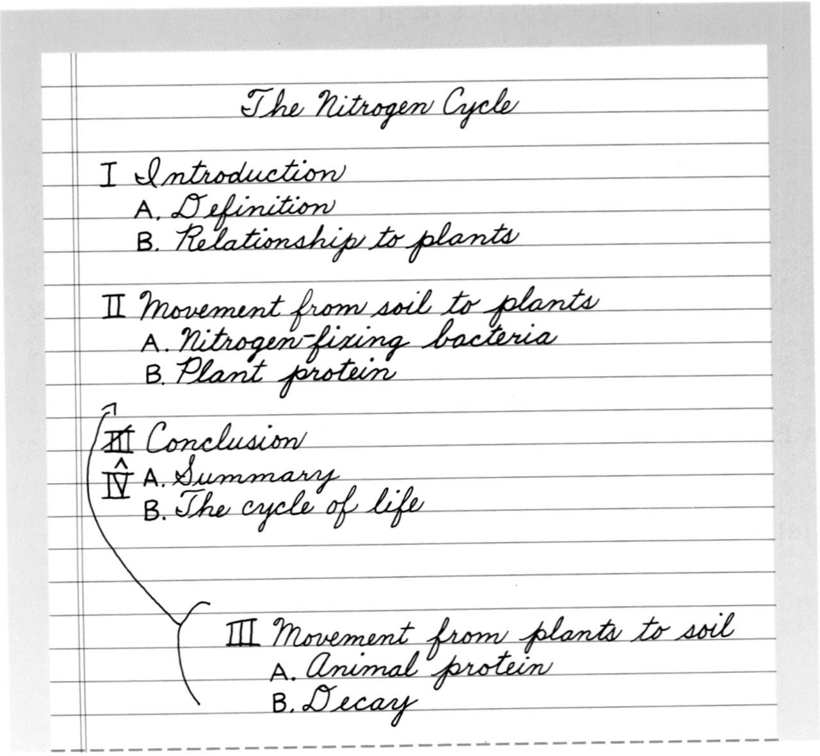
The Nitrogen Cycle

I Introduction
A. Definition
B. Relationship to plants

II Movement from soil to plants
A. Nitrogen-fixing bacteria
B. Plant protein

III IV Conclusion
A. Summary
B. The cycle of life

III Movement from plants to soil
A. Animal protein
B. Decay

- **story organizer** a way to gather ideas and details under headings important for story writing

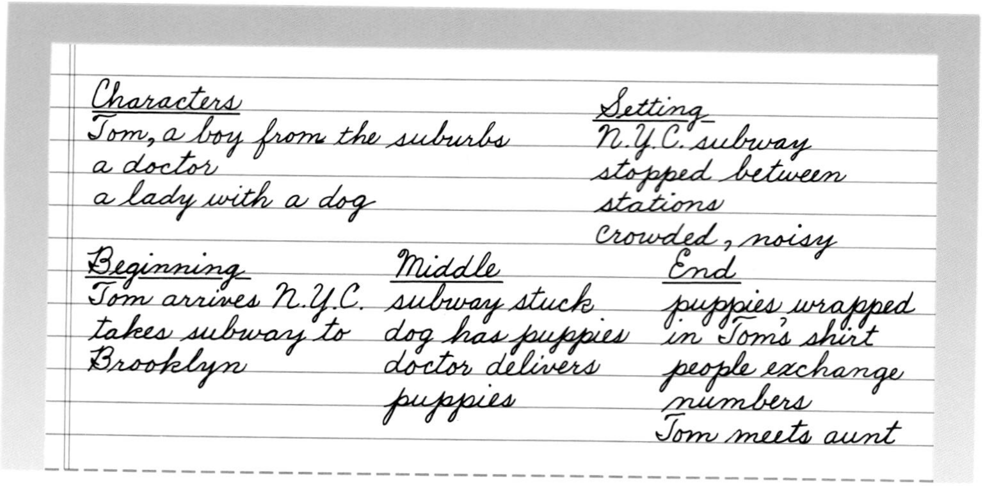

proofread to correct errors in punctuation, capitalization, spelling, and grammar in a writing draft

publish to share a composition with an audience

purpose the writer's reason for writing a composition—for example, to explain, to entertain, or to persuade

revise to improve the first draft of a composition by adding or taking out information, combining and reordering sentences, or changing word choice according to the purpose and audience

sensory details in a description, the details that appeal to the reader's five senses—sight, hearing, touch, taste, and smell

supporting details facts, examples, or sensory details that give more information about the main idea of a paragraph

time order the arrangement of events in a composition according to when they occur in time

topic sentence another name for the **main-idea sentence**

transition words words or phrases that link sentences in a paragraph, such as *finally* and *in the meantime*

writing conference a meeting in which a writer asks and answers questions about his or her writing with the purpose of improving it

writing process the steps for writing a composition, including prewriting, writing a first draft, revising, proofreading, and publishing

GRAMMAR TERMS

action verb a word that expresses action
The horses *leap* over the fence.

adjective a word that describes a noun or a pronoun
Vermont has *cold* winters.

adverb a word that tells more about a verb
The letter arrived *yesterday.*

article the word *a, an,* or *the*
Tell me *a* story.

common noun a noun that names any person, place, thing, or idea
What *country* will you visit?

complete predicate all the words that tell what the subject of a sentence does or is
The strange noises *remained a mystery.*

complete subject all the words that tell whom or what a sentence is about
Strange noises came from that room.

compound sentence a sentence that contains two sentences joined by a comma and the word *and, or,* or *but*
The lights dimmed, and the audience became quiet.

conjunction a word that joins other words or groups of words in a sentence
We will see a movie *or* a play tonight.

direct object a noun or pronoun that receives the action of a verb
The carpenter built a *desk*.

future tense the form of a verb that shows something that has not yet happened
Steve *will speak* to our club tomorrow.

helping verb a verb that helps the main verb to show an action
Ellen *has* finished her homework.

interjection a word or group of words that expresses strong feeling
Wow! What a huge house that is!

irregular verb a verb that does not form the past tense by adding *d* or *ed*
The children *found* a baby robin.

linking verb a verb that links the subject of a sentence to a noun or an adjective in the predicate
The sun *is* brilliant today.

noun a word that names a person, place, thing, or idea
When is the *concert?*

object of a preposition the noun or pronoun that follows the preposition in a prepositional phrase
A bird flew through the *rainbow.*

object pronoun a pronoun that is used as the object of an action verb or after words such as *to, for, with, in,* and *at*
Will you be traveling with *me?*

past tense the form of a verb that expresses action that has already happened
Paul *returned* the book to me last week.

possessive noun a noun that shows ownership
Is this the *teacher's* pen?

possessive pronoun a pronoun that shows who or what owns something
Welcome to *our* house.

preposition a word that relates a noun or pronoun to another word in a sentence
Place the vase *on* the table.

prepositional phrase a group of words that begins with a preposition and ends with a noun or pronoun
The kitten is *in the tree.*

present tense the form of a verb that tells that something is happening now
Eleanor *wants* a new bicycle.

pronoun a word that takes the place of one or more nouns and the words that go with the nouns
She would like a ten-speed bicycle.

proper adjective an adjective formed a proper noun
We love *Italian* food.

proper noun a noun that names a particular person, place, thing, or idea
Carlos is from *Spain.*

run-on sentence two or more sentences that have been joined together incorrectly
The explorers drew maps they made careful studies.

sentence a group of words that expresses a complete thought
The scientist performed an experiment.

sentence fragment a group of words that does not express a complete thought
Came into the kitchen and sat down.

simple predicate the main word or words in the complete predicate of a sentence
Ana *sang* in the chorus last year.

simple subject the main word or words in the complete subject of a sentence

The enormous *tree* towered above us.

subject pronoun a pronoun that is used as the subject of a sentence

They arrived during a snowstorm.

LITERARY TERMS

alliteration the repetition of the same first letter or initial sound in a series of words—for example, "Linda loves to lick labels."

characters the people in a story or play

concrete poem a poem whose shape suggests the subject of the poem

dialogue the conversations that people have in a story or a play

fiction written works such as novels and short stories that tell about imaginary characters and events

haiku a poem that has three lines and usually seventeen syllables, and that frequently describes something in nature

images pictures suggested by a description or a comparison, such as "The stars formed a glittering road in the sky."

nonfiction written works that deal with real situations, people, or events, such as biographies

personification a description in which human qualities are given to something that is not human—for example, "The wind whispered at the door."

plot the sequence of events in a story

setting the time and place in which the events of a story happen

INDEX

I N D E X

Q

R

INDEX

T

U

V

W

Y

George Ancona quote is from *Something About the Author:* Volume 12. Edited by Anne Commire. Copyright © by Gale Research Company. All rights reserved. Reprinted by permission of the publisher. Marjorie Weiman Sharmat quote is from *Something About the Author:* Volume 33. Edited by Anne Commire. Copyright © by Gale Research Company. All rights reserved. Reprinted by permission of the publisher.

Excerpt from "America the Beautiful" by Katharine Lee Bates is from *Poems* by Katharine Lee Bates. First published 1926 in the United States by E. P. Dutton. All rights reserved. Reprinted by permission of the publisher, E. P. Dutton, a division of NAL Penguin Inc.

Brief quotation by Virginia Hamilton is copyright © 1983, 1989 by Virginia Hamilton Adoff. Used by permission of the author.

Brief quotation by C. S. Lewis from the Preface to *Of Other Worlds* by C. S. Lewis. Copyright © 1966 by The Executors of the Estate of C. S. Lewis. Reprinted by permission of Harcourt Brace Jovanovich, Inc.

Quotation by Ezra Jack Keats is reprinted by the Imprints of Macmillan Children's Book Group.

Excerpt and illustration "Drawing Life in Motion" from *Drawing Life in Motion* by Jim Arnosky. Copyright © 1984, 1987 by Jim Arnosky. Copyright © 1984, 1987 by Jim Arnosky. By permission of Lothrop, Lee & Shepard Books, a division of William Morrow & Company, Inc.

"Pixels and Patterns" from *Computer Science* by Allen L. Wold. Copyright © 1984 by Allen L. Wold. Reprinted by permission of Franklin Watts, Inc.

"The Heart" is excerpted from *The Heart* by John Gaskin. Copyright © 1985 Franklin Watts Ltd. Reprinted by permission of Franklin Watts, Inc.

"Tornado" excerpted from *My Prairie Year*, based on the Diary of Elenore Plaisted by Brett Harvey. Text copyright © 1986 by Brett Harvey. Reprinted by permission of Holiday House.

"Shooting Stars" from *The Reasons for Seasons* by Linda Allison. Copyright © 1975 by the Yolla Bolly Press. Reprinted by permission of Little, Brown and Company.

"Mathematics: Counting and Numbers" is excerpted from *The Penguin Book of the Physical World*. Copyright © Penguin Books 1976. Reprinted by permission of the publisher.

ILLUSTRATION CREDITS: Alex Bloch, 284, 464, 465, 466, 467, 468, 469; Cheryl Chalmer, 394, 395, 396, 397, 398, 399, 401; Patrick Merrill, 382; Carl Molno, 298, 357, 440, 441, 488; Jan Pyk, 289 (top), 361 (top), 425 (top), 493 (top); Roger Roth, 332, 333, 334, 335, 336, 337; Blanche Simms, 316, 317; Joel Snyder, 283, 294, 296, 302, 306, 310, 354, 364, 370, 374, 379, 418, 443, 486, 495; Joe Veno, 446; Fred Winkowski, 2, 6, 10, 12, 16, 18, 20, 78, 84, 86, 92, 144, 145, 156, 168, 292, 300, 301, 308, 313, 366, 368, 372, 376, 404, 428, 430, 432, 436, 438; Jenny Tilden Wright, 260, 261, 262, 263, 264, 265; Rusty Zabransky, 272, 274, 275, 276, 278, 279, 282, 342, 344, 346, 347, 348, 350, 351, 408, 410, 411, 412, 414, 415, 472, 476, 478, 479, 480, 482, 483, 486.

PHOTO CREDITS: CLARA AICH: 53, 56, 59, 62, 63, 123, 124, 126, 129, 132, 133, 136, 361, 423. ANIMALS ANIMALS: 147; E.R. Degginger, 7; Breck P. Kent, 81. ART RESOURCE: 289, 439. BETTMANN ARCHIVE: 19, 367. BETTMANN NEWSPHOTOS: 434, 435. BRUCE COLEMAN, INC.: 443; S.L. Craig, 32L; Edgar J. Jones, 487; Charles G. Summers Jr., 241R. COMSTOCK: Tom Grill, 82. CULVER PICTURES: 429. BOB DAEMMRICH: 142. LEO DE WYS, INC.: Steve Vidler, 76; ZEFA, 83. FEDERICO DIAZ: 297. MARJORIE DRESSLER: 491. DRK PHOTO: D. Cavagnaro, 74, 331; M. Philip Kahl, Jr., 330. F/STOP: R. Dudzic. 119R; R. Sanford, 119L; J. Sherman, 48. THE GRANGER COLLECTION: 258, 285, 375, 431. H. ARMSTRONG ROBERTS, INC.: 23R; L. Fritz, 169; A. Geisser, 22. GRANT HEILMAN; 266; William Felger, 471R; Harry Lefever, 143. MICHAL HERON: 218, 343, 346, 349, 352, 353, 407, 411, 413, 416, 417, 420, 425, 475, 478, 481, 484, 485, 494. RICHARD HUTCHINGS: 40, 344. THE IMAGE BANK: Sebastiao Barbosa, 112; Kul Bhatia, 365; Gerald Brimacombe, 49L; Dan Coffey, 403R; Stephen Derr, 240; Joe Devenney, 118, 392; Steve Dunwell, 64, 408; D.W. Productions, xii; Cliff Feulner, 41; Mitchell Funk, 363; Geoff Gove, 94; David W. Hamilton, 340; Jean Pierre Horlin, 149; Don King, 49BR; Sobel/Klonsky, 442; Steve Krongard, 224; Whitney Lane, 3; Hank de Lespinasse, 403L; Elyse Lewin, 199L; Mahaux, 49TR; Eric Meola, 119T, 402; Peter Miller, 54; Co Rentmeester, 75; B. Roussel, 378; Michael Salas, 199R; Marc Solomon, 198; Harald Sund, 71, 290; Maria Taglienti, 1; H. Wendler, 427; Eric L. Wheater, 443R; Art Wolfe, 267R. WOLFGANG KAEHLER: 225, 268, 379R, 406, 471L. JOAN KRAMER & ASSOCIATES: Ed Simpson, 299. KEN LAX: 203, 204, 206, 209, 212, 213, 216, 271, 274, 277, 280, 281. MONKMEYER PRESS: Peter Glass, 190. MUSEUM OF AMERICAN FOLK ART: 73. NASA: 403T. ODYSSEY PRODUCTIONS: Robert Frerck, 259. PHOTOEDIT: 419; Bill Aron, 339L; Robert Brenner, 233; Myrleen Ferguson, 393; Tony Freeman, 17, 113, 191, 303, 305, 339R, 342; Felicia Martinez, 426; Stephen McBrady, 307. PHOTO RESEARCHERS: Michael Austin, 153; Howie Bluestein, 5; Wesley Bocxe, 472; Tom Branch, 52; Van Bucher, 69R, 227; C. Chesher, 93; Junebug Clark, 11; Patricia Caulfield, 236; Melissa Hayes English, 447; Tony Florio, 87; Lowell J. Georgia, 295; Geoff Gilbert, 443L; Farrell Grehan, 437; Dan Guravich, 161; Eunice Harris, 362; Sven Lindblad, 163; Rexford Lord, 379L; Susan McCartney, 171R; Tom McHugh, 245; Lawrence Migdale, 95R; Hans Namuth, 120; Mitch Reardon, 235; Earl Roberge, 69L; Ronald G. Royer, 287; Leonard Lee Rue III, 462; F. St. Clair-Renard, 154; Kjell B. Sanford, 489; Larry West, 267L. EDA ROGERS: 99. FRED R. SCHWARTZ: 122. STOCK BOSTON: Charles Gupton, 199B. THE STOCK MARKET: Peter Beck, 463; Ed Bock, 151, 272; Robert Frerck, 237; Richard Gross, 313L: Randy O'Rourke, 312; Gabe Palmer, 204, 313R; Paul Steel, 383. SUPERSTOCK/SHOSTAL ASSOCIATES: 293, 338; Ernest S. Bernard, 470; Martin M. Bruce, 471T; R. Erdoes, 267T; David Forbert, 339B; Manley Photo, 371; Stanley Rosenfeld, 311. TAURUS PHOTO: Pam Hasegawa, 155; C.B. Jones, 270. VIESTI ASSOCIATES, INC.: Larry Kolvoord, 95L; Kevin Vandiver, 221; Joe Viesti, 89, 369. ROBERT WINSLOW: 230, 241L. WOODFIN CAMP & ASSOCIATES: 170; Timothy Eagan, 166; George Hall, 291; Alon Reininger, 170, 171L.